MW01027487

Immigrant Rights in the Shadows of Citizenship

NATION OF NEWCOMERS

Immigrant History as American History

Matthew Jacobson and Werner Sollors
GENERAL EDITORS

Beyond the Shadow of Camptown: Korean Military Brides in America
Ji-Yeon Yuh

Feeling Italian: The Art of Ethnicity in America
Thomas J. Ferraro

Constructing Black Selves: Caribbean American Narratives and the Second Generation
Lisa D. McGill

Transnational Adoption: A Cultural Economy of Race, Gender, and Kinship
Sara K. Dorow

Immigration and American Popular Culture: An Introduction
Jeffrey Melnick and Rachel Rubin

From Arrival to Incorporation: Migrants to the U.S. in a Global Era
Edited by Elliott R. Barkan, Hasia Diner, and Alan M. Kraut

Migrant Imaginaries: Latino Cultural Politics in the Mexico-U.S. Borderlands
Alicia Schmidt Camacho

The Force of Domesticity: Filipina Migrants and Globalization
Rhacel Salazar Parreñas

Immigrant Rights in the Shadows of Citizenship
Edited by Rachel Ida Buff

EDITED BY RACHEL IDA BUFF

Immigrant Rights in the Shadows of Citizenship

NEW YORK UNIVERSITY PRESS
New York and London

NEW YORK UNIVERSITY PRESS
New York and London
www.nyupress.org

© 2008 by New York University
All rights reserved

Library of Congress Cataloging-in-Publication Data
Immigrant rights in the shadows of citizenship / Edited by Rachel Ida Buff.
p. cm.
Includes bibliographical references and index.
ISBN-13: 978-0-8147-9991-8 (cl : alk. paper)
ISBN-10: 0-8147-9991-4 (cl : alk. paper)
ISBN-13: 978-0-8147-9992-5 (pb : alk. paper)
ISBN-10: 0-8147-9992-2 (pb : alk. paper)
1. Emigration and immigration law—United States—History.
2. Constitutional law—United States. 3. Immigrants—Civil rights—United States—History. 4. Immigrants—Government policy—United States—History. 5. Social integration—Government policy—United States—History. I. Buff, Rachel, 1961–
KF4819.I49 2008
342.7308'2—dc22 2008009839

New York University Press books are printed on acid-free paper, and their binding materials are chosen for strength and durability. We strive to use environmentally responsible suppliers and materials to the greatest extent possible in publishing our books.

Manufactured in the United States of America

c 10 9 8 7 6 5 4 3 2 1
p 10 9 8 7 6 5 4 3 2 1

CONTENTS

ACKNOWLEDGMENTS

I had no idea that editing an anthology could be such a pleasure, or I would have done it a long time ago. My thanks to the hard work, intelligence and commitment of the contributors represented here. Reading their work and corresponding with them on this project was an unanticipated delight.

A fellowship from the Morris Fromkin Research fund at the University of Wisconsin–Milwaukee in 2006 provided time to germinate the idea of doing this anthology and supported the idea that scholarship could and should be socially progressive. A fellowship from the Institute for Research in the Humanities at the University of Wisconsin–Madison, during spring 2007 provided time to work on this book. Invitations from Dorothee Schneider (University of Illinois–Urbana-Champaign) and Frieda Knobloch (University of Wyoming) to present versions of my work on undocumented students and in-state tuition during the spring of 2006 helped develop this project further. Meeting students, like Diane Mora, Yeni Salgado, and Veronica Sotelo, who are deeply engaged in immigrant rights made me realize the importance of this work. And landing in the History Department and Comparative Ethnic Studies Program at UWM has been a stroke of luck. My colleagues here create an atmosphere of creativity and collaboration. I am also grateful for the insights of the many undergraduate and graduate students I have taught here at UWM, in particular, Bri Smith, Will Smith, Jackleen Salem, Dyuti Ailawadi, Nick Hoffman, Todd T. Taylor, Carly Weckworth, Natalie Battle, Anna Conners, Steven Vincent Anderson, Linda Chance, Connoree Russell, Mark Enters, and Xouhoa Ching.

George Lipsitz has always provided a model of politically engaged scholarship, and he made suggestions for this anthology in its early stages. Donna Gabaccia has shared her generative intellect and identified potential contributors. Matthew Frye Jacobson has been a friend of this project and its editor from the get-go and has made key interventions on its behalf. Eric Zinner, editorial director at New York University Press, treated this project with due seriousness when it was merely a drafty proposal and a twinkle in my eye. Emily Park, Ciara McLoughlin, and Aiden Amos, assistant editors, and Despina Papazoglou Gimbel, managing editor at NYU Press, have been models of professionalism throughout. Cynthia Garver adeptly copyedited the manuscript, improving the quality of the prose. Two anonymous readers provided essential suggestions to make this a better book; I have tried to follow them.

My friend Rich Kees provided key assistance in the clutch, as he has frequently been known to do. The Childcare Center at the University of Wisconsin–Milwaukee has been a happy place for our daughters to be while I was working on this volume. My thanks in particular to Patty Zimmerman, Carmen Simpson, and the incomparable Casey Seymour. Wendy Kozol, Jason Loviglio, and Nan Enstad have been sources of intellectual and psychic support in this project, as well as in most others I can imagine undertaking. I am grateful to have them as colleagues and friends.

The intellectual rigor and hard work of my partner, Joe Austin, along with his commitment to our life together, provides the bedrock on which this book and everything else I do rests. Our two daughters, Ruby Lou and Ellie Rae Sylvia Balotovsky, make me reconsider everything I know and make reinventing the world as we know it a glorious and ongoing project. My love to these three.

Finally, I am deeply indebted to everyone at Voces de la Frontera of Milwaukee for their example of political ingenuity and vision. Christine Neumann-Ortiz in particular has been a great friend and ally. I continue to learn from her political savvy and passion. Voces continually asserts the presence and human dignity of contemporary immigrants and, by extension, of anyone who has ever moved anywhere at all.

Introduction

Toward a Redefinition of Citizenship Rights

Rachel Ida Buff

A Long, Global Struggle

Using the following chant, marchers in Milwaukee's second Day without Latinos (May 1, 2007) addressed President George W. Bush directly:

Bush, ¡Escucha!	(Bush, listen!)
Estamos en la lucha.	(We are in the fight.)

Unlike many other such rhymes being chanted bilingually that day, this one was recited only in Spanish. This means either that the 70,000 marchers present were confident of Mr. Bush's fluency in the language or that, by addressing him in Spanish, they wished to indicate a struggle already taking place in realms they understood well, suggesting that he become aware of it.

It is the central contention of this book that the rights of immigrants in the United States have been grounds for a long struggle, indeed. Leaving their prior homes for a multitude of reasons, including war and political upheaval, economic transformations and downturns, religious and gender oppression, cultural and climate change, migrants from all over the world have arrived in nations like the United States. They have come as pioneers and contract laborers, indentured servants and seekers of fortune, enslaved workers and military brides, businesswomen and adoptees, craftsmen and activists, homesteaders and sojourners, students and refugees. In their new homes, they have created communities by imagining new identities and remembering old ones. They have maintained ties to prior homelands, sometimes when places like a sovereign Poland or a free Haiti have no longer existed geopolitically.[1]

These prior homelands have often loomed large in the shaping of ethnic identities. Migrants have returned home, temporarily or to stay. In so doing, they have created connections between countries. These connections, in turn, have transformed the nations to which they return, as well as the United States. The United States defines itself as a "nation of immigrants." The evolution of this definition has been one of many responses to the new arrivals. Migrants to these shores invented an idea of Euroamerican identity while displacing Native American nations during the colonial period, and then they turned around and borrowed from the Iroquois Great Law of Peace to write a national constitution. Since that time, the nation as a whole has dealt with questions of who is to be included in the nation and who is to be kept out. These issues translate, in the present day, into questions of homeland security and border control. They also, crucially, define what citizenship means and who can have it.

The writers represented in this collection consider the ways in which immigrants to the United States have transformed ideas of citizenship and rights through the cultural and political struggles that Lisa Lowe has called "immigrant acts": "the *acts* of labor, resistance, memory and survival, as well as the politicized cultural work that emerges from dislocation and identification."[2]

At this crucial historic moment, in which a militarized national security state surveys the results of an increasingly global economy from atop a ribbon wire fence, immigrants have mobilized in stunning numbers. They have attempted to influence national public policy toward border control and, more broadly, toward the new global economy in which employers and factories are free to relocate but workers are often constrained by national immigration policy.

These mobilizations are only the most recent and visible immigrant acts. This volume tries to understand these recent mobilizations in a comparative historical context, linking immigrant struggles across time and space. Immigrants have imported ideas about politics and have used these ideas to shape their struggles for citizenship and rights on these shores. Through migration, the very ideas of nation and citizen have been reshaped. This struggle, then, has been both long term and global.

This book combines the work of scholars in law, the humanities, and the social sciences with the writings of activists deeply involved in the contemporary immigrant rights movement. Often, writers whose day jobs are as activists write history and cultural criticism. In turn, those teaching at the university find themselves talking to activists and participating in immigrant rights mobilizations. In my own work, a scholarly interest in immigration and citizenship has led me to research the question of who is, and who is not, able to attend public institutions of higher education like the one at which I teach in Wisconsin. In the course of my research on undocumented students' rights to education, I came into contact with students, some of them still in high school, who work for change. Their presence at universities in the Midwest, in turn, has taught me about histories of citizenship and struggle that I would not be aware of had I not met them.

This collection is intended to illustrate the ways our current historical moment creates such opportunities for encounter. There is a crisis taking place, involving economic transformation, the largest migrations in human history, and the question of rights. One of the central aims of this volume is to link geographically, ethnically, and historically disparate struggles for immigrant rights within the United States. Bringing such diverse stories together allows us to consider questions about the status of nationality and rights, not only in the current transnational moment but also from the first legal construction of "citizen" and "alien" in 1790. Additionally, this volume engages the transformation of immigrant and citizenship rights in the wake of the resurgent nationalism characterizing our contemporary Homeland Security state.

The current moment calls for a new dialogue across disciplines and between those working inside and outside of university settings. This book attempts to provide opportunities for starting such conversations: they can easily be continued in many contexts as we look around the present and back at the past.

The New Civil Rights Movement of the Twenty-First Century?

A popular comparison links the recent upsurge of immigrant rights activism to the civil rights movements of the 1950s–1970s. As "the Civil Rights Movement of the 21st Century,"[3] the contemporary immigrant rights movement gives voice to the disenfranchised and aims to reshape a national policy mired in antedated misconceptions and racialized inequalities. Activist, author, and photographer David Bacon invokes this comparison:

> Social change requires a social movement. Rights are only extended in the United States when people demand it. Congress will pass laws guaranteeing rights for immigrants as it did for workers in 1934, or African Americans in 1966—when it has no choice but to recognize that movement's strength.[4]

Like the civil rights movements emanating from the Black struggle, the immigrant rights movement has brought awareness of global inequality to bear on struggles for national citizenship. And, also like the civil rights movement, the immigrant rights movement contends with the ways in which transnational identities are delimited by the nation. This volume explores the limits and possibilities of the analogy comparing the two movements and attempts to foster new ways of thinking about the issues surrounding immigrant rights.

Social movements like the African American civil rights struggle trace their origins to the political and cultural resistance of enslaved and free African Americans in the Western Hemisphere. As the Africana Cultures and Policy Study Institute points out in their contribution to this book (Williams, Smith, Vaught, and M'Baye, chapter 6), enslaved Africans were among the first migrants to the Americas. Their resistance to slavery and subsequent regimes based on racial inequality has crucially transformed the definition of citizenship. Broadly defined, the civil rights movement has shaped the possibilities for social movements in this country.

During the 1960s and early 1970s, the period that has come to be associated with the most visible phase of the civil rights movement, other racialized and marginalized groups staked their claims to equal citizenship, and more, to social power and cultural representation. Asian Americans,

American Indians, Chicano/as and Puerto Ricans; women, gays and lesbians, and others—all mobilized during this period. The movements they created articulated alternative histories and demanded the redress of social, political, and economic inequalities; in so doing, they transformed the national landscape.

Like the contemporary immigrant rights movement, the civil rights (or what some historians call the "new social movements") of the 1960s and 1970s were not internally homogeneous. Movements defined by race and ethnicity were internally diverse because of differences in gender, class, sexuality, and region. Diversity of national origins complicated movements based on shared diasporic identities like "African" or "Latino." Movements in both periods have confronted the challenge of internal equality and democracy. Activist scholars Eunice Cho (chapter 4), Fred Tsao (chapter 15), and Pierrette Hondagneu-Sotelo and Angelica Salas (chapter 9) document in their contributions to this book the ways in which the contemporary immigrant rights movement, often represented in the mass media as entirely comprised of Latino/as, is actually composed of coalitions of immigrants of different national origins.

In forming movements dedicated to equality and justice, these groups have struggled with the claims of immigrants of different sexualities and class backgrounds. A crucial literature on immigration and sexuality has emerged over the past five years, pointing to the ways in which sexuality has defined immigration policy and the ways in which gay, lesbian, and transgender immigrants, in particular, have navigated the border.[5]

Both the civil rights and immigrant rights movements navigate the central issue of citizenship. As Lowe argues, while citizenship is often considered an endpoint of social struggles, it can also represent a loss for people whose transnational identities connect them across state boundaries.[6] A rich recent scholarship has documented the ways in which civil rights movement strategies and alternative histories were sharply delimited by the Cold War.[7] Transnational connections were sundered, often violently, by an ideological and paramilitary counterinsurgency concerned with any expression of internationalism: whether pulpit, pamphlet, or program. This sundering included long-standing ties between civil rights leaders in the United States and anticolonial thinkers around the world, and among activists throughout the African diaspora. The civil rights movement, as Carol Anderson has eloquently argued, focused on national citizenship because it was largely forced to abandon the internationalism implicit in questions of pan-Africanism and global human rights.[8]

The contemporary immigrant rights movement takes place at a time of deep historical transition. As Saskia Sassen points out, foundational social categories of *citizen* and *alien* are being transformed by economic globalization. For Sassen, this transformation holds out the possibility of an emergent political subjectivity for those marginalized in the national order, like undocumented migrants or women who labor in the home, outside formally recognized labor markets.[9] Contributor Monisha Das Gupta (chapter 18), a scholar in women's and ethnic studies, argues in another article that national citizenship by its nature has never offered protection to undocumented women workers and that the neoliberal state rests on their social and economic marginalization. The South Asian domestic workers' movements that Das Gupta studied insist "that the transnationalization of labor must come with the universal recognition of the rights of migrant workers."[10]

Other commentators have seen a grim picture, in which the guarantees of citizenship won in struggles like those of the civil rights movement fall away in the context of an international global order. "What citizenship," asks historian Linda Kerber, "can be claimed by those trapped jobless in the underworld of the globalized marketplace?"[11] Those in this underworld are connected through ties of family and affinity to citizens; they struggle to claim rights that, increasingly, are defined as human as well as national rights.

History impelled the civil rights movement away from international claims on human rights, toward the demands for full national citizenship ratified on paper by the Civil Rights Act of 1964. As did those in the civil rights movement, immigrants have historically struggled for citizenship in their adoptive nation. However, the current moment compels a creative reconsideration of the limits of citizenship. As Mae Ngai argues in her important book, *Impossible Subjects,* the evolution of national citizenship in the United States has entailed the creation of a new category: the undocumented alien.[12] The immigrant rights movement challenges this history.

The memory of the American civil rights movement has had signal importance in transforming the shape of national politics, if not necessarily in the ways activists envisioned at the time. The enunciation of the arrival of a "new civil rights movement," therefore, fixes a specific moment in the

American national past as the epitome of the social transformation. When a television newscaster turns back from footage of hundreds of thousands of immigrants waving American flags and dubs them "the new civil rights movement," she is at once inviting them into a specific idea of American politics and containing the possibilities of social transformation by freezing them in time and associating them with a movement that has been popularly pronounced over and done with.

The parallel with civil rights is a loaded one in a nation that deems itself now colorblind and appropriates insurgent rhetoric to rationalize the demise of federal programs in support of equal opportunity. How, the essays in this collection ask, does the paradigm of civil rights delimit a movement so deeply a consequence of transnational political economies? How does the current, transnational moment draw on new technologies of citizenship? In what ways is such a moment delimited by representations of rights in a nation-based context?

Histories of Citizenship

Legal scholar and contributor John S. W. Park (chapter 1) has written eloquently elsewhere about the contradiction in American political thought "between principles of equality and fairness on the one hand, and principles of national sovereignty with bounded political communities on the other."[13] As Daniel Kanstroom has recently pointed out, laws of exclusion and deportation parallel the development of citizenship in a nation of immigrants. The political and cultural processes of naturalization take place alongside "various historical forms of exclusion and forced removal."[14]

The emergent nature of such long-standing contradictions is as evident at the walls being built at the U.S.-Mexico border as it is at our public universities and statehouses. In 2006, the Wisconsin state legislature joined many other states in complying with the federal REAL ID Act (2005), passing legislation denying undocumented workers drivers' licenses; Governor Jim Doyle vetoed a bill which, consonant with many others in states and towns around the country, would have proscribed access to public assistance, including prenatal care. In 2007, when the New Haven, Connecticut, City Council voted to create municipal identification cards that would allow the undocumented to open bank accounts and get electricity in their homes, the Bureau of Immigration and Customs Enforcement responded two days later with a neighborhood raid, detaining over thirty migrants from Guatemala, Mexico, Guinea, and Ecuador for deportation.[15]

The contradiction between liberalism's commitment to equality and justice for all and the necessity of reinforcing national boundaries accelerates in an increasingly transnational global political economy, intensifying a long-running culture war over the position of "aliens" in the national community. On the one hand, free trade agreements secure the mobility of capital, while the enduring clamor for immigration reform and immigrant responsibility limits the movement of people across borders and, increasingly, within the nation-state. These contradictions produce a class of semipermanently stateless low-wage workers. Immigrant rights' advocates speak of "globalization from below," in which workers would migrate freely, transforming the definitions of citizenship itself as they do so, but national policies have tended to reinforce militarized borders and increasingly limited definitions of citizenship.[16]

Immigration restriction has always entailed control over the mundane and intimate aspects of immigrant lives. Border-control policy in the southwest in the 1920s, for example, ordained that Mexicans living in long-standing Mexican-American communities register with the authorities and appear once a week to bathe at an official immigration station.[17] As Erika Lee points out, immigration exclusion was coeval with the development of a state scrutinizing, counting, and registering its inhabitants. A regime of gatekeeping emerged with Asian exclusion in the early twentieth century, transforming and enlarging the state as an overseer of both citizens and denizens.[18] But recent trends in immigration restriction, like the REAL ID Act, under which undocumented immigrants are ineligible for drivers' licenses, and the many facets of contemporary homeland security and welfare legislation that deny them access to state services, regulate the everyday life of the undocumented by not allowing them to register or to be present in state institutions, hence obscuring their social visibility. The concomitant invisibility experienced by some contemporary migrants is anything but freeing.

The historical evolution of citizenship has always entailed the existence of those who do not benefit from its protections and rights: denizens, who inhabit a nation, sometimes for generations, without the benefit of political representation or cultural recognition. Myriad examples of this in the U.S. context include African Americans, excluded as slaves from the constitutionally mandated census count for representation until included as citizens by the Fourteenth Amendment; Asian immigrants, first allowed to become citizens after World War II;[19] and American Indians, deemed members of "domestic dependent nations" in 1830 and hence excluded from both political representation and diplomatic relations.

The discourse of citizenship has always been presumptively male, including or excluding women as incidental to male political subjectivity. This has relegated women's political subjectivity to what Candace Bredbenner has called "derivative citizenship": political standing is determined by marital status and by specific legal doctrines constraining the status of single women. Until the Cable Act of 1922, federal laws tended to make women's citizenship status dependent on her marital status. The Naturalization Act of 1855 made foreign wives the first and only group of adults to receive U.S. citizenship derivatively.[20] During the same year that southern and eastern European immigration peaked, the Expatriation Act of 1907 ruled that women who married non-U.S. citizens would take the citizenship of their husbands. This, of course, meant that female citizens who married men ineligible to naturalize, like Asian immigrants, would lose their citizenship rights. By controlling women's sexuality through marriage, the state used gender to police the racialized boundaries created by Asian exclusion in the early twentieth century.

Women whose independent citizenship was undermined by the Cable Act were relegated to the shadows of political legitimacy and long-term residence in a nation without access to naturalization and full citizenship. Asian women were denizens by law throughout much of the late nineteenth and twentieth centuries; African American women, though citizens under the Fourteenth Amendment, struggled to gain access to the rights guaranteed them by law. Many "foreign-born white women," a census category that then included Middle Eastern and Mexican women, remained denizens during the first half of the twentieth century. Some remained denizens because of their marital status: they were married to noncitizens, divorced, or widowed. Other single women chose not to naturalize. The citizenship status of women, by law and popular practice, points to the gendered and historical nature of political subjectivity.

While citizenship confers official rights of representation, its absence has not necessarily meant a historical lack of political subjectivity for those who are not legally eligible for citizenship. As Das Gupta argues elsewhere, immigrant politics often compel a critical stance on the limits of citizenship and what she calls "space-making" politics to create transnational political subjectivities.[21] New immigrants have constantly challenged the boundaries of citizenship, in many cases transforming them and in other cases forcing the state to publicly articulate its justification for their ongoing exclusion. Across the history of American citizenship, noncitizens have pressed for representation. In doing so, they have transformed the notion of citizenship itself.

In 1857, Dred Scott claimed before the Supreme Court that, because of his migration from the slave south to the free state of Illinois and the territory of Minnesota, he and his family were free people. The Court responded that, as a slave and as a person of African descent, Dred Scott was ineligible for the rights of citizenship. In this famous case, Dred Scott and his family contended with key issues in the history of migration: the questions of family unification, and, more broadly, of whether their political subjectivity, their status as free people, could be contained by the boundaries of a slave regime.

Seven years after the Dred Scott decision, the Thirteenth Amendment ended the legal enslavement of African Americans. Subsequently, after some debate, Congress ratified the Fourteenth Amendment extending citizenship to "all persons born or naturalized" in the United States. In 1898, Wong Kim Ark, a Chinese American born in San Francisco in 1873 to immigrant parents ineligible to naturalize, successfully sued to be recognized as an American citizen under the Fourteenth Amendment. Recognizing Chinese Americans as birthright citizens, the court ratified a broad construction of the Fourteenth Amendment. It reached back to, among other things, Justice Benjamin R. Curtis's minority opinion in the Dred Scott decision asserting that citizenship may be acquired by place of birth.[22]

This granting of birthright citizenship has occasioned perennial controversy because it effectively limits the duration of denizenship status to one generation. Contemporary opponents of birthright citizenship refer to U.S.-born children as "anchor babies," who exert their infant political heft to pull others into the country. Colorado representative Tom Tancredo asserted last year: "There is a general agreement about the fact that citizenship in this country should not be bestowed on people who are the children of folks who come into this country illegally."[23]

Contemporary ambivalence about the Fourteenth Amendment has deep historical roots. The issue of birthright citizenship that Tancredo finds so anathema is connected to the broader category of immigrant family unification. This category has been central in organizing immigration preference categories since 1965. As media studies scholar and contributor Lisa Marie Cacho points out in this volume (chapter 8), the emphasis of the recent immigrant mobilizations on claiming heteronormative family values threatens to delimit the movement. On the one hand, the existing provisions for family reunification, while predicated on very culturally narrow and heteronormative ideas of what a family is, have allowed immigrants space to claim inclusion, while maneuvering to define families in their own ways. The window left for family unification threatens to close in the near future; immigration legislation proposed in the spring of 2007 would have moved the emphasis of federal policy from family unification to the labor needs of a neoliberal marketplace. On the other hand, a more expansive, nonheteronormative idea of family and desire might alter the map of inclusion altogether. As Siobhan Somerville suggests, both birthright citizenship and naturalization rely on heterosexual ideas of the reproduction of citizenship. "Queering" issues of immigration and naturalization would bring about a transformation of ideas of citizenship and inclusion.[24]

If birthright citizenship has been controversial, the rights of contemporary migrants who lack access to constitutionally established channels to citizenship of birthright or naturalization become highly fraught, particularly in times of controversy over the issue of immigration and national identity. At the same time that it granted citizenship to all those born or naturalized in the United States, the Fourteenth Amendment also extended to *any person* within the jurisdiction of the states the equal protection of law. The Equal Protection Clause extends constitutional protection to everyone physically in the country, and it has been a key source for the protection of the rights of noncitizens. In ratifying the rights of undocumented children to be educated in public K–12 schools in *Plyler v. Doe*, for example, the Supreme Court leaned heavily on this important idea of equal protection. As legal scholar and contributor Victor Romero argues in this volume (chapter 12), this is an example of the ways in which rights may be legislated outside of citizenship.[25]

At the same time that constitutional protections are sometimes extended to noncitizens, the impairment of rights for noncitizens can affect citizenship, particularly for the foreign born. Scott Michaelsen writes powerfully of the continuities between the jurisprudence justifying the internment of citizen Japanese Americans during the 1940s, and the USA PATRIOT Act passed by a nearly unanimous congress in 2001. For Michaelsen, the ongoing militarization of the borderlands between the United States and Mexico has enabled what he calls "'the permanent state of racial emergency' or 'the permanent state of legal racial exception.'" Policing the borders against the continuously racialized threat of undocumented migration requires an escalating discourse of exception to notions of due process and equality. This escalated discourse then becomes grounds for spectacular trespasses against civil liberties, such as the internment of Japanese Americans or the detention without cause of legal immigrants from places or of faiths suspected of terror.[26]

In 1907, the same year that Congress made white women's citizenship dependent on the status of their husbands, the Alien Immigration Act allowed for "the rights of the Government to deport the alien Chinese wife of a Chinese citizen found within three years after entering this country in a house of prostitution."[27] While Asian women were "aliens ineligible for naturalization" as of 1790, and hence did not take on the citizenship status of their husbands, the Alien Immigration Act of 1907 was one of many federal regulations that crisscrossed the lives of these denizens with the risk of legal sanction, and even the potential for deportation.

In *Low Wah Suey v. Backus*, 1912, the Supreme Court reaffirmed the denizen status of Asian wives of American citizens, emphasizing the importance of state sanctioning of their morality over any nascent ties they might be developing to their adoptive nation. Allegations by the defense that Li A. Sim, Low Wah Suey's wife, had not received due process in the California court had little effect, as she was not a citizen.[28] This is an example of the ways in which the Equal Protection Clause has been unevenly applied. Li A. Sim, then, had as little political subjectivity as the prostitutes that had been the centerpiece of federal laws concerning Asian women since 1875. Writing for the majority, Justice Day said: "A married woman may be as objectionable as a single one in the respects denounced in the law."[29]

Legal principles calling for the special surveillance of denizen women were not limited to Asian immigrants. In 1909, the Supreme Court found that Irene Bodi, a Hungarian immigrant living in Chicago, had been imported for the purpose of prostitution and ordered her deportation. The Court proclaimed: "The admission of an alien female under this act may be regarded as only conditional, and for three years she is on probation; and, if within that time she be guilty of the acts therein mentioned she forfeits her rights to remain."[30] The Ohio Supreme Court in 1928 upheld a local tradition of laws by ordering Gertrude Davis to be fined and/or imprisoned for practicing palmistry.[31] Denizens who found any kind of work in places deemed inappropriate or immoral were at risk for deportation or jailing. Li A. Sim might have worked as a waitress in a Chinatown establishment that seemed to Commissioner Backus likely to be connected to prositution. Irene Bodi probably hoped, like many young women, that her emigration from Hungary would lead to better things. Gertrude Davis, like many immigrant women, attempted to make her living at a trade that was deemed to be outside constitutional protections on free speech. No matter: these women's political and social subjectivity was limited by their dual status as noncitizens and as women in the early twentieth century.

Ironically, issues of gender and marriage were part of a general transformation of immigration and citizenship policy in the post–World War II period. War bride policies in World War II and the Korean War were part of a more general transition in immigration policy, from the racialized national origins quotas of 1924 and 1952 to the civil rights–inspired moment of the 1965 Immigration and Nationality Act. This "liberalization" of immigration policy, including the gradual abolition of Asian exclusion, and the transition from national origins quotas to family unity and work preferences, were as much a component of a transnational Cold War order as of a civil rights–inspired change in immigration policy.

Citizenship rights have historically been defined and limited by the category of noncitizen. During the Cold War, for example, the deportation of foreign-born radicals, labor leaders in particular, was anchored by legislation designed in the 1930s to expedite the removal of Mexican American workers from the U.S. economy during the Great Depression. The

Spolansky or Michigan Alien Registration Act of 1931 targeted communist influence in the Detroit Mexican American community and was a precedent for the federal Smith Act of 1940, which compelled the registration of noncitizens and provided for the deportation of anyone who had ever belonged to an organization advocating the violent overthrow of the government. The Spolansky Act was mostly used to deport Mexican Americans, many of whom were actually American citizens, from the Detroit area.[32]

Similarly, in the current period, the deportation terror levied against undocumented laborers shelters under the broad rubric of the "war on terror." Tram Nguyen points out the connections made in national security rhetoric between undocumented people, refugees, and potential terrorists as "clandestine transnational actors."[33] David Cole writes in his contribution to this volume (chapter 16) about the ways that the war on terror has come to blur the distinctions between citizens, like Yasir Hamdi and Jose Padilla, and perceived threats from foreign actors. Just as laws delimiting the activities of Mexican Americans in Detroit in the 1930s came to apply to political activists of diverse national origins after World War II, heightened surveillance of Muslim and Middle Eastern communities after 9/11 has led to increased ideological and financial support for deporting migrant workers. Nguyen writes: "National security concerns have been used as a justification for increased discrimination in arenas of long-standing concern to civil rights activists, including employment, housing and criminal justice."[34]

Lisa Flores has described the ways in which racialized portrayals of immigrants have led, historically, to anti-immigrant sentiment and federal deportation programs. She traces a "uniformity in the public vocabulary surrounding immigration and criminality. Whether invoked directly or indirectly, the figure of the 'illegal alien' is hauntingly consistent, as is the quick turn to deportation."[35] What is crucial about Flores's argument is that this racialization of noncitizens has been an ongoing rhetorical practice. As such, this rhetoric takes on particular meanings at different times. Flores traces a 1920s mass media discourse in which Mexican American laborers appear as docile "peons," offering cheap labor and little threat, while these same migrants turn up in the 1930s as a dangerous criminal element, threatening to upset the economic and social order. This floating rhetoric can target different populations, as is evident in the transition from the Spolansky Act, later declared unconstitutional because of popular protest,[36] to the Smith Act, used widely against foreign-born people, including but not limited to Mexican Americans, during the Cold War.

In 1954, INS Commissioner Joseph Swing, who had served with General John Pershing in the U.S. occupation of Mexico in 1916, implemented Operation Wetback. Functioning at the same time was the Bracero Program, bringing laborers from Mexico to work in fields and factories, Operation Wetback targeted illegal border crossings from Mexico to the United States. Swing drew on the twin discourses of anti-Communism and criminalization in mustering support for the program in Texas and the Southwest, countering demands from employers and migrants for a legalization program. Operation Wetback apprehended about 1 million undocumented migrants in 1954 alone. Undocumented migrants were often arrested and deported along with their citizen children and family members. As Mae Ngai has emphasized, Operation Wetback drove many migrants to renew contracts under the Bracero Program. These short-term contracts ensured that these migrants would not be eligible for citizenship.[37]

In September 2006, First U.S. District Judge Raner C. Collins dismissed a federal case against humanitarian aid workers Shanti Sellz and Daniel Strauss, volunteers with the Tucson faith-based group, No More Deaths. Working under protocols established in concert with the border patrol, the group does humanitarian work at the U.S.-Mexico border. Sellz and Strauss had been charged in July 2005 with illegally transporting migrants across the U.S.-Mexico border, after having been advised by volunteer doctors to follow established border patrol protocol and transport three dehydrated men, who were unable to drink water, out of the 105-degree desert and to a hospital. The three migrants were detained by the U.S. Border Patrol, and Sellz and Strauss were arrested.[38]

The dismissal of the case against the No More Deaths volunteers has been hailed by immigrant rights advocates and humanitarian groups as affirming the importance of humanitarian work at the border. Since 1995, the death rate among border crossers has doubled; from 300 to 400 people a year die while trying to cross.[39] But legal sanctions against humanitarian work on the border have been an important component of recent immigration legislation. The House immigration bill passed in December 2005, sponsored by Wisconsin State Representative James Sensenbrenner, contained antismuggling provisions so severe that they could be construed to mean that unknowing contact with an undocumented person, and any knowing assistance to an undocumented person, constitute a federal offense punishable by up to five years in prison.[40]

Just as Dred Scott and his family constituted nonpersons for the Supreme Court in 1857, undocumented migrants, and even their citizen allies, become in the current moment presumptively suspicious. In 1857, Chief Justice Roger Taney upheld a slave regime most Americans now view as unjust. But the security of the border between the United States and Mexico, the maintenance of national citizenships, and the policing of infractions like undocumented migration are key components of a contemporary regime of homeland security and neoliberal trade policy. Challenging these policies, like crossing the border, violate the boundaries of this regime.

Rights at the Margins

In February 2007, almost a year after the historic mobilizations for immigrant rights of spring 2006, I attended a summit meeting held by Voces de la Frontera, a workers' center and immigrant rights group in Milwaukee. A seminar entitled "Civil Rights" packed a hotel ballroom with a standing room–only crowd. The seminar began with testimonies by workers from the Star packing plant in nearby Whitewater, Wisconsin, which had been raided by Immigrations and Customs Enforcement (ICE) the previous August.[41] Such sweeps of workplaces known to employ undocumented workers have become very common since the spring of 2006.

Two women from Whitewater spoke at the summit. They testified about being told repeatedly that because they had no immigration documents, they had no rights; about being imprisoned and separated from their families; about being strip-searched and physically abused and intimidated.

Subsequently, an immigration lawyer who volunteers in Voces de la Frontera's legal clinic took the floor, accompanied by a translator. He held up a thick book of ICE regulations to demonstrate that raids like the one in Whitewater are, at least in theory, governed by law. In the course of his presentation, the lawyer spoke of the rights undocumented migrants have in the United States, under constitutional and immigration law. He talked about the ways in which undocumented migrants are protected, to some extent, by the Equal Protection Clause, about what legal resources these workers have recourse to in case of a raid, and how they might protect their children in case of their arrest. A majority of people in the audience raised their hands when the translator posed the question in Spanish: "How many people here know someone who is at risk of being deported?"

In many ways, these sweeps against the undocumented are transforming the immigrant rights movement, bringing people who may otherwise have felt safer remaining invisible to the center of current struggles. At this writing, immigrant rights activist Elvira Arellano, who sheltered in a Chicago church with her seven-year-old son for a year, has been arrested and deported back to Mexico. Her American-born son, Saul, remains in the United States. A New Sanctuary Movement, with clear parallels to the Sanctuary Movement of the 1980s, draws the attention of faith-based groups to the issue. As Jeanne Petit illustrates in her contribution to this volume (chapter 14), immigration rights can become a powerful moral issue for religious people.

In attempting to theorize the position of noncitizen immigrants, American courts have been caught between a history of jurisprudence, extending equal protection to all people dwelling within national borders, and manifestations of nativism that delimit the access of noncitizen immigrant to social services and basic civil liberties. And just as Justice Roger Taney negotiated the soon-to-be-sundered borders of a nation made up of slave states and free in 1857, contemporary immigration jurisprudence centers on the significance of a border separating nations that are increasingly connected by transnational politics and economics. The Dred Scott decision and the No More Deaths case signal crises in political subjectivity, moments in which definitions of human, alien, citizen, and property collide and demand rearticulation. Such moments of crisis have been central to ever-changing notions of the citizen and stranger throughout the history of nation-states.

Organization of This Book

This anthology is organized into five sections. Each section contains original essays, with appendices of primary documents drawn from court cases, newspapers, and the archives of various organizations. These primary sources are meant to provide readers with the opportunity to interpret for themselves some of the documents that contributors refer to.

Part I, "Narratives of Refuge and Resistance," traces the interaction between the image of the United States as a shelter for all and the specific experiences of different communities as they seek refuge and rights here. Claiming refuge, even within the limited terms set by public policy, brings individual migrants to challenge ways in which the state frames their identities. In Part II, "Ambivalent Allies, Reluctant Rivals, and Disavowed Deviants," contributors examine the charged politics of coalition and comparison between different immigrant groups and various native-born communities, including indigenous peoples. Contributors to this part examine the ways in immigrants are compared to native-born communities through discourses of race, gender, and sexuality; and the possibilities for alliances between different groups. Part III, "Immigrant Acts," focuses on contemporary immigrant organizing, and the political mobilizations of spring 2006. The essays and documents in this part offer insights into the ways the movement has come together in recent years, the emergence of immigrant leaders, and the relationship between different members of the coalitions that make up the contemporary immigrant rights movement. In Part IV, "Questions of Democracy," contributors examine the ways that immigrant rights issues are part of a broader transformation in democratic politics. Part V, "Afterwords," provides two essays for continued thought on the questions of citizenship, rights, and identity pursued throughout the book.

When thousands of people, with and without the papers certifying their right to be in a particular country at a particular moment, take to the streets bearing signs saying "No Human Being Is Illegal / Ningun ser humano es illegal," they are drawing on a form of social protest that has been used in this country to make claims on the state. But the idea that no human being can be illegal, that states cannot define the undocumented and confine them to an underworld without rights, is an inherently international proposition. The eighteen essays in this book are dedicated to understanding how this contradiction has been expressed historically, what it means now, and where the ongoing redefinition of citizenship will take us.

NOTES

My gratitude to Nan Enstad for an inspired and fast last-minute critique of this introduction.

1. See Matthew Frye Jacobson, *Special Sorrows: The Diasporic Imagination of Irish, Polish, and Jewish Immigrants in the United States* (Berkeley: University of California Press, 2001), and Michel Laguerre, *Diasporic Citizens: Haitian Americans in Transnational America* (New York: Palgrave, 1998).

2. Lisa Lowe, *Immigrant Acts: On Asian American Cultural Politics* (Durham, N.C.: Duke University Press, 1996), 9.

3. This phrase has most often been attributed to Houston Congresswoman Sheila Jackson Lee.

4. "Time for a More Radical Civil Rights Movement," *American Prospect*, July 24, 2007, at http://www.prospect.org (accessed August 8, 2007).

5. For example, Eithne Luibheid, *Entry Denied: Controlling Sexuality at the Border* (Minneapolis: University of Minnesota Press, 2002); Eithne Luibheid and Lionel Cantú, *Queer Migrations: Sexuality, U.S. Citizenship, and Border Crossings* (Minneapolis: University of Minnesota Press, 2005); Gayatri Gopinath, *Impossible Desires: Queer Diasporas and South Asian Public Cultures* (Durham, N.C.: Duke University Press, 2005); Martin Mansalanan, *Global Divas: Filipino Gay Men in Diaspora* (Durham, N.C.: Duke University Press, 2003); Siobhan Somerville, "Notes towards a Queer History of Naturalization," *American Quarterly* 57/3 (September 2005), 659–76; Margot Canaday, "Building a Straight State: Sexuality and Social Citizenship under the 1944 GI Bill," *Journal of American History* 90/3 (2003), 935–57.

6. Lowe, *Immigrant Acts*, 82.

7. For example, Nikhil Pal Singh, *Black Is a Country: Race and the Unfinished Struggle for Democracy* (Cambridge: Harvard University Press, 2004); Carol Anderson, *Eyes Off the Prize: The United Nations and the African American Struggle for Human Rights, 1944–1955* (Cambridge: Cambridge University Press, 2003); and Mary Dudziak, *Cold War Civil Rights: Race and the Image of American Democracy* (Princeton: Princeton University Press, 2002).

8. Anderson, *Eyes Off the Prize*, 5.

9. Saskia Sassen, "The Repositioning of Citizenship: Emergent Subjects and Spaces for Politics," *Berkeley Journal of Sociology* 46 (2002), 4–25.

10. Monisha Das Gupta, "The Neoliberal State and the Domestic Workers' Movement in New York City," *Canadian Woman Studies/Les Cahiers de la Femme*, 22/3–4 (2003), 82; also, Das Gupta, *Unruly Immigrants: Rights, Activism, and Trans-*

national South Asian Politics in the United States (Durham, N.C.: Duke University Press, 2006).

11. Linda K. Kerber, "Toward a History of Statelessness in America," *American Quarterly* 57/3 (September 2005), 744.

12. Mae Ngai, *Impossible Subjects: Illegal Aliens and the Making of Modern America* (Princeton: Princeton University Press, 2004).

13. John S. W. Park, *Elusive Citizenship: Asian Americans and the Paradox of Civil Rights* (New York: New York University Press, 2004), 5.

14. Daniel Kanstroom, *Deportation Nation: Outsiders in American History* (Cambridge: Harvard University Press, 2007), 21.

15. "Feds Arrest Dozens of Illegal Immigrants in New Haven Raids," *Yale Daily News*, June 6, 2007; "ICE Raids Spark Protests in Portland, New Haven" *World War Four*, at http://www.ww4report.com/node/4084 (accessed August 16, 2007).

16. Robert Lovato, "Envisioning Another World: Integración Desde Abajo," *Nation*, March 6, 2006, 22–26; see also Tim Costello, Jeremy Brecher, and Brendan Smith, *Globalization from Below* (Boston: South End Press, 2000).

17. Ngai, *Impossible Subjects*, 70

18. Erika Lee, *At America's Gates: Chinese Immigration during the Exclusion Era, 1882–1943* (Chapel Hill: University of North Carolina Press, 2003).

19. For example, Hiroshi Motomura, *Americans in Waiting: The Lost Story of Immigration and Citizenship in the United States* (New York: Oxford University Press, 2006).

20. Candace Bredbenner, *A Nationality of Her Own: Women, Marriage and the Laws of Citizenship* (Berkeley: University of California Press, 1998), 15.

21. Das Gupta, *Unruly Immigrants.*

22. Curtis resigned from the Supreme Court after the verdict in *Scott v. Sandford.*

23. Stephan Dinan, "GOP Mulls Ending Birthright Citizenship," *Washington Times*, November 4, 2005, at www.washtimes.com (accessed September 15, 2006).

24. Somerville, "Notes towards a Queer History of Naturalization," 672.

25. Victor Romero, *Alienated: Immigrant Rights, the Constitution, and Equality in America* (New York: New York University Press, 2005).

26. Scott Michaelsen, "Between Japanese Internment and the USA PATRIOT Act: The Borderlands and the Permanent State of Racial Exception," *Aztlán* 30/2 (2005), 87–111.

27. Cited in *Low Wah Suey v. Backus*, 225 U.S. 460 (1912).

28. This principle was reiterated by the Circuit Court of Appeals, Ninth District, in *Choy Gum v. Backus*, 223 Fed. 487 (1915).

29. Ibid.

30. *Keller v. U.S.,* 213 U.S. 138 (1909); *Louis Ullman v. United States,* 29 Sup. Ct. 470 (1909).

31. *Davis v. State of Ohio,* Ohio Supreme Court, no. 20569, 1928. Toledo has had a law setting a Fortunetellers and Phrenologists License at the astronomical price of $450 since 1900; I suspect that this is an instance of legal sanctions being both gendered and racialized in delimiting the ways that immigrant women could earn a living.

32. Kanstroom, *Deportation Nation,* 195; also American Committee for the Protection of the Foreign Born, "Deportation Special: Who's Who in Deportations—Brief Biographies of Workers Held for Deportation," September 1935, at the Tamiment Library, American Committee for the Protection of the Foreign Born Collection, Box 1, File "1935–1945"; see also "Selected Immigration Laws," fall 2004, at http://www.lib.umich.edu/socwork/rescue/archive/sw530.html (accessed August 2007).

33. Tram Nguyen, *We Are All Suspects Now: Untold Stories from Immigrant Communities after 9/11* (Boston: Beacon, 2005), xiv.

34. Ibid., xx.

35. Lisa Flores, "Constructing Rhetorical Borders: Peons, Illegal Aliens, and Competing Narratives of Immigration," *Critical Studies in Media Communication* 20/4 (December 2003), 363.

36. American Committee for the Protection of the Foreign Born, "Deportation Special."

37. Ngai, *Impossible Subjects,* 152–58.

38. No More Deaths/No Más Muertes, www.nomoredeaths.org (accessed September 17, 2006).

39. U.S. Government Accountability Office, Report to Bill Frist, *Illegal Immigration: Border Crossing Deaths Have Doubled since 1995; Border Patrol's Efforts to Prevent Deaths Have Not Been Evaluated,* August 1996, athttp://www.gao.gov/new.items/d06770.pdf (accessed February 26, 2007).

40. National Immigrant Law Center, *How Helping an Immigrant Could Become a Crime under HR 4437,* February 2006, at www.nilc.org (accessed September 17, 2006).

41. For example, Carla McCann, "Whitewater Raid Tears Families Apart," *Janesville Gazette,* August 24, 2006, at www.freerepublic.com/focus/f-news/1689576/posts (accessed January 20, 2008).

PART I

Narratives of Refuge and Resistance

The image of the Statue of Liberty is a central one to political culture in the United States. A time-honored narrative of American national identity relates the story of a nation of immigrants, of people who, for so many reasons, needed and claimed refuge here. At the entry points of the nation—at immigration stations, asylum hearings, detention and deportation centers—people seeking to enter the country, or to remain here, also produce narratives of refuge. Sometimes, their stories re-create a familiar plotline, in which America is a sheltering harbor for the persecuted. At other times, the circumstances in which potential immigrants, refugees, and deportees speak create alternative stories about their circumstances and about the true disposition of the United States toward the world's tired, poor, and huddled masses yearning to breathe free. In the current post-9/11 moment, increasingly restrictive attitudes toward immigrants challenge the national narrative of refuge.

Chapter 1 examines the ways in which the harsh federal responses to immigrant claims threaten to transform not only the narrative of the United States as a nation of refuge but also the very practices of democracy. Asian American and legal studies scholar John S. W. Park examines the historical development of what he calls "the fiction of parole": immigrants physically present but not legally admitted into the country. This category originated with the Chinese exclusion laws of the late nineteenth and early twentieth centuries. As Park explains, though, the idea of a federally "paroled" immigrant evolved throughout the twentieth century, often substituting for petitions for refuge. Since 1990, Park argues, the category of the parolee—someone present but without legal claim—has come to define most immigrants to the United States.

Immigrants consistently contest the legal categories that define them. In chapter 2, sociologist Connie G. Oxford explores the ways that the stories told by women seeking asylum in the United States are transformed by asylum attorneys, social workers, and the court system to fit into the standards established by immigration law. Oxford traces the ways that individual asylum seekers resist the transformation of their experiences into standardized legal narratives that often leave out what is most true to them, as well as the ways in which their advocates attempt to intervene on their behalf. She argues that the transformation of individual experiences into narratives acceptable to the state, while necessary, can also become an act of violence against the complexity of refugee experiences.

Family reunification has been a guiding component of immigration law since 1965, although that emphasis has been challenged by legislation proposed in 2007. But lesbian, gay, and transgender petitioners for immigrant status face a pronounced lack of legal recognition of the relationships they call family. In chapter 3, Scott Long, Jessica Stern, and Adam Francouer of Human Rights Watch and Immigration Equality, Inc., review the legal history of U.S. policy toward gay, lesbian, and transgender people. They trace the ways that LGBT immigration is caught in two distinct and long-term culture wars: over the regulation of national boundaries and over the recognition of gay identities and marriage. This article is followed by the transcript of one of the important legal cases governing LGBT immigration, *Boutilier v. Immigration Service*, 1967.

Finally, in chapter 4, Eunice Hyunhye Cho, former Education Director at the National Network for Immigrant and Refugee Rights (NNIRR), explains the political and historical context for the emergence of the draconian immigration restriction bill of 2006. She traces long-term advocacy by immigrant rights groups for less punitive policies that would recognize the ongoing importance of immigrant communities to national economic and social health. Cho presents the challenges of creating alliances between immigrant groups from different nations, living in different regions, and, often, with markedly different concerns and approaches. Such alliance building, she argues, often transformed the vision of individual, localized communities. This article is followed by a series of short documents from the National Network for Immigrant and Refugee Rights' organizing campaigns of spring 2006.

CHAPTER 1

On Being Here and Not Here

Noncitizen Status in American Immigration Law

John S. W. Park

This essay looks at broad developments in the immigration law to point out how the status of all newcomers to the United States has become both more simple and more vulnerable in fundamental ways. I focus on a particular type of status created through federal court precedents, then codified in the federal immigration law since 1952. That status created a category of persons who were physically in the United States, but framed as though they were not "admitted," and thus having the same position as persons just seeking admission from a foreign country. As nonadmitted persons, they were released from the custody of immigration authorities, but they really had no constitutinal rights and no substantive right to be in the country. No matter the length of their stay, these persons could be expelled at the will of executive officials, with minimal or no supervision from the federal courts. When their status first emerged in the late nineteenth century, only a relatively small minority of undesirable Asians and Europeans fell within the power of this legal fiction. This essay attempts to show, however, how that status now describes the condition of most immigrants in the United States.

Beginning in 1875, as Congress began to regulate immigration much more deliberately and forcefully, federal authorities created a wide range of new categories for people coming to the United States. Some were legislative, and others came from the federal courts, many borrowing from existing legal precedents and concepts. All of these classifications had great legal force: after the first of several Chinese Exclusion Acts in 1882, determining a person's status for purposes of immigration had profound consequences for everyone seeking admission into the United States. As Kitty Calavita, Erika Lee, and other scholars have shown, being classified "a returning citizen," a "merchant," or "a laborer" meant the difference between entry, detention, or exclusion.[1] Clearly, after Chinese exclusion, the new federal system of immigration enforcement responded very differently to persons seeking entry, and depending on one's status, various substantive and procedural protections—the right to a hearing, the right to petition the federal courts, the right to invoke the constitution itself—did or did not apply. Because it was *Chinese* exclusion, racial status mattered a great deal, too, and as Hiroshi Motomura and other scholars have pointed out, many Europeans were treated as "citizens in waiting" from the very first day they arrived in the United States, while Chinese and then other Asians languished in immigration detention arguing over their rights.[2]

By the early twentieth century in the United States, federal immigration law envisioned the categories of citizens, persons on their way to citizenship, lawful residents ineligible for citizenship, and persons who were not formally supposed to be here at all. And not everyone among this last category was in the same position: there were those who had entered unlawfully, having avoided or tricked immigration authorities; and there were persons who were inspected, then either detained or "paroled" into the United States. Being paroled was and is a rather odd status. As it appeared originally in federal immigration law, the fiction of parole developed through the federal courts as an analog to the parole in criminal law. The fiction applies most often to someone who is literally free and yet still under the direct jurisdiction of the state.

Parole in both instances was conceived as a privilege, and the state may revoke that privilege either when the parolee has violated the terms of parole or when the state determines other relevant circumstances warranting a change of status. In the criminal law, revoking parole often means a trip back to jail; in the immigration law, losing parole status means detention, then (maybe) a trip back to one's home country. A change in parole status could have opposite consequences: in the criminal law, a parolee who successfully meets the conditions of parole is considered "rehabilitated" and released into society. Similarly, if a federal official or a federal court finds that an immigrant parolee does have a right to be in the United States, that person is released and acquires other rights as a lawful immigrant. Parole can be an odd, liminal status, like purgatory, neither here nor there.

In federal immigration law, the fiction of parole developed over many cases in the late nineteenth and early twentieth centuries. The underpinnings for the fiction began because many presumptively excludable Chinese migrants were claiming that they were either members of an exempt category of migrants or that they were American citizens. Federal authorities detained many more of these persons, interrogated them, and also demanded from Congress a harsher set of rules to enforce exclusion. This was because more and more Chinese detainees had filed habeas corpus petitions in the federal courts, and those claiming citizenship alleged that immigration authorities were violating their constitutional rights.[3] Chinese detainees were filing habeas petitions because they wanted to test the legality of their detention or exclusion before the federal courts, expecting these courts to be more just and fair than hostile immigration officers.[4] From the government's perspective, one solution to this problem was to treat incoming migrants as though they were not within the United States at all, such that the constitution itself did not apply to such persons. The writ of habeas corpus—rooted in due process principles with the Fifth and then the Fourteenth Amendments—would be unavailable.

In 1895, the U.S. Supreme Court addressed the case of a Japanese woman landing in San Francisco. By this time, new congressional rules gave more authority to federal officers to determine a person's admissibility, and Nishimura Ekiu's case tested these new limits. She claimed to be the wife of a lawfully admitted immigrant, but California's immigration inspector, acting as an agent of the federal government, did not believe her and determined that she was excludable. Nishimura's attorney filed a habeas corpus petition, and the same immigration authorities "placed [her] temporarily in the Methodist Episcopal Japanese and Chinese Mission" in San Francisco "in obedience to the . . . writ." Nishimura was thus *in* the United States literally, and she was invoking, through the writ, procedural protections and due process rights that were generally understood as an integral part of the Constitution. The essence of the case, though, was not whether Nishimura should or shouldn't be admitted into the United States but, rather, whether she should have been allowed to file for the writ at all. In other words, if Congress had passed a set of rules giving executive authorities the right to determine admissibility, should the federal courts intervene at all? Did Nishimura have "a right to due process of law" under the Constitution?[5]

The answer to both questions was no. Nishimura's case illustrated how federal judges increasingly framed themselves as "captives of the law," bound by legislative rules that explicitly denied them the authority to review the findings of executive officials in matters of immigration.[6] In matters of immigration, the constitution did not apply in the same way as it would to an American citizen on American territory. Nishimura was on American soil, the Court conceded, but she was certainly not a full member of the community. Speaking through Justice Horace Gray, the Court said that because Nishimura was a foreigner, for whom special exclusion procedures were created specifically by Congress, "the decisions of executive or administrative officers, acting within powers expressly conferred by Congress, are due process of law."[7]

It did not matter, furthermore, that she was physically within the United States:

> Putting her in the mission house, as a more suitable place than the steamship, pending the decision of the question of her right to land, and keeping her there, by agreement between her attorney and the attorney for the United States, until final judgment upon the writ of habeas corpus, left her in the same position, so far as regarded her right to land in the United States, as if she never had been removed from the steamship.[8]

This was a novel fiction in federal immigration law: to treat someone who was within the territorial borders of the United States as though she was still at the cusp of the nation's border. We are to pretend that she was aboard a ship, not yet disembarked.

The fiction appears again in another famous case in 1905. When Ju Toy filed his habeas petition, however, he claimed that he was a native-born American citizen, thus changing one crucial element distinguishing this case from earlier ones following *Nishimura*. The Supreme Court's reply was still the same: even when a petitioner claims to be an American citizen, if the immigration officer does not believe him, the federal courts should not intervene by granting a full hearing through a habeas corpus petition. Ju Toy had exhausted his appeals to executive authorities, but in the first habeas case, the district court agreed with him, "seemingly on new evidence," that he was in fact an American citizen. But Justice Oliver Wendell Holmes agreed with the executive officials that the federal courts should not have intervened at all. In the decision, he repeated the parole fiction: "The petitioner, although physically present within our boundaries, is to be regarded as if he had been stopped at the limit of our jurisdiction and kept there while his right to enter was under debate."[9] Ju Toy was excluded, then admitted, then excluded again.

Two decades later, the parole fiction was pushed to the limit in a sad case involving a Russian girl. The petitioner in *Kaplan v. Tod* (1925) was found "feeble-minded" and thus excludable, but because of World War I, federal authorities could not deport her, and so she was held on Ellis Island for about a year, until June of 1915, when she was "handed over to the Hebrew Sheltering and Immigrant Aid Society." The society allowed the girl to live with her father, and she did so for close to ten years. When federal officials issued final orders of deportation in 1923, her father had become a naturalized citizen; by the time the U.S. Supreme Court issued its decision, his daughter had been in the United States for about eleven years. Her father insisted that by his naturalization, his daughter had also become an American citizen.

But Justice Holmes refused to concede that such a person had been "admitted" for immigration purposes: "Naturalization of parents affects minor children only 'if dwelling in the United States.'" "The appellant could not lawfully have landed in the United States in view of the express prohibition of the [Immigration] Act of 1910 . . . and until she legally landed, 'could not have dwelt within the United States.'" She had been here, but she was not really here:

> While she was at Ellis Island she was to be regarded as stopped at the boundary line and kept there unless and until her right to enter should be declared. When her prison bounds were enlarged by committing her to the custody of the Hebrew Society, the nature of her stay within the

> territory was not changed. She was still in theory of law at the boundary line and had gained no foothold in the United States.[10]

After all that time, despite all the attachments she may have developed during her parole in the United States, the petitioner was deported.

In 1952, Congress passed the Walter-McCarran Act and defined parole in that statute in much the same way as the courts had held for over five decades. Parole was placed within the discretion of the attorney general and his subordinates. A person paroled into the United States had not been admitted, and such a person is legally in the same position as someone not on American territory and seeking admission.[11] In a case testing the statutory construction of parole as a form of admission into the United States, the Supreme Court phrased parole as

> a device through which needless confinement is avoided while administrative proceedings are conducted. It was never intended to affect an alien's status, and to hold that petitioner's parole placed her legally "within the United States" is inconsistent with the congressional mandate, the administrative concept of parole, and the decisions of this Court. Physical detention of aliens is now the exception, not the rule, and is generally employed only as to security risks or those likely to abscond.[12]

The petitioner, Leng May Ma, had claimed to be an American citizen when she arrived in the United States in May 1951; the government disagreed, but she had been paroled into the country in August 1952 while applying for asylum and the Court's decision was dated June 1958. For over seven years, she was within the United States, but again, not really here.

After the Supreme Court affirmed the power of the parole fiction in *Leng May Ma* (1958), "parole . . . became an outstandingly flexible tool in the hands of the executive branch," allowing prospective entrants to be in the United States while severely limiting their rights.[13] In *Leng May Ma,* the Supreme Court didn't necessarily see it this way; because parolees avoided unnecessary detention, "[the] policy reflects the humane qualities of an enlightened civilization."[14] But as we can see from this case and others like it, parolees had a most uncertain status independent of the length of their stay—while they were here, they could reunite with their families, develop other attachments, and even work, but in the event of an adverse finding, they must leave without being able to challenge the finding in the federal courts. In a nation that typically required only five years of lawful residency before an immigrant could petition for citizenship, the fiction of a person "paroled" for at least five years, and yet somehow not "admitted," simply did not fit reality. It would be as though they were here and yet were perpetually insulated from the procedural and substantive protections of the constitution. The fiction of parole remains "good law," both by statute and by ongoing legal precedents.[15]

In more recent decades, critics of the parole fiction have most often complained that executive authorities were using parole too expansively. For the most part, parole was commonly understood to apply to individuals under narrow circumstances: "to permit medical treatment, to allow appearance in litigation or a criminal prosecution, to prevent inhumane separation of families or for other humanitarian reasons, or to permit release pending adjudication of an exclusion case," according to one scholar.[16] However, since the late 1950s, executive officials, including the president of the United States, paroled large numbers of persons who were fleeing persecution or political dislocation in their home countries. Dwight Eisenhower paroled about 30,000 Hungarians into the United States after the Soviet invasion of Hungary in 1956; these persons were most appropriately "refugees," but determining that they were in fact refugees under the prevailing law would have taken much longer than simply paroling them into the country.

Commentators insisted that this was not a good use of the parole power, and they further objected when these refugee parolees asked to be treated as though they had as many procedural or substantive rights as any other parolees.[17] Yet, before 1980, persons from Asia, including the People's Republic of China and Vietnam, were paroled into the United States as refugees in fairly large numbers, again because this avenue was more expedient and flexible. Even after the Refugee Act of 1980, which was designed in part to curtail the use of parole for persons most suitable for refugee status, executive officials still relied on parole in emergency cases for persons most likely to seek asylum in the United States, the most notable cases being the Cuban refugee crises of the 1980s and the Haitian and Cuban refugee crises of the 1990s. Over a quarter of a million persons were paroled into the United States since 1980 in this way.[18]

Many of the most recent parolees from Haiti and Cuba were released to sponsors, but a small fraction of these persons have since been detained because of past criminal records or because of criminal activity after their release. For example, there are about 1,000 Cubans in immigration detention facilities who had originally been paroled into the United States since 1990; because Cuba itself is either unable or unwilling to take back these persons, their detention is "indefinite."[19] Their circumstances are most peculiar, and though the federal courts have upheld the indefinite detention of "non-admitted" persons many times, commentators have objected to the idea that the federal government can hold such persons in this way, all with extremely limited due process rights. Several notable test cases have emerged in recent years, with mixed results, but all tending to favor the idea that parolees do not have the same rights as others "admitted" to the United States.[20]

The more compelling fact might be that the condition of parolees fits most newcomers to the United States since 1990. Indeed, ever since the Immigration Act of 1990, and especially after a set of new immigration rules in 1996, including the Illegal Immigration Reform and Immigrant Responsibility Act, all newcomers to the United States have had a much more limited set of rights. This is true whether they are admitted temporarily, or as permanent residents, or as persons who come without inspection. The Immigrant Responsibility Act changed the basic language of the immigration law: persons were either "admitted" or not admitted, for example; and immigrants and nonimmigrants were not excluded or deported, they were "removed."

In the Immigration Act of 1990, Congress increased the number of skilled workers who could be admitted to the United States, and it then created new categories of temporary skilled workers whose numbers in subsequent years soon exceeded the numbers of skilled immigrants admitted permanently. For those without skills or capital, the years after 1990 were marked by new barriers and fences, some of which might have slowed—but none of which completely stopped—the migration of the relatively poor. Against the new obstacles of the federal immigration law, illegal aliens came anyway, increasing in number from about three or four million to more than three or four times that number. All these people came over the past two decades. And yet all were held aloof, here and not here; all were treated as though they had no firm right to stay; all were cut off from a common social safety net; and all could be removed with relative ease.

Indeed, all newcomers share the anxiety of the new "removal," no matter how long ago they entered the United States. At one point, for example, entering the United States without inspection, and then remaining undetected for a while, could trigger a broader set of rights than being inspected and paroled at the border. How could this be, that an illegal alien could have more rights than a parolee? In a separate line of cases dealing with undocumented aliens, some dating back to the exclusion period, the Supreme Court has long held that persons accused of unlawful entry are still "persons" within the meaning of the Fifth Amendment's Due Process Clause, as well as the Fourteenth Amendment's Equal Protection Clause.[21]

They cannot be denied their liberty without due process of law, and the states may also not discriminate against them without violating the equal protection principle, especially if their entry was long ago or, in the case of undocumented children, not their own fault. In addition, as "persons," when they were facing deportation, they often had access to procedural protections that parolees did not.[22] The rules in 1996 clearly ended this "discrepancy": undocumented aliens may have entered and stayed, but they were no longer regarded as "admitted," and so, according to Linda Bosniak, undocumented aliens "are now subject to the more rigorous grounds of inadmissibility with fewer procedural protections in the administative proceeding itself."[23] In other words, undocumented aliens are now as easily removable as parolees. This is because neither class of persons is regarded as "admitted" under the law.

In addition, in light of the harsh set of rules governing "removal" from the United States, even persons admitted as permanent residents should expect relatively minor criminal convictions to result in the end of their permanent residency. Before 1996, persons convicted of a crime could apply for suspension of deportation, often based on the impact of their deportation on an American citizen; afterward, these same persons are now ineligible for what has become "cancellation of removal." Consequently, more and more persons are removed for a much wider range of offenses —about 200,000 have been removed every year since 2004.[24] Although in recent cases the U.S. Supreme Court has concluded that some criminal convictions should not count as aggravated felonies triggering removal, the Court has retained most of the force of the new removal rules.[25] As a result, many persons who were originally admitted as permanent residents and refugees are now removed to countries that they'd left as minors. They are also removed irrespective of the length of their stay in the United States.[26]

Finally, the new immigration rules have created conditions where thousands of lawfully admitted persons could be forced to leave the United States, not because they've committed a crime but because their status is contingent on continued employment here. The regulation of highly skilled temporary workers is now a regular feature of American immigration law. Ever since the Immigration Act of 1990, these skilled workers have been admitted for three to six years; when their employment ends, though, so does their right to stay in the country. This is because these persons acquired their very right to be admitted into the United States when an American employer sponsored them for a temporary visa. They cannot self-petition for admission.

In all instances, however, when the employer terminates employment for these workers, they fall "out of status," and they must find some other sponsor. Otherwise, they must leave the United States.[27] The sheer number of such persons is staggering, especially compared with the number of persons admitted under permanent resident categories for skilled laborers. Since 1999, over 300,000 persons were admitted as skilled workers in temporary occupations; in 2004, that number exceeded 400,000. By contrast, since 1999, persons admitted permanently under employment categories were about one-half these figures.[28] In short, temporary workers are a much larger fraction of the newcomers to the United States, and the vast majority are highly skilled professionals. And yet their vulnerability to removal from this country is a function of an immigraiton law that systematically favors the interests of their American employers over their own interests. By law, their employers decide how long they can stay here.

Over a hundred years ago, when the federal courts created the fiction of parole, the early protagonists were an odd set of litigants with little in common. Nishimura had just disembarked from her vessel from Japan, Ju Toy claimed American citizenship by birth, and the orphan Kaplan was found to be excludable upon her arrival, although circumstances conspired to keep her in the United States for over a decade. Nishimura alleged no real attachment to the United States, although she did insist that the purpose of her trip was to reunite with her lawfully admitted husband. In the lower federal courts, Ju Toy *proved* his American citizenship, and his case was overturned not because the facts were wrong but because the majority of the Court believed with the government that he should not have had the venue for having proved the facts at all. And there was and still is something incredibly sad and cruel about the fate of the orphan Kaplan: here was a young girl of thirteen at her arrival in the United States; here was her father, an American citizen willing to care for her; and here she had spent about half her life in this country. She was originally excludable, the record tells us, because she was "feeble-minded."[29]

In our own day, American immigration law removes noncitizens with rather thick attachments to the rest of us, people who've been here for decades. Some were admitted lawfully as permanent residents, others "entered" without inspection. Now, all are relatively easily removable, either because they committed crimes or because their presence was always itself a crime. On the other hand, the same immigration law also admits a much wider group of persons, but admits them in a way that their very right to be here is even more precarious, somewhere between the position of Nishimura (the newly arrived) and Ju Toy (the aspiring citizen). They are here when they are necessary, but they must leave when they are no longer useful to their sponsoring companies. Indeed, the early cases about parole have long been regarded as odd exceptions to the broader story of immigration in the United States, a story that long emphasized settlement, attachment, and eventually belonging and citizenship. The status of parole —a status fraught with formal vulnerability before the law, as well as with disconnectedness and anxiety—accurately captures the position of most of our contemporary newcomers.

NOTES

1. For historical background, see Charles McClain, *In Search of Equality: The Chinese Struggle against Discrimination in Nineteenth-Century America* (Berkeley: University of California Press, 1996); Kitty Calavita, "The Paradoxes of Race, Class,

Identity and 'Passing': Enforcing the Chinese Exclusion Acts, 1882–1910," *Law and Social Inquiry* 25 (2000): 1; and Kitty Calavita, "Collisions at the Intersection of Gender, Race, and Class: Enforcing the Chinese Exclusion Laws," *Law and Society Review* 40 (2006): 249.

2. Hiroshi Motomura, *Americans in Waiting: The Lost Story of Immigration and Citizenship in the United States* (New York: Oxford University Press, 2006). See also Gerald Neuman, *Strangers to the Constitution: Immigrants, Borders, and Fundamental Law* (Princeton: Princeton University Press, 1996), and James Kettner, *The Development of American Citizenship, 1608–1870* (Chapel Hill: University of North Carolina Press, 1984).

3. For histories of the exclusion period and Chinese immigrants' response, see Lucy Salyer, *Laws Harsh as Tigers: Chinese Immigrants and the Shaping of Modern Immigration Law* (Chapel Hill: University of North Carolina Press, 1995); Erika Lee, *At America's Gates: Chinese Immigration during the Exclusion Era, 1882–1943* (Chapel Hill: University of North Carolina Press, 2003); and Mae Ngai, *Impossible Subjects: Illegal Aliens and the Making of Modern America* (Princeton: Princeton University Press, 2004).

4. For a thorough discussion of litigation tactics during the exclusion era, see Salyer, *Laws Harsh as Tigers.* See also Christian Fritz, "A Nineteenth-Century 'Habeas Corpus Mill': The Chinese before the Federal Courts of California," *American Journal of Legal History* 32 (1988): 347.

5. *Nishimura Ekiu v. United States,* 142 U.S. 651, 652–656 (1892).

6. Salyer, *Laws Harsh as Tigers.*

7. *Nishimura Ekiu v. United States,* at 660. This aspect of the decision, giving federal authorities a final say for immigration purposes, appears in subsequent cases and in *Lem Moon Sing v. United States,* 158 U.S. 538 (1895).

8. *Nishimura Ekiu v. United States,* at 661.

9. *United States v. Ju Toy,* 198 U.S. 253, 263 (1905). The decision continues: "If, for the purpose of argument, we assume that the Fifth Amendment applies to him and that to deny entrance to a citizen is to deprive him of liberty, we nevertheless are of the opinion that with regard to him due process of law does not require a judicial trial. That is the result of the cases which we have cited and the almost necessary result of the power of Congress to pass exclusion laws."

10. *Kaplan v. Tod,* 267 U.S. 228, 229–230 (1925).

11. *Leng May Ma v. Barber,* 357 U.S. 185, fn. 5 (1958). Section 212 (d)(5) of the Immigration Act of 1952 reads: "The Attorney General may in his discretion parole into the United States temporarily under such conditions as he may prescribe for emergent reasons or for reasons deemed strictly in the public interest any alien applying for admission to the United States, but such parole of such alien shall

not be regarded as an admission of the alien and when the purposes of such parole shall, in the opinion of the Attorney General, have been served the alien shall forthwith return or be returned to the custody from which he was paroled and thereafter his case shall continue to be dealt with in the same manner as that of any other applicant for admission to the United States."

12. *Nishimura Ekiu v. United States*, at 661

13. Thomas Aleinikoff, David Martin, and Hiroshi Motomura, *Immigration: Process and Policy*, 3rd ed. (Minneapolis: West Group, 1995), 382.

14. *Leng May Ma v. Barber*, at 390.

15. For example, *Dimenski v. INS*, 275 F. 3d 574 (7th Cir., 2001). In this case Dragan Dimenski was lawfully admitted as a tourist in 1987, but he overstayed his visa and resided in the United States for over eight years. When he wanted to visit a relative overseas, he sought "advance parole" before his departure; this status allowed him to visit his sick relative and return to the United States, but this status also indicated that he would not have a valid visa to return to the United States. When he did return, he was paroled into the United States. He applied for permanent residency based on his relationship to his American citizen daughter, but the government contended that, as a parolee, he was excludable and thus ineligible for this form of relief from deporation. He was held excludable and barred for ten years from reentering the United States.

16. Aleinikoff et al., *Immigration*, 383.

17. For example, "Aliens: Parole of Hungarian Revolution Refugee Entering Pursuant to Section 212(d)(5) of the Immigration Act Cannot Constitutionally Be Revoked without a Hearing," *Virginia Law Review* 45 (1959): 283.

18. Aleinikoff et al., *Immigration*, 383.

19. David Martin, "Graduated Application of Constitutional Protection for Aliens: The Real Meaning of *Zadvydas v. Davis*," *Supreme Court Review* 47 (2001); and Phillip Riblett, "Calling for an End to Indefinite Detention," *University of Miami International and Comparative Law Review* 13 (2005): 261.

20. For a review of some of these cases, see "Indefinite Detention of Immigrant Parolees: An Unconstitutional Condition?" *Harvard Law Review* 116 (2003): 1868.

21. For example, *Wong Wing v. United States*, 163 U.S. 28 (1896), and *Plyler v. Doe*, 457 U.S. 202 (1982).

22. For example, *INS v. Lopez-Mendoza*, 468 U.S. 1032 (1984), where the Supreme Court ruled that persons facing deportation might have Fourth Amendment protections against unlawful searches and seizures.

23. Linda Bosniak, "A Basic Territorial Distinction," *Georgetown Immigration Law Journal* 16 (2002): 407, 409. Other scholars have seen the disappearance of this discrepancy as an improvement in the law; for example, T. Alexandar Aleinikoff,

"Detaining Plenary Power: The Meaning and Impact of *Zadvydas v. Davis*," *Georgetown Immigration Law Journal* 16 (2002): 365.

24. U.S. Department of Homeland Security, Office of Immigration Statistics, *Yearbook of Immigration Statistics: 2005* (Washington, D.C.: U.S. Government Printing Office, 2006), table 38.

25. Narrow exceptions could include some minor drug offenses, as in *Lopez v. Gonzales*, 127 S. Ct. 625 (2006), or drunk driving convictions, as in *Leocal v. Ashcroft*, 543 U.S. 1 (2004). In a recent case, *Gonzales v. Duenas-Alvarez*, 127 S. Ct. 815 (2007), the Attorney General successfully argued that abetting a theft offense, in this instance, stealing a car, should be grounds for removal of a permanent resident. For more background on the relationship between the criminal law and removal, see Jennifer Welch, "Defending against Deportation: Equipping Public Defenders to Represent Non-Citizens Effectively," *California Law Review* 92 (2004): 541.

26. On the deportation of refugees, especially persons who had been admitted as minors, see Bill Hing, "Detention to Deportation: Rethinking the Deportation of Cambodian Refugees," *U.C. Davis Law Review* 38 (2005): 891, and Bill Hing, *Deporting Our Souls: Values, Morality, and Immigration Policy* (Cambridge: Cambridge University Press, 2006). On the detention and deportation of a permanent resident admitted as a minor, see *Demore v. Kim*, 538 U.S. 510 (2003).

27. See, generally, Edward Park and John Park, *Probationary Americans: Contemporary Immigration Policies and the Shaping of Asian American Communities* (New York: Routledge, 2005), and John Park, "Aliens of Extraordinary Ability, Aliens of Extraordinary Vulnerability: Skilled Professionals and Contingent Status in American Immigration Law," in *Ethnographies of Law and Social Control*, ed. Stacy Lee Burns, vol. 6 of *Sociology of Crime, Law and Deviance* (Amsterdam: Elsevier, 2005), 165–83.

28. U.S. Department of Homeland Security, *Yearbook of Immigration Statistics*, tables 6 and 26.

29. The language evokes another case from the same period, *Buck v. Bell*, 274 U.S. 200. In that case, again speaking through Justice Holmes, the Supreme Court upheld the sterilization of Carrie Buck under a Virginia rule allowing physicians to sterilize "mental defectives."

CHAPTER 2

Acts of Resistance in Asylum Seekers' Persecution Narratives

Connie G. Oxford

Immigration law in the United States treats asylum seekers as a special category of migrants. It enacts a boundary reserving refuge for those who articulate persecution as the motivating decision to cross a national border. Consequently, a narrative of persecution is necessary in order to gain asylum. Asylum is timely because it addresses the recent national anxiety about immigration in our post–September 11th world that questions who should be allowed entry into the United States, regardless of the motivation for migrating. U.S. policy makers have capitalized on Americans' fear of terrorists in order to weaken immigration policies that admit asylum seekers. The United States is increasingly mirroring the policies and practices of fortress Europe in its anti-immigration practices that detain and deport immigrants, including those seeking asylum from persecution.

The implementation of asylum policies and laws illuminates the social processes and practices that shape immigration, citizenship, and human rights in the United States. In this chapter, I draw from ethnographic data to show how asylum seekers, immigration attorneys, immigrant service providers, and asylum officers confront and reproduce hegemonic power structures in the U.S. asylum bureaucracy during the preparation and telling of persecution narratives.[1] When a persecution narrative reproduces hegemonic power, it limits the possibilities about what may be considered harm and *how* stories about the harm should be told in the context of asylum interviews and immigration court hearings. One problem with hegemonic narratives is that they circumscribe asylum seekers' agency by restricting their ability to tell their own stories of persecution.

Hegemonic and Subversive Narratives

Sociolegal scholars Patricia Ewick and Susan Silbey argue that stories are social events.[2] By social event, they mean that telling a story, particularly one in a legal setting, is more than its reenactment—it is itself an event. The institutional setting within which the story is told defines what constitutes a successful narrative. Institutions regulate narratives through various rules, and, consequently, those who tell stories within those institutions create narrative strategies in order to establish agency.[3] During the process of narration, storytellers are expected to engage in performative features that include repetition, vivid concrete details, and coherence of plot. Ultimately, narratives are assumed by those who elicit them to reveal truth about a particular event. In law there are hegemonic stories.[4] Narratives must conform to a story that the law recognizes. According to Ewick and Silbey, the content of a particular story tends to be legally recognizable when it reproduces existing power relations and to be unrecognizable when the content challenges taken-for-granted hegemony. Therefore, the narrative itself emerges as either hegemonic or subversive.

Narratives contribute to hegemony through social control and conformity and through their ability to colonize consciousness through believable plots when the events seem to speak for themselves. For example, the act of female genital cutting, a legally accepted form of persecution, constitutes persecution regardless of the asylum seeker's perception about what her circumcision means to her. This happens, in part, because the law treats female genital cutting as persecution, and therefore those who are responsible for upholding the law, such as asylum officers and immigration judges, are obligated to consider it as such. However, asylum narratives based on female genital cutting contribute toward hegemony not only because of the law itself but also because those who are responsible for applying the law and those who assist asylum seekers with their applications consider it a horrific practice.[5] I elaborate further with an example of how this happens later in the chapter.

Subversive narratives are important because they undermine hegemonic institutional power through resistance. Michel Foucault's affirmation that "power is everywhere; not because it embraces everything but because it comes from everywhere" provides a poststructural account of institutional power.[6] Foucault's argument about the circulation of power as ubiquitous is germane to identifying its sources. Power in asylum adjudication is dispersed in that it circulates through multiple sites. The multiplicity of the possibilities of points of conferral of power, however, does not necessitate its equal dispersion. While power is everywhere, its distribution and depth are disproportionate among its multiple sites. Power in asylum adjudication is concentrated among those who implement the laws, such as asylum officers and immigration court judges. However, in addition to adjudicators, who exert the greatest power over claimants, immigration attorneys, immigrant service providers, and language interpreters engage tactics that reveal a contestation over authority.

In this chapter, I show how power operates in asylum adjudication and illuminates the complicated task of identifying resistance given the complexity of how narratives contribute toward hegemonic and counter-hegemonic power. In asylum hearings, there are rules about what stories should be told and about *how* those stories should be told. In order to gain asylum, asylum officers and immigration judges expect asylum seekers to tell stories with hegemonic content and to tell those stories in such a way that contributes toward what they believe is the required way of telling the story. Immigration attorneys and service providers practice resistance (and sometimes accommodation by conforming to the expectations regarding how stories should be told) by using the rules of asylum to their advantage by teaching asylum seekers to tell hegemonic stories.

Narrating Persecution

Asylum narratives are the stories that migrants tell to attorneys and service providers who help them prepare their asylum applications, and to asylum officers and immigration judges who determine whether they are eligible for asylum. Narratives have a written component that includes the asylum seeker's declaration and other materials such as supporting documents from service providers. Narratives are also spoken when asylum seekers testify during their interviews and hearings. The stories that asylum seekers tell must detail harm that is recognized as severe to constitute persecution according to the standards of asylum law. However, many asylum seekers are initially unaware of the legal narrative that they would be required to articulate in order to gain asylum when they arrive in the United States. Asylum seekers learn how to articulate the required narrative of persecution from their attorneys and service providers.

Asylum seekers are dependent on their attorneys to negotiate the legal system and facilitate the process of applying for asylum. When meeting with clients, attorneys look for certain facts that lend themselves to a narrative of persecution. Attorneys use legal criteria when considering whether to take on a client. They consider whether a case fits the rules of asylum law based on one of the five legally accepted grounds of persecution. These five grounds are race, religion, nationality, political opinion, and membership in a social group. Deciding to take a case based on its legal merits is what John Conley and William O'Barr referred to as having a rules orientation rather than a relationship orientation toward the law.[7] Those who are rule oriented "evaluate their problems in terms of neutral principles whose application transcends differences in personal and social status." Those with a relational orientation toward the law "come to the legal system seeking redress for a wide range of personal and social wrongs. In talking about their problems, they predicate rights and responsibilities on a broad notion of social interdependence rather than on the application of rules."[8] Plaintiffs with a rules approach to articulating their grievance are more likely to receive a favorable decision in court than those who articulate a relationship approach.

The mutually exclusive categories of "rules" and "relationships" is problematic because it neglects the social interaction between clients, who tell their stories, and attorneys, who are responsible for molding those stories into legally presentable narratives. Asylum seekers may construct their stories according to a relationship orientation toward the law, such as telling stories of harm that do not specify whether the harm was because of one of the five legally accepted grounds. However, in order to prevail in court, immigration attorneys must turn asylum seekers' narratives into rule-based narratives of harm. To do so requires multiple visits with the client. Attorneys may require that asylum seekers meet with them three or more times before they submit their applications. During these meetings, attorneys ask general questions about what happened and why they left their country. After eliciting an initial narrative, the attorney follows up with questions that mold the narrative into a rules-oriented approach that conforms to the rules of asylum law.

The following example is from an asylum hearing that reveals the expectations about *how* the story of persecution, in addition to its content, should be told during rape testimony. Asylum seekers are often reluctant to discuss sexual violence during their preparation visits with their attorneys. When I questioned immigration attorneys about rape cases, they voiced frustration with their clients who would not reveal stories of rape during their asylum preparation meetings, yet told these stories during their interview in front of an asylum officer or immigration judge. The attorneys were frustrated because failing to include rape in the asylum application made the asylum seekers appear not to be credible during their interviews. Moreover, this meant the attorneys could not prepare their clients for questioning about the rape. Many attorneys relayed stories of how they assisted asylum seekers with telling stories of rape during their hearings and interviews. During my interview with Michael, an immigration attorney, he discussed a client he represented at an asylum office when he worked for a private organization, as an example of why women do not convey stories of sexual harm during their meetings with their attorneys:

> I was representing an Eritrean woman, and my practice was to always spend a lot of time with the client trying to understand the story so that I could put together a very detailed declaration in the application. We met three times prior to her interview, and I read it back to her and she confirmed it. At no time had there been any mention of sexual harm. In the interview, she starts talking about her rapes while in custody.

> Now I hadn't heard this before and was concerned that it would be held against her on credibility, that she is adding things that aren't a part of her claim. Fortunately, the officer involved understood that it didn't undermine her story and did grant her. We [the asylum officer and Michael] sat and discussed the issue and realized that in the meetings in my office her relative was always there translating. In this interview, they hired a professional to come in and translate.

Michael's depiction of female asylum seekers' reluctance to discuss sexual violence in front of friends and family members resonated across many of my interviews with asylees who omitted their rape as part of their persecution narrative.

This example shows that while the content of a narrative (rape) may be acceptable as a claim of persecution, its initial introduction in the applicant's oral testimony was feared to have deemed her noncredible by her attorney. Ewick and Silbey argue that narratives are situationally produced in that they are told within a particular context. For female asylum seekers who tell stories of sexual violence, the presence of male relatives often determines whether they are willing to divulge information about their rape. Consequently, female asylum seekers who were raped are often noncredible applicants when they appear to change their story. The narrative during the oral interview is one that replicates the content of that found in the written application. When asylum seekers include additional testimony in their oral narrative, they may risk being denied asylum.

The hegemonic narrative is one that is told initially to the attorney, not the asylum officer. It is hegemonic because it supports the institutional assumption that the content of stories do not change when they are told to different people, such as the attorney and the asylum officer. One characteristic of hegemonic asylum narratives is the institutional expectation that stories are verbatim in all of the various contexts within which they are told (e.g., attorney's office, service provider's office, asylum office, immigration court). The narrative that the asylum seeker told in her oral interview is counterhegemonic because it resists the assumption embedded in the institutional power structure of the U.S. asylum bureaucracy that stories are uniform across the different settings in which they are told.

One consequence of telling counterhegemonic narratives is that those who adjudicate asylum claims tend to assume that asylum seekers who articulate different narratives to different people are not telling the "truth." Therefore, subversive persecution stories risk being interpreted by adjudicators as fraudulent claims. This assumption provides fodder for the anti-immigrant sentiment found in the policies and practices of the U.S. immigration bureaucracy that has become increasingly suspicious of immigrants' veracity since the September 11th terrorist attack.

In addition to immigration attorneys, immigrant service providers also assist asylum seekers by providing the documentation necessary for successful applications. Many immigration attorneys refer their clients to immigrant service providers to provide psychological counseling. The service provider meets with the asylum seeker and then writes a report that is included in the asylum application. Service providers often testify in immigration court as expert witnesses regarding the asylum seeker's mental health status. The following examples show how two service providers, Nicole and Margaret, assist asylum seekers by preparing legally expected stories of persecution. Nicole and Margaret are similar in that they both consider themselves advocates who work toward the goal of helping immigrants gain asylum. What is interesting about these stories is that they show how different motivations for engaging in tactics that encourage asylum seekers to tell expected stories can contribute to hegemonic narratives. These examples support Foucault's well-circulated adage that "where there is power there is resistance."[9] However, working toward the goal of helping immigrants gain asylum can take on different forms of resistance that may reproduce rather than undermine hegemonic institutional power.

Nicole, a psychologist who is employed by an organization that works with torture survivors, provides counseling for asylum seekers, writes reports that are included in her clients' applications, and often testifies on their behalf in immigration court. During our interview, Nicole discussed how she diagnoses post-traumatic stress disorder (PTSD) and its relevance in asylum applications:

> Clients come to us with many psychosocial problems that typically include major depression and panic attacks. PTSD is just one of the possible diagnoses that someone might have. But it's a diagnosis that the adjudicators, the INS, and the judges seem to be looking for.

In her authoritative position on psychosocial disorders, Nicole conveyed that she emphasizes PTSD in her reports because she knows that it is the diagnosis with which asylum officers and immigration judges are familiar. She was clear that she does not fabricate reports or embellish testimony, but that she merely emphasizes PTSD in clients who have multiple psychosocial diagnoses in order to facilitate their ability to gain asylum. Nicole's behavior contributes toward reproducing a hegemonic narrative about PTSD as the primary clinical diagnosis for asylum seekers. Her justification is rooted in her social position as an advocate for asylum seekers, not because PTSD is the only or primary diagnosis that explains her clients' behaviors. Nicole's motivation may not be to reproduce a hegemonic narrative, yet that is the outcome based on the reports she submits in asylum applications.

Margaret, too, encourages hegemonic narratives in an effort to facilitate asylum seekers' ability to gain asylum. A physician who documents torture and writes affidavits that are included in asylum seekers' applications, Margaret works with an immigrant organization that serves many female clients who have been circumcised. During our interview, she discussed how she documents these cases and her own response to this practice:

> Most of my cases are with women who have been raped after they were circumcised. They have so much scar tissue, and it's just horrifying and sorrowful to see that. When the labia is removed, you see nothing, it's just smooth between the vaginal opening and the rectum. And when I see that, I feel like crying. I walk out of the room to collect myself. I've actually looked at my own anatomy more to appreciate it and just say: Oh my God, they have destroyed the rose, they have depetaled the rose.

Margaret explained how she often gives her patients a copy of Alice Walker and Pratibha Parmar's *Warrior Marks,* a book that chronicles Walker's documentary film on female circumcision and makes clear that the practice is torture.[10] She continued with her position on female circumcision by articulating the mother's responsibility in this practice and her own anxiety about treating the "torturer":

> It's usually the mother or another female relative who performs it [circumcision]. Sometimes it's not the mother, but she is implicated by

> virtue of her facilitating the taking of the child [to the circumciser]. I've had a few families where I knew the mother, and I heard the story [from the daughter] and it really angered me. I thought how am I going to deal with this mother? What if they bring her to me as a patient?

Margaret insists that women tell stories of female circumcision in ways that portray them as victims of a barbaric practice. Although Margaret did not indicate that she refuses to treat women who have circumcised their daughters, her grave disapproval of the practice and of the mother's compliance makes her reluctant to work with certain immigrants.

Nicole's and Margaret's descriptions of how they assist torture survivors provides insight into how asylum seeker's narratives, in their reporting of persecution, are remolded to fit a hegemonic narrative, in these cases by suggesting PTSD symptomology as a psychosocial disorder and female circumcision as torture compared with the experience of an "anatomically normal" uncircumcised woman. Nicole and Margaret share a spirit of client advocacy and desire to see their clients gain asylum. They act on the asylum seeker's behalf by emphasizing legally recognizable forms of harm that those who wield institutional power, such as asylum officers and judges, "are looking for" in asylum applications. Yet in doing so, they contribute toward hegemonic power by reproducing legally accepted narratives of harm. While their motivation for contributing toward a hegemonic narrative may differ in that Nicole's appears intentionally strategic and Margaret's seems naively orientalist, their behavior is one of accommodation, not resistance of hegemonic power.

The shaping of persecution narratives can involve not just asylees, their attorneys, and advocates but even those who are supposed to be impartial, like asylum officers and immigration judges, some of whom were previously activists for asylum. One argument among scholars of transnational human rights movements is that human rights activism emerges from *outside* of the state.[11] A basic tenet in this scholarship is the widely accepted human rights/state sovereignty dichotomy. These scholars argue that international law and policy provide universal standards of personhood and notions of humanness that transcend how any particular nation-state might conceptualize these terms. Consequently, state sovereignty is eroded because power and control emerge from outside the nation-state.

The problem with this argument is that it ignores the diversity within the state or within human rights organizations and consequently treats each as monolithic. Unlike other departments within U.S. asylum bureaucracy, the asylum corps has a large number of employees who identify as human rights advocates. The introduction of the INS asylum corps in 1991 restructured the hiring process for asylum officers to include the transfer of bureaucrats previously employed by INS, as well as the new hire of human rights advocates, most of whom were trained in human rights law.

During my interviews with asylum supervisors and former asylum officers, they described how the human rights advocates clashed with the bureaucrats, whom they referred to as the "old guard," over the politics of immigration. Many of the asylum supervisors and former asylum officers I interviewed considered themselves activist bureaucrats in that they actively worked toward granting asylum cases.

During my interview with Walter, an asylum officer, he described the division between the old guard bureaucrats and the human rights advocates:

> In the beginning, in New York, all of the supervisors were former airport inspectors from Kennedy [JFK airport]. These were old guard INS, and they didn't trust people. All of my supervisors were jaded people from inspections from JFK. They didn't think that most [asylum seekers] were credible. A person whose background was INS inspections was cynical. They assumed most of the people coming in were lying. These people were much more reluctant to sign off on a grant [of asylum]. In the beginning, it was the lawyers versus the airport people. In my office there was a culture. It was us against them.

Walter's understanding of the division within the asylum office—the "us against them" culture between asylum officers who understand asylum within a human rights framework and those who view adjudicating claims as a gatekeeping function—demonstrates the multiplicity of ways that asylum officers view their position. The variation among how asylum officers view their role within the state apparatus in part determines how one judges asylum applicants during interviews. Asylum officers can facilitate or impede asylum seekers' ability to gain asylum.

Walter's critique of his colleagues' anti-immigrant position reveals the problem with simplistic depictions of the asylum process that posit participants' actions as either reproducing hegemonic institutional power (those who work *inside* the state, such as government employees) or resisting institutional power (those who work *oustide* the state, such as the attorneys, service providers, and other activists) based on their location vis-à-vis the state. This example complicates Foucault's claim that "where there is power there is resistance" by considering acts of resistance to hegemonic power by those who are situated inside state institutions.

Immigration attorneys, immigrant service providers, and asylum officers may draw from a vast array of experiences in their understanding of the asylum bureaucracy because of their relationship to the asylum process with regard to their employment status. Conversely, asylum seekers tend to have the most limited knowledge about the system they are negotiating because their visits to their attorneys, service providers, and the asylum office are only in reference to their own claim. Therefore, acts of resistance on the part of immigration attorneys, service providers, and asylum officers may occur more often than acts of resistance from the asylum seekers themselves.

The following is an example of how an asylum seeker engaged in an act of resistance during her asylum interview. Asylum seekers are often asked to identify political and religious figures to determine whether they are knowledgeable about a particular place or practice. During my interview with Amina, an Ethiopian asylum seeker, she discussed how she was questioned during her asylum interview about the current government in Ethiopia. During her asylum interview, which was conducted with the aid of an interpreter, she relayed the following story of how her interpreter translated her answer incorrectly. Her own knowledge of English enabled her to act on her own behalf during her interview:

> He [the asylum officer] asked me about the new government, but after I went to Saudi there was another government. I gave him the one I knew before I went to Saudi. During that time, there was a new president every three or four months. Even right now I don't know who the president is. And the translator told me he's not the president now [during the interview]. When he [the asylum officer] was asking me, I told her [the translator] the answer. But she [the translator] told a different

> answer. I was getting angry and said no to the interview guy, "that's not what I said. I understand English."

Language ability can determine the outcome of a case. Interviews are often conducted with the aid of an interpreter. According to the INS lesson plan, the role of the interpreter is to "interpret verbatim as much as possible, using the asylum officer's and applicant's choice of words, rather than using the interpreter's choice of words."[12] This statement (along with other criteria) is read to the interpreter at the beginning of the interview. It is nearly impossible for asylum officers to know whether the interpreter is translating correctly. Unlike immigration court hearings which are recorded and in which a transcription of the proceedings is made available to the judge, no such recordings are made available during asylum interviews for the applicant's attorney and the attorney representing the INS. Therefore, asylum seekers with limited or no English skills cannot intervene on their own behalf regarding correct translation.

Amina's familiarity with English gave her the opportunity to intervene on her own behalf by correcting the translator's answer about the president of Ethiopia. In this example, Amina was able to tell the expected narrative because of her fluency in English and therefore could correct the interpreter during her interview. She had a consciousness of opportunity that she turned to her own advantage. While Amina's claim was denied at the asylum office, in part, because of her "incorrect" answer about who occupied the Ethiopian presidency, her claim was granted in immigration court.

While I was conducting interviews with asylum supervisors, I inquired whether they intervene during interviews when they think there may be problems with language translation.While all of them cited the INS policy regarding adequate translation during interviews, they indicated that intervention may be problematic in practice. During our interview, Walter described how uncooperative responses by asylum supervisors discouraged intervention by asylum officers:

> There were times when I thought that the translator was not competent, and I told them [the asylum seeker] that this isn't to your advantage; you need to come back and bring somebody with you who can translate properly. When I did this, supervisors frowned on it, especially

> when I had a big backlog and the pressure was to move cases. Others of us [asylum officers] did this as well, but those who routinely did it were talked to.[13]

Walter's willingness to intervene on behalf of asylum seekers is an example of how he engaged in resistance against institutional authority. His identification of translation incompetence shows how he attempted to shift the power dynamic in favor of asylum seekers. Ewick and Silbey argue that "through everyday practical engagements, individuals identify the cracks and vulnerabilities of institutionalized power."[14] Walter is an example of how asylum officers work within the bureaucracy to resist hegemonic power, not reproduce it.

Conclusion

How stories of persecution are told is as important as the story itself. In this chapter, I demonstrate the complexity in storytelling that contributes to a legally accepted narrative of persecution. I argue that storytelling is as important as the story itself. I have expanded Ewick and Silbey's focus on narrative content by arguing that stories, and how they are told, are not simply hegemonic or counterhegemonic. Moreover, unlike Ewick and Silbey's work that emphasizes agency and resistance among the claimants who bring forth grievances, I have included how differently situated participants, such as asylum officers, immigration attorneys, and immigrant service providers, engage acts of resistance and confront institutional power structures on behalf of those who are unfamiliar with the asylum bureaucracy.

Yet not all asylum officers expect a hegemonic narrative of harm. Nor do they all expect a narrative be told in way that is hegemonic. In this chapter, I argue that Michel Foucault's notion of power can illuminate resistance *within* state institutions, such as the asylum bureaucracy. The examples offered show how asylum officers, attorneys, and service providers engage in acts of resistance in order to undermine hegemonic power. In his role as asylum officer, Walter alerted asylum seekers to problems with language translation. As an immigration attorney, Michael engaged with an asylum officer about why his client introduced her rape during her asylum interview and not during her preparation. Nicole, a psychologist with an immigrant service organization, diagnosed PTSD as the primary disorder in order to facilitate a grant of asylum. These examples show how asylum officers, attorneys, and service providers work against institutional power on behalf of asylum seekers, even when doing so means encouraging hegemonic stories. Consequently, a pro-immigrant position does not preclude one from encouraging hegemonic narratives of harm. Some of these participants do so, in part, because they identify as human rights activists. And in doing so, they often work toward reproducing, not undermining, institutional power.

NOTES

1. References to interviews in this chapter are from Connie Oxford, "Gender-Based Persecution in Asylum Law and Policy in the United States" (Ph.D. dissertation, University of Pittsburgh, 2006). Interviews were conducted in Los Angeles between September 2001 and March 2003. This material is based on work supported by the National Science Foundation under Grant No. 0211694 and by a fellowship from the International Migration Program of the Social Science Research Council with funds provided by the Andrew W. Mellon Foundation.

2. Patricia Ewick and Susan Silbey, "Subversive Stories and Hegemonic Tales: Toward a Sociology of Narrative," *Law and Society Review* 229/2 (1995), 197–211.

3. Patricia Ewick and Susan Silbey, "Narrating Social Structure: Stories of Resistance to Legal Authority," *American Journal of Sociology* 108/6 (2003), 1328–72.

4. Ibid.

5. For the precedent case on female genital cutting and asylum in the United States, see *Matter of Kasinga*, 21 I and N, Dec. 357 (BIA 1996). For a critique of the treatment of female genital cutting asylum claims, see Connie G. Oxford, "Protectors and Victims in the Gender Regime of Practices," *NWSA Journal* 17/3 (2005), 18–38.

6. Michel Foucault, *The History of Sexuality: An Introduction* (New York: Vintage, 1995), 1:93.

7. John M Conley and William M. O'Barr, *Rules versus Relationships: The Ethnography of Legal Discourse* (Chicago: University of Chicago Press, 1990).

8. Ibid.

9. Foucault, *History of Sexuality,* 1:95.

10. Alice Walker and Pratibha Parmar, *Warrior Marks: Female Genital Mutilation and the Sexual Blinding of Women* (New York : Harcourt Brace, 1993).

11. Saskia Sassen, *Globalization and Its Discontents* (New York: New Press, 1999); Saskia Sassen, *Guests and Aliens* (New York: New Press, 1999); Margaret E. Keck and Kathryn Sikkink, *Activists beyond Borders: Advocacy Networks in International Politics* (Ithaca: Cornell University Press, 1998); Yasemin Nuhoğlu Soysal, *Limits of Citizenship: Migrants and Postnational Membership in Europe* (Chicago: University of Chicago Press, 1994).

12. Immigration and Naturalization Service "Working with an Interpreter," *Asylum Officer Basic Training* (Washington, D.C.: U.S. Government Printing Office, 1998).

13. Ewick and Silbey, "Narrating Social Structure."

14. Ibid.

CHAPTER 3

Family, Unvalued

Sex and Security: A Short History of Exclusions

Scott Long, Jessica Stern, and Adam Francouer

Richard Adams, a U.S. citizen, was in love with Anthony Sullivan, an Australian national. They lived together in Colorado in 1975. With Anthony's visa about to expire, Adams tried to sponsor him for permanent residency in the United States. The written answer of the Immigration and Naturalization Service made its position clear:

> Your visa petition . . . for classification of Anthony Corbett Sullivan as the spouse of a United States citizen [is] denied for the following reasons: *You have failed to establish that a bona fide marital relationship can exist between two faggots.*[1]

Three decades later, what has changed? "Faggot" relationships remain invalid within the system. And even the word resurfaces. One man wrote us:

This chapter is an excerpt from *Family, Unvalued: Discrimination, Denial and the Fate of Binational Same-Sex Couples under U.S. Law* (New York: Human Rights Watch and Immigration Equality, 2006). Reprinted with permission.

> While traveling abroad I met the person I would spend the rest of my life with, and eventually start a family with. Bogdan is a citizen of . . . the former Yugoslavia. Because of both of our countries' treatment [of] its own gay citizens, it's been impossible to be together at some points. Most of the time I've had to go to Serbia, because after Bogdan tried obtaining a visa at the American Embassy in Belgrade, he was denied, because "they don't give visas to fag couples," as we were told by the visa officer. . . . I, being an American, had the preconception that my country was the true land of the free. I guess I was wrong.[2]

Immigration, Gender, and Sexuality in U.S. History

Lesbian or gay noncitizens trying to join their U.S. partners, and transgender people trying to see their relationships acknowledged, are caught between two forces: escalating panic about "porous" borders, and intensifying battles over the legal status of partnerships between people of the same sex.

These pincers convey an unmistakable message: *You do not belong.* Yet neither ferocious anti-immigrant feeling nor fear of sexuality and sexual "deviance" is new in U.S. politics or society. Nor is it novel for them to meet. Fantasies about immigrants' sexualities figured heavily in nineteenth-century and early-twentieth-century anti-immigrant prejudice—from pornographic imprecations against Irish convents as scenes for orgies[3] to a lurid literature on "white slavery."[4] At the end of the nineteenth century, these bogeymen took on both legal and scientific garb. The 1875 Page Act was the first major federal measure restricting entry; prostitutes were a key category of "undesirables" it excluded, and sensational stories about sex workers from China led to further bans on Chinese immigration.[5]

Meanwhile, Francis Walker, an influential statistician and superintendent of two successive U.S. censuses, warned of "immigrants from southern Italy, Hungary, Austria, and Russia" who "are beaten men from beaten races; representing the worst failures in the struggle for existence."[6] Such racist notions played on a distorted Darwinism. Immigrants became a biological threat, defined by their prolific sexuality and perverse vigor. The emerging pseudoscience of eugenics—the belief that societies should keep the "unfit" from breeding—bolstered anti-immigrant sentiment.[7] Not only the crude rural racists of the Ku Klux Klan but also urban intellectuals and self-styled progressives argued that immigration and immigrants' reproduction had to stop.[8]

Groups opposing immigration spread and spawned: a "Race Betterment Foundation," the "Committee on Selective Immigration," a "National Committee for Mental Hygiene."[9] The word "hygiene" is suggestive. Immigrants were a racial peril but also a menace to healthy masculinity, enervating men of the "native stock." As one congressman said in 1896, immigration restriction was needed "to preserve the human blood *and manhood* of the American character by the exclusion of depraved human beings."[10] The proximity of immigrants, with their exuberant, excessive sexuality, jumbled gender relations—producing an "impotent, decadent manhood."[11]

A sweeping "red scare" took place in 1919–1920, when a federal attorney general and an ambitious aide named J. Edgar Hoover warned that anarchist immigrants intended revolution—and deported hundreds. Existing fears thus drew new power from the specter of terrorism. From 1917, a new wave of laws restricted immigrant intake. They culminated in the Immigration Act of 1924. It clamped an overall numerical cap on immigration; national quotas within that figure were fixed according to percentages of national origin in the U.S. population. The framers particularly meant to choke the flow from southern and eastern Europe; immigration from Italy, for instance, plummeted more than twentyfold, from over 200,000 in 1921 to just over 8,000 in 1926.[12] The act also effectively ended legal immigration from Asia. One triumphant nativist exulted at the time that it "marks the close of an epoch in the history of the United States."[13]

The golden door Emma Lazarus had lauded slammed shut.

From McCarthyism to the "HIV Ban"

In the 1950s, anxiety gripped American society over the sudden suspicion of homosexuals in its midst—and the sexual hysteria moved in tandem with a new "red scare." Homosexuals were seen as susceptible to blackmail, easy to enlist in treason. Moreover, to the McCarthyite mind, they shared with Communists the qualities of being gregarious yet secretive, concealing their true selves and loyalties, creating coteries and collectives that evaded surveillance. Republican Senate leader Kenneth Wherry said, "You can't hardly separate homosexuals from subversives. . . . A man of low morality is a menace in the government, and they are all tied up together."[14]

The panic prompted a campaign to drive homosexuals out of government service, as well as burgeoning and sometimes brutal FBI and police witch-hunts against ordinary people.[15] And it saw lesbian and gay immigrants banned from the United States by law. The bar dates from the 1952 Immigration and Nationality Act (INA), pushed through by Senator Pat McCarran of Nevada, a livid anti-Communist crusader.

The bill still stands as the basis for U.S. immigration policy—which it sweepingly revised. Slightly distancing itself from the whites-only past, it reinstated a trickle of Asian immigrants for the first time since 1924 (partly to improve the U.S.'s image as the Cold War militarized the Pacific); but it held to a lopsided bias for northern European groups. By building into national quotas favorable treatment for immigrants with special skills, and for relatives of people already in the country, it laid the groundwork for the employment-based and family-sponsored preference categories of today.[16]

However, the act also allowed the government to ban people from the country on ideological grounds.[17] Moreover, it barred "aliens afflicted with *psychopathic personality,* epilepsy or *mental defect.*"[18] Congress made clear that this was meant to exclude "homosexuals and sex perverts," even seeking an opinion from the U.S. Public Health Service that the term was broad enough to do so.[19] In 1965, the INA was amended, with new language prohibiting the entry of persons "afflicted with . . . *sexual deviation.*"[20] With slight variations in the phrasing, for almost forty years the U.S. banned lesbians and gays from entering the country.

The ideological provisions of McCarran's immigration act finally were repealed in 1990—after denying entry over the years to such figures as Yves Montand, Gabriel Garcia Marquez, and Pierre Trudeau. The same 1990 reform also eliminated the bar against homosexuals and the references to "psychopathic personality or mental defect." [21] The change in immigration law came late.[22] The United States was the last industrialized country to cling to a complete ban on homosexuals' entry.

The 1990 Immigration Act also quietly authorized the Department of Health and Human Services to remove a ban, in effect since 1987, on the entry of foreign nationals with HIV. When President Bill Clinton tried to do so three years later, however, a thunderous backlash ensued—much of it following nineteenth-century channels, identifying immigrants with disease and closed borders with immunity and health. In 1993, Congress wrote the ban back into law, specifying that excludable conditions "include infection with the etiologic agent for acquired immune deficiency syndrome."

One observer writes that "the U.S. Immigration and Naturalization Service currently conducts the largest mandatory HIV-testing program in the world. Every applicant for permanent residence over the age of fifteen is required to undergo HIV testing, and largely without informed consent or pre- and post-testing."[23] Applicants for nonimmigrant entry are questioned on their HIV status, and if they admit to being positive, can be refused admission.[24] If the government suspects them of HIV infection, it can require an HIV test; people entering the United States with HIV medications in their luggage can be questioned or expelled. Nonimmigrants who are HIV-positive can request (and can be denied) a waiver for short trips under limited conditions. U.S. policy on HIV and travel has been called "one of the most unenlightened in the world."[25]

The United Nations International Guidelines on HIV/AIDS and Human Rights notes that "there is no public health rationale for restricting liberty of movement or choice of residence on the grounds of HIV status."[26] Two experts observe:

> HIV is well-established everywhere in the world, and attempts to halt its spread by controlling the movement of infected or potentially infected persons have proven futile and expensive besides causing considerable hardship.[27]

Preserving the myth that HIV/AIDS is a threat external to the U.S.'s borders, the ban encourages a false sense of safety, damaging public health rather than defending it. It feeds on, and further feeds, archaic associations between immigration and contamination, the alien and the unclean. Finally, the ban exposes lesbian, gay, bisexual, and transgender immigrants and visitors to particular harassment, given stereotypes that associate them with HIV infection. The fears that locked the "golden door" and defined deserving immigrants as "mentally defective" still run strong.

Defended from What?

On September 10, 1996, by a huge margin, the Senate approved the Defense of Marriage Act (DOMA). Passed in haste, and signed in an almost furtive late-night ceremony by President Clinton ten days later, the measure was an election-year reaction to the possibility that Hawaii might become the first state to recognize equality in civil marriage. (Seven years later, Massachusetts did.)

The bill did two things. It declared that no state was obliged to recognize "a relationship between persons of the same sex that is treated as marriage" by any other state or jurisdiction. And it defined marriage, for all purposes of the federal government, as "only a legal union between one man and one woman as husband and wife." The word "spouse" now refers "only to a person of the opposite sex who is a husband or wife."[28] This foreclosed the possibility that foreign, permanent same-sex partners of U.S. citizens could be recognized as "spouses" under current U.S. immigration law.

The constitutionality of DOMA remains uncertain.[29] As a panicked reaction to the mere prospect of a state recognizing same-sex relationships, however, it was telling—and foretelling. Since then, nineteen states have approved constitutional amendments barring equality in civil marriage.[30] Some prohibited giving *any* legal status to relationships other than heterosexual marriage. The results are devastating. Ohio's draconian amendment, for instance, forced a judge in 2005 to void part of the state's domestic violence law. He threw out a felony charge against a man accused of abusing his unmarried *heterosexual* partner—because the state constitution now barred any law or ruling that would "create or recognize a legal status for relationships of unmarried individuals."[31]

Amid the furor, President George W. Bush in 2004 endorsed a national constitutional amendment banning equality in marriage. Many want this to go further, and, like Ohio's, to bar civil unions and all forms of recognizing unmarried relationships, anywhere in policy or law.[32]

Lesbian, gay, bisexual, and transgender people's relationships are thus central, not collateral, casualties in a raging culture war. The moral panic reaches beyond them. "Gay marriage" is a wedge issue, wielded to restrict other forms of personal autonomy. Most of the groups in the trenches opposing it also fight to eliminate abortion, and many support laws restricting divorce.[33] Nearly all agitate for curbs on legal immigration.

Striking in this culture war is the cultural defensiveness: the notion that people who want to enjoy the dignity and benefits of marriage seek to destroy it, or that people who admire the United States and want to enter its borders are inevitably its invading enemies. The rhetoric of invisible foes, values endangered, redoubts taken, and battles lost is heard everywhere. It mimics the pessimism of a Francis Walker or a Madison Grant, men who saw lifeways beleaguered by difference.

Indeed, many anti-immigrant activists sound like time-capsule transmissions from the 1880s or the 1920s, with minor changes. *Then,* the aliens who menaced "American values" were largely Slavs, Jews, or Italians; *now* those groups are seen as safely assimilated, and the enemy Other has grown darker and more distant. But the stereotypes, the fears of sterility and decline, are the same.[34]

When lesbian, gay, bisexual, and transgender people's rights involve the country's borders, then the response will likely be furious. One conservative warned that the Uniting American Families Act "would make the United States a magnet for homosexuals to come to our shores."[35] When a Texas congressman supported the act, opponents charged him with "allowing homosexuals . . . a free pass to bypass our immigration laws by bringing over anyone they say is their 'partner'"—people "who will not only take American jobs but also worsen the AIDS epidemic (including free health care once they get here)."[36]

In the wake of the September 11 attacks—much as in the 1920s—anxiety over terrorism has twisted all immigration debates. The 2001 Patriot Act revived forms of ideological exclusion. Antiterrorist rhetoric insinuates itself into arguments over sexual rights as well. When the Supreme Court struck down sodomy laws in 2003, Lou Sheldon, a right-wing activist, said, "This is a 9/11, major wake-up call that the enemy is at our doorsteps."[37] When border officials halted a Canadian same-sex married couple because they tried to use the same customs form—like any other spouses—the conservative group Concerned Women for America declared:

> Many have feared that lax border security would allow terrorists to easily enter the United States from Canada. However, U.S. Customs officials

at Pearson International Airport in Toronto were able to stop the latest pair of "domestic terrorists."[38]

What threat did that family represent? And what needs to be defended?

A National Threat?

Tony, forty and a denizen of Atlanta, Georgia, met Asa, thirty-three, during a vacation in Britain in early 2002. They fell in love, and, like many other couples, immediately faced a quandary: How to be together?

At the time, U.K. immigration laws gave residency to unmarried foreign partners of British citizens—but only after the couple had lived together for two years. Tony had commitments to his U.S. business, so they needed to demonstrate their cohabitation through Asa spending as much time as possible in the United States. "I went to the INS," Asa says, "and they told me there was no limit to how often I could come in and out of the U.S. legally, as long as I don't overstay. So I would go in and out of the country every ninety days." He continues:

> I spent the majority of my time during those two years in the U.S. . . . While I was forced to quit my job in Britain to spend time in the States, I could not work, drive, own a cell phone or even a bank account in America—all the things most people take for granted. My partner was powerless to do anything to help. . . . One of our major hurdles was that I had to live in America [to prove to the two-year U.K. cohabitation requirement], but I couldn't do so legally in the U.S.'s eyes. We had to walk this fine line.

Still, Asa left every three months and remained legal. In 2004, having met the requirements, they resettled in London, where Tony got a new job. In June 2005, Tony had to return to the states for an eight-week business trip:

> We said I'd go there [to the U.S.] on holiday for two weeks [at the end of Tony's trip], and [we'd] fly back together. Tony asked me if I was worried

about coming into the country. Ironically, every other time I was horrified coming into the U.S. This time, I wasn't worried at all.

At the Atlanta airport

I got to immigration. They asked me the standard series of questions: last time I was here, what I was here for—a holiday. I kept the answers as simple as possible. They put my passport in an orange folder, so I knew. They took me into another room.

They asked details about me. I told them the hundred percent truth. I said I'm in a same-sex relationship, we live in the U.K., we transferred our lives there. . . . It was blatantly obvious to me that the questioning was homophobic. He asked me questions about our landlord when we had lived in San Francisco. Were they already investigating us? He told me that he didn't think I'd be let into the country.

I said, "don't do this to me." They never said, "You have been refused entry because." And I never actually asked, "Why aren't you letting me in?" I just said, "please, don't do this to me." I was given a refusal, and made to sign. The flights to the U.K. were all booked. They didn't think they could permit me to fly back to another E.U. country. They found a London flight leaving in a couple of hours, with one seat in first class—for $5,000. I bought that. When my flight came up, I got escorted there by a Homeland Security office and boarded onto the plane.

Meanwhile, Tony waited hours for Asa to emerge—then waited for him to call when he got back to London that night. He remembers:

At 10 or 11 A.M. the next morning, someone was banging on my door—two officers standing there, cars sitting in front of my house. I was shocked. But I knew who it was. Homeland Security.

[The agents] didn't want any pleasant communication. They informed me of my rights—I could have an attorney present; they recorded everything. I told them all they asked for. They wanted to know what my relationship to Asa was. I knew he'd already told them, so I told them the same.

They knew things about our relationship. We had moved to San Francisco for about a year. We'd signed a lease there, so we had both

> our names on it. Sitting in my house, they had the documentation: they asked about our landlords in San Francisco by name; "Did Asa live with you for the year?" I explained that no, he'd been doing it legally, leaving and entering every ninety days. They didn't believe me. They asked, "Where are you living now?" I said London. Obviously, they didn't believe I was living anywhere but Atlanta, because I still owned a house there. The line of questioning was: when did we meet; how long was he in the U.S.; did I know that it was a violation of law if I let him live with me and if I harbored an illegal immigrant? They asked me how Asa supported himself in the U.S. They knew he didn't have a job in the U.K. "So he lives there but you pay all the bills?"

By coincidence or not, Tony says:

> One or two weeks later, I got an Internal Revenue audit. That's still going on. . . . I'm not at risk, but—I suspect that they're making sure that I didn't pay Asa.
>
> We never did anything that should have flagged us. Honestly, I love my country; if we could live in America tomorrow, I would want to come home. . . . Our home is there. My family is there. He and I are here alone in London.

And yet, Tony says, "they treat me so well over here [in the U.K.], almost to the point that it freaks you out. It's the other side of the spectrum. You don't see any hate here. It's really nice."[39]

Legal Protections against Unequal Treatment

Nondiscrimination means, in essence: *everyone belongs;* everyone is entitled to the same rights protections. It takes constitutional form in the Fourteenth Amendment—which guarantees the "equal protection of the laws" to all people in the U.S.'s jurisdiction.[40] The Supreme Court employed it in the landmark case of *Romer v. Evans* to overturn a Colorado law that voided any protections against discrimination based on sexual orientation.

The case of *Lawrence v. Texas* (invalidating laws against consensual homosexual conduct) was decided on grounds of "the liberty protected by the fourteenth amendment," rather than equal protection per se. However, the majority held that "equality of treatment and the due process right to demand respect for conduct protected by the substantive guarantee of liberty are linked in important respects," observing that sodomy laws are "an invitation to subject homosexual persons to discrimination both in the public and in the private spheres."[41]

International law recognizes the rights of nations to define their immigration policies. It is nonetheless inconsistent with human rights principles for a state to frame its immigration policies in a way that denies human rights on a basis of proscribed discrimination. When a government allows such discrimination to destroy its own citizens' right to a family life, separating partners at national borders on account of their sexual orientation and HIV status, it strikes intolerably at the idea of equality. The European Court of Human Rights in 1985 held that discrimination against immigrant spouses on the basis of sex was a violation of the right to family life; the European Court also recognizes sexual orientation as an unacceptable basis of discrimination.[42]

The U.N. Human Rights Committee—the authoritative body responsible for interpreting the International Covenant on Civil and Political Rights (ICCPR) and monitoring countries' compliance with their covenant obligations—notes that according to the ICCPR, while a country has the authority to expel aliens from its territory in accordance with domestic law, it must apply the law in accordance with "such requirements under the Covenant as equality before the law (art. 26)." Furthermore, the committee notes that "in certain circumstances, an alien may enjoy the protection of the Covenant even in relation to entry or residence, for example, when considerations of non-discrimination, prohibition of inhumane treatment and respect for family life arise."[43]

With specific bearing on the U.S. ban on entry of persons who are HIV-positive, the U.N. Commission on Human Rights, until this year the central U.N. body charged with monitoring rights violations and interpreting standards, has made clear that HIV status is categorically protected from discrimination under international human rights law. In a 1995 resolution, the commission held that "discrimination on the basis of AIDS or HIV status, actual or presumed, is prohibited by existing international human rights standards, and that the term 'or other status' in non-discrimination provisions in international human rights texts can be interpreted to cover health status, including HIV/AIDS."[44]

The United States can also draw lessons from other countries—both near and far—which have taken stands against inequality based on sexual orientation. In the 1998 case of *Vriend v. Alberta,* Canada's Supreme Court held:

> It is easy to say that everyone who is just like "us" is entitled to equality. Everyone finds it more difficult to say that those who are "different" from us in some way should have the same equality rights that we enjoy. Yet so soon as we say any . . . group is less deserving and unworthy of equal protection and benefit of the law all minorities and all of Canadian society are demeaned. It is so deceptively simple and so devastatingly injurious to say that those who are handicapped or of a different race, or religion, or colour or sexual orientation are less worthy. . . . It can never be forgotten that discrimination is the antithesis of equality and that it is the recognition of equality which will foster the dignity of every individual.[45]

The United States can also learn from South Africa. In 1996, emerging from the abysses of apartheid, that country became the first to enshrine sexual orientation in its constitution as a status protected from discrimination. One of the earliest decisions by South Africa's Constitutional Court based on this provision guaranteed immigration rights for any citizen's permanent partner, whether of the same or opposite sex. To disregard or discount same-sex relationships for immigration purposes, the Court said, sent a message

> that gays and lesbians lack the inherent humanity to have their families and family lives in such same-sex relationships respected or protected. . . . The impact constitutes a crass, blunt, cruel and serious invasion of their dignity. . . .
>
> The sting of past and continuing discrimination against both gays and lesbians is the clear message that it conveys, namely, that they, whether viewed as individuals or in their same-sex relationships, do not have the inherent dignity and are not worthy of the human respect possessed by

> and accorded to heterosexuals and their relationships. This discrimination occurs at a deeply intimate level of human existence and relationality. It denies to gays and lesbians that which is foundational to our Constitution . . . namely that all persons have the same inherent worth and dignity as human beings, whatever their other differences may be.[46]

"The Hopes and Expectations of Humanity": Law and the Forms of Family

Debates in the United States over how to recognize relationships tend to assume that "marriage" and "the family" have a single character that has not changed over time: the institutions have taken the same shape, and the same people have always had a right to them. Expanding their legal definition to other forms of affiliation thus seems a social change of tectonic importance.

Obviously, this is untrue. Casting an eye over a world map or through the Bible is enough to show that over miles and through millennia, families take divergent configurations and have meant many things. United States law only very recently came to recognize in heterosexual marriage a value so universally acknowledged as to be deserved by, and protected for, all.

For generations, for example, marriages between slaves had no legal effect.[47] After slavery, state after state passed "miscegenation" laws barring interracial marriages. These enforced the segregation system; surviving into the twentieth century, they become one of many weapons in the eugenicists' arsenal—hindering the supposedly "unfit" from marrying.

Marriage also was a means of defining citizenship—and of defining certain people out. These laws were widely used to limit immigration. By the nineteenth century's end, a dozen states forbade whites to marry Asians; nine specifically targeted Filipinos. Arizona, one historian notes, "prohibited whites from marrying 'Hindus' and . . . Oregon prohibited whites from marrying Native Hawaiians, or Kanakas."[48] In 1907, Congress mandated that any U.S. woman marrying a foreigner who was ineligible (on racial or other grounds) for U.S. immigration be stripped of her own citizenship without trial.

In a large part of the United States, then—not unlike apartheid South Africa[49]—a web of restrictions on marriage and relationships upheld a racially exclusive definition of national identity. In declaring marriage "a fundamental right of free men"; in stating that "the right to marry is the right to join in marriage with the person of one's choice" (as the California Supreme Court did in overturning a "miscegenation" law in 1948),[50] courts were not just confirming the legal ability to contract a partnership. They were nailing libratory theses to the door about the character of their country and its ability to imagine an open rather than a branded and biased future. Likewise, other steps in this century toward ensuring justice in married relationships—eliminating child marriages, campaigning against domestic violence, guaranteeing the legal and economic rights of both partners, and protecting the rights of the child—also guarantee that family relations will not be a private, insular exception to the public values of dignity and fairness.

A future president of the United States wrote in 1900, "Family methods rest upon individual inequality, state methods upon individual equality. Family order rests upon tutelage, state order upon franchise."[51] Law in the succeeding century strained to erode that invidious division and make the family a place of choice and justice. It is certainly true that "marriage is more than a contract," as some conservatives complain.[52] The way relationships are treated—whether furthering equality or fathering privilege—draws a line between inside and outside, valued and unvalued, on many levels. It not only encapsulates how power is allotted between individuals and state; it embodies a vision of how society will develop.

In 1967, in *Loving v. Virginia*, the Supreme Court finally struck down laws against interracial marriage.[53] It said:

> Marriage is one of the "basic civil rights of man," fundamental to our very existence and survival. To deny this fundamental freedom on so unsupportable a basis as the racial classifications embodied in these statutes, classifications so directly subversive of the principle of equality at the heart of the Fourteenth Amendment, is surely to deprive all the State's citizens of liberty without due process of law.[54]

This affirmed the reach of the Equal Protection Clause. It also was a step in the Court's progress toward identifying a realm of intimate decision-making as a basic part of liberty. In *Lawrence v. Texas,* the Court maintained:

> Liberty presumes an autonomy of self that includes freedom of thought, belief, expression, and certain intimate conduct. . . . When sexuality finds overt expression in intimate conduct with another person, the conduct can be but one element in a personal bond that is more enduring. The liberty protected by the Constitution allows homosexual persons the right to make this choice.[55]

Current U.S. immigration law, bound by a restrictive concept of family relationships excluding lesbian and gay partners, denies those persons that right and that choice. This sends a devastating message to them about their dignity and worth. It sends the wrong message about U.S. society and what it wants to become.

Liz, with her Jaimaican partner Carly, put it in simpler but more heartfelt words when she wrote: "We are in love. This country needs more love. Why my country fights so hard to interfere with my right to pursue happiness and live in peace and harmony with all is beyond me. It saddens me deeply. Recognizing our relationships would only strengthen our nation."[56]

Lesbian and Gay Immigrants in the Courts: A Summary

Despite right-wing claims that "judicial activism" favors lesbian, gay, bisexual, and transgender people, the immigration rights of LGBT people were consistently given scant support in jurisprudence from the 1950s to the 1980s. However, *Hill v. INS* in 1983 effectively took the teeth out of the Immigration and Nationality Act's exclusion of lesbian and gay people from the United States—and pointed toward the emerging protections for LGBT people's rights in more recent, nonimmigration-related jurisprudence.

Boutilier v. Immigration Service, 1967

In this case, the Supreme Court decided whether lesbian and gay people were covered by the definition of "psychopathic personality." Twenty-one-year-old Clive Boutilier, a Canadian, had moved to the United States in 1955 to join his mother, stepfather, and three siblings who already lived there. In 1963, he applied for U.S. citizenship, admitting that he had been arrested for sodomy in 1959. He was ordered deported.[57]

The case eventually reached the Supreme Court, which, in a 6–3 decision, upheld his deportation. The majority found that "Congress was not laying down a clinical test, but an exclusionary standard which it declared to be inclusive of those having homosexual and perverted characteristics. . . . Congress used the phrase 'psychopathic personality' not in the clinical sense, but to effectuate its purpose to exclude from entry all homosexuals and other sex perverts."[58] Dissenting, Justice William Douglas observed, "The term 'psychopathic personality' is a treacherous one like 'communist' or in an earlier day 'Bolshevik.' A label of this kind when freely used may mean only an unpopular person."[59]

Boutilier was torn from his partner of eight years. According to one historian, "Presumably distraught about the Court's decision . . . Boutilier attempted suicide before leaving New York, survived a month-long coma that left him brain-damaged with permanent disabilities, and moved to southern Ontario with his parents, who took on the task of caring for him for more than twenty years." He died in Canada on April 12, 2003, only weeks before that country at last moved to legalize same-sex marriage.[60]

Adams v. Howerton, 1980

Richard Adams, a U.S. citizen, lived in Colorado with his partner Anthony Sullivan, an Australian national. When Sullivan's visitor's visa expired, they persuaded their local county clerk to issue them a marriage license. Adams then asked the INS to classify Sullivan as his spouse for immigration purposes.[61] The INS refused to acknowledge a relationship between "faggots"—as told above. The case eventually reached the Ninth Circuit Court of Appeals. The court addressed two issues: whether for the purposes of immigration, a U.S. citizen's spouse must be a person of the opposite sex, and, if so, whether such limitation is constitutional. The court concluded that Congress had intended to restrict the term "spouse" to opposite-sex married couples. The court then found that it was within Congress's plenary power thus to limit access to immigration benefits, stating that the Supreme Court "has upheld the broad power of Congress to determine immigration policy in the face of challenges" based on constitutional claims.[62] The Supreme Court refused to hear an appeal.

Hill v. INS, 1983

On August 2, 1979, the U.S. surgeon general issued a new policy stating that the U.S. Public Health Service should no longer consider "homosexuality per se to be a 'mental disease or defect,'" citing "current and generally accepted canons of medical practice with respect to homosexuality."[63] Since the exclusion of homosexuals was based on the Public Health Service's findings, this created problems for the Immigration and Naturalization Service. In response, in 1980 the INS issued its own "Guidelines and Procedures for Inspection of Aliens Who Are Suspected of Being Homosexual." Noncitizens would no longer be asked about their sexual orientation, but if one admitted to being gay or the fact was revealed during inspection, the INS would not need medical certification. The admission could be used to deport him or her.

In 1980, Carl Hill, a British citizen, arrived at San Francisco International Airport and told immigration authorities he was gay. His resulting exclusion led to a court case that came before the Ninth Circuit Court in 1983. The court decided that noncitizens could not be shut out of the country based solely on their own admission to homosexuality. The law required Public Health Service certification, and the INS could not circumvent this through its own, different guidelines.[64]

The decision indicated that future denials of entry to homosexuals would face serious legal scrutiny. However, not until the Immigration Act of 1990 was the issue finally settled: Congress decided that lesbians and gays could no longer be excluded based on their sexual orientation.

NOTES

1. Letter from Immigration and Naturalization Service to Richard Adams (November 24, 1975) (in Stephen H. Legomsky, *Immigration and Refugee Law and Policy,* 2nd ed. [New York: Foundation Press, 1997], 139).

2. E-mail to Immigration Equality (names withheld or changed at the author's request), May 29, 2005.

3. Martha Butt Sherwood's *The Nun,* published in the United States in 1834, was an early tract claiming that convents were virtual brothels; it helped incite an enraged nativist mob to burn an Ursuline convent in Charlestown, Massachusetts, the same year. Other scandalous volumes, such as *The Awful Disclosures of Maria Monk, as Exhibited in a Narrative of Her Sufferings during a Residence of Five Years as a Novice and Two Years as a Black Nun, in the Hotel Dieu Nunnery in Montreal* (published in 1836) fed anti-Irish and anti-Catholic sentiment throughout the century. See Marie Anne Pagliarini, "The Pure American Woman and the Wicked Catholic Priest: An Analysis of Anti-Catholic Literature in Antebellum America," Religion and American Culture 9/1 (Winter 1999), 97–128.

4. An inflammatory and extensive campaign excited racist fears by charging immigrants with smuggling European women into the United States, or American women abroad, and forcing them into sex work—so-called white slavery.

5. Eithne Luibheid, *Entry Denied: Controlling Sexuality at the Border* (Minneapolis: University of Minnesota, 2002), 31–51. The Chinese Exclusion Act of 1882 imposed overtly racist restrictions on Asian immigration, which were progressively tightened in succeeding revisions; it barred all Chinese immigrants from naturalization.

6. Francis A. Walker, "Restriction of Immigration," *Atlantic Monthly* 77/464 (June 1896), 822–29, at http://www.faculty.fairfield.edu/faculty/hodyson/courses/city/wlker/walker.htm (retrieved January 17, 2008).

7. Wendy Kline, *Building a Better Race: Gender, Sexuality, and Eugenics from the Turn of the Century to the Baby Boom* (Berkeley: University of California Press, 2001), also traces ancestral connections between early "scientific racism" and contemporary movements to "defend the family."

8. Donald K. Pickens, *Eugenics and the Progressives* (Nashville: Vanderbilt University Press, 1968).

9. Annie L. Cot, "'Breed Out the Unfit and Breed In the Fit': Irving Fisher, Economics, and the Science of Heredity," *American Journal of Economics and Sociology*64/3 (July 2005), 793–826.

10. Congressman John Corliss, quoted in Jeanne Petit, "Breeders, Workers, and Mothers: Gender and the Congressional Literacy Test Debate, 1896–1897," *Journal of the Gilded Age and Progressive Era* 3/1 (2004), 73; emphasis added.

11. Gail Bederman, *Manliness and Civilization: A Cultural History of Gender and Race in the United States, 1866–1917* (Chicago: University of Chicago Press, 1996), 200.

12. U.S. Bureau of the Census, *Historical Statistics of the United States: Colonial Times to 1957* (Washington, D.C.: U.S. Bureau of the Census, 1960), 56.

13. John B. Trevor, quoted in Jon Higham, *Strangers in the Land* (New York: Atheneum, 1968), 324.

14. Max Lerner, "The Senator and the Purge," *New York Post,* July 17, 1950, quoted in Jonathan Katz, *Gay American History: Lesbians and Gay Men in the U.S.A.* (New York: Harper Colophon, 1976), 95.

15. For example, David K. Johnson, *The Lavender Scare: The Cold War Persecution of Gays and Lesbians in the Federal Government* (Chicago: University of Chicago Press, 2004), and John D'Emilio, *Sexual Politics, Sexual Communities: The Making of a Homosexual Minority in the United States, 1940–1970* (Chicago: University of Chicago Press, 1983), 38–56. D'Emilio in particular suggests that the "lavender scare," like the anti-immigrant panics of earlier years, was connected to fears of changing gender roles and family structure, particularly after the shifts of the war years: "Because the war removed large numbers of men and women from familial —and familiar—environments, it freed homosexual eroticism from some of the structural restraints that made it appear marginal and isolated" (38).

16. Alicia J. Campi, *The McCarran-Walter Act: A Contradictory Legacy on Race, Quotas, and Ideology,* immigration policy brief by the American Immigration Law Foundation, at http://www.ailf.org/ipc/policy_reports_2004_mccarranwalter.asp (retrieved December 26, 2005). For an explanation of these categories, see chapter 3 in this volume.

17. President Harry S. Truman vetoed the bill, calling it "neither a fitting instrument for our foreign policy nor a true reflection of what we stand for, at home and abroad, " but Congress easily overrode him. See Michael Ybarra, *Washington Gone Crazy: Senator Pat McCarran and the Great American Communist Hunt* (New York: Steerforth, 2004), 132.

18. Immigration and Nationality Act, § 212(a)(4), 66 Stat. at 182; emphasis added.

19. The Senate Judiciary Committee had recommended in 1950 that "the classes of mentally defectives" barred from entry in existing legislation "should be enlarged to include homosexuals and other sex perverts" (S. Rep. No. 1515, 81st Cong., 2d Sess., p. 345). The proposed Immigration and Nationality Act thus originally contained an additional phrase expressly providing for the exclusion of aliens "who are homosexuals or sex perverts." These words were omitted from the law as passed, because—as the Senate Judiciary Committee explained—"The Public Health Service has advised that the provision for the exclusion of aliens afflicted with psychopathic personality or a mental defect . . . is sufficiently broad to provide for the exclusion of homosexuals and sex perverts. This change of nomenclature is not to be construed in any way as modifying the intent to exclude all aliens who are sexual deviates" (S. Rep. No. 1137, 82d Cong., 2d Sess., p. 9). See *Boutilier v. Immigration Service,* 387 U.S. 118 (1967).

20. 1965 Amendments, Pub. L. No. 89-236, 79 Stat. 911 (1965); emphasis added.

The 1965 legislation represented another broad restructuring of immigration. It finally abolished the 1924 act's national quotas: with the civil rights movement combating racism at home, discriminating by national origin no longer seemed compatible with the U.S.'s expressed values.

21. Robert Foss, "The Demise of the Homosexual Exclusion: New Possibilities for Gay and Lesbian Immigration," *Harvard Civil Rights–Civil Liberties Law Review* 29 (1994), 439–46.

22. The American Psychological Association had removed homosexuality from its roster of psychiatric disorders in 1973.

23. Alana Klein, *HIV/AIDS and Immigration: Final Report,* (Toronto: Canadian HIV/AIDS Legal Network, 2001), 27.

24. The language of affliction clearly recalls the ban on people "afflicted with . . . sexual deviation."

25. William B. Rubenstein, Ruth Eisenberg, and Lawrence O. Gostin, *The Authoritative ACLU Guide to the Rights of People Living with HIV Disease and AIDS* (Carbondale: Southern Illinois University Press, 1996), 315. The biannual International AIDS Conference, the most important gathering of experts and activists combating the disease, is no longer held in the United States because of the ban. The WHO has a policy of not sponsoring international meetings to discuss AIDS in countries with HIV/AIDS-specific short-term travel restrictions. See World Health Organization, "WHO policy of Non-sponsorship of International Conferences on AIDS in Countries with HIV/AIDS-Specific Short Term Travel Restrictions," February 1993, with reference to World Health Assembly Resolution WHA41.24 (1988) ("Avoidance of discrimination in relation to HIV-infected people and people with AIDS").

26. Office of the United Nations High Commissioner for Human Rights and the Joint United Nations Programme on HIV/AIDS, *HIV/AIDS and Human Rights-International Guidelines (from the second international consultation on HIV/AIDS and human rights, 23–25 September 1996, Geneva),* U.N. Doc. HR/PUB/98/1 (Geneva, 1998).

27. Josef Decosas and Alix Adrien, quoted in Klein, *HIV/AIDS and Immigration,* 51.

28. Defense of Marriage Act, Pub. L. No. 104-199, 100 Stat. 2419 (September 21, 1996), codified at 1 U.S.C. § 7 and 28 U.S.C. § 1738C.

29. Article 4, section 1 of the U.S. Constitution states, "Full Faith and Credit shall be given in each State to the public Acts, Records, and judicial Proceedings of every other State" and that "Congress may by general Laws prescribe the Manner in which such Acts, Records, and Proceedings shall be proved and the Effect thereof." In a range of decisions, the Supreme Court has not fully clarified

the extent to which a state can decline "full faith and credit" on the grounds of its own strong public policy or the extent to which Congress' permitted regulation of "the effect thereof" includes the ability to retract it. See Paige Chabora, "Congress' Power under the Full Faith and Credit Clause and the Defense of Marriage Act of 1996," *Nebraska Law Review* 76 (1997), at http://www.lexisnexis.com/us/lnacademic/search/journalssubmit.fan.do (retrieved January 31, 2008), and Julie L. B. Johnson, "The Meaning of 'General Laws': The Extent of Congress's Power under the Full Faith and Credit Clause and the Constitutionality of the Defense of Marriage Act," *University of Pennsylvania Law Review* 145 (1997), 1611–30.

30. This includes amendments in Louisiana and Nebraska that have been overturned and are still subject to litigation.

31. "Judge: Domestic Violence Law for Marrieds Only: Backlash from Anti-gay Marriage Amendment," Associated Press, March 24, 2005, at http://peaceandjustice.org/article.php/20050325120409728 (retrieved January 31, 2008).

32. For example, Michael Farris, *Critical Decision on Text of Constitutional Amendment Protecting Marriage,* February 5, 2004, at http://www.cwfa.org/articles/5208/CWA/family/ (retrieved January 2, 2005).

33. Bridget E. Maher, *Why Marriage Should Be Privileged in Public Policy,* Family Research Council, at http://www.frc.org/index.cfm?i=IS03D1&f=WU03J07 (retrieved December 15, 2004). See also *Anti-Gay Groups Active in Massachusetts: A Closer Look,* National Gay and Lesbian Task Force, at http://www.TheTaskForce.org/marriagecenter (retrieved November 11, 2004). The same paper points out that the website of Concerned Women for America, a powerful conservative group that describes itself as a "public policy women's organization," "had 602 documents on its website that contained the word 'homosexual,' but only 97 referring to 'health care,' 80 with the word 'poverty' . . . and six containing 'child support.'" Only seventy-one documents referred to "rape," nineteen to "domestic violence," and none at all to "pay equity."

34. David H. Bennett, *Party of Fear: From Nativist Movements to the New Right in American History* (New York: Knopf, 1995), argues for direct continuity between nineteenth-century racism and xenophobia and contemporary anti-immigrant and fundamentalist movements. In the present day, Pat Buchanan blames U.S. "decline" on immigrants: "America is ceasing to be one country." But gender and sexuality propel population shifts. The problem, he says, is Western women: "We know how they are not having children—birth control or abortion or sterilization or whatever. But the reasons why are the economy and culture and feminism, and the women are doing what they want to do. I don't know how politically, in a democratic society . . . we can force changes upon women and upon men as well. But I do have some ideas." See "How the West Was Lost: Pat Buchanan Discusses

His New Book with Geoff Metcalf," *World Net Daily,* December 23, 2001, at http://www.worldnetdaily.com/news/article.asp?ARTICLE_ID=25797 (retrieved January 4, 2003).

35. Robert Knight, director of the Culture and Family Institute of Concerned Women for America, quoted in Jeff Johnson, "Congressman Promotes Immigration Privileges for Homosexuals," *Christian News Service,* at http://www.cnsnews.com/ViewPrint.asp?Page=%5CPolitics%5Carchive%5C200209%5CPOL20020923d.html (retrieved October 31, 2004).

36. Tom Owens, "Why Rep. Nick Lampson Is 'Bought and Paid For' by the Homosexual Lobby," at http://www.liberallampson.com, and "The Shocking Truth about Nick Lampson's Connections to the Homosexual Lobby," mailing distributed to voters, at http://www.liberallampson.com/lampsonmailer.pdf (retrieved November 25, 2005). The Uniting American Families Act (UAFA) in no way offers "free health care" or any other benefit save immigration recognition.

37. Quoted in Robert B. Bluey, "Court's Ruling on Sodomy Fuels Fight for Same-Sex Marriage," *Christian News Service,* June 27, 2003, at http://www.newsmax.com/archives/articles/2003/6/27/120250.shtml (retrieved June 28, 2003).

38. James Kimball, "Homosexuals Pose New Threat to U.S. Border Security," press release from Concerned Women for America, September 24, 2003, at http://www.csfa.com/printerfriendly.asp?id=4629&department+cwa&categoryid=family (retrieved September 25, 2003).

39. All quotations in this discussion are from a Human Rights Watch/Immigration Equality telephone interview with Asa and Tony (last names withheld at their request), January 5, 2006, and an email from Asa to Human Rights Watch, January 5, 2006.

40. Technically, the Equal Protection Clause directly applies only to states and not the federal government. However, discrimination at the federal level has been held similarly to violate the Due Process Clause in the Fifth Amendment.

41. *Lawrence and Garner v. Texas,* 539 U.S. (2003), at 14.

42. *Abulaziz, Cabales and Balkandali v. United Kingdom,* European Court of Human Rights 471 (May 28, 1985).

43. Human Rights Committee, *General Comment 15, The Rights of Aliens under the International Covenant on Civil and Political Rights,* HRI/GEN/1/Rev.7, para. 9 and para. 5, at http://www.unhchr.ch/tbs/doc.nsf/(Symbol)/bc561aa81bc5d86ec12563ed004aaa1b?Opendocument (retrieved August 8, 2007).

44. U.N. Commission on Human Rights, "The Protection of Human Rights in the Context of Human Immunodeficiency Virus (HIV) and Acquired Immune Deficiency Syndrome (AIDS)," resolution 995/44, E/CN.4/1995/176.

45. *Vriend v. Alberta,* Supreme Court of Canada, File No. 25285, at 69.

46. *National Coalition for Gay and Lesbian Equality and Others v. Ministry of Home Affairs and Others,* Constitutional Court of South Africa, CCT 10/99, at 54 and 42.

47. "It is clear that slaves have no legal capacity to assent to any contract. With the consent of their master they may marry, and their *moral* power to agree to such a contract or connection cannot be doubted; *but while in a state of slavery* it cannot produce any *civil effect,* because slaves are deprived of all civil rights. Emancipation gives to the slave his civil rights, and a contract of marriage, legal and valid by the consent of the master, and moral assent of the slave, *from the moment of freedom, although dormant during slavery,* produces all the effects which result from such contract among free persons." (Opinion of Judge Matthews, case of *Girod v. Lewis,* May term, 1819; *Martin's Louisiana Reports,* vol. 6, p. 559.)

48. Peggy Pascoe, "Why the Ugly Rhetoric against Gay Marriage Is Familiar to This Historian of Miscegenation," *History News Network,* at http://hnn.us/articles/4708.html (retrieved December 14, 2005).

49. Among the first steps in establishing apartheid in South Africa were banning interracial marriages (in 1949) and all interracial sex (in 1950). This paralleled similar moves in building a racial regime in Nazi Germany in the 1930s.

50. *Perez* v. *Sharp,* 32 Ca1.2d 711, 198 P.2d 17 (1948).

51. Woodrow Wilson, *The State: Elements of Historical and Practical Politics* (Boston: Heath, 1900), 638.

52. David Coolidge, "What Is Marriage?" *Crisis Magazine,* July 15, 1996, 27–29.

53. The statute in question, Virginia's Racial Integrity Act of 1924, outlawing intermarriage, was itself illustrative. Virginia had been a hotbed of eugenicist pseudoscience and practice; Madison Grant, the Jeremiah of "mongrelization" (see chapter 2 in this volume) was consulted as the law was drawn up. The bill, requiring racial registration certificates, was clearly meant to promote racial classification across the whole population. (This also corresponded to national trends: in 1920, the U.S. Census eliminated the category of "mixed race" for the first time in seven decades, forcing people to class themselves as either "black" or "white.") The act defined a "white person" as one who "has no trace whatever of any blood other than Caucasian; but persons who have one-sixteenth or less of the blood of the American Indian and have no other non-Caucasic blood shall be deemed to be white persons." The latter exception was added because sixteen members of the Virginia legislature, who proudly claimed partial descent from Pocohontas, feared being legally leached of their whiteness by a more constricting definition. See Paul Lombardo, "Miscegenation, Eugenics and Racism: Historical Footnotes to *Loving v. Virginia,*" *University of California Davis Law Review,* 21 (1988), 421–52.

54. *Loving v. Virginia,* 388 U.S. 1 (1967), at 13.

55. *Lawrence and Garner v. Texas,* 539 U.S. (2003), at 6.

56. Email to Immigration Equality from Liz (names changed at her request), October 18, 2003.

57. Chris Duenas, "Coming to America: The Immigration Obstacle Facing Binational Same-Sex Couples," *Southern California Law Review* 73 (2000), 811–41.

58. *Boutilier v. Immigration Service,* 387 U.S. 118 (1967).

59. Ibid.

60. Mark Stein, "Forgetting and Remembering a Deported Alien," *History News Network,* November 3, 2003, at http://hnn.us/articles/1769.html (retrieved December 26, 2005).

61. Duenas, "Coming to America," 80.

62. *Adams v. Howerton,* 673 F.2d 1038 (1980).

63. Board of Immigration Appeal, No. A-2420404969, *Matter of Hill,* quoted from opinion.

64. *Hill v. INS,* 714 F.2d 1472 (1983).

PRIMARY SOURCE

Boutilier v. Immigration Service, 1967

As Scott Long, Jessica Stern, and Adam Francouer argue, Boutilier v. Immigration Service, *in 1967, was an important case in the history of lesbian, gay, and transgender immigrant rights. In this case, the Supreme Court drew on psychological research stigmatizing homosexuality and found that homosexuality constituted grounds for exclusion and deportation under the 1952 McCarran-Walter Immigration Act. The pathologization of sexual identity in this case marks the first time that homosexuality is referred to specifically in immigration law. The issues raised by this important case still affect immigrant rights for LGBT people.*

U.S. Supreme Court

BOUTILIER V. IMMIGRATION SERVICE, 387 U.S. 118 (1967)

BOUTILIER V. IMMIGRATION AND NATURALIZATION SERVICE.

CERTIORARI TO THE UNITED STATES COURT OF APPEALS FOR THE SECOND CIRCUIT.

No. 440.

Argued March 14, 1967.

Decided May 22, 1967.

Petitioner, an alien who at the time of his entry into the United States was a homosexual, held excludable under 212 (a) (4) of the Immigration and

Nationality Act of 1952, as one "afflicted with [a] psychopathic personality," a term which Congress clearly intended to include homosexuals. Pp. 120–125.

363 F.2d 488, affirmed.

Blanch Freedman argued the cause for petitioner. With her on the briefs was Robert Brown.

Nathan Lewin argued the cause for respondent. On the brief were Solicitor General Marshall, Assistant Attorney General Vinson and Philip R. Monahan.

Briefs of amici curiae, urging reversal, were filed by David Carliner, Nanette Dembitz and Alan H. Levine for the American Civil Liberties Union et al., and by the Homosexual Law Reform Society of America.

MR. JUSTICE CLARK delivered the opinion of the Court.

The petitioner, an alien, has been ordered deported to Canada as one who upon entry into this country was a homosexual and therefore "afflicted with psychopathic personality" and excludable under 212 (a) (4) of the Immigration and Nationality Act of 1952, 66 Stat. 182. 8 U.S.C. 1182 (a) (4).* Petitioner's appeal from the finding of the Special Inquiry Officer was dismissed by the Board of Immigration Appeals, without opinion, and his petition for review in the Court of Appeals was dismissed, with one judge dissenting. 363 F.2d 488. It held that the term "psychopathic personality," as used by the Congress in 212 (a) (4), was a term of art intended to exclude homosexuals from entry into the United States. It further found that the term was not void for vagueness and was, therefore, not repugnant to the Fifth Amendment's Due Process Clause. We granted certiorari, 385 U.S. 927, and now affirm.

I. Petitioner, a Canadian national, was first admitted to this country on June 22, 1955, at the age of 21. His last entry was in 1959, at which time

* "SEC. 212. (a) Except as otherwise provided in this Act, the following classes of aliens shall be ineligible to receive visas and shall be excluded from admission into the United States. . . ." (4) Aliens afflicted with psychopathic personality, epilepsy, or a mental defect. . . ." Section 241 (a) (1) of the Immigration and Nationality Act, 66 Stat. 204, 8 U.S.C. 1251 (a) (1), provides that: "Any alien in the United States . . . shall, upon the order of the Attorney General, be deported who (1) at the time of entry was within one or more of the classes of aliens excludable by the law existing at the time of such entry. . . ."

he was returning from a short trip to Canada. His mother and stepfather and three of his brothers and sisters live in the United States. In 1963 he applied for citizenship and submitted to the Naturalization Examiner an affidavit in which he admitted that he was arrested in New York in October 1959, on a charge of sodomy, which was later reduced to simple assault and thereafter dismissed on default of the complainant. In 1964, petitioner, at the request of the Government, submitted another affidavit which revealed the full history of his sexual deviate behavior. It stated that his first homosexual experience occurred when he was 14 years of age, some seven years before his entry into the United States. Petitioner was evidently a passive participant in this encounter. His next episode was at age 16 and occurred in a public park in Halifax, Nova Scotia. Petitioner was the active participant in this affair. During the next five years immediately preceding his first entry into the United States petitioner had homosexual relations on an average of three or four times a year. He also stated that prior to his entry he had engaged in heterosexual relations on three or four occasions. During the eight and one-half years immediately subsequent to his entry, and up to the time of his second statement, petitioner continued to have homosexual relations on an average of three or four times a year. Since 1959 petitioner had shared an apartment with a man with whom he had had homosexual relations.

The 1964 affidavit was submitted to the Public Health Service for its opinion as to whether petitioner was excludable for any reason at the time of his entry. The Public Health Service issued a certificate in 1964 stating that in the opinion of the subscribing physicians petitioner "was afflicted with a class A condition, namely, psychopathic personality, sexual deviate" at the time of his admission. Deportation proceedings were then instituted. "No serious question," the Special Inquiry Officer found, "has been raised either by the respondent [petitioner here], his counsel or the psychiatrists [employed by petitioner] who have submitted reports on the respondent as to his sexual deviation." Indeed, the officer found that both of petitioner's psychiatrists "concede that the respondent has been a homosexual for a number of years but conclude that by reason of such sexual deviation, the respondent is not a psychopathic personality." Finding against petitioner on the facts, the issue before the officer was reduced to the purely legal question of whether the term "psychopathic personality" included homosexuals and if it suffered illegality because of vagueness.

II. The legislative history of the Act indicates beyond a shadow of a doubt that the Congress intended the phrase "psychopathic personality" to include homosexuals such as petitioner.

Prior to the 1952 Act the immigration law excluded "persons of constitutional psychopathic inferiority." 39 Stat. 875, as amended, 8 U.S.C. 136 (a) (1946 ed.). Beginning in 1950, a subcommittee of the Senate Committee on the Judiciary conducted a comprehensive study of the immigration laws and in its report found "that the purpose of the provision against 'persons with constitutional psychopathic inferiority' will be more adequately served by changing that term to 'persons afflicted with psychopathic personality,' and that the classes of mentally defectives should be enlarged to include homosexuals and other sex perverts." S. Rep. No. 1515, 81st Cong., 2d Sess., p. 345. The resulting legislation was first introduced as S. 3455 and used the new phrase "psychopathic personality." The bill, however, contained an additional clause providing for the exclusion of aliens "who are homosexuals or sex perverts." As the legislation progressed (now S. 2550 in the 82d Congress), however, it omitted the latter clause "who are homosexuals or sex perverts" and used only the phrase "psychopathic personality." The omission is explained by the Judiciary Committee Report on the bill:

"The provisio[n] of S. 716 [one of the earlier bills not enacted] which specifically excluded homosexuals and sex perverts as a separate excludable class does not appear in the instant bill. The Public Health Service has advised that the provision for the exclusion of aliens afflicted with psychopathic personality or a mental defect which appears in the instant bill is sufficiently broad to provide for the exclusion of homosexuals and sex perverts. This change of nomenclature is not to be construed in any way as modifying the intent to exclude all aliens who are sexual deviates." (Emphasis supplied.) S. Rep. No. 1137, 82d Cong., 2d Sess., p. 9.

Likewise, a House bill, H.R. 5678, adopted the position of the Public Health Service that the phrase "psychopathic personality" excluded from entry homosexuals and sex perverts. The report that accompanied the bill shows clearly that the House Judiciary Committee adopted the recommendation of the Public Health Service that "psychopathic personality" should be used in the Act as a phrase that would exclude from admission homosexuals and sex perverts. H.R. Rep. No. 1365, 82d Cong., 2d Sess. It quoted at length, and specifically adopted, the Public Health Service report which recommended that the term "psychopathic personality" be used to "specify such types of pathologic behavior as homosexuality or sexual perversion." We, therefore, conclude that the Congress used the phrase "psychopathic personality" not in the clinical sense, but to effectuate its purpose to exclude from entry all homosexuals and other sex perverts.

Petitioner stresses that only persons afflicted with psychopathic personality are excludable. This, he says, is "a condition, physical or psychiatric, which may be manifested in different ways, including sexual behavior." Petitioner's contention must fall by his own admissions. For over six years prior to his entry petitioner admittedly followed a continued course of homosexual conduct. The Public Health Service doctors found and certified that at the time of his entry petitioner "was afflicted with a class A condition, namely, psychopathic personality, sexual deviate. . . ." It was stipulated that if these doctors were to appear in the case they would testify to this effect and that "no useful purpose would be served by submitting this additional psychiatric material [furnished by petitioner's doctors] to the United States Public Health Service. . . ." The Government clearly established that petitioner was a homosexual at entry. Having substantial support in the record, we do not now disturb that finding, especially since petitioner admitted being a homosexual at the time of his entry. The existence of this condition over a continuous and uninterrupted period prior to and at the time of petitioner's entry clearly supports the ultimate finding upon which the order of deportation was based.

III. Petitioner says, even so, the section as construed is constitutionally defective because it did not adequately warn him that his sexual affliction at the time of entry could lead to his deportation. It is true that this Court has held the "void for vagueness" doctrine applicable to civil as well as criminal actions. See Small Co. v. Am. Sugar Ref. Co., 267 U.S. 233, 239 (1925). However, this is where "the exaction of obedience to a rule or standard . . . was so vague and indefinite as really to be no rule or standard at all. . . ." In short, the exaction must strip a participant of his rights to come within the principle of the cases. But the "exaction" of 212 (a) (4) never applied to petitioner's conduct after entry. The section imposes neither regulation of nor sanction for conduct. In this situation, therefore, no necessity exists for guidance so that one may avoid the applicability of the law. The petitioner is not being deported for conduct engaged in after his entry into the United States, but rather for characteristics he possessed at the time of his entry. Here, when petitioner first presented himself at our border for entrance, he was already afflicted with homosexuality. The pattern was cut, and under it he was not admissible.

The constitutional requirement of fair warning has no applicability to standards such as are laid down in 212 (a) (4) for admission of aliens to the United States. It has long been held that the Congress has plenary power to make rules for the admission of aliens and to exclude those who possess those characteristics which Congress has forbidden. See The Chinese Exclusion Case (1889). Here Congress commanded that homosexuals not be allowed to enter. The petitioner was found to have that characteristic and was ordered deported. The basis of the deportation order was his affliction for a long period of time prior to entry, i. e., six and one-half years before his entry. It may be, as some claim, that "psychopathic personality" is a medically ambiguous term, including several separate and distinct afflictions. Noyes, Modern Clinical Psychiatry 410 (3d ed. 1948). But the test here is what the Congress intended, not what differing psychiatrists may think. It was not laying down a clinical test, but an exclusionary standard which it declared to be inclusive of those having homosexual and perverted characteristics. It can hardly be disputed that the legislative history of 212 (a) (4) clearly shows that Congress so intended.

But petitioner says that he had no warning and that no interpretation of the section had come down at the time of his 1955 entry. Therefore, he argues, he was unaware of the fact that homosexual conduct engaged in after entry could lead to his deportation. We do not believe that petitioner's post-entry conduct is the basis for his deportation order. At the time of his first entry he had continuously been afflicted with homosexuality for over six years. To us the statute is clear. It fixes "the time of entry" as the crucial date and the record shows that the findings of the Public Health Service doctors and the Special Inquiry Officer all were based on that date. We find no indication that the post-entry evidence was of any consequence in the ultimate decision of the doctors, the hearing officer or the court. Indeed, the proof was uncontradicted as to petitioner's characteristic at the time of entry and this brought him within the excludable class. A standard applicable solely to time of entry could hardly be vague as to post-entry conduct.

The petitioner raises other points, including the claim that an "arriving alien" under the Act is entitled to medical examination. Since he is not an "arriving alien" subject to exclusion, but a deportable alien within an excludable class who through error was permitted entry it is doubtful if the requirement would apply. But we need not go into the question since petitioner was twice offered examination and refused to submit himself. He can hardly be heard to complain now. The remaining contentions are likewise without merit.

Affirmed.

MR. JUSTICE BRENNAN dissents for the reasons stated by Judge Moore of the Court of Appeals, 363 F.2d 488, 496–499.

MR. JUSTICE DOUGLAS, with whom MR. JUSTICE FORTAS concurs, dissenting.

The term "psychopathic personality" is a treacherous one like "communist" or in an earlier day "Bolshevik." A label of this kind when freely used may mean only an unpopular person. It is much too vague by constitutional standards for the imposition of penalties or punishment.

Cleckley defines "psychopathic personality" as one who has the following characteristics:

(1) Superficial charm and good "intelligence." (2) Absence of delusions and other signs of irrational "thinking." (3) Absence of "nervousness" or psycho-neurotic manifestations. (4) Unreliability. (5) Untruthfulness and insincerity. (6) Lack of remorse or shame. (7) Inadequately motivated antisocial behavior. (8) Poor judgment and failure to learn by experience. (9) Pathologic egocentricity and incapacity for love. (10) General poverty in major affective reactions. (11) Specific loss of insight. (12) Unresponsiveness in general interpersonal relations. (13) Fantastic and uninviting behavior with drink and sometimes without. (14) Suicide rarely carried out. (15) Sex life impersonal, trivial and poorly integrated. (16) Failure to follow any life plan. Cleckley, The Mask of Sanity 238–255 (1941).

The word "psychopath" according to some means "a sick mind." Guttmacher & Weihofen, Psychiatry and the Law 86 (1952):

"In the light of present knowledge, most of the individuals called psychopathic personalities should probably be considered as suffering from neurotic character disorders. They are, for the most part, unhappy persons, harassed by tension and anxiety, who are struggling against unconscious conflicts which were created during the very early years of childhood. The nature and even the existence of these conflicts which drive them restlessly on are unknown to them. When the anxiety rises to a certain pitch, they seek relief through some antisocial act. The frequency with which this pattern recurs in the individual is dependent in part upon the intensity of the unconscious conflict, upon the tolerance for anxiety, and upon chance environmental situations which may heighten or decrease it. One of the chief diagnostic criteria of this type of neurotically determined delinquency is the repetitiveness of the pattern. The usual explanation, as for example, that the recidivistic check-writer has just 'got in the habit of writing bad checks' is meaningless." Id., at 88–89.

Many experts think that it is a meaningless designation. "Not yet is there any common agreement . . . as to classification or . . . etiology." Noyes, Modern Clinical Psychiatry 410 (3d ed. 1948). "The only conclusion that seems warrantable is that, at some time or other and by some reputable authority, the term psychopathic personality has been used to designate every conceivable type of abnormal character." Curran & Mallinson, Psychopathic Personality, 90 J. Mental Sci. 266, 278. See also Guttmacher, Diagnosis and Etiology of Psychopathic Personalities as Perceived in Our Time, in Current Problems in Psychiatric Diagnosis 139, 154 (Hoch & Zubin ed. 1953); Tappan, Sexual Offences and the Treatment of Sexual Offenders in the United States, in Sexual Offences 500, 507 (Radzinowicz ed. 1957). It is much too treacherously vague a term to allow the high penalty of deportation to turn on it.

When it comes to sex, the problem is complex. Those "who fail to reach sexual maturity (hetero-sexuality), and who remain at a narcissistic or homosexual stage" are the products "of heredity, of glandular dysfunction, [or] of environmental circumstances." Henderson, Psychopathic Constitution and Criminal Behaviour, in Mental Abnormality and Crime 105, 114 (Radzinowicz & Turner ed. 1949).

The homosexual is one, who by some freak [accident], is the product of an arrested development:

"All people have originally bisexual tendencies which are more or less developed and which in the course of time normally deviate either in the direction of male or female. This may indicate that a trace of homosexuality, no matter how weak it may be, exists in every human being. It is present in the adolescent stage, where there is a considerable amount of undifferentiated sexuality." Abrahamsen, Crime and the Human Mind 117 (1944).

Many homosexuals become involved in violations of laws; many do not. Kinsey reported:

"It is not possible to insist that any departure from the sexual mores, or any participation in socially taboo activities, always, or even usually, involves a neurosis or psychosis, for the case histories abundantly demonstrate that most individuals who engage in taboo activities make satisfactory social adjustments. There are, in actuality, few adult males who are particularly disturbed over their sexual histories. Psychiatrists, clinical psychologists, and others who deal with cases of maladjustment, sometimes come to feel that most people find difficulty in adjusting their sexual lives; but a clinic is no place to secure incidence figures. The incidence of tuberculosis in a tuberculosis sanitarium is no measure of the incidence of tuberculosis in the population as a whole; and the incidence of disturbance over sexual activities, among the persons who come to a clinic, is no measure of the frequency of similar disturbances outside of clinics. The impression that such 'sexual irregularities' as 'excessive' masturbation, pre-marital intercourse, responsibility for a pre-marital pregnancy, extramarital intercourse, mouth-genital contacts, homosexual activity, or animal intercourse, always produce psychoses and abnormal personalities is based upon the fact that the persons who do go to professional sources for advice are upset by these things.

"It is unwarranted to believe that particular types of sexual behavior are always expressions of psychoses or neuroses. In actuality, they are more often expressions of what is biologically basic in mammalian and anthropoid behavior, and of a deliberate disregard for social convention. Many of the socially and intellectually most significant persons in our histories, successful scientists, educators, physicians, clergymen, business men, and persons of high position in governmental affairs, have socially taboo items in their sexual histories, and among them they have accepted nearly the whole range of so-called sexual abnormalities. Among the socially most successful and personally best adjusted persons who have contributed to the present study, there are some whose rates of outlet are as high as those in any case labelled nymphomania or satyriasis in the literature, or recognized as such in the clinic." Kinsey, Sexual Behavior in the Human Male 201–202 (1948).

It is common knowledge that in this century homosexuals have risen high in our own public service, both in Congress and in the Executive

Branch, and have served with distinction. It is therefore not credible that Congress wanted to deport everyone and anyone who was a sexual deviate, no matter how blameless his social conduct had been nor how creative his work nor how valuable his contribution to society. I agree with Judge Moore, dissenting below, that the legislative history should not be read as imputing to Congress a purpose to classify under the heading "psychopathic personality" every person who had ever had a homosexual experience:

"Professor Kinsey estimated that 'at least 37 per cent' of the American male population has at least one homosexual experience, defined in terms of physical contact to the point of orgasm, between the beginning of adolescence and old age.[1] Kinsey, Pomeroy & Martin, Sexual Behavior in the Human Male 623 (1948). Earlier estimates had ranged from one per cent to 100 per cent. Id. at 616–622. The sponsors of Britain's current reform bill on homosexuality have indicated that one male in 25 is a homosexual in Britain.[2] To label a group so large 'excludable aliens' would be tantamount to saying that Sappho, Leonardo da Vinci, Michelangelo, Andre Gide, and perhaps even Shakespeare, were they to come to life again, would be deemed unfit to visit our shores.[3] Indeed, so broad a definition might well comprise more than a few members of legislative bodies." 363 F.2d 488, 497–498.

The Public Health Service, from whom Congress borrowed the term "psychopathic personality" (H.R. Rep. No. 1365, 82d Cong., 2d Sess., 46–47) admits that the term is "vague and indefinite." Id., at 46.

If we are to hold, as the Court apparently does, that any acts of homosexuality suffice to deport the alien, whether or not they are part of a fabric of antisocial behavior, then we face a serious question of due process. By that construction a person is judged by a standard that is almost incapable of definition. I have already quoted from clinical experts to show what a wide range the term "psychopathic personality" has. Another expert[4] classifies such a person under three headings:

Acting: (1) inability to withstand tedium, (2) lack of a sense of responsibility, (3) a tendency to "blow up" under pressure, (4) maladjustment to law and order, and (5) recidivism.

Feeling: they tend to (1) be emotionally deficient, narcissistic, callous, inconsiderate, and unremorseful, generally projecting blame on others, (2) have hair-trigger emotions, exaggerated display of emotion, and be irritable and impulsive, (3) be amoral (socially and sexually) and (4) worry, but do nothing about it.

Thinking: they display (1) defective judgment, living for the present rather than for the future, and (2) inability to profit from experience, i. e., they are able to realize the consequences intelligently, but not to evaluate them.

We held in Jordan v. De George, 341 U.S. 223, that the crime of a conspiracy to defraud the United States of taxes involved "moral turpitude" and made the person subject to deportation. That, however, was a term that has "deep roots in the law." Id., at 227. But the grab-bag "psychopathic personality" has no "deep roots" whatsoever.[5] Caprice of judgment is almost certain under this broad definition. Anyone can be caught who is unpopular, who is off-beat, who is nonconformist.

Deportation is the equivalent to banishment or exile. Fong Haw Tan v. Phelan, 333 U.S. 6, 10. Though technically not criminal, it practically may be. The penalty is so severe that we have extended to the resident alien the protection of due process. Wong Yang Sung v. McGrath, 339 U.S. 33 (1950). Even apart from deportation cases, we look with suspicion at those delegations of power so broad as to allow the administrative staff the power to formulate the fundamental policy. See Watkins v. United States, 354 U.S. 178, 203–205; Kent v. Dulles, 357 U.S. 116 (1958). In the Watkins case we were protecting important First Amendment rights. In the Kent case we were protecting the right to travel, an important ingredient of a person's "liberty" within the meaning of the Fifth Amendment. We deal here also with an aspect of "liberty" and the requirements of due process. They demand that the standard be sufficiently clear as to fore-warn those who may otherwise be entrapped and to provide full opportunity to conform. "Psychopathic personality" is so broad and vague as to be hardly more than an epithet. The Court seeks to avoid this question by saying that the standard being applied relates only to what petitioner had done prior to his entry, not to his postentry conduct. But at least half of the questioning of this petitioner related to his postentry conduct.

Moreover, the issue of deportability under 212 (a) of the Immigration and Nationality Act of 1952 turns on whether petitioner is "afflicted with psychopathic personality." On this I think he is entitled to a hearing to satisfy both the statute and the requirement of due process.

One psychiatrist reported:

"On psychiatric examination of Mr. Boutilier, there was no indication of delusional trend or hallucinatory phenomena. He is not psychotic. From his own account, he has a psychosexual problem but is beginning treatment for this disorder. Diagnostically, I would consider him as having a Character Neurosis, believe that the prognosis in therapy is reasonably good and do not think he represents any risk of decompensation into a dependent psychotic reaction nor any potential for frank criminal activity."

Another submitted a long report ending as follows:

"The patient's present difficulties obviously weigh very heavily upon him. He feels as if he has made his life in this country and is deeply disturbed at the prospect of being cut off from the life he has created for himself. He talks frankly about himself. What emerged out of the interview was not a picture of a psychopath but that of a dependent, immature young man with a conscience, an awareness of the feelings of others and a sense of personal honesty. His sexual structure still appears fluid and immature so that he moves from homosexual to heterosexual interests as well as abstinence with almost equal facility. His homosexual orientation seems secondary to a very constricted, dependent personality pattern rather than occurring in the context of a psychopathic personality. My own feeling is that his own need to fit in and be accepted is so great that it far surpasses his need for sex in any form.

"I do not believe that Mr. Boutilier is a psychopath."

In light of these statements, I cannot say that it has been determined that petitioner was "afflicted" in the statutory sense either at the time of entry or at present. "Afflicted" means possessed or dominated by. Occasional acts would not seem sufficient. "Afflicted" means a way of life, an accustomed pattern of conduct. Whatever disagreement there is as to the meaning of "psychopathic personality," it has generally been understood to refer to a consistent, lifelong pattern of behavior conflicting with social norms without accompanying guilt. Cleckley, supra, at 29.[6] Nothing of that character was shown to exist at the time of entry. The fact that he presently has a problem, as one psychiatrist said, does not mean that he is or was necessarily "afflicted" with homosexuality. His conduct is, of course, evidence material to the issue. But the informed judgment of experts is needed to make the required finding. We cruelly mutilate the Act when we hold otherwise. For we make the word of the bureaucrat supreme, when it was the expertise of the doctors and psychiatrists on which Congress wanted the administrative action to be dependent.

NOTES

1. "Homosexual activity in the human male is much more frequent than is ordinarily realized. . . . In the youngest unmarried group, more than a quarter (27.3%) of the males have some homosexual activity to the point of orgasm. . . . The incidence among these single males rises in successive age groups until it reaches a maximum of 38.7 per cent between 36 and 40 years of age. "High frequencies do not occur as often in the homosexual as they do in some other kinds of sexual activity. . . . Populations are more homogeneous in regard to this outlet. This may reflect the difficulties involved in having frequent and regular relations in a socially taboo activity. Nevertheless, there are a few of the younger adolescent males who have homosexual frequencies of 7 or more per week, and between 26 and 30 the maximum frequencies run to 15 per week. By 50 years of age the most active individual is averaging only 5.0 per week. "For single, active populations, the mean frequencies of homosexual contacts . . . rise more or less steadily from near once per week . . . for the younger adolescent boys to nearly twice as often . . . for males between the ages of 31 and 35. They stand above once a week through age 50." Kinsey, Sexual Behavior in the Human Male 259–261 (1948).

2. Report, Committee on Homosexual Offenses and Prostitution (1957).

3. Sigmund Freud wrote in 1935: "Homosexuality is assuredly no advantage, but it is nothing to be ashamed of, no vice, no degradation, it cannot be classified as an illness; we consider it to be a variation of the sexual function produced by a certain arrest of sexual development. Many highly respectable individuals of ancient and modern times have been homosexuals, several of the greatest men among them (Plato, Michelangelo, Leonardo da Vinci, etc.). It is a great injustice to persecute homosexuality as a crime, and cruelty too. If you do not believe me, read the books of Havelock Ellis." Ruitenbeek, The Problem of Homosexuality in Modern Society 1 (1963).

4. Caldwell, Constitutional Psychopathic State (Psychopathic Personality) Studies of Soldiers in the U.S. Army, 3 J. Crim. Psychopathology 171–172 (1941).

5. See Lindman & McIntyre, The Mentally Disabled and the Law 299 (1961).

6. There is good indication that Congress intended the term "afflicted with psychopathic personality" to refer only to those individuals demonstrating "devel-

opmental defects or pathological trends in the personality structure manifest[ed] by lifelong patterns of action or behavior. . . ." U.S. Public Health Service, Report on Medical Aspects of H.R. 2379, U.S. Code Cong. & Admin. News 1700 (1952). The provision for exclusion of persons afflicted with psychopathic personality replaced the section of the 1917 Act, 39 Stat. 875, providing for the exclusion of "persons of constitutional psychopathic inferiority." The purpose of that clause was "to keep out 'tainted blood,' that is, 'persons who have medical traits which would harm the people of the United States if those traits were introduced in this country, or if those possessing those traits were added to those in this country who unfortunately are so afflicted.'" The Immigration and Naturalization System of the United States, S. Rep. No. 1515, 81st Cong., 2d Sess., 343 (1950). The Senate subcommittee which had been charged with making an investigation of the immigration laws concluded that "the exclusion of persons with 'constitutional psychopathic inferiority' was aimed at keeping out of the country aliens with a propensity to mental aberration, those with an inherent likelihood of becoming mental cases, as indicated by their case history." Ibid. It concluded that "the purpose of the provision against 'persons with constitutional psychopathic inferiority' will be more adequately served by changing that term to 'persons afflicted with psychopathic personality,' and that the classes of mentally defectives should be enlarged to include homosexuals and other sex perverts." Id., at 345. Senate Report 1515 accompanied Senate bill 3455, which included among excludable aliens "[a]liens afflicted with psychopathic personality," and "[a]liens who are homosexuals or sex perverts." The bill was redrafted and became S. 716, with its counterpart in the House being H.R. 2379; the material provisions remained the same as in S. 3455. In response to the House's request for its opinion on the new provisions, the Public Health Service noted that: "The conditions classified within the group of psychopathic personalities are, in effect, disorders of the personality. They are characterized by developmental defects or pathological trends in the personality structure manifest by lifelong patterns of action or behavior, rather than by mental or emotional symptoms. Individuals with such a disorder may manifest a disturbance of intrinsic personality patterns, exaggerated personality trends, or are persons ill primarily in terms of society and the prevailing culture. The latter or sociopathic reactions are frequently symptomatic of a severe underlying neurosis or psychosis and frequently include those groups of individuals suffering from addiction or sexual deviation." U.S. Code Cong. & Admin. News 1700 (1952). The letter setting forth the views of the Public Health Service went on to say, with respect to the exclusion of "homosexuals or sex perverts": "Ordinarily, persons suffering from disturbances in sexuality are included within the classification of 'psychopathic personality with pathologic sexuality.' This classification will specify such types of pathologic behavior as homosexuality or sexual perversion which includes sexual sadism, fetishism, transvestism, pedophilia, etc." Id., at 1701. The bill which was finally enacted, H.R. 5678, provided for exclusion of "[a]liens afflicted with psychopathic personality," but did not provide for exclusion of aliens who are homosexuals or sex perverts, as had its predecessors. The House Report, H.R. Rep. No. 1365, which accompanied the bill incorporated the full report of the Public Health Service (H.R. Rep. No. 1365, 82d Cong., 2d Sess., at 46–48) and indicated that the "recommendations contained in the . . . report have been followed." Id., at 48. This legislative history indicates that the term "afflicted with psychopathic personality" was used in a medical sense and was meant to refer to lifelong patterns of action that are pathologic and symptomatic of grave underlying neurosis or psychosis. Homosexuality and sex perversion, as a subclass, are limited to the same afflictions.

CHAPTER 4

Beyond the Day without an Immigrant

Immigrant Communities Building a Sustainable Movement

Eunice Hyunhye Cho

It is without question that the immigrant rights protests of 2006 marked a milestone in U.S. history. Within the space of only a few weeks, millions of immigrants and their supporters marched in over 100 cities in almost every state in the country. The sheer magnitude of these mobilizations against H.R. 4437, or the Border Protection, Antiterrorism, and Illegal Immigration Control Act of 2005, set records as the largest immigrant rights demonstrations in U.S. history. In spite of the historic protests, and perhaps as an ominous hint of things to come, Congress closed its session after approving a new 700-mile fence along the U.S.-Mexico border and provided funding for 1,500 new border patrol agents; new technology, such as portable imaging machines, cameras, sensors, and automated targeting systems along the border; a $626 million increase to support detention and removal efforts; and the addition of 6,000 new detention beds.[1]

Congress' ability to pass these anti-immigrant provisions into law only months after the massive demonstrations took place suggests the critical need to support a sustainable, popular movement with a long-term vision for immigrant rights. The 2006 mobilizations demonstrated the potential power of the immigrant rights movement, as well as the vital role played by immigrants in the United States. While immigrant communities have organized to protect their rights in the past, these mobilizations signalled a shift in popular perceptions of immigration as an issue. The unique factors that brought about the demonstrations in 2006 and the lessons learned by organizers and participants thus deserve attention. In this article I examine the political context for these protests, including anti-immigrant trends and policies in recent years. I also explore debates within the immigrant rights movement around attempts to achieve reform, including legalization of undocumented immigrants, and around divergent tactics and strategies during the 2006 mobilizations. I also trace Congress's failed attempts to pass immigration reform in 2007 and reflect on possibilities for the future. Finally, I report on the successes, challenges, and lessons on building principled, sustainable, and strategic alliances across lines of ethnicity, race, and sexual orientation and on the movement's growing recognition and strategic vision for global justice.

Immigrant Communities under Attack: The Context for Mobilization

Throughout its history, U.S. immigration policy has served as a way to regulate the "character of the nation," by limiting entry, citizenship, enfranchisement, and economic access. Immigration policy not only reflects whom the state views as a model subject or potential citizen but also serves as a vehicle to exclude those who do not fit into the ideal. In addition, immigration policies serve to control the flow of labor for the needs of capital.[2] As Isabel Garcia observes, "changing administrative strategies around immigration reflects the state's shifting interpretation of the particular role or political threat posed by immigrants."[3]

These themes continue to color public dialogue: immigrants have become the scapegoat for social ills such as unemployment, crime, environmental devastation, failure of public institutions and services, and, most recently, terrorism.[4]

Since the administrative creation of the "illegal alien" in 1921,[5] immigrants living in the United States, particularly those who are undocumented, have faced increasing peril. After the passage of the 1965 Immigration and Nationality Act, which eliminated the national origins quota system favoring European migration, Congress has passed measures to curtail immigration and target undocumented immigrant communities. Most notably, the 1986 Immigration Reform and Control Act (IRCA) established the regime of employer sanctions, the statutory cornerstone that continues to enable the sustained vulnerability of immigrant workers. While a compromise provision within IRCA allowed for a limited amnesty of undocumented immigrants present in the United States at the time, it also required employers to keep records of employees' immigration status, imposing fines on those who would hire undocumented workers. Employee sanctions provisions, however, are rarely enforced against employers; the real impact of the law continues to fall on undocumented workers, who face increasing vulnerability to exploitation, decreased wage levels, immigration raids, and deportation due to this law.[6]

During the 1990s, policymakers increasingly drew a distinction between the rights of documented and undocumented immigrants, a pattern that continues to persist today. While Republicans, particularly social conservatives opposed to racial equality, supported proposals that called for the reduction of immigration quotas and the elimination of benefits to all noncitizens, including legal permanent residents, Democrats objected, drawing on the rhetoric of "America as a nation of immigrants." However, the Democratic Party still supported reforms that targeted undocumented immigrant communities, supporting policies that strengthened law enforcement and heightened militarization of the U.S.-Mexico border. Immigration reforms passed in 1996, including the Illegal Immigration Reform and Immigrant Responsibility Act (IIRIRA), and the Anti-Terrorism and Effective Death Penalty Act increased the use of detention, incarceration, and deportation as an enforcement strategy against undocumented immigrants. In 1996, welfare reform provisions also eliminated many federal public benefits for immigrants, fueled largely by gendered stereotypes of immigrant women swarming over the border for welfare.[7]

This distinction between the rights of legal and undocumented migrants also divided the immigrant rights movement. Community groups, particularly those who provided services or organized directly with immigrants, opposed enforcement measures targeting the undocumented. However, other organizations working on behalf of immigrants chose to defend only legal immigrants, arguing that the strength of anti-immigrant force in congress necessitated some concessions in order to at least preserve the rights of a subset of immigrants living in the United States. The position taken by the National Immigration Forum, a Washington, D.C.–based lobbying organization, exemplifies this choice. In its lobbying guide around the 1996 immigration reforms, the forum instructed advocates that "legal immigration is not the same as illegal immigration" and that "the American people want the federal government to take decisive and effective action to control illegal immigration."[8]

Post-1996 legislation views immigration policy primarily as an enforcement regime. The Bureau of Immigration and Customs Enforcement is now the largest armed law enforcement agency in the United States, surpassing both the FBI and the U.S. Bureau of Prisons; immigrants and asylum seekers are now among the fastest-growing incarcerated population in the United States.[9] Border militarization strategies along the U.S.-Mexico border and strategies of containment have escalated human rights abuses against migrants and border communities and have lead to the death of over 4,000 people crossing the desert by 2006.[10] Since the passage of the 1996 legislation, the U.S. government has detained and deported over 1.6 million immigrants and forced over 12 million voluntary departures.[11]

In the aftermath of the 1996 reforms, a call for amnesty, or legalization of undocumented immigrants, emerged as a priority at the grassroots level. Legalization would allow undocumented immigrants to gain legal permanent resident status, obtain authorization to live and work in the United States, and travel more freely to and from their countries of origin. This demand gained added viability in 2000 as the executive council of the AFL-CIO issued an appeal for blanket amnesty to undocumented immigrants and for an end to employer sanctions.[12] This resolution marked a profound shift for the AFL-CIO. In 1986, the AFL-CIO originally supported the passage of employer sanctions, reflecting the federation's cold war policies. At the time, the AFL-CIO argued that employer sanctions would encourage immigrant workers to return to their native countries, thus strengthening rights for native workers. In its call for legalization, the federation recognized that employer sanctions had not stopped the flow of migrants to the United States but, rather, had became a tool for corporations to thwart labor organizing in industries dominated by immigrant workers—a growing sector of strength for the labor movement.[13] Hopes for the passage of a legalization proposal remained high: in preparation for talks with Mexican President Vincente Fox, President George W. Bush began to indicate support for a legalization plan for Mexican immigrants. On September 1, 2001, Bush announced that he would endorse a general set of principles and framework for regulating the flow of migrants.[14] Only ten days later, the events of September 11, 2001, dashed hopes for a new policy.

Almost immediately after planes crashed into New York City's World Trade Center, a wave of anti-immigrant fear swept the country. Taking advantage of this climate, restrictionist groups lost little time in recasting immigration as a national security issue. As a result, anti-immigrant policy initiatives passed through Congress with little controversy and with astonishing speed. In the weeks following September 11, the Department of Justice encouraged the public's vigilance in reporting "any suspicious activity" that could be associated with "acts of terror." The Immigration and Naturalization Service (INS) subsequently rounded up, secretly detained, and denied legal counsel to more than 1,200 South Asian, Arab, and Muslim men.[15] In November 2001, the Department of Justice announced its policy of voluntary interviews with a list of 5,000 additional South Asian, Arab, and Muslim men, requiring local police officers to interrogate local immigrants about their ties to terrorist organizations.[16]

The INS also conducted visible raids at high-profile public events such as the Super Bowl ("Operation Game Day") and the 2002 Salt Lake City Winter Olympics. In November 2002, the Aviation and Transportation Security Act mandated the replacement of over 28,000 immigrant airport screeners with U.S. citizens slated to earn much higher wages.[17] Critics within law enforcement agencies, however, noted the role of immigration enforcement as image control for the government's national security program and the extent to which racial profiling played a part in post-9/11 immigration practice. A memo leaked to the press revealed that the FBI leadership had issued explicit directives establishing numerical quotas for counterterrorism investigations and secret wiretaps in Arab and Muslim communities—based on geographic regions with a high concentration of mosques. In a public letter, veteran Coleen Rowley, who gained recognition when she testified to the agency's inaction on intelligence gathered prior to September 11, highlighted the use of immigration policy. "From what I have observed, particular vigilance may be required to head off undue pressure to detain or "round up" suspects—particularly those of Arabic origin," she stated; "after 9/11, Headquarters encouraged more and more detentions for what seemed to be essentially PR purposes."[18]

Post–September 11 immigration legislation such as the USA PATRIOT Act, the Enhanced Border Security and Visa Reform Act, and the REAL ID Act also reflected the long-held policy agenda of the anti-immigrant right. These policies, passed since September 11, heightened border militarization and enhanced interior enforcement personnel, increased the capacity of immigrant detention centers, denied drivers' licenses to undocumented immigrants, and increased funding for worksite law enforcement.[19] The Immigration and Naturalization Service also moved under the auspices of the newly formed Department of Homeland Security, consonant with the logic of immigrants as "national security threat."[20]

Immigrant communities also faced heightened xenophobia at the local and state levels. In November 2004, Arizona voters passed Proposition 200, which criminalized state employees who provided services to undocumented immigrants and increased discrimination against voters of color. Its success sparked a wave of copycat bills around the country, where local cities and states began to pass xenophobic resolutions and policies.[21] The Minutemen, an anti-immigrant vigilante group promoted by white supremacist organizations, garnered considerable coverage in the popular news media for its harassment of local immigrant communities and patrols along the U.S.-Mexico border.[22] Organizers in immigrant rights movement settings reported an increasing number of anecdotes of harassment and death threats to local immigrant community leaders.[23]

Given the rise of anti-immigrant sentiment, and faced with flagging public support due to domestic policy failure around Hurricane Katrina, administrative scandal, and growing dissatisfaction with the war in Iraq, Republican leadership began to view immigration reform as an area of viable success. Assuming that immigration had become sufficiently synonymous with national security, Republicans calculated that appearing tough on immigration would buoy their chances in midterm elections. Despite party divisions between corporate interests (who argued for a guest-worker policy to enable the importation of cheap labor) and ideologues (who supported full-scale restrictions on immigration), Republicans believed that strengthened anti-immigrant enforcement measures would resonate with voters. "Democrats will find it hard to get traction on this issue because it goes to law enforcement and security, and that is not traditionally a level playing field for them," stated one Republican consultant.[24] On December 6, 2006, Representative Sensenbrenner (R-WI) introduced H.R. 4437; the Republican-controlled House of Representatives passed the bill only ten days later. While many parts of H.R. 4437 continued a long-term policy strategy of controlling immigrant labor through heightened militarization of the U.S.-Mexico border, stringent detention and deportation policies, and increased authority of local police departments to enforce federal immigration statues, this bill went even further. H.R. 4437 also classified the estimated 12 million undocumented immigrants living in the United States as felons and made it a felony for anyone to provide services—even medical, legal, or pastoral aid—to undocumented immigrants.[25]

While a majority of Democrats voted against the bill, the party ultimately supported increased enforcement against immigrant communities. Even after massive rallies had begun across the country against H.R. 4437, Democratic National Committee Chairman Howard Dean announced that his party would consider border security the top priority in immigration reform. "The first thing we want is tough border control . . . we have to do a much better job on our borders than George Bush has done," he said.[26] Two months later, however, while courting Latino voters, Dean shifted his rhetoric. "Immigrant bashing and scapegoating of any American is wrong, and we won't do it. . . . We will do better than Republicans will if you will give us the chance," he said.[27] Although they offered a friendlier face to immigrant communities, the Democratic Party still supported measures that maintained the vulnerability of immigrant communities, violated civil and human rights, and strengthened militarization of the border.

"Enforcement Only" and "Enforcement Plus": Trading Off Immigrant Rights

In the months before the passage of H.R. 4437, Congress considered several legislative proposals addressing immigration. Congressional debate and negotiations centered on a few key issues, most notably guest-worker programs, legalization of undocumented immigrants, and anti-immigrant law enforcement. These issues became a site of contention and divided both the right and left. Divergent outlooks, strategies, and political visions within various sectors of the immigrant rights movement influenced the planning and course of the 2006 mobilizations themselves, as well as the political aftermath of the marches. These tensions and debates continue to shape discourse within the immigrant rights movement and have led to central questions over strategy and vision as the movement grows with increased support and interest from private foundations, along with greater participation and engagement of grassroots immigrant community members.

These tensions are perhaps best reflected in debates around the Safe, Orderly, Legal Visas and Enforcement (SOLVE) Act (S. 1033/H.R. 2330), or the Secure American and Orderly Immigration Act of 2005, introduced by Senator John McCain (R-AZ) and Senator Edward Kennedy (D-MA). Supporters of the bill hailed it as an influential bipartisan effort for immigration reform with the strongest chance of gaining congressional consensus. The SOLVE Act provided a limited opportunity for undocumented immigrants to gain legal status after six years, as well as a guest-worker policy that would allow employers to hire 400,000 immigrant workers under temporary worker visas, where immigrants' legal status would be linked to their employer. Anti-immigrant forces objected to the legalization and guest-worker programs, and they raised objections to any increase in the authorized flow of migrants to the United States. Various industries, including the National Chamber of Commerce, however, supported the opportunity for a pool of expanded labor who would depend on their employers for legal status, with limited wage and worker protections.[28]

The guest-worker issue similarly divided the immigrant rights movement. Some sectors of the movement, including Washington, D.C.–based immigration advocacy groups and select labor unions within the newly formed Coalition for Comprehensive Immigration Reform alliance pursued a "left-right" coalition strategy and offered their support for the SOLVE Act.[29] These groups argued that, given a congressional climate hostile to immigrants, any chance for positive reforms, such as legalization, depended on the inclusion of guest-worker provisions and heightened enforcement. The inclusion of administrative protections in the bill, they claimed, would include provisions for workers' rights. Aligning themselves with organizations such as the Manhattan Institute, a right-wing think tank, these groups engaged in a strategy dependent on focus groups, lobbying, and media messaging to hone their political platform. At the same time, philanthropic organizations infused unparalleled amounts of funding into the immigrant rights movement, influencing organizational decisions to support the legislative strategy.[30]

The resulting strategy portrayed the issue of immigration as a contest between two competing doctrines: "enforcement-only" and "enforcement plus." Enforcement-only, the alliance argued, represented a hard-line stance that ignored the practical impossibility of deporting 12 million undocumented immigrants from the United States. In contrast, they contended that an enforcement-plus strategy, or a combination of increased enforcement in exchange for earned legalization, resonated with focus groups such as Republican voters. "New public opinion data indicates that Republican voters do not think it is possible to deport the illegal immigrants already in the country and do not favor an enforcement-only approach often preached by hard-line conservatives. On the contrary, the [Republican] rank and file want realistic solutions to deal with future immigrants and the millions of undocumented workers already here," proclaimed a Manhattan Institute press release, reporting on the results of their commissioned poll.[31]

Washington, D.C.–based immigration advocacy groups echoed this message in the halls of Congress. During Senate hearings on immigration reform, the National Immigration Forum, for example, underscored its willingness to trade off future enforcement policies for the possibility of attaining even a limited legalization for undocumented workers: "We are fully prepared to support and fight for a combination of tough and smart enforcement measures if combined with simultaneous reforms to our admissions policies that bring undocumented immigrants out of the shadows and provide a sufficient number of worker and family reunification visas for the future flow."[32] In short, these groups sought to frame congressional and national media dialogue about immigration around these options, with the assumption that any viable legalization provisions for undocumented immigrants would require some compromise on enforcement and guest-worker provisions.

Many local and grassroots immigrant community groups, as well as the AFL-CIO, rejected this position, contending that a guest-worker program would degrade the labor rights and wages of both immigrant and non-immigrant workers and would unfairly bind immigrant workers to potentially abusive employers due to their conditional status. Pointing to past examples such as the Bracero Program of the 1940s, these groups maintained that guest-worker programs would enable widespread exploitation and human rights abuses of temporary migrant workers. In addition, community groups with fewer resources and access to Congress worried that giving any support for a guest-worker policy would suggest wholesale endorsement of guest-worker programs and increased enforcement. Worker protections and legalization for the undocumented, they feared, could be later eliminated in congressional negotiations.[33] Arab, Muslim, and South Asian groups argued that these proposals also further eroded civil rights in a post–September 11 period. Enforcement measures in SOLVE allowed the government to expand its use of secret evidence to deny citizenship based on a vague definition of "terrorist activity and security related grounds," a practice long opposed by Arab and Muslim American groups.[34]

These fears became reality after the passage of H.R. 4437: as the Senate struggled to pass a bill compatible with that of the House, Republicans and Democrats reached a compromise by integrating parts of the SOLVE Act with more regressive legislation, resulting in the Martinez-Hagel bill, or S. 2611. The Senate's final version strengthened anti-immigrant law enforcement, limited labor protections for specific classes of workers, and established a multitiered system of legalization for undocumented immigrants. As the AFL-CIO concluded in a press release:

> Instead of raising working standards for all workers by providing a fair path to citizenship to the 12 million undocumented workers currently living in our communities, the Senate adopted the framework of the fatally flawed Martinez-Hagel compromise, which creates an undemocratic, unjust and unworkable three-tiered society that denigrates and marginalize millions of immigrant families. That three-tiered approach creates a caste society in which millions of hard-working immigrants are driven further into the shadows of American society, leaving them vulnerable to exploitation. We are also disappointed that the Senate

> adopted the greedy corporate model of addressing our nations' future needs for workers—guestworker programs—instead of crafting a mechanism to ensure that future foreign workers come into the U.S. with full rights and as full social partners.[35]

The House and Senate ended the 109th congressional session without reaching a compromise on the two bills, thus stalling immigration reform. The immigrant rights movement, emboldened by the success of the 2006 massive mobilizations, reflected on strategies, tactics, and vision for the future.

"The Day without an Immigrant!" The Mass Mobilizations of 2006

On March 10, 2006, over 100,000 people filled the streets of Chicago in protest against H.R. 4437. The biggest march ever seen in the city's history, this massive turnout surpassed expectations of most participants and organizers. This first demonstration set the stage for a national surge of mass protests, rallies, and marches for the next three months: in the coming weeks, organizers in cities across the United States created ad hoc coalitions to plan marches and rallies that would result in the largest immigrant rights mobilizations in the history of the country. A first wave of protests took place in the latter weeks of March, including an estimated 5,000 in Charlotte, North Carolina; 10,000 people in Milwaukee, Wisconsin; 20,000 in Phoenix, Arizona; 50,000 in Denver, Colorado; and over 500,000 people in Los Angeles, California.[36] On April 10, 2006, over 100 cities held record-breaking rallies in a national day of action, ranging from small towns such as Hyde Park, New York, and Garden City, Kansas, to larger cities such as Dallas, San Diego, Miami, Boise, and Atlanta.[37] Mobilizations peaked on May 1, 2006, when over 1.1 million people marched in cities across the United States, causing temporary shutdowns in multiple industries.[38] A "perfect storm" of factors—including a sense of urgency created by the passage of H.R. 4437 in the House, unilateral opposition to the bill by virtually all sectors of the immigrant rights movement, and enhanced institutional support from actors such as the Catholic Church and ethnic media—enabled the mobilization of millions of people into the streets.[39]

"We had never seen anything go that far," recalled Lisa Duran, director of Rights for All People, an immigrant-based organizing project in Denver. "We had never seen any legislation so dangerous, that would criminalize all undocumented immigrants in our midst."[40] While her organization had closely followed legislative debate around H.R. 4437, the bill's passage by the House of Representatives shocked the group's membership. Local advocacy and service groups across the country also grew alarmed. "It hit home for a lot of groups when they found out that any assistance to any undocumented person could be considered a felony," remembered Rashida Tlaib of the Arab Community Center for Economic and Social Services (ACCESS) in Dearborn, Michigan; "they realized that that they would have to police who came in for services, and that it would jeopardize their organizations."[41] Yet fear seemed to be the most powerful motivator for many immigrants at the grassroots level. "People had licenses that were about to expire, and more raids were taking place," noted Pancho Argüelles of Colectivo Flatlander, in Houston, Texas. "People are used to the fear of being deported every day. When we asked people what the main challenges facing immigrants was—they always said 'overcoming fear.'"[42]

Tensions in the movement, however, emerged as a number of Washington, D.C.–based organizations and well-resourced regional advocacy groups announced the formation of the We Are America Alliance on April 10, 2006. Many of these organizations had supported earlier compromises on guest-worker programs and enforcement in the SOLVE Act, and this announcement further exacerbated mistrust.[43] When differing sectors of the immigrant rights movement began to call for an economic boycott and work stoppage on May 1, 2006, members of the We Are America Alliance publicly opposed this tactic. Alliance members such as the Catholic Church, select labor unions, and radio DJs who had mobilized immigrants for massive protests only weeks earlier argued that a boycott would create a mainstream backlash against immigrants, and they encouraged workers and students to protest only after work or school.[44]

These divisions played out differently in local organizing efforts around the country. In many towns, organizers compromised by holding separate activities in different locations or by avoiding the language of "boycotts." "We weren't impacted by national divisions around the boycott," remembered Maria Jimenez, a special projects coordinator at the Center for Central American Resources in Houston, describing planning around May 1st protests; "we decided to promote the event by saying that if you leave your job without permission, that you might be fired because Texas is an at-will state. So we never said boycott, but it was understood." Jimenez further noted the impossibility for any single community institution to claim credit for the political capital developed by the protests: "There was no way that we as organizers had the capacity to tell people whether or not to boycott; people were doing it on their own. Even though the leadership was split on the issue, ultimately, it was the sentiment of people in the community not to work. That is why we can't take credit for it."[45]

Compounding this tension was a fear that the massive mobilizations and boycotts would enable mainstream immigration advocacy groups to more strongly present their trade-off agenda rather than represent opposition to repression against immigrants. Alexis Mazon, with the Coalicion de Derechos Humanos, recalled that "there was a disagreement in Tucson around the boycott, and some of the groups that participated in the April 10 mobilizations decided they would not participate on May 1." While the participation of local Spanish-language radio stations also waned in the days preceding the boycott, protesters still turned out in record numbers. "A lot of the D.C. groups told us not to march, not to make a fuss or use aggressive tactics; they said that marches that would anger people in the center," Mazon noted. "But now they are trying to take credit for turning out millions of people."[46] Organizers in other cities echoed this sentiment. Monami Maulik, director of DRUM: Desis Rising Up and Moving in New York City, recalled messages sent by regional advocacy groups. "They didn't want us to use the word amnesty, call for a boycott, and they didn't endorse or come to the marches," she said: "The strategy the policy groups took was effective at undermining the grassroots' message. While there was a massive turnout for our march on May 1, policy and advocacy groups held a smaller event, but got the bulk of messaging opportunities. The mainstream press didn't see the difference between the two events."[47]

While the May 1 mobilizations unquestionably demonstrated the growing power and influence of immigrant communities in the United States, they also served to activate anti-immigrant sentiment. Sandra Sanchez, director of the American Friends Service Committee's Project Voice chapter in Des Moines, Iowa, reflected on changes after the May 1 activities. "At first, many people in Des Moines didn't understand that we were protesting—they thought it was a Mexican holiday! Even though we were doing a lot of education, there were many misconceptions," she recalled. Local politicians, including both Republicans and Democrats, however, began to present anti-immigrant platforms in preparation for the November 2006 mid-term elections, and "after May 1, we felt a backlash. In some cases, co-workers refused to work with immigrants or called them names; some were fired the next day. Lots of immigrants reported a changed environment everywhere—in schools, workplaces, and stores." In addition, by the end of the year, immigration enforcement officials conducted raids on local meatpacking plants, which had shut down in support of immigrant workers during the May 1 mobilizations. "The raids were seen as a retaliation by the government," Sanchez noted; "but the sad reality is that we don't even have enough immigration lawyers in town to represent the cases here." Sanchez's group, however, has decided that it must build alliances with local citizens in order to advance its goals: "We came to the conclusion that whatever work we do with immigrants is meaningless without the support of non-immigrant voters. We have to continue doing education work with citizens."[48]

After the events of May 1, 2006, the rhythm of mass mobilizations began to wane. During this time, multiple proposals for future action emerged. In July 2006, the We Are America Alliance announced the launch of "Democracy Summer," a coordinated effort to naturalize immigrants and register voters in time for the 2006 midterm elections. By September, the alliance scheduled a series of protests around the country in time for Labor Day weekend. While the campaign successfully registered thousands of voters, participation in its rallies fell well below predictions. "After May 1, national leadership wasn't united, and it played a role in demobilizing the community," reflected Jimenez: "Most of the base that turned out for the mobilizations were youth, undocumented or had TPS [Temporary Protected Status], so voting and citizenship drives excluded them. We participated in these events, but we always felt that this strategy eliminated the base that gave the body of mobilization."[49]

Instead of relying exclusively on a short-term voter registration campaign, some organizers argued that long-term strategies for leadership development and capacity building were also necessary. "Voter registration and mobilization have been important, but it is a singular strategy," noted

Maricela Garcia, a founding member of the National Alliance of Latin American and Caribbean Communities (NALACC): "We need multiple approaches. There was a lot of money for voter registration offered by foundations, but not a lot of funding to help build the leadership capacity of people who were organizing the marches."[50] Mazon also echoed the need for deeper political education and empowerment. "We need leadership development, but not in the way that is often done by non-profits, where only staff members of organizations are trained. We need thousands of spokespeople," she said.[51]

Other organizers viewed the 2006 mobilizations as a new opportunity for the immigrant rights movement. "There was a break between groups in the movement. Those who work more directly with immigrant communities broke from the strategies of traditional advocacy groups and decided to form their own coalitions," noted Argüelles. "I don't think we are a consolidated movement," said Elizabeth Sunwoo, coordinator of the Multi-Ethnic Immigrant Organizing Network (MIWON) in Los Angeles:

> There is a difference of strategy and tactics. Across the movement, there isn't a lot of trust, so there are a lot of assumptions being made. But I think there is more willingness from folks in the D.C.-based groups to reach out more to grassroots organizations. It doesn't mean we don't have disagreement, but it doesn't mean we have to stop the dialogue. It would hurt the movement otherwise.[52]

Argüelles agreed, but noted the need for a clear process to base decision-making in the hands of the most vulnerable: "We have to build a movement from bottom to top; the strategic decision making has to be guided by those directly affected. We need intermediary groups to work with decision-makers, but we cannot confuse them as the real leadership of the movement."[53]

Building Alliances for a Sustainable Movement

Even before the 2006 mobilizations, immigrant community organizers realized the strategic need to build alliances. While the participation of

Latinos far outnumbered other groups in the 2006 national mobilizations, most rallies, protests, and media events to some extent reflected the diversity of immigrant communities in the United States. Many organizations, recognizing the potential for historic divisions to weaken their work, have taken conscious steps toward building meaningful solidarity. Developing solidarity and a sense that no one's interests will be sold off, activists argue, is key to building a sustainable movement. As Rashida Tlaib of ACCESS noted: "Not one issue is owned by a particular group; all of these issues affect us in some way. When Michigan passed a ban on affirmative action, it was seen as an African American issue. National security is seen as an Arab issue and immigration is viewed as a Latino issue. But people need to realize that it will touch us all in some way."[54]

In a time where immigration proposals encourage the exchange of benefits such as legalization for the elimination of other civil and human rights, organizers recognize the critical importance of building alliances across lines of difference. They have also emphasized the need for grassroots immigrant community members to develop processes to analyze and strategize around legislative policy, instead of depending on advocacy organizations for instruction and analysis. In New York, a grassroots coalition of immigrant community membership-based groups has begun such a process. Immigrant Communities in Action, originally comprised of four membership organizations, first came together to create a campaign to protect drivers' licenses for undocumented immigrants in Queens, New York. As the New York Civic Participation Project, DRUM: Desis Rising Up and Moving, Centro Hispano, and New Immigrant Community Empowerment (NICE) realized the centrality of comprehensive immigration reform in their community organizing work, the coalition began to organize community consultations, or *consultas,* in order to define its political platform.

"A lot of membership participated in the *consulta* process because they felt for the first time that they had an opportunity to shape the platform from the beginning, instead of being told what to support in terms of policy," observes Monami Maulik, director of DRUM. Organizers began to realize the deep organizational investment of its membership in the process, along with the unique space created by the consultations. While many groups in New York worked under the rubric of immigrant rights, the specific issue areas covered by individual organizations resulted in artificial divisions and segregated different immigrant ethnic groups from one another. South Asian, Arab, and Muslim groups, for example, often focused on the impact of post–September 11 policies, while Latino organizations often worked around worker rights and enforcement issues. "A lot of the Latinos in the group started out using slogans such as 'We aren't terrorists.' After talking to South Asian immigrants about the effects of September 11, this began to change," notes Maulik; "South Asians in the group also had ideas about undocumented immigrants, especially Mexicans. They would say that they deserved citizenship because they had come to the U.S. legally on a plane, instead of crossing the border." These *consultas* enabled members of the coalition to develop a vision of comprehensive immigration reform that responded to the particular needs and vulnerabilities of different communities.[55]

"Most people have a general wish to work with other communities," notes Liz Sunwoo, who coordinates the Multi-Ethnic Immigrant Organizing Network (MIWON) in Los Angeles. The network, comprised of five immigrant rights organizations—the Korean Immigrant Workers Advocates (KIWA), the Coalition for Humane Immigrant Rights of Los Angeles (CHIRLA), the Pilipino Workers' Center (PWC), the Garment Workers' Center (GWC), and the Institute of Popular Education of Southern California (IDEPSCA)—works to build the power of immigrant workers for better living and working conditions. Misconceptions of the economic condition of other ethnic groups, however, remain one of the basic challenges to building effective solidarity between workers of different ethnicities. "It's the whole discussion of who is more oppressed, and who takes the worst jobs," Sunwoo observes: "We try to take the focus away from that. For example, Latino workers will be surprised to see a Korean worker who makes less than they do, especially if they both work for Koreans. We try to build alliances across our city on the basis of class, rather than simply ethnic lines."

Focusing on shared working conditions, however, is only the beginning of the work to build effective multiethnic alliances. Sunwoo notes that "there are complexities to all of our communities, and most other communities don't understand the immigration experience or political situations of home countries of groups other than themselves." Introducing an analysis of globalization and its influence on workers has proved an effective tool in deepening a common vision among groups. Over the past few years, immigrant community organizations have increasingly identified global justice issues as a key component of their struggle. Recent discussions at training sessions held with grassroots organizations by the National Network for Immigrant and Refugee Rights also suggest a growing awareness of globalization and structural adjustment policies as part of a migrant rights agenda. In an activity asking participants to identify their priorities for the immigrant rights movement, several participants listed a change in U.S. economic policy with countries in the Global South as a long-term priority for the immigrant rights movement.[56] International policies dealing with the roots of migration also form a key part of the National Alliance of Latin American and Caribbean Communities' agenda. As Maricela Garcia says, "Part of our mission is to look at policies that deal with the roots of migration, because we don't want migration to be the only way for our communities to survive. We have to look at what international policies need to be in place so people have a future."[57]

Immigrant rights organizers have also found discussions of the global economy as a useful starting point to open discussions, particularly when attempting to build connections across movements. Trishala Deb, a staff member at the Audre Lorde Project (a community-organizing center for lesbian, gay, bisexual, two spirit, transgender and gender-nonconforming people of color in New York City), recalls the value of discussing global justice in discussions around immigration reform within the LGBT movement. As immigrant rights protests began to gain attention in early spring 2006, Jasmyne Cannick, a respected black lesbian journalist, provoked alarm when she published an article titled "Gays First, Then Illegals," on *Advocate.com,* a popular LGBT news site. She wrote:

> It's a slap in the face to lesbian, gay, bisexual, and transgender people to take up the debate on whether to give people who are in this country illegally additional rights when we haven't given the people who are here legally all of their rights. Immigration reform needs to get in line behind the LGBT civil rights movement, which has not yet realized all of its goals. . . . As a black lesbian, I find it hard to jump on the immigration reform bandwagon when my own bandwagon hasn't even left the barn.[58]

In response, several dozen LGBT activists of color posted an open letter to Cannick on the website to express their disagreement: "We are painfully aware that lesbian, gay, bisexual, and transgender communities still lack many basic protections under law in this country . . . nevertheless, supporting immigrant rights, while we continue to work for LGBT liberation, does nothing to hurt our cause."[59]

Instead of signing the letter, Deb contacted Cannick directly. "One of the best lessons I learned is that the worst way to begin the conversation is to dismiss the argument that black folks lose jobs to immigrants," she recalls: "We need to talk about globalization and the fact that people coming here will work for low wages due to the global economy, not to undermine people's wages. We have to point out that this problem is due to the policies of the U.S., and reframe the conversation about U.S. global complicity to poverty."[60]

Deb, however, notes how what had begun as part of a healthy debate in the LGBT community over the movement's support of immigrant rights quickly became framed as a conflict between African Americans and immigrants.[61] Before H.R. 4437, the mainstream LGBT movement largely assumed that "if marriage is passed for LGBT folks, then LGBT immigrants could become legalized through marriage," she observes. Immigrant rights mobilizations "helped to shift consciousness that a focus on marriage wouldn't necessarily deal with the core issues of what is a crisis around immigration in the country."[62]

The New Civil Rights Movement?

The recent mobilizations for immigrant and refugee rights have been hailed as a resurgence of the "civil rights movement" of the twentieth century; in many instances, immigrants have joyfully celebrated by comparing successful mobilizations to the African American struggle.[63] The immigrant rights movement has self-consciously borrowed iconography from the African American civil rights movement. Examples include the 2003 Immigrant Worker Freedom Rides, a national campaign largely underwritten by the Hotel Employees and Restaurant Employees International Union in reference to the voting rights and desegregation crusades of the

1960s. Immigrant community organizers also study and draw comparisons between organizing tactics and movement dynamics between the African American civil rights movement and the current immigrant rights movement as an interpretive tool. Limited dialogues between immigrant community organizers and African American groups have highlighted the need to build stronger alliances with one another, and for immigrant communities to recognize the ongoing struggle of African Americans for full enfranchisement and equality.[64]

More immigrant community organizers also acknowledge the critical role taken by African Americans in any debate over citizenship, national inclusion, and civil rights. "There has to be an immigrant rights movement that incorporates and addresses the issues of racial justice in a new way, and that advocates for something beyond immigration," notes Arnoldo Garcia of the National Network for Immigrant and Refugee Rights: "African American communities are strategic . . . around the debate around immigration. We also have to recognize that the African American community is not homogeneous: it contains immigrants and non-immigrants."[65] Since the 2006 mobilizations, many immigrant rights organizers have reflected on the negative stereotypes of African Americans perpetuated by messages popularly used by in the protests. "As we move forward, we need to have a better understanding of positions we won't stand for, and this applies to messaging, such as 'we aren't criminals or terrorists'; 'we take jobs that no Americans will take'; or 'we worked hard, so we deserve legalization,'" reflects Sunwoo.[66]

Congressional bills such as the Save America Comprehensive Immigration Act of 2005 introduced by Rep. Sheila Jackson-Lee (D-TX) serves as a model for potential legislation that addresses the needs of both immigrant and African American communities. This bill, developed in consultation with both immigrant and African American community groups, includes provisions for immigrants to legalize their status and restores many civil and due process rights stripped away by the 1996 immigration reforms. Without establishing a guest-worker policy, the bill also provides funds for job creation and training to communities with a historically high percentage of unemployment and discrimination.[67]

A New Chapter for the Immigrant Rights Movement

In 2007, the 110th Session of Congress again attempted to address the issue of immigration reform. The 2006 mobilizations, as well as growing pressure from anti-immigrant restrictionist groups, lent new urgency to the issue as a legislative priority. This heightened intrest in passing an immigration bill ultimately resulted in what became the main vehicle for immigration reform in the Senate, the Secure Borders, Economic Opportunity and Immigration Reform Act of 2007 (SBEOIR).[68] The result of a fragile compromise negotiated by Senators Kennedy (D-MA) and Kyl (R-AZ), the bill attempted to satisfy both immigrant communities and anti-immigrant activists.

The initial bill contained provisions that would have fundamentally restructured U.S immigration policy. These provisions attempted to satisfy a broad range of interests in the immigrant rights debate. To address the anti-immigrant lobby, and senators wanting to appear tough on national security, the bill included provisions to heighten enforcement at the U.S.-Mexico border, by adding 370 miles of fencing and increasing the number of border patrol agents to 20,000. In addition, the bill proposed an "Employment Eligibility Verification System," a central database to track the immigration eligibility of all workers in the United States. The bill also addressed the interests of industry, by including a guestworker program and, with mixed reception, the replacement of the family reunification basis for immigration with a merit-based point system weighted toward high-skilled imigrants.

Senator Kennedy, who had been championed as a supporter of immigrant rights, defended the compromise as a political calculation: concessions on enforcement and employment issues would allow for greater support of legalization provisions.[69] As the legislative session continued, debates over amendments to the bill indicated that the bill would only continue to worsen for immigrant rights. Yet the compromise bill was ultimately doomed to failure. While the Senate gained consensus on heightening immigration enforcement, the bill's passage halted around the issues of legalization and, to a lesser extent, on passing a guestworker program.[70]

These negative provisions of SBEOIR—such as the replacement of employer-based visas with a merit-based point system weighted toward high-skilled immigrants, a radical restructuring of family reunification policies, the inclusion of a guestworker program, and a legalization scheme that erected prohibitively high barriers to citizenship—left the boarder movement disillusioned.[71] Even groups who had labored for the inclusion of progressive provisions that would allow undocumented youth to gain legal status through higher education and protection of agricultural workers decried the bill.[72] The immigrant rights movement unified in its opposition to the bill, and groups across the spectrum breathed a collective sigh of relief when the compromise broke, dooming the bill's negative provisions to failure.[73]

In the wake of Congress's failure to pass an immigration reform bill that protects the rights of immigrants, communities continue to organize in self-defense against raids, enforcement, and anti-immigrant sentiment. Immigrant rights groups across the political spectrum view this time as a chance to mend fences and build further unity and strength. Many organizers view the failure of the 2007 reform as a chance to reevaluate strategies and to strengthen the capacity of the immigrant rights movement for the long haul. "We have an opportunity to write a new chapter on immigration reform," concludes Catherine Tactaquin, executive director of the National Network for Immigrant and Refugee Rights:

> We have even more challenges to protect the rights of immigrants against a backlash. If we move toward another period of immigration reform, which may not significantly emerge for another five years or so, we may have a movement of communities and groups "in the field" that will have greater capacity to promote fair and just immigration reforms, rather than to allow power brokers to negotiate away key principles and values.[74]

Ultimately, organizers recognize that even the passage of a legalization bill will not end the work of the movement. "At the end of the day, we are working for a social justice agenda," notes Maricela Garcia.[75] "Even if everyone gets a green card, we still have a community that has bad housing, schools, and is in poverty. We have a social justice agenda that must be broader than just immigration reform." The work of building a sustainable, long-term movement is careful and transformative work. As Pancho

Argüelles puts it, "We need to engage in strategic work with those who share our values on what we want to build, based on our own histories and values. We have to build our own kind of strength, not based on the oppression of others but based on our humanity."[76]

NOTES

Social movements produce collective knowledge and analysis that cannot be claimed by any individual. Any insight or analysis should be credited to the interviewed organizers and immigrant communities with whom they work, while any errors, inaccuracies, or biases should be attributed to the author. Thanks to Tomas Aguilar, Pancho Argüelles Paz y Puente, Mariana Bustamente, Trishala Deb, Lisa Duran, Arnoldo Garcia, Maricela Garcia, Lucas Guttentag, Maria Jimenez, Dan Kesselbrenner, Monami Maulik, Alexis Mazon, Sandra Sanchez, Elizabeth Sunwoo, Catherine Tactaquin, and Rashida Tlaib for their assistance with this article.

Research for this article was supported in part by a grant from the Paul and Daisy Soros Fellowships for New Americans. The program is not responsible for the view expressed.

1. Executive Office of the President, Office of Management and Budget, *Analytical Perspectives: Budget of the United States Government, Fiscal Year 2007* (Washington, D.C.: U.S. Government Printing Office, 2006), 23, at http://www.whitehouse.gov/omb/budget/fy2007/pdf/spec.pdf (accessed January 14, 2007).

2. Bill Ong Hing, *Defining America through Immigration Policy* (Philadelphia: Temple University Press, 2004), 2.

3. Isabel Garcia, Coalición de Derechos Humanos, Tucson, Arizona; interview August 5, 2006.

4. The portrayal of immigrants as threats to national security is hardly new to U.S. history. Examples of past immigration legislation include the Immigration Act of 1903, which permitted exclusion or deportation of aliens who believed in or advocated the overthrow of the U.S. government by force; the Anarchist Act of 1918; and the Palmer Raids of the 1920s. See Kevin Johnson, *The "Huddled Masses" Myth: Immigration and Civil Rights* (Philadelphia: Temple University Press, 2004), 62–63.

5. Mae M. Ngai, *Impossible Subjects: Illegal Aliens and the Making of Modern America* (Princeton: Princeton University Press, 2004).

6. David Bacon, "Employer Sanctions: Making It a Crime to Work without Documents in the U.S.," in *From the Borderline to the Colorline: A Report on Anti-*

immigrant Racism in the U.S., ed. Eunice Cho (Oakland, Calif.: National Network for Immigrant and Refugee Rights, 2001), 44.

7. Grace Chang, Disposable Domestics: Immigrant Women Workers in the Global Economy (Boston: South End Press, 2000), 36.

8. National Immigration Forum, *Local Lobby Days to Defend Immigration* and *What's Wrong with the House Immigration Bill (HR 2202)* (Washington, D.C.: National Immigration Forum, 1995), as cited in David Bacon, "For an Immigration Policy Based on Human Rights," in *Immigration: A Civil Rights Issue for the Americas*, ed. Suzanne Jonas and Suzie Dod Thomas (Wilmington, Del.: Social Justice, 1999), 158.

9. Roberto Lovato, "Immigrants Regroup," *Nation*, November 13, 2006, at www.thenation.com (accessed January 17, 2008), and Barbara Rider, "Letter from America, Still the Land of the Free?" *Borderlands Journal* 4/1 (2005), at http://www.borderlandsejournal.adelaide.edu.au/vo14no1_2005/franz_letter.htm (accessed June 13, 2006).

10. Karl Eschbach, Jacqueline Hagan, and Nestor Rodriguez, *Deaths during Undocumented Migration: Trends and Policy Implications in the New Era of Homeland Security*, 2003, at http://www.uh.edu/cir/death.htm (accessed January 11, 2007); and Migration Information Source, "The US-Mexico Border," June 1, 2006, at www.migrationinformation.org/USFocus/display.cfm?ID=407 (accessed January 9, 2007).

11. U.S. Department of Homeland Security, *2005 Yearbook of Immigration Statistics* (Washington, D.C.: U.S. Department of Homeland Security, Office of Immigration Statistics, 2006), 95.

12. Steven Greenhouse, "Labor Urges Amnesty for Illegal Immigrants," *New York Times*, February 17, 2000, A26.

13. Bacon, "Employer Sanctions," 46.

14. Eric Schmitt, "No Agreement Yet with Mexico on Immigration Plan, U.S. Says," *New York Times*, September 1, 2001, A1.

15. Somini Sengupta and Christopher Drew, "A Nation Challenged: The Immigration Agency," *New York Times*, November 12, 2001, A8; Human Rights Watch, *Presumption of Guilt: Human Rights Abuses of Post-September 11 Detainees* (New York: Human Rights Watch, 2002).

16. Thomas Farragher and Kevin Cullen, "Plan to Question 5,000 Raise Issue of Racial Profiling," *Boston Globe*, November 15, 2001, A1.

17. Michael Tackett, "Airport Net Caught Small Fry: Washington-Area Sweep Yielded No Terror-Related Charges," *Chicago Tribune*, October 6, 2002, A1; "Pro Football—Cab Drivers and Guards Detained in Three Month Immigration Swap," *New York Times*, January 25, 2003, sports, 4; Fred Tsao, *Losing Ground: The Loss*

of Freedom, Equality, and Opportunity for America's Immigrants since September 11 (Chicago: Illinois Coalition for Immigrant and Refugee Rights, 2002).

18. Colleen Rowley, "Rowley Letter to FBI Director, February 26, 2003," *Minneapolis Star Tribune,* March 6, 2003, 1A.

19. Stephen Camorata, The Open Door: How Militant Islamic Terrorists Entered and Remained in the United States, 1993–2001 (Washington, D.C.: Center for Immigration Studies, 2001).

20. Michael Riley and Mike Soraghan, "INS Set to Join Homeland Security," *Denver Post,* March 2, 2003, B4.

21. Megan Izen, "Attempts to Disenfranchise Voters of Color," *Colorlines Magazine,* September–October 2006.

22. Leonard Zeskind, "The New Nativism," *American Prospect,* October 23, 2005, A15, at www.prospect.org/cs/articles?article_id=10485 (accessed June 7, 2007); and ACLU of Arizona, *Creating the Minutemen: A Misinformation Campaign Fueled by a Small Group of Extremists* (Phoenix: ACLU of Arizona, 2006), 4.

23. Eunice Cho, *2nd Annual Immigrant and Refugee Rights Training Institute Report* (Oakland, Calif.: National Network for Immigrant and Refugee Rights, 2005), 17–18.

24. David Drucker, "GOP Frets on Immigration," *Roll Call,* October 11, 2005, at www.rollcall.com (accessed February 7, 2008).

25. Nina Bernstein, "In the Streets, Suddenly, An Immigrant Groundswell," *New York Times,* 27 March 2006, at www.nytimes.com (accessed February 7, 2008).

26. Quoted in Ralph Hollow, "Dean Calls the Border Top Priority, Surprises GOP with Seeking 'Tough' Control, *Washington Times,* April 20, 2006, A1.

27. Quoted in Greg J. Borowski, "Parties Court Hispanic Voters at LULAC Event: GOP and Democratic Leaders Trade Barbs over Immigration Issue," *Milwaukee Journal Sentinel,* June 29, 2006, B News, at www.jsonline.com (accessed February 7, 2008).

28. Rachel L. Swarns, "Chamber and 2 Unions Forge Alliance on Immigration Bill," *New York Times,* January 19, 2006, at www.nytimes.com (accessed February 7, 2008).

29. For example, the New American Opportunity Coalition—headed by representatives of the National Immigration Forum (Washington, D.C.), the National Council of La Raza (Washington, D.C.), the Center for Community Change (Washington, D.C.), Service Employees International Union, UNITE-HERE, and the New York Immigration Coalition—led in support of SOLVE. At www.cirnow.org (accessed February 7, 2008).

30. For example, Atlantic Philanthropies, *Legislative Advocacy Principles,*

September 1, 2004, at http://atlanticphilanthropies.org/news/reports/legislative-advocacy-principles (accessed September 20, 2007). Between 2004 and 2007, Atlantic Philanthropies provided CCIR with $10 million in core support funds, an unprecedented amount of funding for the immigrant rights movement; at http://atlanticphilanthropies.org/grantees/results?programme=®ion=5&year=&keywords=immigration&x=14&y=18&sort=grantee (accessed September 20, 2007).

31. Manhattan Institute, "Earned Legalization and Increased Border Security Is Key to Immigration Reform According to Republican Voters: New Poll," press release, October 17, 2006.

32. Committee on the Judiciary, *Comprehensive Immigration Reform,* 109th Cong., 2nd sess., October 18, 2005, D1047.

33. Rosita Choy, "Translating Grassroots Organizing into Policy Change," *Peaceworks Magazine,* July/August 2004, 21.

34. Rashida Tlaib, "Immigration Matters: Bills' Dangerous Provisions Hidden in Plain Sight," *New American Media,* August 10, 2006, at http://news.newamericamedia.org/news/view_article.html?article_id=8f2c43730f05079cf54e0f3dfd631221a (accessed January 13, 2008); and Dan Kesselbrenner and Sandy Lin, "An Immigrant's Worst Nightmare: Facing the U.S. Legal System," in *From the Borderline to the Colorline* (Oakland, Calif.: National Network for Immigrant and Refugee Rights, 2001), 31–32.

35. AFL-CIO, *Statement by AFL-CIO President John Sweeney on the Senate's Immigration Bill* (Washington, D.C.: AFL-CIO, 2006).

36. Richard Fausset, "A New Immigrant Rights Movement Builds Slowly in the South," *Lexington Herald Leader,* March 31, 2006, A3; Yvonne Wingett and Daniel Gonzalez, "Immigrants Protest in Valley, Cities across the U.S." *Arizona Republic,* March 28, 2006, A1; Mike Littwin, "Awe Inspiring Marches Jolt Politicians," *Rocky Mountain News,* March 28, 2006, 7A; Teresa Watanabe and Hector Becerra, "Answering DJ's Call to March: How DJs Put 500,000 Marchers in Motion," *LA Times,* March 28, 2006, Domestic News.

37. Maria Newman, "Immigrants Display Boldness in U.S. Rallies," *International Herald Tribune,* April 11, 2006, News, 6.

38. Gillian Flaccus, "Across Country, 1 Million Turn Out,," *St. Louis Post-Dispatch,* May 2, 2006, A1.

39. For example, Randal C. Archibald, "Strategy Sessions Fueled Immigrant Marches," *New York Times,* April 12, 2006, A16.

40. Lisa Duran, interview by Eunice Hyunhye Cho, Berkeley, California, January 3, 2007.

41. Rashida Tlaib, interview by Eunice Hyunhye Cho, Berkeley, California, January 2, 2007.

42. Pancho Argüelles Paz y Puente, interview by Eunice Hyunhye Cho, Berkeley, California, January 6, 2007.

43. Monami Maulik, interview by Eunice Hyunhye Cho, Tucson, Arizona, December 27, 2006.

44. Teresa Watanabe and Anna Gorman, "Rally Organizers Differ on Boycott," *LA Times,* April 20, 2006, Domestic News.

45. Maria Jimenez, interview by Eunice Hyunhye Cho, Berkeley, California, January 2, 2007.

46. Alexis Mazon, interview by Eunice Hyunhye Cho, Berkeley, California, January 4, 2007.

47. Maulik interview.

48. Sandra Sanchez, interview by Eunice Hyunhye Cho, Berkeley, California, December 19, 2006.

49. Jimenez interview.

50. Garcia interview.

51. Mazon interview.

52. Elizabeth Sunwoo, interview by Eunice Hyunhye Cho, Berkeley, California, December 18, 2006.

53. Argüelles interview.

54. Tlaib interview.

55. This and following quotations from Sunwoo interview.

56. Eunice Hyunhye Cho, *Northwest Regional Immigrant and Refugee Rights Training Institute Report* (Oakland, Calif.: National Network for Immigrant and Refugee Rights, 2006), 9–11.

57. Garcia interview.

58. Jasmyne Cannick, "Gays First, Then Illegals," *Advocate.com,* April 4, 2006, at http://www.advocate.com/exclusive_detail_ektid28908.asp (accessed January 14, 2007).

59. 55 LGBT Activists, "We 55 Respectfully Disagree," *Advocate.com,* April 11, 2006, at http://www.advocate.com/exclusive_detail_ektid29496.asp (accessed January 14, 2007).

60. Trishala Deb, interview with Eunice Hyunhye Cho, Tucson, Arizona, December 27, 2006.

61. This framing, of course, does not address the need for the immigrant rights movement to address sexism, transphobia, and homophobia as critical issues.

62. Deb interview.

63. Bernstein, "In the Streets," A14.

64. National Network for Immigrant and Refugee Rights, *2nd Annual BRIDGE*

Trainers Bureau Meeting Report (Oakland, Calif.: National Network for Immigrant and Refugee Rights, 2006), 15–20.

65. Arnoldo Garcia, interview by Eunice Hyunhye Cho, Berkeley, California, January 6, 2007.

66. Sunwoo interview.

67. *Save America Comprehensive Immigration Act of 2005*, 109th Congress (May 4, 2005): H.R. 2092.

68. S. 1349, 110th Cong. (2007).

69 Julie Hirschfeld Davis, "Kennedy Critized on Immigratio," *Newark Star Ledger,* June 26, 2007, A3.

79. Stephen Dinan, "Immigration Bill Quashed," *Washington Times,* June 29, 2007, A1.

71. Catherine Tactaquin, interview by Eunice Hyunhye Cho, Berkeley, CA, September 20, 2007.

72. For example, Press Release, Asian American Justice Center, "Asian American Leaders Announce Overwhelming Opposition to Anti-Family Immigration Proposal," March 30, 2007; Press Release, National Immigration Law Center, "NILC Opposes Current Sennate Bill because It Would Preclude Real reform," June 25, 2007.

73. Klaus Marre, "45–53, Immigration Bill Goes Down in Defeat," *The Hill,* June 28, 2007.

74. Tactaquin interview.

75. M. Garcia interview.

76. Argüelles interview.

PRIMARY SOURCE

Documents from the National Network on Immigrant and Refugee Rights, 2006

The following are documents from groups participating in NNIRR's spring 2006 mobilization. These documents include statements from diverse human rights, legal, faith-based, and labor organizations. The Center for Human Rights and Constitutional Law is a non-profit, public-interest legal foundation specializing in immigration and poverty law. Formed in 1955, the American Federation of Labor–Congress of International Organizations is a voluntary federation of fifty-five national and international unions representing over 10 million workers; the AFL-CIO has led pro-immigrant labor organizing since the mid-1990s. Combining litigation, education, and advocacy, the Asian American Legal Defense and Education Fund has promoted human rights since 1974. One of the earliest legal centers to focus on immigrants rights, the Immigrant Legal Resource Center was founded in 1979 in San Francisco. Founded by Quakers to help civilian casualties of war in 1917, the American Friends Service Committee is dedicated to peace and social justice work.

The primary documents included here represent a small sample of the groups involved in the mobilizations of 2006 and 2007. Reading these documents illuminates the different emphases of these groups and the ways they come into coalition around specific issues and policies.

Center for Human Rights and Constitutional Law
For Immediate Release: May 27, 2006
Statement by Peter Schey, President, Center for Human Rights and Constitutional Law
While Immigrants Rise Up, Congress Falls Down

As the principal legal organization that has represented hundreds of thousands of immigrants in court cases seeking legalization under the Immigration Reform and Control Act of 1986 (IRCA), and having assisted the Congress when it addressed IRCA in 1986 and again when it drafted the LIFE Act in 2000, and having worked over the past several months with members of the Senate and local coalitions and community-based organizations to arrive at a comprehensive immigration reform package, we are deeply disappointed with and must now oppose the Senate's immigration bill unless it is dramatically improved in a Conference Committee, the chances of which are exceptionally slim.

We are fully dedicated to and recognize the urgent need for comprehensive immigration reform that fully protects U.S. and foreign-born workers within our borders and addresses the nation's legitimate national security concerns, The bill adopted by the Senate on Thursday entirely fails to satisfy these fundamental goals.

Nevertheless, with immigrants and others in favor of fair and rational immigration reform now on the march throughout the country, we believe that the drive for positive immigration reform is irreversible. Upcoming elections could well change the complexion of the House of Representatives making real immigration reform much more likely. We will work with local coalitions, community-based and national organizations, and concerned members of Congress to make sure that the goal of comprehensive immigration reform remains on the legislative table until it is accomplished.

While some have applauded the architecture of the Senate immigration bill, a careful review of the entire bill discloses one disastrous and irrational provision after another. Taken as a whole, the bill will not come close to legalizing the majority of undocumented immigrants. In fact, it will increase the size of the undocumented population over time because of its draconian enforcement measures that block traditional avenues for undocumented immigrants to legalize their status. If the bill becomes law, it wouldn't be surprising if within 20 years the undocumented population reaches about 20 million. Enactment of the bill will drive undocumented immigrants deeper underground and intensify their fugitive status, which will increase their exploitability and whatever adverse impact they have on U.S. workers.

The three-tier legalization program is absurdly complex, unworkable, and will likely not include even half the undocumented people residing permanently in the U.S. No more than 3 million immigrants (according to reliable IRCA data) will qualify for tier one legalization based upon more than five years of continuous residence. *Even these immigrants will only obtain "temporary" status for eight years (given current visa backlogs of over 20 years), and will wait about 16–18 years to become citizens and be able to vote for the first time.* Relatively few migrants will qualify for permanent residence under the second tier "temporary worker" and third tier "guest-worker" programs because they will not have the necessary family relationships or qualifying low-skilled jobs to win permanent resident status. Last year the DOL approved about 5,000 low-skilled worker visas. For those who do succeed, they must wait well over 20 years before they can become citizens and participate in the democratic process. This is an obstacle course to legalization and citizenship, not a reasonable path.

The Senate's interior enforcement provisions will criminalize all immigrants who entered the country unlawfully, although making them guilty of misdemeanors, rather than felonies as proposed by the House in the Sensenbrenner bill. Evading inspection is made a "continuous" crime that doesn't end until the immigrant is "discovered." With other provisions and laws that encourage local police to get involved in immigration enforcement, the criminalization of those who enter without inspection will likely result in mass warrantless arrests and detentions of Latino and other people of color in communities throughout the country.

The Senate bill also criminalizes the use of false or altered documents to obtain jobs, and makes any immigrant who worked using someone else's name or social security number ineligible for visas in the future. These provisions will impact most undocumented workers. They will become criminals because they used someone else's name or documents to obtain employment in order to survive and feed their families. They will be ineligible for visas in the future, but are unlikely to ever leave the country. These provisions, like many other iron-fist measures in the bill, will not force people to leave the country. These measures will simply drive immigrants deeper underground, make them more exploitable, and over the next several years increase the size of the undocumented population.

The Senate bill overturns recent Supreme Court decisions in order to permit the "indefinite detention" of immigrants believed to be removable. It forces immigrants to abandon their right to appeal erroneous deportation decisions in order to preserve their right to "voluntary departure." It makes it even more difficult for legitimate asylum seekers to win protection from deportation to countries where they face torture and imprisonment. It broadens the definition of "aggravated felonies" to crimes that are neither felonies nor aggravated, and then provides for mandatory detention and deportation of all such "felons" regardless of their present immigration status or length of residence in the country. It will cause the deportation of thousands of immigrants who have United States citizen children. It will substantially increase the militarization and criminalization of the U.S.-Mexico border, destroying border communities and further ramping up border deaths and criminal violence.

It also strips the federal courts of their historic role in reviewing and correcting unlawful policies enforced by immigration officials in violation of laws enacted by Congress, as well as erroneous decisions reached in individual cases. No judge will have authority to address unconscionable delays in the processing of applications, or the policies adopted in adjudicating applications. These court-stripping measures will permit prejudice, ignorance of the laws, and even wide-scale lawlessness to permeate the decisions and policies of immigration officials.

If the Senate bill included only its legalization provisions, as flawed and short-sighted as they are, we would support such a bill as offering something that was better than nothing. If the bill offered only the Dream Act to legalize the status of certain immigrant students, we would fully endorse it. If the bill included only provisions to increase the availability of visas and reduce the current massive visa backlogs, we would unquestionably support it. However, as presently constructed, the bill offers a hopelessly flawed legalization as a velvet glove to some immigrants, and a sledgehammer approach to all other immigrants. This approach may grant something akin to indentured servitude to a few million immigrants, but it will drive the majority, as well as new entrants, far deeper underground, intensify their fugitive status, increase their exploitability, and over time substantially expand the size of the undocumented population. That's a combination that we, as a human rights organization, are bound to reject.

Statement by AFL-CIO President John Sweeney
On the Senate's Immigration Bill
May 26, 2006

We are deeply disappointed that the Senate missed a historic opportunity to fix our nation's broken immigration system in a just, meaningful and comprehensive way. We strongly believe that America deserves an immigration system that protects all workers within our borders and at same time guarantees the safety of our nation without compromising our fundamental civil rights and liberties. The bill adopted by the Senate yesterday failed to satisfy those fundamental principles.

Instead of raising working standards for all workers by providing a fair path to citizenship to the 12 million undocumented workers currently living in our communities, the Senate adopted the framework of the fatally flawed Martinez-Hagel compromise, which creates an undemocratic, unjust and unworkable three-tiered society that denigrates and marginalize millions of immigrant families. That three-tiered approach creates a caste society in which millions of hard-working immigrants are driven further into the shadows of American society, leaving them vulnerable to exploitation.

We are also disappointed that the Senate adopted the greedy corporate model of addressing our nations' future needs for workers—guestworker programs—-instead of crafting a mechanism to ensure that future foreign workers come into the U.S. with full rights and as full social partners. We are heartened by the fact that the Senate substantially reduced the size of the new H2C guestworker program and added many worker protections that were missing from earlier versions of the proposed legislation. Clearly, the Senate recognized the exploitative nature of guestworker programs and their detrimental effects on U.S. workers and foreign workers alike.

We echo the concerns expressed by civil rights, religious and community leaders about the erosion of civil liberties and other fundamental rights embodied in the Senate bill. Further, we stand behind immigrant workers and immigrant communities around the country, who have expressed deep concerns with the Senate bill because, among other things, it creates deep divisions within immigrant communities and leaves millions of immigrants in the shadows.

This is not the time to start popping champagne corks. Our work is far from over. As the only national organization in our country dedicated exclusively to standing up for working people, we will continue to fight for workers' rights and for a strong blanket standard of treatment that makes no exceptions and that benefits the middle-class as a whole.

Asian American Legal Defense and Education Fund
For Immediate Release
May 24, 2006
AALDEF Statement Opposing Hagel-Martinez Bill (S. 2611)

The convoluted debate in the Senate over "comprehensive immigration reform" has made one thing abundantly clear: we must oppose passage of the Hagel-Martinez bill (S. 2611).

The Hagel-Martinez bill is neither reform nor comprehensive policy for immigration. As we suspected, the political climate of the debate has converted this immigration bill into a Trojan horse into which lawmakers have crammed anti-immigrant and undemocratic policies. Instead of opportunities of legalization for all with full workers' rights and protections, S. 2611 in its basic form proposes to divide our communities by dividing the undocumented into three groups based on how long they have been in the U.S., which would likely bar more than half the undocumented population from adjusting their status from within the U.S. It also vastly increases detention and deportation practices and further militarizes the border.

None of the above proposals will become law as a result of this compromised debate if we stop the passage of Hagel-Martinez. We know that if the Senate were to pass Hagel-Martinez, Congress must reconcile it with the House of Representatives' enforcement-only H.R. 4437 in order for it to become law. In effect, pushing a flawed bill through the Senate would result in the dilution of any meaningful protections for immigrants remaining in the Senate bill, and leave our immigration system even worse off than it was in 1986, when Congress last enacted large-scale immigration reform.

The Senate has also passed an unnecessary amendment to S. 2611 that declared English as our "national language" and that could undercut immigrants' access to government services and communication in multiple languages.

Instead, our communities have proposed ten principles for comprehensive immigration reform. Broadly, any legislation lawmakers consider must honor all of the following:

Adjustment to legal status for undocumented immigrants.
Clearing of the immigration backlog.
Expansion of legal immigration opportunities to account for both family-based immigration and the needs of our economy.
Provisions that keep families together.
Stronger protections for workers—including repeal of employer sanctions, no new guestworker programs, and path to citizenship for future workers.
Ending of all detention for mere civil immigration violations and repeal of mandatory deportation.
Stronger civil rights standards for enforcement efforts, including ending of racial and ethnic profiling and selective targeting of communities.
Full due process rights and judicial review for individuals in removal proceedings.
No state and local enforcement of immigration laws.
Reasonable, just, and humane enforcement and border policies.

If any law or policy does not meet the above principles that we have set as a starting point, we must voice our opposition and demand nothing less than "comprehensive" immigration reform.

AALDEF urges communities to call their Senator immediately at (202) 224-3121 to oppose passage of Hagel-Martinez.

The Asian American Legal Defense and Education Fund (AALDEF), founded in 1974, is a national organization that protects and promotes the civil rights of Asian Americans. By combining litigation, advocacy, education, and organizing, AALDEF works with Asian American communities across the country to secure human rights for all.

Immigrant Legal Resource Center
For Immediate Release: May 25, 2006
The Senate Immigration Reform Bill
They Didn't Get It Right!

SAN FRANCISCO, CA: After much debate and discussion, the Senate by a vote of 62 to 36 passed S. 2611, a measure that would profoundly reform our immigration laws. Unfortunately and tragically, they did not get it right: unfortunately, because our nation desperately needs good reform; and tragically because the positive provisions in the bill have been fatally compromised by the negative measures included in the bill. Moreover, in a conference with the House, we expect that the bill's positive provisions will be further eroded, if not eliminated, and the negative provisions made more draconian and unfair.

This has been a difficult debate, and we applaud those Senators who spoke out in support of immigrants and the positive contributions immigrants are making to our nation. We thank them for standing up for immigrants on the Senate floor every day and for speaking out loudly and clearly against the restrictionist and nativist sentiments that have erupted during this debate.

What are the provisions of most concern to the ILRC that are in the Senate bill?

- A fundamentally unworkable three tiered legalization program with exorbitant fees that will be a nightmare to implement.
- Local and state police encouraged to enforce federal civil immigration law, a body of law that most do not understand and the enforcement of which will dramatically hamper community policing and discourage victims and witnesses of crime from coming forward. Contracts between the Department of Homeland Security (DHS) and local police in every state will be promoted so that local police will enforce

immigration laws and immigration information will be entered into NCIC, the federal criminal database.

- U.S. Mexico border militarized: An additional 370 miles of triple-layered fencing will be added along the U.S.-Mexico border as well as 500 miles of vehicle barriers.
- People, including persons with green cards, will be detained without bond for failing to file a change of address card, even though the federal government does not even have the capacity to process all these filed changes.
- Increased number of people deported for minor crimes and misdemeanors, changing the rules in the middle of the game: Long time legal permanent residents will be mandatorily deportable for minor crimes such as having three DUI's (Driving under the Influence) no matter how long ago they were convicted and despite their rehabilitation, extensive family ties, and length of time in this country.
- U.S. citizens and legal permanent residents criminalized for helping family members or friends.
- The number of youth who could be found deportable and ineligible for any immigration benefits expanded based on the sole finding that the child is or was a member of a gang, with no requirement that any criminal act was committed or there was actual gang activity or involvement.
- American businesses challenged by requiring employers to verify every single worker, when the only employer verification system that exists is rife with error, and a new, comprehensive database is years away.
- Faster deportation of people allowed and the court doors closed so that people are prohibited from ever seeing a judge, even if they have lived here for years.
- New hurdles created to citizenship by changing the test to require applicants to know key U.S. inventors and artists and information about the Federalist Papers.
- All U.S. citizens subject to long criminal background checks in petitioning a family member and some precluded from sponsoring their immediate relatives altogether.
- I-9 document requirements that undermine legalization. (We need to review the Manager's Amendment that was introduced today to determine if this issue was resolved.)

Although S. 2611 includes positive provisions that would reduce the backlog in family-based immigration, as well as AgJobs, DREAM Act, and a well-intentioned, but flawed, legalization program, the measures noted above dramatically undermine these provisions. As if that weren't bad enough, the "enforcement" provisions in the bill will cost Americans billions of dollars, will overwhelm the Department of Homeland Security, and will not accomplish its stated goals.

We will continue to fight for immigration reform that works for America, immigrants, and communities nationwide. Our country deserves something better than what has come out of the process to date.

AFSC Calls for Substantive Immigration Policy Solutions Senate Leaders Falter: Immigrants and Border Communities Become National Security Scapegoats

PHILADELPHIA (MAY 24)—

. . .

In what have been difficult days packed with bipartisan rhetoric, emotionally charged and tough talk, the U.S. Senate has repeatedly failed to produce substantive immigration reform measures. Instead of comprehensive and coherent policies, Senate leaders have charged ahead with short-term, punitive measures or enforcement-only provisions, such as the total militarization of the border and provisions for the construction of miles of multi-layered fences. Some argue for an "apartheid-like" tiered legalization process.

"What is being fashioned in the halls of Congress does not represent what is in the best interest of our nation," notes Esther Nieves, interim director of Project VOICE, the American Friends Service Committee immigrant rights initiative. "The tone and tenure of the debate has focused on pre-election political convenience, one-upmanship and demagoguery. We urge our legislators not to succumb to partisan shortsightedness that ultimately only divides families and destroys communities."

An amendment imposing English-only requirements moves the bar for eventual citizenship even higher. Studies have consistently documented that immigrants consider learning to speak and communicate in English of critical importance. To bar immigrants from accessing resources or becoming legal residents because of English proficiency is a damaging indictment. Indeed, a more sensible solution would be the allocation of resources to conduct English and civic classes rather than the imposition of an English-only litmus test.

"The measures that have been presented are troubling. As proposed, the process leading to permanent residency and eventual citizenship will be quite cumbersome, punitive and unrealistic," observed Christian Ramirez, AFSC Project VOICE national base-building coordinator. "Long-term solutions that address structural flaws in the immigration system have been lost in the discourse."

The Bush administration has set in motion a multibillion-dollar federal contract process and has solicited bids from major contractors to increase security on the southern border. Taking a chapter from its warfare-building arsenal, the administration recently requested $1.95 billion from Congress to "fix the problem of immigration." However, the continued build-up of the border and the infusion of dollars to further militarize the region by adding National Guard troops, more enforcement agents and new technology has no impact on the long-term policies that are needed to bring 12 million undocumented workers and their families out of the shadows.

The continued build up of the border and the infusion of dollars—more than $30 billion in the past decade—have not deterred border crossings. Instead 4,000 people have died crossing the desert in the past 12 years.

"Congress and the current administration must acknowledge that there are 12 million undocumented workers who have established deep roots in the United States," emphasizes Joyce Miller, AFSC assistant general secretary for justice and human rights. "They work, they pay taxes, they live here, they have married and have children here, they shop here, and they worship in local churches and are an asset to local economies. The Senate is steadily chipping away at this historic juncture—that is, to bring millions of immigrants out of the shadows."

"It is ludicrous to use taxpayers' dollars to continue to build fences, erect barriers, and impose punitive and mean-spirited policies. These are tremendously difficult issues that our national leaders must tackle. The discrepancy over who has health coverage in this country, the rising cost of medication, the skyrocketing gasoline prices, a coherent energy plan, the dwindling resources of the nation's working and middle class families, and other basic quality of life concerns would be a wiser use of our national budget resources," Ramirez concluded.

The American Friends Service Committee supports the rights and dignity of all people, regardless of their immigration status. AFSC's Project VOICE works to uplift immigrant voices and strengthen efforts of immigrant-led organizations to set an agenda for fair and humane national public policies. Backed by an 89-year history working for peace, justice and reconciliation in troubled areas of the world, the American Friends Service Committee is a faith-based organization grounded in Quaker beliefs respecting the dignity and worth of every person. The AFSC has worked in Mexico on rural and urban development projects and with migrant farm workers in California since 1940. In 1977 AFSC's U.S.-Mexico Border Program was created.

Groups Endorsing the National Network for Immigrant and Refugee Rights, Spring 2006

Adhikaar (Staten Island, NY)
Alliance of South Asians Taking Action (ASATA) (Oakland, CA)
American-Arab Anti-Discrimination Committee—Massachusetts Chapter (Boston, MA)
American Friends Service Committee (AFSC) (Philadelphia, PA)
American Friends Service Committee–Austin (Austin, TX)
Applied Research Center (Oakland, CA)
Arab American Family Support Center (Brooklyn, NY)
Arab Community Center for Economic and Social Services (ACCESS) (Dearborn, MI)
Asian Immigrant Women Advocates (Oakland, CA)
Asian Pacific Environmental Network (Oakland, CA)
Asociación Latina (Clarksville, TN)
Audre Lorde Project (New York, NY)

Aztlan Media Kollective (East Los Angeles and San Francisco, CA)
Black Workers for Justice (North Carolina)
Bonilla Community Services (Durham, NC)
Border Agricultural Workers Project (El Paso, TX)
Building Opportunities for Self-Sufficiency (Berkeley, CA)
CAA: Chinese for Affirmative Action/Center for Asian American Advocacy (San Francisco, CA)
CAAAV Organizing Asian Communities (New York, NY)
California Services (Anaheim, CA)
CASA Latina (Seattle, WA)
Center for Constitutional Rights (New York, NY)
Center for Immigrant Families (New York, NY)
Central Valley Progressive PAC (Fresno, CA)
Centro Hispano "Cuzcatlán" (Jamaica, NY)
Chicano Consortium (Sacramento, CA)
Chinese Progressive Association (San Francisco, CA)
Coalición de Derechos Humanos (Tucson, AZ)
Coalición de Trabajadores de Immokalee (Immokalee, FL)
Comite NO NOS VAMOS (Fresno, CA)
Community HIV/AIDS Mobilization Project (CHAMP) (Providence, RI)
Derechos Humanos (Tucson)
Desis Rising Up and Moving (DRUM) (New York, NY)
Eastern Massachusetts Jobs with Justice
Esperanza Peace and Justice Center (San Antonio, TX)
Farmworker Legal Services of NY (Rochester, NY)
Filipino Civil Rights Advocates (FilCRA) (Oakland, CA)
Filipinos for Affirmative Action (Oakland, CA)
Frente Continental (Los Angeles, CA)
Frente Indígena de Organizaciones Binacionales (FIOB) (Fresno, CA)
Fuerza Unida (San Antonio, TX)
Gay Men's Health Crisis (New York, NY)
Gente Unida/San Diego Border Coalition for Human Rights (Chula Vista, CA)
Gustavus Myers Center for the Study of Bigotry and Human Rights (Boston, MA)
Health Initiatives for Youth (San Francisco, CA)
Hispanic Organizations Leadership Alliance (Washington, DC)

Iglesia Metodista Unida Summerfield (New York, NY)
Iglesia San Romero de Las Americas–United Church of Christ (New York, NY)
Immigrant Communities in Action (New York, NY)
Immigrant Justice Solidarity Project (Brooklyn, NY)
Immigration Equality (New York, NY)
Inmigrantes Latinos en Acción (Austin, TX)
Jews for Racial and Economic Justice (New York, NY)
Junta Centro Mujer Dominicana (New York, NY)
Korean Americans United for Peace (Bay Area, CA)
Korean Community Center of the East Bay (Oakland, CA)
Korean Immigrant Workers Alliance (KIWA) (Los Angeles, CA)
Korean Youth Cultural Center (Oakland, CA)
Labor Council for Latin American Advancement—Massachusetts Chapter (Boston, MA)
La Raza Centro Legal, SF Day Labor Program (San Francisco, CA)
Latino Union of Chicago (Chicago, IL)
Los Angeles Coalition to End Hunger and Homelessness (Los Angeles, CA)
March 25 Coalition (a group of 100 political and immigrant rights organizations who called for the Great American Boycott of 2006)
Mexican American Political Association (California)
Migrant Worker Solidarity of Douglas County (Eudora, KS)
Migration Policy and Resource Center/Occidental College (Los Angeles, CA)
National Association of People with AIDS (NAPWA) (Silver Spring, MD)
National Immigration Project of the National Lawyers Guild (Boston, MA)
National Network for Arab American Communities (NNAAC) (Dearborn, MI)
National Network for Immigrant and Refugee Rights (Oakland, CA)
North Carolina Justice Center (Durham, NC)
Nuestra Casa (East Palo Alto, CA)
Oakland Institute (Oakland, CA)
Orange County Peace and Freedom Party (Anaheim, CA)
Pilipino Workers Center of Southern California (Los Angeles, CA)
Project Voice New England—American Friends Service Committee (Boston, MA)

San Francisco Day Labor Program Women's Collective of La Raza Centro Legal (San Francisco, CA)
Section of Christian Social Responsibility, Women's Division, United Methodist Church (New York, NY)
South Asian Network (Artesia, CA)
Southwest Network for Environmental and Economic Justice (Albuquerque, NM)
Southwest Organizing Project (Albuquerque, NM)
Southwest Workers' Union (San Antonio, TX)
Speak Out—Institute for Democratic Education and Culture (Emeryville, CA)
Student/Farmworker Alliance (Immokalee, FL)
ThinkingPeople (Mount Pleasant, SC)
Third World Majority (Oakland, CA)
United for a Fair Economy (Boston, MA)
U.S.-Mexico Border Program / American Friends Service Committee (San Diego, CA)
Voluntarios de la Comunidad (Sacramento, CA)

PART II

Ambivalent Allies, Reluctant Rivals, and Disavowed Deviants

As a political movement, immigrant rights necessarily involve coalition building. Just as immigration policy has often created odd categories to describe people—for example, the "Asian barred zone" operative throughout most of the twentieth century, which mapped the undesirability of all "Asian" people, from East Asia to Afghanistan—people from different places, living in different regions, with different languages and access to resources reach across what divides them to advocate for more just treatment of all people called "immigrants."

While most of the articles in this collection deal with questions of alliance in some way, the articles in this section are particularly concerned with the ways that immigrants forge connections to one another, across what divides them.

In chapter 5, ethnic studies scholar Dustin Tahmakera illuminates the ways in which nineteenth-century ideas about the racial inferiority of indigenous peoples came to be used to delimit the legal rights of Chinese immigrants on the West Coast. He traces the progress of the ideas expressed in one decision, *People v. Hall* (1854), in which the Supreme Court ruled that the testimony of indigenous people could not be heard in court. Tahmakera's insistence that immigrants and indigenous peoples share historical and contemporary cause is amply demonstrated by the provisions in the Comprehensive Immigration Reform bill passed by the Senate in April 2006 that could abridge tribal sovereignty on reservation land along the U.S.-Mexico border to enable the militarized presence of Homeland Security. The text of *People v. Hall* follows the article.

Writing from the Africana Cultures and Policy Studies Institute (ACPSI), historians Zachery Williams, Robert Samuel Smith, and Seneca Vaught, with literary critic Babacar M'Baye, make the crucial observation in chapter 6 that African peoples were early, though unwilling, immigrants to the Americas. Regulation of the slave trade, for these scholars, constituted immigration policy long before the writing of federal documents delimited certain nonnative peoples as "aliens ineligible to citizenship." The first Black immigrants, then, were slaves. From this standpoint, these writers examine the experiences of African Americans with subsequent cohorts of Black immigrants from Africa and the Caribbean, arguing that each group is compelled by the ongoing necessity of the struggle for civil rights.

In chapter 7, media studies scholar Isabel Molina examines the Elián Gonzalez incident of 1999. Usually, she explains, the particular stories of women and children immigrants are overshadowed by mass media attention to either family unification, or presumptively male, solitary immigration. But in the case of Elián Gonzalez, Molina argues, the U.S. mass media and the Cuban exile community competed to interpret this light-skinned child as either a motherless refugee from a ruthless dictatorship or a lost son to be returned to his father in Cuba. This competition, in turn, she argues, led to a change in the ways Cubans in the United States are represented as citizens, exiles, and refugees.

Interdisciplinary scholar Lisa Marie Cacho's powerful essay, chapter 8, from which the title of Part II is drawn, brings the section to a close. Focusing on media coverage of conflict between Blacks and Latino/as over the issue of immigrant rights, Cacho argues that advocates for both groups have often been pressured to assert their normalcy. In particular, she argues, immigrant and civil rights groups have responded to the criminalization of Blacks and Latino/as by emphasizing law-abiding, heterosexual and nuclear family-oriented identities, to the exclusion of alternative family formations and the realities of "illegal" immigration. Cacho's essay explores the complexities of coalition building, and the ways that the politics of alliance are often impeded by the cultural politics of mass media.

CHAPTER 5

"Pale Face 'Fraid You Crowd Him Out"

Racializing "Indians" and "Indianizing" Chinese Immigrants

Dustin Tahmakera

On the front cover of the February 8, 1879, edition of *Harper's Weekly: A Journal of Civilization* is a drawing titled "Every Dog" (No Distinction of Color) "Has His Day" (Fig. 5.1). Artist Thomas Nast depicts a peculiar-looking male "Indian" leaning towards the attentive ear of a Chinese male caricature. Covered in tattered blankets and rubbing his chin in sagacious thought, the "Indian" stands slightly over the long-haired, hollow-eyed immigrant. Anti-Chinese flyers, such as "PROHIBIT CHINESE IMMIGRATION," are posted on a wall behind them. Seated to their left in the background is an inattentive black man with the words "MY DAY IS COMING" scrawled on the wall near his head. The "Red Gentleman" utters a few wise words to the "Yellow Gentleman": "Pale face 'fraid you crowd him out, as he did me." The Red Gentleman's sentence refers to the fear and paranoia that many white men, or "pale faces," felt toward the

Fig. 5.1. Thomas Nast, "Every Dog (No Distinction of Color) Has His Day," cover of *Harper's Weekly*, February 8, 1879. The subtitle reads "Red Gentleman to Yellow Gentleman: 'Pale face 'fraid you crowd him out as he did me.'"

presence of the Chinese during the 1870s and exemplified through the 1882 Chinese Exclusion Act. His statement also notes the irony and hypocrisy that whites feared a Chinese invasion and an attempt to take all of white America's resources and means for livelihood as Europeans and Euro-Americans did in their invasion of "America" and its Indigenous Peoples.[1]

As Nast's Red Gentleman suggests, whites' anti-"Indian" fear became a basis for anti-Chinese paranoia. On February 26, 1879, less than three weeks after "Every Dog" first appeared, President Rutherford Hayes expressed his personal paranoia: "Our [white American] experience in dealing with the weaker races—the Negroes and Indians, for example,—is not encouraging. . . . I would consider with favor any suitable measures to discourage the Chinese from coming to our shores."[2] Echoing Irish-born Denis Kearney's 1877 summation, "The Chinese must go,"[3] Hayes spoke to a common sentiment among California's white population, which accounted for 87 percent of the state's residents.[4]

Despite the stereotypical portrayals of each figure and the seriocomic tone, "Every Dog" goes beyond the typical white/"other" binary to situate two "others"—Indigenous Peoples and Chinese immigrants—next to each other. Furthermore, the cartoon serves as an opening to discuss legislation enacted by white politicians acting on their fear(s),[5] as referred to by Nast's Red Gentleman, that "others" will physically (Indigenes) or economically (Chinese) harm them, occupy "their" territory, and thus, "crowd [them] out." In addition to coining the Red Gentleman's words, Nast's drawing of an "Indian" forcibly going west and the Chinese going east suggests imagined and inevitable geographical intersections between the two. Yet little scholarship has revealed these sites.[6]

In this chapter I compare the California courts' racialization of Chinese immigrants and Indigenous Peoples through legislation in the 1850s.[7] Ironically, Chinese and Indigenes intersected politically through the California Supreme Court's expanding definition of "Indian." In *People v. Hall* (1854),[8] the Chinese were racialized as "Indian" based on falsehoods and an unproven theory about Indigenes, who had not been allowed to testify in California since 1850. Through the court's "Indianization" of Chinese, the new immigrants could not testify, either. For instance, if only Indigenes or Chinese witnessed an Indigene or Chinese man being physically harmed by a white male, the only person who could testify was the white attacker. He could say anything without fear of protest or rebuttal by the victim.

Unlike earlier studies, my work explores not only the inhumanity committed by the California Supreme Court against Chinese immigrants but also the court's perpetuation of historical racist presuppositions about Indigenes. In *People v. Hall*, the court viewed the Chinese through a framework that had previously been reserved for assailing "Indians." In an examination of the court's racialization of Indigenes and the subsequent "Indianization" of Chinese, I try to contribute to scholarship in comparative ethnic studies. In *Immigrant Acts*, Lisa Lowe attempts "to place the specific history of Asian American racialization in relation to other forms of racialization," including "those of . . . Native Americans . . . in order to open possibilities of cross-race and cross-national projects."[9] While Lowe does not specify who should conduct such projects, Ruby Tapia calls for, as phrased in part by Yen Le Espiritu, "scholars of color to study 'our own' by studying other 'others.'" Espiritu agrees with Tapia that such "comparative projects permit us to highlight the *differentiating* functional forces of racialization" and to "discover commonalities."[10]

In conversation with Lowe, Tapia, and Espiritu, I conclude this essay with remarks on comparative ethnic studies between Asian Americans and Indigenous Peoples. Potential comparative projects entail important alliance-building work for Asian Americans, Indigenes, and allies. These coalitions, in turn, can bring strong collective voices in support of immigrant and migrant rights. Rather than enacting a discourse of division, I opt for a dialogue that moves seemingly disparate groups toward unity and toward a comparative awareness of how they are related to each other. The resulting united formations of Asian Americans and Indigenous Peoples can increase political and social strength for all.

Racialization

According to Michael Omi and Howard Winant, *racialization* signifies "the extension of racial meaning to a previously racially unclassified relationship, social practice or group."[11] Historically in the United States, racialization often has occurred through immigrant groups being racialized as "blacks" or "Negroes." As Ronald Takaki has noted, Irish immigrants have been called "Irish niggers,"[12] and Najia Aarim-Herrot says, "The marginalization of the Chinese . . . can be traced to their 'racialization.'"[13] In line with Omi and Winant's definition, I contribute to the discourse of racialization by asking how the Chinese were racialized as "Indian" by the California Supreme Court in 1854. Moreover, what are the implications of the "savage Indian" and "heathen Chinee" identities, synonymous with "foreigners" and non-U.S. citizens in White America, being remanipulated and resituated by American courts as one "Indian" entity?[14]

Anti-Chinese sentiment in California began very soon after Chinese people reached the mainland in 1848. By 1852, nearly 10,000 Chinese were in California. As the number of immigrants increased, so did the antagonism toward them. In particular, the Chinese were willing to work for less pay than whites. Fearing labor competition and other sites of interaction with Chinese immigrants, white Americans saw the "yellow peril" as an opposition to forming a nation of white American citizens. Thus, the Chinese soon experienced discrimination in comparable ways to the racism enacted against Indigenes.

Whites continued to encroach on Indigenes' lands and resources and to dehumanize Indigenes as intellectually inferior and uncivilized savages. Both Chinese and Indigenes fit into the related category of a despised, exoticized, and misunderstood "other." Extermination campaigns against Indigenes and exclusion efforts against Chinese became essential work for many whites. Whereas Chinese immigrants were seen as a nonviolent threat to whites' economic *livelihood,* Indigenous Peoples were viewed as a violent threat to whites' *lives.* Historian Daniel Liestman agrees: "Whites often perceived American Indians to be the greater menace, because Indians were seen as life threatening."[15] In fact, in 1854—the same year as *People v. Hall*—whites in California could be charged with a misdemeanor for selling guns or ammunition to "Indians."

Prohibiting Indigenous and Chinese Testimony

In 1850, the year that California became a state, California passed the Act for the Government and Protection of Indians. "Protection" was a misleading word for an act that effectually prohibited the testimony of Indigenes against white males in California courts. Section 6 read: "In no case shall a white man be convicted on any offence upon the testimony of an Indian." Curiously, Section 12 stated: "In all cases of trial between a white man and an Indian, either party may require a jury."[16] Why was it *illegal* for an "Indian" to testify in court to a jury that he or she was *legally* allowed to "require"? This act for further marginalizing Indigenes became the legal basis for upcoming anti-Chinese legislation.

In 1853, Chinese leaders began to speak out against certain California courts' refusals to hear their testimony. Crimes against the Chinese in mining districts had increased, and often the only witnesses were the victims. Banishing Chinese testimony was part of the overall effort in the 1850s and later decades to remove Chinese immigrants from America, to discourage potential future arrivals to the United States from China, and to diminish Chinese lives. The Chinese outcry against the courts' injustices did no good, as Chinese testimony became officially excluded for almost twenty years in *People v. Hall.*[17]

In October 1853, three Chinese and one white testified for the state of California during the four-day trial of George W. Hall, who—along with his brother and another white male—was accused of murdering Ling Sing, a local Chinese immigrant. Basing its decision largely on the testimony by the Chinese, the grand jury in Nevada County found Hall guilty. Hall's counsel appealed the verdict and cited Section 14 of California's Criminal Proceedings Act: "No black or mulatto person, or Indian, shall be permitted to give evidence in favor of, or against, any white person."[18] Attempting to discredit and remove the Chinese testimony from its client's trial, the counsel tried to prove that "Chinese" could mean "Indian" or "black." The California Supreme Court previously had never been presented with the need to determine whether the Chinese should be allowed to testify in a court of law. The appeal was in favor of Hall as the court's reading of Section 14 racialized the three Chinese witnesses as "Indian." Thus, Christopher Columbus's geographical confusion and subsequent misnomer and scientists' Bering Strait theory became the bizarre bases for racializing the Chinese as "Indian" in the mid-nineteenth century.

Chief Justice Hugh C. Murray, responsible for the reinterpretation of the law, identified the Chinese as Mongolian, Asiatic, and Indian to disallow Chinese testimony. He relied on a racial theory commonly accepted at the time of what he called "the early history of legislation." "The American Indians and the Mongolian, or Asiatic," Murray explained, "were regarded as the same type of the human species" because Columbus erroneously thought he had landed on "an island in the China sea." Unaware that he was not in the West Indies, Columbus identified the natives he saw in the "New World" as "Indian." The chief justice proclaimed that since 1492, "the name of Indian . . . has been used to designate, not alone the North American Indian, but the whole of the Mongolian [or Asiatic] race, and that the name, though first applied probably through mistake, was afterwards continued as appropriate on account of the supposed common origin [from Asia]."

Columbus *definitely,* not *probably* as Murray stated, made a mistake, one which arguably carries on today with each use of "Indian" to refer to the Indigenous Peoples of North America. Yet Murray reasoned that early American legislation accepted the common use of "Indian" and, therefore, "it was used and admitted in its common and ordinary acceptation, as a generic term, distinguishing the great Mongolian race, and as such, its meaning then became fixed by law." He argued, then, that "in construing statutes the legal meaning of words must be preserved."[19]

Murray's next major reliance on questionable history, as he alluded to in his acceptance of "Indian" "on account of the supposed common origin," was the Bering Strait theory. Scientists and anthropologists attempted to prove that North American Indigenes originated from Asia and that they traveled across Beringia when Asia was connected to the "New World" thousands of years ago. In Murray's estimation, "It has been supposed, and not without plausibility, that this continent was first peopled by Asiatics, who crossed Behring's [*sic*] Straits."[20] Despite its possible lack of belief in the Bering Strait theory, the court system continued to use it. White male scientists conceptualized it, and the court perpetuated it.

If "Indians," according to Murray and other whites, come from Asia, and hence, "Indians" and Asians are related peoples, then whites in the nineteenth century—despite showing up thousands of years after "Indians" supposedly crossed Beringia—could have argued that they had as much of a right to the land. As Joy Harjo (Mesquakie) has asked, "If we [Indigenes] were recent immigrants too, who were we to make such [land] claims"?[21] For Indigenes to be categorized as immigrants, as Justice Murray did, could provide whites with less guilt and more justification for taking the lands. When Murray then "Indianizes" the Chinese, that racist justification extends to *protecting* the lands from Chinese immigrants, who, unlike European Americans, did not desire to dominate the lands and resources of Native Peoples.

Even if the Bering Strait theory had not been reputable for Murray and if Indigenes' testimony had not previously been banned, Murray had yet another argument for disallowing Chinese testimony.[22] In merging what Daniel Kanstroom observes as "crude racial theorizing" and "public policy concerns,"[23] Murray expressed *fear* of what admittance to the witness stand might lead to, including the Chinese "at the polls, in the jury box, upon the bench, and in our legislative halls." He did not wish to allow "a race of people whom nature has marked as inferior, and who are incapable of progress or intellectual development beyond a certain point" to receive such power in an arena where white males, like Murray, dominated. "The court, confronted with an odious law, had chosen to expand rather than restrict its application."[24] Expansion is the obvious choice in light of nineteenth-century white American beliefs in racial and sovereign superiority over Chinese immigrants and Native Peoples.

As might be expected, violence against the Chinese, like that against Indigenes in 1850, increased after the court decided to deny their testimony. "Few Americans," Robert Heizer and Alan Almquist noted, "were ever brought to court to answer for the homicidal . . . acts in killing Indians."[25] "In the isolated, rural mining fields," notes Leigh-Wai Doo, "on which the first waves of Chinese immigrants worked, hundreds of Chinese were murdered and numerous more robbed with only a minuscule number of the offenders brought to trial and convicted."[26] Without the right for Indigenes and Chinese to testify, murderers, rapists, and thieves increased their chances for being found not guilty—if they were even brought to trial—in cases involving Indigenous and Chinese victims.

The court's racialization of Chinese as "Indian" prompted outrage from the Chinese community. Lai Chun-Chuen, a Chinese business owner in San Francisco, expressed his dismay to Governor Bigler in 1855 at being identified as Indian: "[The politicians] have come to the conclusion that we Chinese are the same as Indians. . . . And yet these Indians know nothing about the relations of society; they know no mutual respect; they wear neither clothes nor shoes; they live in wild places and in caves."[27] Despite the fact that Chun-Chuen's rhetoric was racist toward "Indians," what was more disturbing was how much his response corresponded with whites' ideas of the "civilized" white society and "savage" Indigenous population. Unfortunately, little is known about Chinese thought toward Indigenes at that time. Thus, to extend Chun-Chuen's retort outward to other Chinese feeling is speculative. If Chun-Chuen's retort was representative of other Chinese sentiment, the possibilities for alliances between the oppressed

Chinese and Indigenes were slim. Instead, anti-"Indian" discourse by the Chinese followed in line with what they may have heard, and been influenced by, from racist whites, who did not recognize or respect the tribally diverse, long-standing traditions and philosophies of Indigenes. Still, Chun-Chuen, who migrated from an industrious and developing country, did not emphasize that he was *like* whites in their racism toward Indigenes but that the Chinese were civilized in a hierarchical comparison to Indigenes.

Over the next fifteen years, the courts largely dismissed Chun-Chuen's and other Chinese calls for immigrant rights. Finally, in December 1869, Senator William Stewart of Nevada, the prosecutor in *People v. Hall*, introduced a resolution for "all persons within the jurisdiction of the United States" to "have the same right . . . to . . . give evidence."[28] Stewart's work would become, with slight revisions, Section 16 of the Civil Rights Act of 1870, which granted "full and equal benefit of all laws and proceedings . . . as is enjoyed by white citizens." Legislation, Takaki explains, enforcing "equal protection . . . had little or no effect on what happened in society."[29] Anti-Chinese sentiment continued, reaching its nineteenth-century climax with the Chinese Exclusion Act of 1882.

Ironically, previous racializations in the 1850s eventually led to *all persons* being allowed to testify in the early 1870s. In particular, racializing "Indians" and Chinese into one racial formation, "Indian," in the 1850s became a foundation for granting rights in state courts to both in the 1870s. After California's exclusion of "Indian" testimony in the 1850 Act for the Government and Protection of Indians, *People v. Hall* in 1854 racialized the Chinese as "Indian" to ban Chinese testimony, too. It was not until the Civil Rights Act of 1870 and the more enforced Civil Procedure Code in 1872 that Indigenes and Chinese were legally allowed to testify. Thus, both heterogeneous groups were equally unequal from 1854 to 1869, and both simultaneously gained equality in the courts in the early 1870s.

Political Relations

Despite Murray's "truly remarkable display of ignorance and racism,"[30] including his support of the Bering Strait theory, Indigenes and Asian

Americans are, politically speaking, related. Indigenes and Asian Americans worked together, for example, in civil rights campaigns in the 1960s and 1970s. As Liestman explains, their interactions date further back, including the peaceful business relations in the late 1800s between Wong Sing, a Chinese merchant, and the Utes at Fort Duchesne. In 1856, Wong Ying, a Chinese miner, and Native Peoples in southern Idaho "even speculated that they shared a common ethnic heritage," but this is the only "evidence," according to Liestman, that Chinese and Indigenes "discussed a common genetic heritage."[31]

Imagine, though, if the Bering Strait theory had held and was accepted as truth by the majority of today's Asian Americans and Indigenous Peoples. Asian Americans and Indigenes could be closer and likely more powerful today as a result of the conglomeration of Chinese, Japanese, Koreans, Filipinos, Vietnamese, Thai, Cambodians, and South Asian Indians as Asians and Asian Americans merging with the gathering of Comanches, Apaches, Cherokees, Osages, Mohawks, Seminoles, Choctaws, and the hundreds of other Indigenous Nations collectively known as Indigenous Peoples. Regardless of immigration and migration theories, however, future work on the political relations between Asian Americans and Indigenes can be done in ways to unite, not to divide.

A comparative study can involve, for instance, a cross-cultural examination of the Immigration Act of 1924 and the [American] Indian Citizenship Act of 1924. The former excluded Asians from the United States; the latter worked toward assimilating Indigenes into becoming Americans. What motives did America have to reject one heterogeneous group from its shores and welcome its native inhabitants into American citizenship in the same year? Both acts arguably excluded immigrants and natives. The Immigration Act excluded migrants geographically by preventing Asians from entering the United States. The Citizenship Act dismissed tribal sovereignty and traditional indigenous identities. It encouraged "Indians" to be Americans first, not tribally identified Indigenes.

While here I have largely discussed how the white court system treated Chinese immigrants and "Indians," I have looked for connections in their treatment by the dominant society to bridge the gap between Chinese Americans and Indigenous Peoples that continues to exist 150 years after the decision in *People v. Hall.* Although Indigenes have the unique

U.S.-based status of dual citizenship and tribal sovereignty, their struggles against racism and injustice today can effectually lead to a common bond with other marginalized peoples in their similar causes to be heard and to be treated justly. When the historical racism toward one group of people intersects with or serves as the rationale for racism against another group, such as was the case in *People v. Hall,* possibilities open up for contemporary alliances.

As Devon Mihesuah and Angela Cavender Wilson ask, "What are the links between the struggles of Indigenous peoples and other marginalized populations in this hemisphere and throughout the world? How can we work toward solidarity that acknowledges our differences (including the reality of colonialism) while fighting for our shared concerns?"[32] The stories of colonization and oppression told by the colonized and oppressed of different ethnicities and cultures often share commonalities. Harjo writes poetically:

> As an [American] Indian woman in this country, I often find that
> I have much in common with many of the immigrants
> from other colonized lands who come here to make a
> living.[33]

Harjo's words, Rachel Buff observes, reveal that "histories of colonization and resistance often connect individuals from disparate parts of the globe."[34] The coming together, rather than the separation, of Indigenes and Asian Americans can further disrupt the predominantly white structure whose dominant position in the United States is increasingly being challenged by marginalized groups. Indigenes must not only unite with Asian Americans and other non-Native allies but also unite with each other as Indigenous Peoples. And, as Frank Wu explains, "Asian Americans must be united as Asian Americans, but we must be united with whites, African Americans, Latino/as, Native Americans, and others who have the same commitments and passions. Each of us has an individual role, but together we have the greater role in the pursuit of racial justice."[35]

NOTES

1. In this chapter, the terms "Indigenous Peoples" and "Indigenes" are used interchangeably to refer to the original inhabitants of the land now known as North America. "Indian," a European invention and a misnomer rooted in colonialism and easily recognized in the United States as a linguistic identifier to refer to Indigenous Peoples, is placed in quotes when it is used here.

2. Quoted in Stuart Miller, *The Unwelcome Immigrant: The American Image of the Chinese, 1875–1882* (Berkeley: University of California Press, 1969), 190.

3. Quoted in Ronald Takaki, *A Different Mirror: A History of Multicultural America* (Boston: Back Bay Books, 1994), 156.

4. Ronald Takaki, *Strangers from a Different Shore: A History of Asian Americans* (Boston: Back Bay Books, 1998), 40.

5. The singular or plural use of "fear" is debatable. On the one hand, if whites imagined sharing a collective white national identity, then perhaps they could imagine sharing a collective national "fear" of nonwhites. On the other hand, "fears" denotes each of the numerous fears, such as the loss of lives in conflicts with Indigenes and loss of jobs due to increases in immigrant populations.

6. Daniel Liestman, "Horizontal Inter-Ethnic Relations: Chinese and American Indians in the Nineteenth-Century American West," *Western Historical Quarterly* 30(3) (1999): 327–49, offers a rare comparative look.

7. While here I am focusing on the racialization of Chinese as "Indian," other anti-Chinese legislation was ongoing in the courts at the same time. A series of taxes and ordinances directed *only* at Chinese immigrants was part of the overall collective effort by white Americans to force Chinese to leave America—thus freeing up, whites thought, more jobs—or to abide by the increased costs of living if staying in America. Such anti-Chinese measures also intended to prevent more Chinese from immigrating to America.

8. *People v. Hall*, 4 Cal. 399 (1854).

9. Lisa Lowe, *Immigrant Acts* (Durham, N.C.: Duke University Press, 1996), 173.

10. Quoted in Yen Le Espiritu, *Home Bound* (Berkeley: University of California Press, 2003), 12.

11. Michael Omi and Howard Winant, *Racial Formations in the United States from the 1960s to the 1990s* (New York: Routledge, 1994), 64.

12. Takaki, *Strangers from a Different Shore*, 150.

13. Najia Aarim-Herrot focuses her study on the "Negroization" of the Chinese, but she acknowledges that the Chinese were "Indianized," or racialized as "Indian," too (*Chinese Immigrants, African Americans, and the Racial Anxiety in the United States, 1848–82* [Urbana: University of Illinois Press, 2006], 10).

14. In the 1857 *Dred Scott v. Sandford* case, Justice Roger Taney spoke of "Indian governments . . . as foreign governments, as much so as if an ocean had separated the red man from the white" (quoted in David Wilkins, *American Indian Politics and the American Political System* [New York: Rowman and Littlefield, 2002], 52).

15. Liestman, "Horizontal Inter-Ethnic Relations," 342.

16. Quoted in Robert Heizer and Alan Almquist, *The Other Californians: Prejudice and Discrimination under Spain, Mexico, and the United States to 1920* (Berkeley: University of California Press, 1977), 224. In 1851, individuals with at least one-quarter "Indian" blood could not testify in state civil cases. In 1863, the law was modified to apply to those with at least one-half "Indian" blood. In 1872, all "Indians" were allowed to testify.

17. As Charles McClain notes, "The ban . . . applied only to the state courts. The United States District Court for the Northern District of California had begun to receive Chinese testimony on an unrestricted basis as early as 1851 and continued to do so throughout the period" (*In Search of Equality: The Chinese Struggle against Discrimination in Nineteenth-Century America* [Berkeley: University of California Press, 1996], 23).

18. Quoted in Heizer and Almquist, *The Other Californians,* 230.

19. Ibid., 230–31.

20. Ibid., 230.

21. Joy Harjo, "There Is No Such Thing as a One-Way Land Bridge," in *Native Voices: American Indian Identity and Resistance,* ed. Richard Grouns, George Tinker, and David Wilkins (Lawrence: University Press of Kansas, 2003), 243–44.

22. Without the racial category "Indian," Judge Murray still could ban Chinese testimony through his interpretation of the term "black." As Aarim-Herrot explains: "Citing the 1850 California criminal statute that provided that 'no black . . . shall be allowed to give evidence in favor, or against, a white man,' Murray argued that the framers of the statue used 'black' as a generic term. . . . He concluded that while 'white' excluded black, yellow, and all other colors, the term *black* should be construed as the opposite of white or Caucasian. Excluding blacks therefore entailed the debarment of all non-Caucasians" (*Chinese Immigrants,* 44).

23. Daniel Kanstroom, *Deportation Nation: Outsiders in American History* (Cambridge: Harvard University Press, 2007), 99.

24. Quoted in McClain, *In Search of Equality,* 21, 22. In *Speer v. See Yup Co.* (1859), the California Supreme Court also banned Chinese testimony against whites in civil cases.

25. Heizer and Almquist, *The Other Californians,* 200.

26. Leigh-Wai Doo, *Dispute Settlement in Chinatown* (Cambridge: Harvard Law School, 1973), 631.

27. Quoted in McClain, *In Search of Equality,* 22.

28. Ibid., 38.

29. Takaki, *Strangers from a Different Shore,* 115.

30. Kanstroom, *Deportation Nation,* 99.

31. Liestman, "Horizontal Inter-Ethnic Relations," 346, 330, 349.

32. Devon Mihesuah and Angela Cavender Wilson, *Indigenizing the Academy: Transforming Scholarship and Empowering Communities* (Lincoln, Neb.: Bison Books, 2004), 233.

33. Joy Harjo, "Letter from the End of the Twentieth Century," *The Woman Who Fell from the Sky: Poems* (New York: Norton, 1996), 38.

34. Rachel Buff, *Immigration and the Political Economy of Home: West Indian Brooklyn and American Indian Minneapolis, 1945–1992* (Berkeley: University of California Press, 2001), 7.

35. Frank Wu, *Yellow: Race in America beyond Black and White* (New York: Basic Books, 2003), 315.

PRIMARY SOURCE

People v. Hall, 1854

Dustin Tahmakera argues that the silencing effects of this case migrated from indigenous peoples to Asian immigrants. The racialized language used to describe both Chinese immigrants and American Indians was a component of an evolving social order in mid-nineteenth-century California and the United States as a whole. Twenty-one years before the Page Act initiated the exclusion of Asian immigrants, this case set legal precedents, as well as ratifying a racialized inequality among inhabitants of the United States.

THE PEOPLE, RESPONDENT, V. GEORGE W. HALL, APPELLANT.
Supreme Court of the State of California, 1854.

Mr. Ch. J. Murray delivered the opinion of the Court. Mr. J. Heydenfeldt concurred.

The appellant, a free white citizen of this State, was convicted of murder upon the testimony of Chinese witnesses.

The point involved in this case is the admissibility of such evidence.

The 394th section of the Act Concerning Civil Cases provides that no Indian or Negro shall be allowed to testify as a witness in any action or proceeding in which a white person is a party.

The 14th section of the Act of April 16th, 1850, regulating Criminal Proceedings, provides that "No black or mulatto person, or Indian, shall be allowed to give evidence in favor of, or against a white man."

The true point at which we are anxious to arrive is the legal signification of the words "black, mulatto, Indian, and white person," and whether the Legislature adopted them as generic terms, or intended to limit their application to specific types of the human species. . . .

The Act of Congress, in defining that description of aliens may become naturalized citizens, provides that every "free white citizen," etc. . . .

If the term "white," as used in the Constitution, was not understood in its generic sense as including the Caucasian race, and necessarily excluding all others, where was the necessary of providing for the admission of Indians to the privilege of voting, by special legislation?

We are of the opinion that the words "white," "Negro," "mulatto," "Indian," and "black person," wherever they occur in our Constitution and laws, must be taken in their generic sense, and that, even admitting the Indian of this continent is not of the Mongolian type, that the words "black person," in the 14th section, must be taken as contradistinguished from white, and necessarily excludes all races other than the Caucasian.

We have carefully considered all the consequences resulting from a different rule of construction, and are satisfied that even in a doubtful case, we would be impelled to this decision on ground of public policy.

The same rule which would admit them to testify, would admit them to all the equal rights of citizenship, and we might soon see them at the polls, in the jury box, upon the bench, and in our legislative halls.

This is not a speculation which exists in the excited and overheated imagination of the patriot and statesman, but it is an actual and present danger.

The anomalous spectacle of a distinct people, living in our community, recognizing no laws of this State, except through necessity, bringing with them their prejudices and national feuds, in which they indulge in open violation of law; whose medacity is proverbial; a race of people whom nature has marked as inferior, and who are incapable of progress or intellectual development beyond a certain point, as their history has shown; differing in language, opinions, color, and physical conformation; between whom and ourselves nature has placed an impassable difference, is now presented, and for them is claimed, not only the right to swear away the life of a citizen, but the further privilege of participating with us in administering the affairs of our Government.

These facts were before the Legislature that framed this Act, and have been known as matters of public history to every subsequent Legislature.

There can be no doubt as to the intention of Legislature, and that if it had ever been anticipated that this class of people were not embraced in the prohibition, then such specific words would have been employed as would have put the matter beyond any possible controversy.

For these reasons, we are of opinion that the testimony was inadmissible.

The judgment is reversed and the cause remanded.

CHAPTER 6

A History of Black Immigration into the United States through the Lens of the African American Civil and Human Rights Struggle

The Africana Cultures and Policy Studies Institute: Zachery Williams, Robert Samuel Smith, Seneca Vaught, and Babacar M'Baye

Long before the controversy over the militarization of the U.S.-Mexico border, national origins quotas, and a national identification system, the nation faced a problem with undesirable Black immigrants. Even though the issue was introduced by a European initiative in the Americas, Black immigration has historically been perceived as being culturally invasive and distinctly alien. To be a Black immigrant is to be subject to a rigid set of attitudes, assumptions, and policies with regard to culture and place. Much of this legacy is owed and directly attributable to the era of slavery and slave trading. Discourse on Black migration was linked to the forced migration by the African slave trade until more recent scholarship revised such antiquated approaches. In fact, Black diasporic immigration was hampered by the "invisibility, nonparticipation, passiveness, immobility, and homogeneity often attributed to them in the literature."[1]

Voluntary immigration on the part of Black populations has garnered less attention than the migrations of other racial and ethnic groups in scholarship. Even less scholarly attention has been aimed at Black, multiethnic solidarity as an extension of Black immigrant and native Black sociocultural and political exchange. Yet, against these social odds, Black immigrants in the United States have found ways to unite and resist the prejudice they have faced internally and within the broader American society. Similarly, with major spikes in Black immigration numbers, new scholarship has emerged, making room for a more balanced depiction of Black immigration patterns and intergroup relations between native Black Americans and Black diasporic immigrants to the United States.

Using three case studies, in this essay we discuss, first, the history of Black immigration to the United States and the impact of American policy of alienation. Second, we explore the contributions of Caribbean immigrants to the history of African American civil and human rights struggles. Third, we examine the current relations between East African immigrants and African Americans in King County, Seattle. Fourth, we show how Charlotte, North Carolina, poses an interesting example of interaction between native Blacks and diasporic immigrants stemming from a burgeoning, urban, center in the contemporary South.

"Why Increase the Sons of Africa?": Black Immigrants and the American Policy of Perpetual Alienation

Revealing a deep concern about the issues of Black immigration through the transatlantic slave trade, which was remarkably different in character than that of the present, Benjamin Franklin wrote, "Why Increase the Sons of Africa, by Planting them in America, where we have so fair an Opportunity, by excluding all Blacks and Tawneys, of increasing the lovely White and Red?"[2] At the heart of colonial immigration policy for Blacks, Franklin revealed a horrible predicament. The American project, an emerging nation destined for revolutionary processes of acculturation and assimilation, had no place for Blacks, whose culture and color seemed too defiling and whose numbers were too threatening for the American colonies to absorb.[3]

Yet, the introduction of such a racially identifiable and cheap—indeed, free—labor force dramatically altered social conditions by injecting a direct threat to the cultivation of white supremacy in a fledging nation. Such labor patterns would make for interracial hostilities between poor whites and Blacks but would simultaneously produce the ingredients for multiclass, multiracial cohesion, despite the racial antipathy encouraged by America's codification of Black racial inferiority.

Moreover, Blacks have historically remained distinctly alien and illegal when they attempt to mainstream themselves as citizens. The host of early American policy that sought to restrict the movement and importation of Blacks was essentially immigration policy (e.g., the Fugitive Slave Act of 1793 and prohibition of the slave trade in 1808). Yet, as the system of domestic slave trading peaked in the United States, European immigration patterns had already begun to impact the employment status of free Blacks. As early as 1820, free Black artisans of New York City were "relegated to more menial trades such as longshoremen, white-washers, domestic servants, and boot-blacks," due in large part to the migratory patterns of Irish immigrants.[4]

Indeed, during the 1830s, most domestic servants in New York City were African American. Yet, by the 1850s, most were Irish. Such "discrimination" in favor of non-Black immigrants was not lost on Black spokespersons. As Frederick Douglas remarked, "every hour sees the black man elbowed out of employment by some newly arrived emigrant, whose hunger and whose color are thought to give him a better title to the place."[5]

In the nineteenth century, discourses of Black migration reflected the alienation and exclusion of African Americans from mainstream national life. Repatriation, the policy of sending Blacks back to Africa, was regularly articulated by both Blacks and Whites, but for different reasons.[6] In defiance of immigration policies designed to curtail their freedom and mobility, Blacks developed counterstrategies, policies, and emigration movements. Blacks chartered their own course of African repatriation and colonization, relocated to Canada via the mechanism of the Underground Railroad and Florida during the eighteenth and nineteenth centuries, and aggressively argued for full citizenship in a nation still clinging to race-based enslavement.[7]

Despite the policy-derived and socially constructed patterns of exclusion aimed at Blacks, something distinctly American was to endure. The melding of multiple cultural facets of the African diaspora into a Black American experience would forever maintain justification for Black permanence in the United States. Commenting on this historical irony in his classic early-twentieth-century work on immigration, *Our Foreigners,* Samuel Peter Orth discovered that by 1920 Blacks were American immigrants but not *really* American:

> The negro's melodies, his dialect, and his banjo, have always been identified with America. Even Americans do not at once think of the negro as a foreigner, so accustomed have they become to his presence, to his quaint mythology, his soft accent, and his genial and accommodating nature. . . . The negro, however, is racially the most distinctly foreign element in America. He belongs to a period of biological and racial evolution far removed from that of the white man.[8]

Since Blacks have historically been considered foreign within America, their movements into, outside and within the borders can and should be discussed as an act of immigration. Movement of Africans *within* America has usually been associated with some form of protest, resistance, or response to local conditions. During and immediately after World War I, following a northern demand for labor, over 1 million Black southerners migrated to the North and another 1.5 million relocated to the North each decade from 1940 to 1970.[9] This regional move was nearly as significant to the culture and character of Black southerners as international migration was to other ethnic groups traversing the Atlantic.

Examining movements of the African American post-transatlantic slave trade experience as immigration policy also reveals much about the "imagined communities" of American nationalism(s).[10] While the importation or forced immigration of American Blacks into the British North American colonies was a small fraction of the overall distribution to the Caribbean and South America, it is ironic that the very process through which Africans (e.g., Ibo, Wolof, Yoruba, et al.) were brought in served to exclude them under the categorization of Black from the rest of American society. This artificial homogenization, which has had numerous cultural effects on the development of white identity and nationalism in the United States, is essentially an immigration policy.

Whereas historical factors in the twentieth century have created a tension between Black city dwellers and white ethnic immigrants, additional forces of white flight and gentrification pose significant glimpses into the continued trends of the immigration of American Blacks.[11] The situation of African Americans has historically been tied to those of incoming streams of immigrants and in a racial climate and culture prone to increasing tension and economic competition between "assimilable" ethnic communities and Blacks—a process now further complicated by charges of internecine tensions between African Americans and new Black immigrants.[12]

Cultural Influences of Caribbean Immigrants on African American Civil and Human Rights Struggles

What would the American civil rights and freedom movements be without the contributions of countless known and unknown migrants from various areas of the Caribbean islands and the Spanish Caribbean? Historian Irma Watkins-Owens offers that the majority of residents in Harlem, New York, in 1915 originated from the following areas: Jamaica, Barbados, Montserrat, Antigua, Bermuda, the Bahamas, the Virgin Islands, Martinique, Haiti, Guadeloupe, Puerto Rico, Cuba, Panama, Suriname, and others. Watkins-Owens goes on to say that most immigrants, once arrived, chose to settle "in already existing or evolving African American communities."[13]

Once settled in those particular communities, many West Indian migrants passed on the virtues of obtaining a good education, maintaining a strong work ethic, pursuing excellence, providing discipline, respecting elders, and focusing on sustaining a keen ethnic identity. But second-generation and third-generation West Indians have struggled to maintain a sense of identity in a country that exhibits a tendency to place all people of African descent into one category: Black. The spatial location of the United States confronts young West Indians, in particular, with a sort of double consciousness whereby they attempt to forge a muted Caribbean identity in reconciliation with anti-Black discrimination and racism.

In response, 40 percent choose a Black American identity, 30 percent choose a West Indian ethnic affiliation, and the remaining 30 percent exist as merely "immigrants." Many who took on a West Indian ethnic orientation eschewed the realities of white racism against Blacks, as well as noticeable affiliations with the latter, choosing instead to emphasize the ideals of education, work ethic, and desire over and above pan-African linkages. The last group adheres to the immigrant label without pressure to immediately assimilate to either end of the white/Black race binary. In New York, for instance, the latter two groups have identified themselves based on their ethnic affiliation as Trinidadians, Grenadians, and Jamaicans. In each sense, both assimilation and acculturation processes fuse with transnational cultural customs and continually influence overall identity.[14]

Caribbean immigration to the United States evidenced a continuous flow into the United States. It developed in four distinct phases. Phase one occurred during the seventeenth century, due mainly to the enslavement of Barbadians in South Carolina. Phase two of occurred around the turn of the twentieth century, as a considerable influx of British West Indian migrants inhabited various locales of the United States. Phase three, the years 1930 to 1965, witnessed a resurgent increase in Caribbean migration to the nation, following a previous lull due to racist congressional legislation. Since World War II, Caribbean immigration has increased and reflected more diverse points of origin. During phase four, after 1965, the nation's immigration policy reflected an even greater growth of Caribbean peoples. Regardless of whether these new arrivals identified with the resident black population, what is certain is that many maintained some sense of historical, cultural, and ethnic connection.[15]

Perhaps the most important contribution of Caribbean migrants and their descendants to African American freedom struggles has been through participation and leadership of various social movements, most notably during the twentieth century. The list includes countless persons. Jamaican-born Marcus Mosiah Garvey was responsible for developing and leading the largest mass movement of people of African descent, and the Honorable Elijah Muhammad, Malcolm X, and Louis Farrakhan built on the Universal Negro Improvement Association (UNIA) to undergird twentieth-century efforts of Black nationalism. The scholarly community has been enriched by the contributions of noted thinkers and activists such as W. E. B. Du Bois, Hubert Harrison, Richard B. Moore, Claude McKay, Shirley Chisholm, Paule Marshall, June Jordan, Audre Lorde, Michele Wallace, and many others.[16]

Du Bois, pan-Africanist and leading twentieth-century intellectual, greatly influenced the global Black civil and human rights struggle. He also had significant Caribbean roots, as his father, Alfred, hailed from Haiti. Du Bois himself spent a lifetime working to unite displaced peoples of African descent via his writings, activism with numerous pan-African congresses, and nurturing of relationships with intellectuals and cultural workers on the African continent and throughout the diaspora.[17]

Born in St. Croix in 1883, self-styled Harlem intellectual Hubert Harrison, contemporary to Du Bois, McKay, and Garvey, worked as editor of the UNIA's *Negro World,* while also serving as New York commissioner of education. Harrison spoke and wrote on themes pertaining to black radicalism, civil rights, and socialism, and he contributed to noted periodicals of the day from the *Messenger,* the *Call,* the *New York World,* and the *New York Times.* In fact, Harrison's Black radicalism, most evidenced in his "race first" slogan, inspired the work of Garvey, A. Philip Randolph, and Chandler Owen.

Jamaican-born writer and poet Claude McKay became one of the most important voices of the Harlem Renaissance, penning two autobiographies, *A Long Way from Home* (1937) and *Harlem: Negro Metropolis* (1940); three novels; and two books of poetry, *Harlem Shadows* (1922) and the posthumous *Selected Poems* (1953). While attending school in Charleston, South Carolina, McKay was exposed to very intense racism, prompting the accelerated formation of his racial consciousness. This consciousness was further ignited as McKay read Du Bois's *Souls of Black Folk*

Caribbean immigrant intellectual Richard B. Moore, was born in Barbados in 1893. Moore was a member of the Communist Party USA before being expelled in 1942. His cultural politics also included lecturing and writing for various news outlets and he served as vice president of the West Indies' National Council; he also owned the Frederick Douglass bookstore in New York.[18]

Shirley Chisholm, born to a Barbadian mother and a Guyanese father, became an uncompromising champion for civil and human rights for people of African descent, serving as the influential congresswoman of New York's twelfth district. In addition to her straight talk, bold leadership, and audacious personality, Chisholm became the first African American woman elected to Congress in 1968 and the very first African American to make a serious run for the presidency of the United States in 1972.

Paule Marshall, a child of Barbadian parents, went on to become one of the most celebrated novelists of her time. In addition to early poetic pieces, Marshall became known for her signature stories of black life and culture, including *Brown Girl, Brownstones.*[19]

June Jordan, political activist, professor of African American studies, writer, and essayist, was born to Jamaican immigrant parents. Jordan's activism infused the Black studies movement with her courageous political writings and autobiographical reflections. Audre Lorde, born in 1934 to West Indian parents, was significantly involved in the civil rights, feminist, and antiwar movements of the 1960s and 1970s. As an influential poet and cultural critic, Lorde was not afraid to address controversial subjects such as love and lesbianism. Openly embracing her sexual identity, she affirmed her own personal politics and spoke to a community wrestling with what had been a taboo subject.

Michele Wallace, professor, author, and daughter of noted artist Faith Ringgold, penned perhaps the signal piece of Black feminist criticism, *Myth of the Black Superwoman,* which took to task evident sexism in the Black nationalist movement.[20]

Harry Belafonte and Stokely Carmichael infused the civil rights and Black power movement with a good deal of its ideological force. Belafonte, of Jamaican background, has been an important cultural ambassador throughout his life and career, beginning as a noted calypso singer and voice for civil rights and equality for oppressed peoples the world over. Belafonte was influenced by the example of Paul Robeson in terms of his adherence to Black cultural politics and support of civil and human rights causes. Stokely Carmichael, later in his life known as Kwame Ture, was one of the signal leaders of the Student Non-violent Coordinating Committee (SNCC) under the leadership of visionary activist Ella Baker. After experiencing growing disillusionment with perceived gradualist tactics of civil rights leaders, Carmichael led the movement of youthful civil rights workers clamoring for Black power. Even though Congressman Adam Clayton Powell Jr. is first credited with coining the term, Carmichael, who studied briefly at Howard University, is centrally identified as one of the seminal figures of the movement. He, among other leaders, is largely credited with internationalizing the term Black as a form of popular identity.[21]

Many of these figures represent instances where sons and daughters of Caribbean immigrants have worked in tandem with African Americans to advance social movements and common goals. In addition to civil rights and Black power, pan-Africanism and hip-hop culture would be decidedly different without the central impact of Afro-Caribbean influences functioning alongside African American ones. Following Garvey's lead with the Universal Negro Improvement Association, in 1934, Elijah Muhammad continued the work of Master W. D. Fard Muhammad to strengthen the parallel movement of the Nation of Islam, emphasizing a synthesis of Islam, Christianity, and elements of cultural symbolism. This movement of religious nationalism, designed to liberate the minds and beings of Black people in North America from centuries of oppression, was continued by two disciples of Muhammad, Malcolm X and Louis Farrakhan.

Malcolm, whose parents were active Garveyites, was initially baptized into the politics of Black nationalism as a child. His mother, having been born in Grenada, further solidified his Afro-Caribbean genealogical links. After the assassination of his father by members of the Ku Klux Klan in 1931, Malcolm's family was further disrupted by his mother's mental illness. Sent to foster care, Malcolm was subjected to increasing levels of white supremacy, eventually leading him to a life of crime. In this sense, Malcolm was deprived of the highly affirming familial life of Afro-Caribbean religio-cultural nationalism and was left without both a father and a mother to nurture his continued maturation. Elijah Muhammad provided the missing connection of a paternal example that Malcolm longed for. In 1952, after a stint in prison, Malcolm joined the Nation of Islam and soon became the national minister and assistant to Muhammad. With Malcolm's leadership and dedication, he injected tremendous growth into the organization, as the main spokesman for Muhammad. Even with the painful personal and ideological rift that separated the two, their collective influence on the cultural psyche of activists pressing for twentieth-century and twenty-first-century Black civil and human rights activists is undeniable.[22]

Malcolm's protégé and Muhammad's pupil, Louis Farrakhan, also had deep Caribbean roots. Farrakhan's mother emigrated from St. Kitts and Nevis, and his father was a Jamaican immigrant. The effect of the teachings of Elijah Muhammad and the example of Malcolm impressed Farrakhan so much so that he became a member of the Nation of Islam in July 1955. Farrakhan's impact on the nation increased after Malcolm was assassinated in February 1965. In 1977, after the death of Elijah Muhammad in 1975, Farrakhan revived the original structure of the Nation of Islam, embarking on path that would see the organization rise again to levels of prominence of the years that Malcolm served a national minister. Most recently, Farrakhan spearheaded the Million Man, Million Family, and the Millions More movements. The effect of Malcolm and Farrakhan on Black cultural life and politics remains strong to this day, despite a lingering controversy over the involvement of Farrakhan on Malcolm's assassination.[23]

To be sure, much has been made about the enduring and often troublesome relationship among Afro-Caribbeans and African Americans. Considering the lineage of most current African Americans, it is apparent that Caribbean immigration has played a monumental role in the biological and cultural construction of African American people from slavery to the present day. In light of that fact, the reality of the matter provides a complex set of relationships that deserve careful and close analysis rather than reliance on mere conjecture and stereotype. One aspect of this complexity is discovered in the relations between Afro-Caribbean and recent African immigrants as they seek assimilation into American society. Many have come to the realization of a conflict between myths and realities of racism, thus injecting a measure of unsettling and abrupt racial consciousness into their cultural psyche. Upon arrival in the United States, Caribbean immigrants, many from the West Indies, have harbored visions of a color-blind America, due in large measure to prior experiences of low levels of racial tension in their homeland regions.[24]

Based on this previous experience, as well as on overblown stereotypes about American Blacks, some West Indians have, on occasion, asserted that African Americans are too preoccupied with race, only to find out through personal experience the all-too-painful effects of racism on anyone of African descent with dark skin, whether born in the United States or abroad. "Over time," Milton Vickerman writes, "continued exposure to racial discrimination causes many West Indians to shift their paradigm from a nonracial one to one that is more explicitly racial."[25] Vickerman elaborates on his original point:

> By this, one means that West Indians: (1) come to understand that race permeates all facets of American life; (2) expect to have unpleasant encounters because of race, and (3) often become pessimistic that the United States will become "colorblind" anytime soon. In other words, the understanding that they may have had about race prior to migrating goes from being fairly abstract to being experiential and more consciously life-shaping.[26]

In evaluating such findings, one can conclude that the exposure and experience of racism socializes West Indian migrants to the same reality understood by most American-born Blacks, which is that race matters, as Cornel West opined. The same bias and criticism can also be applied to other Afro-Caribbean immigrants who once espoused similar beliefs of a color-blind America.[27]

There is no question that the salience of American race and racism has contributed, one way or another, to the linkage of Caribbean Americans to African American struggles for civil and human rights. Whether some were drawn by the exigencies of civil rights, Black power, and the Black women's movement—or repelled by them—none were immune to the manner in which their race would change their American experience.[28]

Relationships between East African Immigrants and African Americans in Seattle's Central District

The relations between African immigrants and African Americans is a taboo subject, because it unfolds unexplored conflicts between two groups that tend to emphasize differences of cultures and language rather than common links. A few examples of such conflicts are noticeable in Seattle's Central District, where troubling incidents that occurred in the summer of 2006 brought East African immigrants and African Americans at odds against each other. This area of the South Puget Sound is home to 30,000 to 40,000 East Africans, including Ethiopians, Eritreans, and Somalis.[29]

This population is quite sizable in comparison with that of African Americans in King County which, in the 2000 census, was estimated at 93,875.[30] Yet tensions arose between the two groups, raising central issues that can be understood only when the taboos and spirit of solidarity between the two communities are exposed.

The *Seattle Post-Intelligencer* reports that on July 12, 2006, an African American woman shot an Ethiopian cab driver named Berhane Haile, who was nearby, when she and three African American men attacked Zenebe Worota, another East African cab driver who had told them that he could not take them on a ride because he was on a break. This tragic incident brought the African Americans and East Africans of Seattle's Central District together as they attempted to bridge the misunderstanding that weakens their relationships. Among the African American leaders, Charlie James, a longtime activist in Seattle, made honest remarks addressing the tension between African Americans and East Africans in Seattle while pointing out the need for collaboration between the two groups. At a meeting between members of the two communities held in the Urban League of Metropolitan Seattle on July 20, 2006, James located the divide between the two groups in the assumptions that some African Americans make about African immigrants. He said:

> The appearance of success (among recent African immigrants). . . . People (immigrants) are opening businesses. They're coming into areas that are dilapidated and run down and revitalizing it. . . . The perception is they have access to resources outside of America. . . . Some African Americans see themselves as having been left out, and people who have been in Kenya (and other African countries) don't understand the African American struggle.[31]

These perceptions do not represent the views of all African Americans. Yet, they are pervasive among African Americans who view Africans as people who pretend to be better them.

In an interview with Robert William and his friend, two African Americans sitting at a table in an Ethiopian restaurant of Seattle called the Blue Nile, World radio correspondent Chana Joffe-Walt learned what the two persons think of African immigrants: "They think when they get out here [that] they are better than African Americans that live here already and who have been here." His anonymous friend added: "Because all you have to do is once they look at you. You know what they think of you 'I am better than you!' 'You are nothing.'"[32] This interview shows that the perception of some African Americans toward Africans is based on fear and prejudice rooted in the assumption that African immigrants think they have more stable families and connections to Africa than African American have. This stereotype is sometimes fed by many African immigrants themselves, who easily internalize the prejudice that many European Americans have toward African Americans, such as the notion that many African Americans celebrate violence, carry guns, play basketball, and have no connections with Africa.

In an interview with Chido Nwangwu and Charlie James, news correspondent Phyllis Fletcher of Seattle radio station KUOW uncovered some of the other stereotypes of many African immigrants toward African Americans. Nwangwu is a Nigerian and the founder and publisher of USAfricaonline.com, which is the first and most respected African-owned and U.S.-based newspaper to be published on the internet. He said that many Africans look at African Americans with condescension and view them as being less human than them.

Such stereotypes that both groups have toward each other prevent them from knowing and appreciating their shared cultural heritage and history of resistance against oppression. Furthermore, while many Africans respect this heritage, study it, and even teach it in American universities, others greatly need to learn and value the history of resistance and struggle against racism and discrimination of African Americans. As Bill Fletcher, the founder of Trans-Africa, pointed out, the divide between African Americans and African immigrants can be resolved "only if African immigrants are educated on the racial dynamics in the U.S." and if African Americans begin to "de-demonize Africa."[33]

Charlotte, N.C.: Post–Civil Rights Era Possibilities in an Urban City in the Contemporary South

North Carolina, like most of the nation, has received a large influx of Latino immigrants since the early 1990s. While North Carolina's immigrant demography does not reflect the higher-end threshold as other states, the numbers are staggering nonetheless.[34] However, amid the robust entry of Latinos has been a quieter, though significant, steady trickling of African and Caribbean immigrants to the Queen City. Charlotte's growth as a city and its ever-rising influence as a southern metropolis make it an interesting place to explore the connectedness of diasporic immigrants and native Blacks.

Charlotte has emerged as an economically viable southern urban space, encouraging and stimulating various related immigration trends. The city is home to a vibrant corporate community, stabilized largely by the banking industry, and it offers a booming housing market. Such economic developments have pulled large numbers of economically mobile Blacks to the city, increasing its native Black population from the resulting remigration of African Americans to southern locales.[35] Next, Charlotte can brag of having a simmering civil rights community, with holdovers serving as leaders of post–civil rights era legal developments.[36] Leaders of this community openly encourage interdiasporic cultural cooperation and collaboration. Finally, Charlotte's Black immigrant communities have forged key institutions to help stabilize and support one another. Collectively, these social networks and conditions could breed successful, domestically bound, transnational linkages.

Census data show that of the nearly one million African immigrants in the United States, more than 50 percent entered and settled in the country between 1990 and 2000. While some have charged that the numbers are underreported by hundreds of thousands, the 40,000 African immigrants arriving annually suggest one basic reality: more African immigrants are finding their way to the United States, particularly to metropolitan areas.[37] In Charlotte, African immigrants total roughly 4,700 citizens, with Caribbean immigrants hovering around 2,500. These numbers seem too low for effective comparative analysis, but the presence of these immigrant populations and the social networks and institutions they have created provide room for critique.

As in many communities, diasporic immigrants to Charlotte have created culturally specific clubs and organizations, as well as important sociocultural programming that emphasizes their cultural distinctiveness. Economically, the entrepreneurial, medical, and corporate presence of diasporic immigrants is obvious. And, through the efforts of Charlotte's International House, which works with nearly all of the city's immigrant communities, many of the legalities facing immigrants are effectively managed. These organizations provide social support services and community empowerment to the African immigrant community. However, the key development has been the recent push to coordinate intradiasporic dialogues, relationships, and culturally based activities to promote broader awareness and interaction between native Blacks and diasporic immigrants.

In recent years, several grassroots organizations have emerged whose aims are to connect the local African diaspora communities housed in the Queen City.[38] These fledgling organizations have maintained momentum largely because the immigrant community leaders are well educated, economically stable, and politically well-connected spokespersons. Similarly, the native Black leaders in direct contact with the immigrant leadership are comparably educated, with some serving as university faculty, and economically stable. And, the native Black leadership advancing a diaspora-based social agenda includes former civil rights attorneys, former sit-in leaders, and former social activists in general. In subsequent years, Charlotte, North Carolina, might emerge as a leader in intradiasporic group connectedness. The foundation for such success is indeed already in place.

Conclusion

Despite the current tension revealed between African American and Black African and Caribbean immigrants, the history of the second generation of Black immigrants into the United States folds in the same dilemma of Black Americans in the historical and political trajectory of American society. Yet, the experiences of Black African and Caribbean immigrants reveal a distinct set of problems that complicate the already existing scenario with African Americans. The immigration policy toward Black Africans, already disadvantaged by a lack of resources that could help them come to the United States, raises serious questions about the future role of the historical trajectory of perpetual alienation as the unequal practices of racial discrimination at the borders remain.

Recommendations:

- A scholarly push to emphasize community-based diasporic relations is needed. The injection of digestible diasporic literature can encourage social education and awareness to complement the work of community-based organizations.
- In cities experiencing recent spikes in Black immigrants, more community programming and initiatives emphasizing interconnectedness of distinctiveness of diasporic populations are desperately needed.
- Collaborative corporate involvement with social programming will be useful. As more and more companies have begun to welcome a more diversified vision and mission, such programming will be of interest.

NOTES

1. Roy Simon Bryce-Laporte, "Voluntary Immigration and Continuing Encounters between Blacks," in *The Immigration Reader: American in a Multidisciplinary Perspective,* ed. David Jacobson (New York: Blackwell, 1998), 183.

2. Benjamin Franklin, "Observations Concerning the Increase of Mankind," in *Autobiography and Other Writings,* ed. Ormond Seavey (New York: Oxford University Press, 1998), 260.

3. The number of Blacks in the colonies is estimated at 59,000 in 1714, according to Sidney Mary Sitwell, *The Growth of the English Colonies* (London: Rivingtons, 1884), 62. Citing Bancroft, Orth contends that the numbers increased to 78,000 in 1727, to 263,000 in 1754, and to 697,624 in 1790 (Samuel Peter Orth, *Our Foreigners: A Chronicle of Americans in the Making* [New Haven, Conn.: Yale University Press, 1920], 47). This increase, according to Orth, "was not due alone to the fecundity of the negro. It was due, in large measure, to the unceasing slave trade" (47). These numbers marked the effect of the Black colonial "immigration" policy.

4. Quoted in Jeff Diamond, "African American Attitudes toward United States Immigration Policy," *International Migration Review,* 32/2 (Summer 1998), 452. Douglas, while frustrated over the dislocation of Black workers, was a proponent of fair and open immigration policy. Such stances by liberal, civil, and human rights advocates would be consistent over the next two centuries and into the new millennium. Black leaders regularly supported nonbiased immigration policy, despite

the clear conflict among Blacks and other working-class populations, white and nonwhite.

5. Ibid.

6. Some philanthropists and Blacks wanted to return to Africa as a humane policy of emancipation. Others endorsed this policy of emigration as a means to rid the blossoming American nation of disproportionate numbers of Blacks. Sending free Blacks to Africa was also a response to the growing numbers of German and Irish immigrants and to the national impulse to make the complexion of the nation a white one (Eric Burin, *Slavery and the Peculiar Solution: A History of the American Colonization Society,* [Gainesville: University Press of Florida, 2005]).

7. A discussion of these Black émigrés, referred to as *estelusti,* is in Daniel F. Littlefield, *Africans and Seminoles: From Removal to Emancipation* (Jackson: Banner Books, University Press of Mississippi, 2001), 4–6. Others returned to the continent of Africa.

8. Orth, *Our Foreigners,* 45–46.

9. Eric Arnesen, *Black Protest and the Great Migration: A Brief History with Documents* (Boston: Bedford/St. Martin's, 2003), 1, 36.

10. The use of the term "imagined communities" is in reference to the concept discussed by Benedict Anderson that suggests, in his words, "the members of even the smallest nation will never know most of their fellow-members, meet them, or even hear of them, yet in the minds of each lives the image of their communion" (*Imagined Communities: Reflections on the Origin and Spread of Nationalism,* rev. ed. [New York: Verso, 1991], 6). Anderson argues that nations are imagined as limited, sovereign, and a community.

11. Forecasting future conflict between African Americans and European Americans while typecasting both, Orth stated: "His [the African American's] happy-go-lucky ways, his easy philosophy of life, the remarkable ease with which he severs home ties and shifts from place to place, his indifference to property obligations—these negative defects in his character may easily lead to his economic doom if the vigorous peasantry of Italy and other lands are brought into competition with him" (*Our Foreigners,* 65).

12. For a controversial and important discussion of the assimilation politics among Blacks and other immigrants, see Nathan Glazer and Daniel P. Moynihan, *Beyond the Melting Pot: The Negroes, Puerto Ricans, Jews, Italians, and Irish of New York City,* 2nd ed. (Cambridge: MIT Press, 1974). On the emerging problems of inassimilability, see Matthew Frye Jacobson, *Roots Too: White Ethnic Revival in Post-Civil Rights America* (Cambridge: Harvard University Press, 2006), 180–83. The Fourteenth Amendment granted citizenship to Blacks born in the United States and did not extend the same privilege to those born in the Caribbean or Africa.

Perhaps this was the first dividing wedge between future debates between Black Caribbean immigrants and American-born Blacks. A discussion of grievances between Africans and African Americans is taken up in Godfrey Mwakikagile, *Relations between Africans and African Americans: Misconceptions, Myths and Realities* (Johannesburg, South Africa: Continental Press, 2006), esp. 94–99.

13. Irma Watkins-Owens, *Blood Relations: Caribbean Immigrants and the Harlem Community, 1900–1930* (Bloomington: Indiana University Press, 1996), 2, 4.

14. Holger Henke, *The West Indians* (Westport, Conn.: Greenwood, 2001), 129–31; Mary C. Waters, *Black Identities: West Indian Immigrant Dreams and American Realities* (Cambridge: Harvard University Press, 1999), 48–49.

15. Howard Dodson and Sylviane Diouf, *In Motion: The African American Migration Experience* (Washington, D.C.: National Geographic Society, 2004), 162; Center for AfroAmerican and African Studies, *Black Immigration and Ethnicity in the United States: An Annotated* Bibliography. Westport, Conn.: Greenwood, 1985. For a brilliant study of Caribbean immigration to colonial South Carolina, see Peter H. Wood, *Black Majority: Negroes in Colonial South Carolina from 1670 through the Stono Rebellion* (New York: Norton, 1996).

16. Watkins-Owens, *Blood Relations,* 92, 149; Winston James, *Holding Aloft the Banner of Ethiopia: Caribbean Radicalism in Early Twentieth-Century Radicalism* (New York: Verso, 1998).

17. David Levering-Lewis, *W. E. B. Du Bois: Biography of a Race, 1868–1919* (New York: Henry Holt, 1993); Levering-Lewis, *W. E. B. Du Bois: The Fight for Equality and the American Century, 1919–1963* (New York: Henry Holt, 2000).

18. Jeffrey B. Perry, ed., *A Hubert Harrison Reader* (Middletown, Conn.: Wesleyan University Press, 2001), 1–30; W. Burghardt Turner and Joyce Moore Turner, eds., *Richard B. Moore, Caribbean Militant in Harlem: Collected Writings, 1920–1972* (Bloomington: University of Indiana Press, 1988).

19. Jill Pollack, *Shirley Chisholm* (New York: F. Watts, 1994); Dorothy Hamer Denniston, *The Fiction of Paule Marshall: Reconstructions of History, Culture, and Gender* (Knoxville: University of Tennessee Press, 1995), 8–32.

20. Valerie Kinloch, *June Jordan: Her Life and Letters* (Westport, Conn.: Praeger, 2006); June Jordan, *Some of Us Did Not Die: New and Selected* Essays (New York: Basic Civitas, 2002); Alexis De Veaux, *Warrior Poet: A Biography of Audre Lorde* (New York: W.W. Norton, 2004); Michele Wallace, *Black Macho and the Myth of the Superwoman* (New York: Verso, 1999).

21. Stokely Carmichael with Ekwueme Michael Thelwell, *Ready for the Revolution: The Life and Struggles of Stokely Carmichael* (*Kwame Ture*) (New York: Scribner, 2003); Jesse Carney Smith, ed., *Black Heroes* (Detroit: Visible Ink Press, 2001).

22. Dennis Walker, *Islam and the Search for African-American Nationhood:*

Elijah Muhammad, Louis Farrakhan, and the Nation of Islam (Atlanta: Clarity, 2005); Claude Clegg, *An Original Man: The Life and Times of Elijah Muhammad* (New York: St. Martin's, 1997); Louis A. DeCaro, *"On the Side of My People": A Religious Life of Malcolm X* (New York: New York University Press, 1996), 90–110; James Cone, *Malcolm, Martin, and America: A Dream or a Nightmare* (Maryknoll, N.Y.: Orbis, 1991).

23. Clarence Taylor, *Black Religious Intellectuals: Fight for Equality from Jim Crow to the 21st Century* (New York: Routledge, 2002); Mattias Gardell, *In The Name of Elijah Muhammad: Louis Farrakhan and the Nation of Islam* (Durham, N.C.: Duke University Press, 1996).

24. One major scholarly debate was indeed the question of "cultural" influences on the relative success of Caribbean immigrants versus native U.S. Blacks (Kristin F. Butcher, "Black Immigrants in the United States: A Comparison with Native Blacks and Other Immigrants," *Industrial and Labor Relations Review* 47/2 [1994], 265–84). While such assertions have been debunked of late, belief in such arguments and continued labor debates helped maintain conflictual relations between African Americans and Caribbean immigrants.

25. Milton Vickerman, *Crosscurrents: West Indian Immigrants and Race.* (New York: Oxford University Press, 1999), 112–13.

26. Ibid., 113.

27. Cornel West, *Race Matters* (Boston: Beacon, 1993).

28. Rachel Buff, *Immigration and the Political Economy of Home: West Indian Brooklyn and American Indian Minneapolis, 1945–1992* (Berkeley: University of California Press, 2001).

29. Vanessa Ho, "Kids' Troubles Shake Seattle's East Africans: Yearlong Inquiry by Gang Task Force Led to Indictments," *Seattle Post-Intelligencer,* April 12, 2006, at http://seattlepi.nwsource.com/local/266361_eastafrican12.html (accessed November 23, 2006).

30. *Census 2000 PHC-T-14: Ranking Table for Counties by Race Alone, Race Alone or in Combination, and Two or More Races Population,* U.S. Census, 2000, at http://www.census.gov/population/cen2000/phc-t14/tab06.pdf (accessed November 23, 2006).

31. Kery Murakami and Mary Andom, "Shooting Puts Light on Ethnic Divide between African Americans, Immigrants," *Seattle Post-Intelligencer,* July 20, 2006, at http://seattlepi.nwsource.com/local/278195_african20.html (accessed November 22, 2006).

32. Chana Joffe-Walt, *Africans in Seattle Report,* August 29, 2006, at http://theworld.org/?q=node/3900 (accessed November 23, 2006).

33. Jennifer H. Cunningham, "Tensions between African Americans and Africans Surface Again," *New York Amsterdam News,* February 3, 2005, 6, 48.

34. In the last decade, Raleigh received 72,580 new Latino immigrants (a 1,180 percent increase), Greensboro received 62,210 (a 962 percent increase), and Charlotte received 77,092 (a 932 percent increase). Statistics borrowed from the Latin American Coalition of Mecklenburg County.

35. This remigration is most evident in Atlanta, but Charlotte, Richmond, Orlando, Jackson (Miss.), and other southern cities are experiencing similar demographic changes and patterns.

36. The centerpiece of Charlotte's civil rights community rests with its legal community. However, Black community mobilization around urban renewal and school desegregation or resegregation suggests a moderate degree of social activism on the part of Black Charlotteans. Similarly, civil rights activists have typically supported more open immigration policies and have been more receptive to the particular challenges facing immigrants of color. For example, Diamond, "African American Attitudes toward United States Immigration Policy"; see also Franco Ordoñez, "Blacks Fret over Immigrant Gains: Latino Population Surge Puts Wage, Jobs, Clout at Risk, Some Say," *Charlotte Observer,* May 21, 2006, A2.

37. "African Immigrants to U.S. Make Presence Known in Some American Communities," Voice of America, at www.voanews.com/english/archive/2005-05/2005-05-02-voa50.cfm (accessed January 15, 2008).

38. The minutes to one group, the African Council, suggests that it assists with "housing, healthcare, jobs, and education," just to name some of its services. Other organizations such as African Diaspora Dialogues offer similar opportunities to encourage cultural exchange.

CHAPTER 7

Rescuing Elián

Gender and Race in Stories of Children's Migration

Isabel Guzman Molina

In June 2004, the Puerto Rican government reached a compromise with the Russian Consulate over the much-disputed fate of nine-year-old Arnas Gaurlicikas.[1] Maritza Ramos, a Supreme Court judge, adopted the boy, who was born in Lithuania with Russian citizenship and abandoned by his mother on the island in 2002. Ramos had cared for the child since his case appeared before her family court, and she claimed the boy's adoption was fair and legal. However, after a two-year battle, his maternal grandparents successfully sued to bring him back to Lithuania. The transnational custody battle between Russia and Puerto Rico over "el niño ruso" commandeered the island's newspaper and television headlines.[2]

In February 2004, the Taiwanese government stormed the paternal home of Iruan Ergui Wu on a court-mandated order to return the young nine-year-old boy to his Brazilian grandmother.[3] Iruan Wu, whose Uruguayan mother and Taiwanese father had both died, was left in the middle of a transnational custody dispute. The maternal grandmother in Brazil had legal custody of the child, but a paternal uncle in Taiwan who claimed custody of the child during a holiday visit refused to turn him over. After a three-year court battle, the Taiwanese government forcibly removed the child from the uncle's home, and Iruan Wu left Taiwan for Brazil in his grandmother's care as hundreds waved goodbye.

Both of these conflicts followed perhaps the most famous international child custody dispute to date—that of young Elián González, the six-year-old rescued at sea after watching his mother drown. At the center of the transnational custody conflict was his U.S. Cuban uncle and cousin and his Cuban father and grandparents. The case involving "the world's most famous refugee" brought U.S. and international attention to the issue of child immigration law, paternal rights, and racial inequities in U.S. immigration law. Indeed, writing about the Elián case, one associated press reporter asked: "What if adorable little light-skinned Elián who washed up on U.S. shores from Cuba had been adorable little dark-skinned Elián from Haiti? Some lawmakers don't like the answer they believe they would get."[4] Nevertheless, it is precisely the answer to that question that this essay explores.

By examining the general-market and Spanish-language coverage of the Elián case, I set out to explore three questions:

1. How did the media report on the issue of child immigration?
2. What were the differences between how Cuban/Latina/o child immigrants and other child immigrants were constructed in the journalistic narratives?
3. What do the journalistic narratives tell us about the symbolic role of children immigrants in the United States?

Gendered Narrative of Immigration

Women and children's immigration stories are rarely told outside of the masculine-oriented narrative of family unification, even as the rate of women immigrants and the number of children immigrating without adults continues to grow.[5] According to the U.S. Department of Homeland Security's Office of Immigration Statistics, 69,113 children immigrants were admitted into the country in 2004. Of those admitted, 16,037 arrived orphaned or alone.[6] Yet, stories about these children are rarely told.

The fantastical reporting about the Elián case might be grounded in the hyperemotional dimensions surrounding the tale of a young, beautiful, light-skinned Cuban woman and her motherless only son. Elisabet's racial identity and narrative of single motherhood might have resonated ideologically with general-market journalists and audiences. While some might find it difficult to identify with the brown faces of Mexican children crossing the border or the black faces of Haitian children floating to safety, sympathizing with the lighter face of the only child of a young single mother is much easier.

The fact that Elián was a boy and an only child positioned him as the symbolic son of *La Patria Cubana* and the rallying cry for an exiled nation.[7] As a point of contrast, throughout the Elián case, Arienne Horta, another survivor of the shipwreck, was fighting for reunification with the two young daughters she had leftwith their maternal grandmother in Cuba, but rarely did audiences hear of Horta's story or her young daughters. Elián's narrative is compelling because he is the son of the father, the future patriarch. More important, he is the heir of collective imaginings, of national longings and belongings, whether here or there.

Elisabet's status as a light-skinned Cuban and the dead mother of an only son insulated her from the racialized and gendered discourse of hyperfertility and poverty through which other Caribbean and Latina women and children who illegally journey to the United States are often inscribed.[8] After all, Elisabet is a dead sexually nonreproductive body while Elián is a boy who cannot physically give birth. Within the general-market news narratives, it is only the living bodies of racialized Latinas who remain marked as fertile and reproductively dangerous.

Racialized Narrative of Immigration

In an article on the politics of race and ethnicity in contemporary immigration, Ruben Rumbaut argues that the U.S. policy toward Cuban immigration has a historical racial bias:

> Color, Cold War foreign policies, and the political clout of the Cuban ethnic communities in the United States have helped shape a contradictory reception accorded to recent escapees from Cuba and Haiti who make

> it to the United States: the Cubans fleeing an economic crisis deepened by the 1989 collapse of the Soviet Union and a tightened U.S.-imposed trade embargo, are generally guaranteed political asylum, and under the Cuban Adjustment Act of 1966, become eligible for permanent residency a year after the arrival; the Haitians, fleeing political terrorism of a military regime that deposed the democratically elected president in 1991, are detained and subject to deportation as economic migrants.[9]

As Rumbaut observes, despite the economic exigency driving recent Cuban immigration, policies toward Cuban refugees continue to be informed by the Cold War politics of U.S. foreign policy. The unquestioned construction of Elisabet and Elián as Cuban political exiles within the early general-market news coverage is based on a historical pattern of implicit racial privilege and social status—the status of exceptional Cubans—a status still accorded to Cuban refugees, despite the dominant influx of working-class black Cubans during the 1980s and 1990s.[10] Not coincidentally, it is precisely Elián's perceived race and ethnic identity as a light-skinned Cuban and the preferential immigration treatment accorded to Cubans that eventually became contested ground in both the general-market and Spanish-language media.[11]

During the same time frame as the Elián news coverage, print and television journalists covered several stories emphasizing the racial and ethnic politics of differential immigration policies toward other children from Latin America and the Caribbean. Contrasting the warm reception of Cuban children during the 1960s' *Operacíon Pedro Pan,* a *Christian Science Monitor* report focused on the impending deportation of a young Honduran boy with no living relatives in the United States or Honduras.[12] A few months later, the *New York Times* published a front-page story about undocumented Haitian immigrants faced with deportation and the decision whether to take or leave their children, who have legal U.S. citizenship status.[13] According to the U.S. Haitian Refugee Immigration Fairness Act of 1998, only dependents are able to apply for citizenship, which means that undocumented parents faced with deportation must choose: either leave their children alone in the United States as legal citizens or take them back to Haiti, a place few of their children know.

Both the *Christian Science* and *Times* stories emphasize the general invisibility surrounding non-Cuban immigrants, in particular black Haitian immigrants and immigrants from other parts of Latin America and the Spanish Caribbean. Again, this begs the possibility that had Elisabet and Elián not been Cuban and light-skinned we might have never learned of the story. Political leaders within the Miami exile community and the Cuban news press gambled that the white identity of Elisabet and Elián would insulate the story within the realm of the exceptionally political and protect the community from the more racializing discourse of the Cuban Marielitos or Balseros. But this was a gamble that did not pay off for the exiled U.S. Cuban community. For the national and local general-market media, the focus of the journalistic narrative shifted from Cold War politics to racial inequality.[14]

As the conflict between the U.S. Cuban community and the U.S. federal government reached its climax, the Miami Cuban exiles were increasingly presented in the general-market news as lawless outsiders, culturally foreign, and racial "others." Simultaneously, this opened a narrative space from which journalists could question the racial bias of the U.S. government's Cuban immigration policy. Journalists began to pit conservative Cuban politicians against U.S. black politicians in order to introduce narratives of Cuban racial privilege. For example, an April 2000 segment of CNN's *Late Edition with Wolf Blitzer* had as guests U.S. Congresswoman Maxine Waters, a black democrat, and Ileana Ros-Lehtinen, a Cuban republican, and here is part of their exchange:

> *Waters*: Haitians are treated quite differently. I have not mentioned them, but since you brought it up, had that been a Haitian child, he would have been repatriated immediately, and you know that.
>
> *Ros-Lehtinen*: We have been very helpful to the Haitian community, when they have been seeking equality, and we will continue to do so. However, I think that people are correct when they say . . .
>
> *Waters*: Well, they don't receive the same treatment as Cubans. You know that, they don't.[15]

The unmasking of the racialized privilege accorded to Cuban refugees highlights Elisabet's and Elián's whiteness and ethnic specificity within broader representation of Latina/o immigration.[16]

The narrative of racial privilege and inequality became even more apparent in the Spanish-language newspaper coverage about the case: both

New York's *La Prensa* and Los Angeles's *La Opinion* criticized Miami's Cuban exile community and the unprecedented national attention given to Elián as a sign of the continuing political double-standard used to treat Cubans and other Latina/o immigrants.

Child Immigrants, National Identity, and the Rule of Symbolic Law

For conservative Cuban exiles and the Cuban press in Miami, keeping Elián was pivotal to the cultural reproduction of exile *Cubanidad,* the customs, values, and traditions associated with being and performing Cuban identity in exile, an identity that is both cultural and deeply political.[17] Thus, not surprisingly, Miami's Cuban media maintained a focus on Castro and Cuba's communist policies toward children in order to reaffirm the nostalgic emphasis on the bygone era of the Cold War. By highlighting the U.S.-Cuba immigration agreement and other foreign policy issues, the U.S. Cuban press implicitly encoded the U.S. Cuban community as an exile community in need of U.S. political protection rather than a racialized ethnic community.[18] For the U.S. Cuban media, Elián and Elisabet were constructed as members of the exceptional model Latino "minority"—different, but important, members of the imagined nation.

Not only did claiming Elián within the discourse of nostalgia locate U.S. Cubans within a politically privileged deracialized space, but it also functioned to create ideological cohesion within an increasingly fractured Miami Cuban community. The growing number of Afro-Cubans, Cuban émigrés sympathetic to the Cuban revolution, and apolitical second-generation and third-generation U.S. Cubans created fissures within a community that once had been defined more by its homogeneity than by its differences.[19] Amid these concerns, particularly the need to incorporate young U.S.-born Cubans into the conservative political ideology of older conservative Cuban exiles, the arrival of Elián proved to be an unexpected but fortuitous event: "Within hours of the boy's rescue from Florida waters, CANF [Cuban American National Foundation] converted Elián into a poster child, distributing thousands of leaflets of him at the World Trade

Organization meeting in Seattle, beneath the headline 'Another child victim of Fidel Castro'"[20] Despite the political backlash suffered by the U.S. Cuban community, Elián and the symbolism surrounding his immigration case reaffirmed U.S. Cuban solidarity and politicized previously disengaged younger Cubans.

In the end, rather than producing an assimilated ethnic identity or unified panethnic Latino identity, the U.S. Cuban media constructed an imagined community grounded in the nostalgic symbols, practices, and ideology associated with conservative Cuban identity and culture. The news coverage also provided a political outlet for disseminating an image of Cuban identity that challenged the boundaries of U.S. national identity while it simultaneously sought to rewrite the meaning of U.S. citizenship.

However, by the time Elián landed on Miami's shore in 1999, the conservative Cuban community's discourse of exceptionalism, so effective in the 1960s and 1970s, was becoming increasingly dissonant with general-market journalists and a public more preoccupied with the "browning of America" and the related shifting constructs of national identity than with Cuba's communist threat. The long-term presence of more than one million Cuban immigrants (the fifth largest immigrant population in the United States) and growing numbers of U.S.-born Cubans contributed to the general-market media's gendering and racialization of Cubans as ethnic exiles rather than politic exiles.[21] Cuban politicians, conservative activists, and media found themselves facing a world in which their difference was no longer defined by ethnic-specific symbols but by their relation to other ethnic and racial groups.

Conclusion

With increasing national and local anxieties about Latino immigration and demographic growth, the Elián case pushed Miami's general-market and Spanish-language media into the middle of an emotional and complicated contemporary ethnic and racial crisis, bringing long-standing and simmering ethnic and racial hostilities between non-Cubans and Cubans to a boil and creating unusual coalitions of Anglo American, African American, and non-Cuban Latino residents.[22] On one side, the U.S. Cuban news coverage actively affirmed the nostalgic ideology of Cold War Cuban exceptionalism by maintaining an editorial anti-Castro stance supportive of the conservative Cuban exile community. On the other side, Miami's general-market language media sought the cover of neutral ground by being critical of both the Miami relatives' bid to keep Elián and U.S. policies and actions toward the Miami family.[23] The routinized journalistic practices of objectivity with its focus on event-centered coverage, conflict over analysis, and "pro and con" sourcing practices[24] contribute to an ideological narrative grounded in dominant "white" definitions of law, order, and citizenship. Such a narrative embeds U.S. Cubans within the meaning of anti-immigration discourses prevalent in general-market news through two strategies: the construction of U.S. Cuban actions as outside the law, and the construction of U.S. Cubans as embodied by Elián as ethnic outsiders.

The converging politics of immigration and race has long muddied the waters for racial politics in Miami. Since 1985, most of the growth in Miami's African American population has been the result of Afro-Caribbean migration. However, Afro-Caribbean immigrants from Cuba, Dominican Republic, Haiti, Jamaica, and Puerto Rico, among other places, have resisted identifying as African American, even as they have met with the brunt of contemporary racial discrimination in Miami.[25] Anglo Miamians, who fled the city during the 1980s and 1990s, constitute less than 30 percent of Miami County's population but retain control of a majority of the economic and political institutions. In this period, Miami has had more violent racial disturbances than any other urban city in the United States, and many in Miami's African American community maintain that, despite the gains made by U.S. Cubans, little has changed for African Americans.[26] Ultimately, underlying the news coverage and columns is uneasiness with how immigration, and Cuban immigration in particular, is challenging notions of the nation-state and traditional definitions of U.S. citizenship based on Anglo-linguistic practices, ethnicity, history, and culture.

Feminist postcolonial scholars suggest that cultural representations of women are often burdened as the symbolic bearers of national identity, such that when representations of women transgress they rupture collective and imagined notions of community and nation. I would like to suggest that immigrating "Native Sons" function similarly, although embedded in a patriarchal logic that foregrounds both gender and race in the collective project of constructing national identity.

NOTES

1. "Investigación contra Maritza Ramos," *El Nuevo Dia,* February 20, 2004, at http://buscador.endi.com (retrieved December 15, 2005).

2. A search of the *El Nuevo Dia* website for articles published during 2004 about Gaurlicikas and Ramos yielded 128 items.

3. J. Chuang, "Brazilian Boy's Taiwanese Family Desperate for Help," *Taipei Times,* January 17, 2004, 2, at http://www.taipeitimes.com/News/taiwan/archives/2004/01/17/2003091687 (retrieved December 15, 2005).

4. Paul Shepard, Associated Press, *AP Online,* April 8, 2000 (accessed January 20, 2008).

5. S. Pedraza, "Women and Migration: The Social Consequences of Gender," *Annual Review of Sociology* 17 (1991): 303–25.

6. Office of Immigration Statistics, "Yearbook of Immigration Statistics," *Department of Homeland Security* (Washington, D.C.: National Technical Information Services, 2004), 14 (table 4).

7. I. Molina Guzmán, "Gendering Latinidad through the Elián News Discourse about Cuban Women," *Latino Studies* 1 (2005), 1–26.

8. Cuban studies scholars have documented the negative media representation and political backlash surrounding the Mariel boatlift in April–October 1980 that brought 125,000 Cubans to Miami and the Balseros immigration of the early 1990s. While most of the refugees were working-class laborers, media images focused attention on black Cubans, homosexual Cubans, and the small percentage of refugees with criminal records. For an in-depth discussion of race and the Mariel and Balsero exiles, see R. Rumbaut, "Origins and Destinies: Immigration to the United States since World War II," *Sociological Forum* 9 (1994), 583–617. For an in-depth discussion of the political and economic impact of the Mariel exiles, see Alejandro Portes and Alex Stepick, *City on the Edge: The Transformation of Miami* (Berkeley: University of California Press, 1994), and Alex Stepick, Guillermo Grenier, Max Castro, and Marvin Dunn, *This Land Is Our Land: Immigrants and Power in Miami* (Berkeley: University of California Press, 2003).

9. Rumbaut, "Origins and Destinies," 586.

10. For a discussion of the racialization of Mexican women, see M. Ruiz,

"Border Narratives, HIV/AIDS, and Latina/o Health in the United States: A Cultural Analysis," *Feminist Media Studies* 1 (2002). 37–62, and O. Santa Ana, *Brown Tide Rising: Metaphors of Latinos in Contemporary American Public Discourse* (Austin: University of Texas Press, 2002).

11. I. Molina Guzmán, "Covering Ethnic Conflicts: Tracing the Discourses of Race, Ethnicity and Difference in the Local Press," *Journalism: Theory, Practice, Criticism* 7 (2006), 262–80.

12. S. Baldauf, "Elián's Peers Treated Differently: Most Illegal-Immigrant Children Face Deportation and Detention—Not TV," *Christian Science Monitor,* January 18, 2000, A-1. During the 1960s, more than 14,000 Cuban children were sent to the United States without their parents through the program *Operacíon Pedro Pan* (M. Torres, *In the Land of Mirrors: Cuban Exile Politics in the United States* [Ann Arbor: University of Michigan Press, 1999]).).

13. R. Bragg, "Haitian Immigrants in U.S. Face a Wrenching Choice," *New York Times,* March 29, 2000, A-1.

14. Molina Guzmán, "Covering Ethnic Conflicts," 283.

15. Transcript available at http://transcripts.cnn.com/TRANSCRIPTS/0001/04/cf00.html (accessed January 20, 2008).

16. Ironically, one of the unintended consequences of the Elián story was the formation of white and black community coalitions against the "real" and "perceived" preferential treatments given to Miami Cubans (Stepick et al., *This Land Is Our Land,* 127).

17. M. García, *Havana USA: Cuban Exiles and Cuban Americans in South Florida: 1959–1993* (Berkeley: University of California Press, 1996); Torres, *In the Land of Mirrors.*

18. For examples of stories that highlight U.S.-Cuba foreign policy elements, see Staff, "Ultimatum de Castro a EU" (Castro gives the U.S. an ultimatum), *El Nuevo Herald,* December 6, 1999, 1A; R. Ferreira, "Castro añade a la guerra por Elián una nueva batalla contra la Ley de Ajuste" (Castro wages a new battle on the Cuban Adjustment Act in his war for Elián), *El Nuevo Herald,* March 10, 2000, 2A; and P. Alfonso, "Castro rompe la luna de mile con Washington" (Castro breaks his honeymoon with Washington), *El Nuevo Herald,* April 20, 2000, 1A.

19. Torres, *In the Land of Mirrors.*

20. Stepick et al., *This Land Is Our Land,* 52.

21. Molina Guzmán, "Gendering Latinidad."

22. Stepick et al., *This Land Is Our Land,* 24.

23. Attempts to straddle a middle ground are most apparent in editorials criticizing the actions of Miami's Cuban community while also calling into question the federal government's decision. For examples, see Staff, "Divisive Tactics Won't

Work, Protests Must Aim to Build Support," *Miami Herald,* January 8, 2000, 6B; Staff, "The Littlest Refugees Merit Better Treatment from INS," *Miami Herald,* January 9, 2000, 4L; and Staff, "A Shocking Raid, A Call for Calm," *Miami Herald,* April 23, 2000, 1A.

24. Michael Schudson, *The Sociology of News* (New York: Norton, 2003).

25. Guillermo J. Grenier and Alex Stepick, *Miami Now: Immigration, Ethnicity and Social Change* (Gainesville: University Press of Florida, 1992).

26. Stepick et al., *This Land Is Our Land,* 24–25.

CHAPTER 8

The Rights of Respectability

Ambivalent Allies, Reluctant Rivals, and Disavowed Deviants

Lisa Marie Cacho

In the spring of 2006, we witnessed a national mass mobilization opposing House Bill 4437, the Border Protection, Antiterrorism and Illegal Immigration Control Act, also known as the Sensenbrenner Bill. Among the many undemocratic measures proposed, this bill, if passed and enacted, would increase crimes considered aggravated felonies, intensify mandatory punishments, allow indefinite detentions, and deny entry to all nationals from countries that either deny or delay accepting deportees. People of all colors across the nation organized to oppose H.R. 4437. Referred to as the immigrant rights movement, activists coordinated demonstrations, marches, walkouts, rallies, and a nationwide boycott referred to as "A Day without an Immigrant." The movement incorporated people of all ages and various political leanings; protestors' demands ranged from humane immigration reform to full amnesty for undocumented immigrants. Unquestionably, an inspiring moment for antiracist, pro-immigrant activists, artists, and academics of all colors, it was also a moment that could not help but be haunted by the many national mobilizations, demonstrations, and protests that should have happened, but never did.

For some, the hope evoked by the Immigrant Movement aggravated rather than abated the tensions, resentments, and anxieties between and among racial and ethnic groups. We witnessed such media representations during and after the demonstrations and protests for immigrant rights as exemplified in news headlines, such as "Growing unease for some blacks on immigration"; "The black-brown divide: An alliance seems natural, but what separates Latinos and African Americans has to be examined first"; "Immigrants, other minorities must find unity"; and "Blacks split on support for illegal immigrations: Many are backers, but fight for jobs spurs foes."[1] Sharing a similar socioeconomic status, but conferred differential access to jobs and resources, working-class African Americans and undocumented Latinas/os are structurally and ideologically positioned to be both ambivalent allies and reluctant rivals.[2]

Although both undocumented Latina/o immigrants and working-class African Americans are consigned to low-wage work in the service economy, they are not necessarily provided equal access to the jobs within that realm, nor are they necessarily paid comparable wages for very similar occupations. On the one hand, it seems that their collective class struggles could easily form the basis for cross-racial alliances to fight against common adversaries (such as the prison industrial complex) or to fight for improving access to social resources (such as more equitable funding for public education). On the other hand, their different social positions in those classed struggles—as citizens or immigrants, as overexploited or chronically unemployed—also situate both aggrieved groups as competitors over the same low-wage jobs and limited social resources, players within a zero-sum game.

But Latinas/os and African Americans are not only potential economic competitors. Various processes of globalization, international policies, U.S. government regulations, and cultural representations have also differently criminalized both aggrieved groups and differently denied them full social membership and political participation in the United States. Any argument for civil or immigrant rights cannot be disentangled from racialized and gendered discourses of (Black) criminality and (Latina/o) illegality. African Americans and Latinas/os necessarily must negotiate their respective exclusions from political and legal rights in relation to one another. To counter implicit or explicit stereotypes of criminality or illegality, writers and activists represent both aggrieved groups as members of heterosexual families, which not only repudiates racialized criminality or illegality but also recuperates respectable domesticity. For example, those who support amnesty for undocumented immigrants often represent the undocumented population as desperately hard-working families, which redefines border crossing without papers from an irrefutable "crime" to one of many necessary sacrifices that immigrants' make for their families.

These representations, however, leave intact racialized, gendered, and classed assumptions of criminality. In other words, even by disentangling "illegality" from "criminality," the faulty and dangerous logic that legitimates and justifies increased surveillance, incarceration, deportation, and state regulation is not challenged, only the stereotype. Consequently, those considered socially or sexually "deviant" must be erased and negated because the pressures to assume "respectability" make it necessary to exclude certain men and women of color from the "moral grammar" of rights discourse all together.[3]

Respectable Representations

According to comparative race scholar Helen H. Jun, "the institution of citizenship constitutes a narrow discursive field within which differentially racialized groups are forced to negotiate their exclusion in relationship to others." Along these lines, she reminds us that relational analysis needs to displace individualist notions of "intention" or attitude" because racial and ethnic groups must engage racialized and gendered institutions and discourses in their struggles for "humanity and citizenship."[4]

In this section I examine the ways in which racialized and gendered discourses of criminality, illegality, and respectability frame and limit how Black-Latino relations can be spoken about and represented in relation to civil rights, immigration rights, and citizenship rights. As forced to distance the two aggrieved groups from stereotypes of criminality and illegality in order to represent either as "respectable" and, therefore, deserving of rights, writers supporting African Americans or Latinas/os construct these racial groups through ideals of gender and sexuality. The emerging debates regarding undocumented immigration, amnesty, and rights illustrate the ways in which the institution of citizenship demands that people of color prove that they are "worthy" and "deserving" of rights by demonstrating "respectable domesticity" through ties to properly gendered, heterosexual, nuclear families.[5]

For undocumented immigrants and African Americans, connections to heterosexual, nuclear families were key to portraying both aggrieved groups as deserving of U.S. citizenship, as well as its rights and privileges. This is due to the salience of heterosexual reproduction to the institution of citizenship.[6] Sexual practices and gendered identities that fall outside the accepted, respectable, heterosexual family are interpreted not only as threats to respectability but also as "irresponsible citizenship."[7] Constant references to the family or descriptions of informants as family members (e.g., a "father of seven"[8]) function ideologically to code Latinas/os and African Americans as responsible and loyal citizens. Nuclear families provide each group with private obligations synonymous with national interests.[9]

Articles favorably representing the immigrant rights movement attempted to de-link "illegality" from "criminality" by representing undocumented immigrants as hardworking, family oriented, and in the process of actively assimilating to U.S. American culture. The following quote from Silvio Poot, a community college student in Portland, Oregon, constructs the potential new laws (from H.R. 4437) as arbitrarily, unfairly, and nonsensically creating criminals: "What is one day of school if the law is going to treat their families, friends, parents and maybe them, as criminals?"[10] In this article printed by the *Oregonian,* Poot justifies the school walkouts as a necessary sacrifice ("What is one day of school?") that students need to make for their "families, friends, parents." Employing familial ties in this way serves to characterize undocumented immigrants as responsible, respectable members of U.S. society, who are unjustly and wrongly being "treated" as (but not embodying or becoming) criminals.

In another example, Eduardo Sotelo, known as Piolin on Los Angeles radio, argued that providing undocumented immigrants with legality or amnesty would enable them to fulfill their familial duties in Mexico. As he told Mireya Navarro of the *New York Times,* "Our people suffer when they don't have documents. Our relatives die in Mexico, and we can't go to bury them. To hear immigrants called criminals pains me."[11] In addition to evoking very emotional sentiments and experiences of family, images of burying relatives operate symbolically to depict life in Mexico as undocumented immigrants' past that will necessarily end, implying that future familial obligations will reside in the United States.

The same article spoke about how Piolin and other Los Angeles radio personalities went one step further in depicting undocumented immigrants as respectable and worthy of U.S. citizenship. Navarro wrote that radio hosts "urged listeners not only to march but also to make a good impression: they asked participants to wear peaceful white T-shirts, wave American flags, and bring trash bags to pick up after themselves."[12] Undocumented Latina/o immigrants were asked to represent themselves physically as racially unmarked ("white T-shirts") and assimilated ("wave American flags"). These called for actions attempted to counter racial stereotypes of Latinas/os as "dirty" or as people whose language and culture "contaminate" English and U.S. American culture by "bring[ing] trash bags to pick up after themselves." Leaving no trace of Latina/o culture at the sites of protests or even on their bodies, this political tactic literally illustrated that whiteness signifies U.S. citizenship.

As the Los Angeles radio hosts anticipated, the white T-shirts, trash bags, and American flags all attempted to resignify Latina/o bodies as already fit for U.S. citizenship, suggesting that the conferral of U.S. citizenship to undocumented immigrants would not change the United States in any significant way. These political strategies would characterize Latinas/os generally as deserving of citizenship by visually divesting their bodies and the spaces their bodies inhabited of any cultural, racial, or ethnic traits.

These physical un-markings complement the representations of undocumented Latina/o immigrants' strong ties to their nuclear families because "family" presupposes heterosexuality, proper gendered roles, and respectable domesticity—all of which erase undocumented immigrants' diverse gender and sexual formations and various living arrangements, such as transnational families, mixed-status families, or family structures altered by live-in work. The tactics deployed by some protestors elucidated but also substantiated that the "universality" demanded by U.S. citizenship is actually premised on the particularities of the most privileged (white, straight, middle-class men) in U.S. society.[13]

According to mainstream media, some organizers and organizations that supported immigrant rights did not support "A Day without an Immigrant" because they felt that work stoppage, consumer boycotts, and school walkouts were not respectable methods of protest. The Catholic Church's Justice for Immigrants campaign recommended that people "attend work and school, but also to some sort of activity in support of immigrants on their own time."[14] Going to school, going to work, and even going shopping are all construed as activities that take place during not-their-own-time, so that the majority of one's "time" actually belongs to either the state, in the form of public education, or corporations. Holly K. Hacker, in the *Dallas Morning News,* wrote that student activists were telling peers to stay in school on May 1st because "skipping class . . . sends the wrong idea."[15] To prove that undocumented Latina/o immigrants are "worthy" of U.S. citizenship, they and their supporters in some areas of the country felt compelled to perform obedience, subservience, and compliance.

These carefully constructed representations of Latina/o activists as peaceful, assimilated, and obedient are implicitly devised in relation to imaginings of African American activism. For instance, in a *Los Angeles Times* article regarding union contracts, African Americans were portrayed as disadvantaged in the job market because they were "too expensive and, well, too activist." African American activism was characterized as a detriment to employment *because it was successful,* resulting in "better wages, greater health coverage."[16] The clean, white T-shirt, American flag image that many protestors presented contrasted the militant imagery of the power movements, evoking instead the peaceful, nonviolent images of the civil rights movement.

In fact, disassociating the immigrant rights movement from the civil rights movement was a rhetorical tactic used to criminalize undocumented immigrants in other news articles. To establish this disconnect, many reporters and writers portrayed African Americans as authentically possessing authority over civil rights history. In this way, media positioned African Americans as minority rights authorities in order to discredit and trivialize the immigrant rights movement. As printed in the *New York Times*:

> But despite some sympathy for the nation's illegal immigrants, many black professionals, academics and blue-collar workers feel increasingly uneasy as they watch Hispanics flex their political muscle while assuming the mantle of a seminal black struggle for justice. Some blacks

> bristle at the comparison between the civil rights movement and the immigrant demonstrations, pointing out that black protesters in the 1960s were American citizens and had endured centuries of enslavement, rapes, lynchings and discrimination before they started marching.[17]

In this passage, anti-Latina/o nativism is displaced onto African Americans (who "feel increasingly uneasy" or "bristle at the comparison"), disproportionately and deceitfully holding African Americans accountable for anti-Latina/o nativism while simultaneously diminishing the political significance of the marches ("black protestors . . . had endured centuries of rapes, lynchings, and discrimination before they started marching"). Representations like this one construe civil rights as inherently belonging to U.S. citizens *even when those rights are denied,* functioning to construct the struggle for political inclusion as a right of citizenship rather than as a response to its denial. The passage also represents the struggle for immigrant or civil rights in masculine terms, rendering African Americans as emasculated or impotent as "they watch Hispanics flex their political muscle."

Indeed, much of the so-called conflict between African Americans and Latinas/os has been rendered in masculine language and imagery, figuring resource and job competition through narratives of castration, emasculation, and impotence. An article from the *Christian Science Monitor* reported, "In cities where almost half of the young black men are unemployed, a debate is raging over whether Latinos—undocumented and not—are elbowing aside blacks for jobs in stores, restaurants, hotels, manufacturing plants, and elsewhere."[18] In this quote, Latinos are represented as muscling their way past ("elbowing aside") young African American men to be the first pick of employers.

Similar references were sometimes deployed to discipline young African American men, suggesting that they do not hold the right values to be successful or that they are not using their privileges of U.S. citizenship, like getting an education, to become more competitive:

> But he [James Banks, an African American store manager in Lynn, Mass.] doesn't blame the immigrants: They're just feeding their families. Banks, 36, says the fault lies with a generation of young African-American men

> who would rather "walk their sneakers up and down the street" then step up on a stage to collect high school diplomas.
>
> "Immigration is going to set the black community back 25 years," he said. "Because they'll let it."[19]

In contrast to Latina/o immigrants who are construed as overexploited and "just feeding their families," young African American men are characterized in this passage as socially "deviant," shunning education, and possibly turning toward an underground economy on "the street." By implication, these young men are disconnected from familial stability and decent work, located on "the street" as opposed to a home, workplace, or school. According to Banks, the two groups should not be competing for jobs because young African American men should not be unskilled and undereducated, only needing "to collect high school diplomas." Unlike immigrants, young African American men are depicted as not "stepping up" to become men, which is figured as graduating from high school so that they would be able to acquire decent jobs and provide for their families. Banks implies that without the commitment to family and community (that Latinas/os seem to have), young African American men would not participate in the reproduction, development, or progress of African America, letting immigration effectively castrate an entire generation.

On the other hand, articles seeking to argue for greater work opportunities for African Americans constructed African Americans as equivalent to Latinas/os. In the *Milwaukee Journal Sentinel,* Emily McDonald, a 29-year-old African American who could not find steady employment, was quoted as interpreting her frustrating work situation as the fault of employers: "It [employer preference for immigrant labor] does bother me," McDonald said, "because we have families just like they [Latina/o immigrants] do."[20] She disputes that familial duties can be attributed to one's racial or ethnic background, and she calls into question the assumptions that young African American men are the only ones affected by changes in the economy or are even the primary providers in families. To construct herself and other African Americans as worthy and deserving of job opportunities, she must engage the racialized and gendered stereotypes used to discipline young African American men, which justify and naturalize their exclusion. Unlike Banks, McDonald attempts to depathologize dominant perceptions of African American families as dysfunctional or broken by simply equating African American families with Latina/o families, in which gendered roles are imagined to be more traditional and, therefore, more respectable.

While McDonald revised the script of African American male unemployment and nontraditional family structure by essentially reframing African Americans as equivalent to Latinas/os, especially in work and family, other articles emphasized Latina/o "illegality" in order to argue that "criminals" should never be preferred over citizens. Such a hierarchy of values in which law-abiding citizens should be provided preference in employment failed to take into account the very detrimental effects of a criminal justice system that consistently and disproportionately targets African Americans. In other words, priming audiences to disdain "illegality" contributes to racial stereotypes of African Americans, too—the same stereotypes that justify their exclusion from employment preference. For instance, an article in the *Boston Globe* reported that "some [African Americans] see no reason why people who cross the border illegally should be given leniency, when young black men who break laws receive so little leeway."[21] In this case, staff writer Yvonne Abraham appealed to the reading audience's values of fairness, justice, and equality while also evoking disdain for law-breaking, criminality, and illegality. Unfortunately, the disdain for law-breaking encourages equal punishment rather than equal and increased leniency.

In this brief analysis I do not aim to provide a comprehensive overview of immigrant rights media coverage; rather, I indicate the ways in which narratives of Black-Latino conflict are consistently framed through claims and assertions of respectability. In media, as well as other forms of mainstream and popular culture, "respectability" functions as an ideological shorthand for the values, ethics, and attributes of a person residing in the United States, who *deserves* to be legally protected. As such, any argument for civil or immigrant rights cannot be disentangled from racialized and gendered discourses of criminality and illegality. African Americans and Latinas/os, as historically and currently associated with these discourses, are further disadvantaged because stereotypes of criminality and illegality are inscribed on their bodies.

For this reason, Latinas/os and African Americans, as represented in journalism, are compelled to discredit, disavow, and deny the "criminal" and/or "illegal" populations within their communities to re-present themselves fitting the ideals and standards of "respectability." However, disassociating black and brown bodies from stereotypes of criminality or illegality in order to represent the majority of the group as "respectable" reinforces the logic that justifies economic and political exclusions in the first place because "the narratives teach us how to abandon people."[22] In other words, to make the argument that a marginalized population deserves rights, writers and organizers had to represent that group of people as worthy and deserving of U.S. citizenship, as respectable, and, most important, as not criminal. Unfortunately, disavowing criminality or illegality does not challenge the logic of crime and punishment but actually strengthens, sustains, and substantiates it. This logic leaves those who are most legally vulnerable in both communities with very few allies.

Creating Criminals

Because neither population of either aggrieved group has been conferred full social membership and political participation in the United States, the emerging debates and discourses regarding citizenship and immigration consistently center on "respectability." As demonstrated, to argue for political rights to be conferred or for civil rights to be upheld, both aggrieved groups must be represented as conforming to U.S. ideals of "respectability," which demands disavowing those members of both communities whose ways of living do not conform to U.S. notions of family, domesticity, gender, and sexuality. However, the U.S. economy makes it all but impossible (and even impracticable and inadvisable) for working-class, poor, or legally vulnerable people of color to assimilate to these standards. In fact, the needs of capital for cheap labor create "criminal" and "illegal" populations within and across borders.

African Americans and Latinas/os have been differently racialized and differentially criminalized by local and global economies. As more corporations set up shop overseas, fewer jobs are available to people living in the United States.[23] Transnational and multinational corporations not only exploit the native women, men, and children in other nations, but they also displace those countries' local businesspersons and farmers, contributing to higher levels of national unemployment, which potentially initiates or exacerbates emigration. The 1994 North American Free Trade Agreement

(NAFTA) promised to stabilize farmers' incomes through opening new export markets, but only large agribusinesses benefited. In Mexico, NAFTA undid eighty years of land reform policy; approximately 15 million farmers have been displaced, exacerbating unemployment and underemployment in Mexico and, consequently, facilitating the migration of people beyond Mexico's borders.[24]

Similarly, the 2004 DR-CAFTA (Dominican Republic–Central America Free Trade Agreement) required participating countries (Dominican Republic, El Salvador, Guatemala, Nicaragua, Honduras, and Costa Rica) to significantly change their laws. The radical restructuring of these nations' legal systems resulted in more working poor, unemployed, and landless, and it created so-called criminal populations. Ways of making a living that were not illegal or criminal before DR-CAFTA became criminal under the legal reforms required by the agreement to protect the interests of multinational corporations. For example, the changes in intellectual property laws made piracy illegal, which many people in El Salvador depended on to make a living. Under DR-CAFTA, vendors and purchasers of pirated CDs, DVDs, clothes, shoes, and the like are not only under stricter surveillance but also face imprisonment and fines.[25]

U.S. foreign policies, along with the World Trade Organization and international finance institutions like the World Bank and the International Monetary Fund, have also created "criminal" populations in Mexico, Central America, South America, and the Caribbean (as well as in Asia and Africa), destroyed the means of living for millions in the underground economies and the agricultural sectors, and displaced millions from their homes due to law "reforms," unemployment, or extreme poverty. New patent laws will result in thousands of unnecessary deaths that could be easily prevented with access to generic, affordable medicine.[26] In the United States, the advocates for both NAFTA and DR-CAFTA claimed that undocumented immigration in the United States would decrease because multinational corporations would provide jobs in Mexico, the Dominican Republic, and Central America, providing incentives for people to remain in their countries of origin, but since the implementation of NAFTA in 1994, the undocumented immigrant population increased dramatically, from 2.2 million (pre-NAFTA) to 11 million in 2005.[27] The vicious cycles of unemployment, poverty, migration, and emigration will continue as U.S. products flood Mexican and Central American markets, rapidly putting many entrepreneurs who cannot compete with the low prices out of business. The poor in Latin America have been criminalized through international trade policies, and if they cross the U.S. border without authorization, U.S. immigration laws render them "illegal" as well.

The ongoing loss of jobs in the United States to capital flight, along with deindustrialization, also increases the surplus population in the United States, which is disproportionately African American. Similar to the law reforms imposed on NAFTA and DR-CAFTA countries by the United States, criminal laws in the United States are expanded and extended every year at the local, state, and federal levels. The vast majority of these laws either criminalize recreational activities of the poor of color, such as using specific drugs, or create harsher penalties for crimes already on the books, such as crimes considered gang-related. As reported by the Bureau of Justice Statistics, drug offenders and public-order offenders (which includes breaking immigration laws) accounted for 87 percent of the growth in the federal inmate population between 1995 and 2003.[28] In 2005, black men accounted for 40 percent of the state and federal male inmate population, who had been sentenced for over one year,[29] but African Americans constituted only 13 percent of the civilian population.[30] Hence, the rising Prison Industrial Complex in the United States continues to expand in order to create, contain, and regulate the criminalized, surplus population of color, disproportionately targeting African Americans but increasingly expanding to Latinas/os, too, whether legal immigrant, undocumented, or citizen. In addition to H.R. 4437, the bill that sparked so many protests, U.S. immigration laws not only criminalize immigrants but do so in unforgiving ways. The 1996 Illegal Immigration Reform and Immigrant Responsibility Act (IIRIRA), for instance, enables the *retroactive* deportation of so-called criminals, regardless of time passed, severity of crime, or rehabilitation.[31]

Conclusion

Activists face an ongoing dilemma with the battles for immigrant rights, civil rights, and citizenship rights as local and global economies and policies continue to criminalize and render illegal the racial/ethnic populations that are already marginalized in so many ways. Arguments for U.S.

citizenship as framed by respectability mobilize U.S. American values that are used to discipline, regulate, contain, incarcerate, and deport people of color. As compelled to negotiate their respective exclusions and exploitations through relationally racialized and gendered discourses of criminality, illegality, and respectability, African Americans and Latinas/os are required to disavow the "deviants" within their communities. Consequently, such rhetorics imply that aggrieved communities deserve social resources, political rights, or steady employment because they, too, hold dear the values, morals, and ethics that sustain and maintain racial/ethnic exclusion, gender stratification, sexual regulation, and middle-class privilege.

Aspiring to attain respectability demands disciplining criminality and immorality, and it demands disavowing those labeled as criminal, immoral, deviant, and illegal. This is because in order to garner public support for racial and ethnic rights, the representative victims for each group need to be respectable in order to be sympathetic. It is difficult to argue for amnesty or leniency for those considered "morally wanting," sexually or socially "deviant," criminal, or illegal. But the victims of immigration law and an exclusionary economy are not always as respectable as they need to be imagined.

Many of the people who are most vulnerable in both the African American and Latina/o communities are those who work (whether voluntarily or out of necessity) in underground economies, such as gang members, prostitutes, or drug dealers. In both communities, the men and women whose means of living and working are criminalized are some of the most legally vulnerable populations—whether they are citizens, legal immigrants, or undocumented, African American or Latina/o. The same structures of capital exploitation that create differentially disadvantaged populations also create surplus populations that cannot be incorporated into the legal economy at all. This population is marked as socially or sexually deviant precisely because these men and women need to make a living outside legal and lawful boundaries. Perhaps rather than countering stereotypes of criminality and illegality, we need to question the law and order, discipline and punishment culture of U.S. society.

NOTES

1. Rachel L. Swarns, "Growing Unease for Some Blacks on Immigration," *New York Times,* May 4, 2006, A1; Erin Aubry Kaplan, "The Black-Brown Divide: An Alliance Seems Natural, but What Separates Latinos and African Americans Has to Be Examined First," *Los Angeles Times,* May 24, 2006, B13; María Blanco, Eva Paterson, Hector Preciado, and Van Jones, "Immigrants, Other Minorities Must Find Unity," *San Francisco Chronicle,* May 7, 2006, E1; Oscar Avila, "Blacks Split on Support for Illegal Immigrations: Many Are Backers, but Fight for Jobs Spurs Foes," *Chicago Tribune,* April 23, 2006, 1.

2. In this essay, I refer to identity categories as they are deployed by mainstream media to be consistent. Media representations rely on discrete racial identity and status categories (i.e., Black citizen and Latino immigrant); they cannot incorporate the vast numbers of Afro-Latinas/os, Latina/o citizens, or African immigrants into this framework. "Latinas/os" refers to all Latinas/os regardless of legal status; I use this term when I am speaking about processes of racialization.I use "undocumented immigrant" or "Latina/o immigrant" to refer to the noncitizen Latina/o populations of the United States. Unfortunately, in some news articles, undocumented Latina/o immigration and immigration regardless of means of entry are used interchangeably. For an excellent collection of work that destabilizes the identity categories of Black and Latino, see Anani Dzidzienyo and Suzanne Oboler, eds., *Neither Enemies nor Friends: Latinos, Blacks, Afro-Latinos* (New York: Palgrave Macmillan, 2005).

3. The term "moral grammar" is borrowed from Roderick A. Ferguson, *Aberrations in Black: Toward a Queer of Color Critique* (Minneapolis: University of Minnesota Press, 2004), 124. For excellent analyses of the ways in which the pressures of attaining and maintaining respectability have mitigated the politics of people of color, see these other sources as well: Beth Richie, *Compelled to Crime: The Gender Entrapment of Battered Black Women* (New York: Routledge, 1996); Cathy J. Cohen, *The Boundaries of Blackness: Aids and the Breakdown of Black Politics* (Chicago: University of Chicago Press, 1999); Nayan Shah, *Contagious Divides: Epidemics and Race in San Francisco's Chinatown* (Berkeley: University of California Press, 2001); E. Frances White, *Dark Continent of Our Bodies: Black Feminism and the Politics of Respectability, Mapping Racisms* (Philadelphia: Temple University Press, 2001). See also the special issue of *Social Text* edited by David L. Eng, Judith Halberstam, and José Esteban Muñoz, *What's Queer about Queer Studies Now? Social Text* 84–85 (Fall/Winter 2005).

4. Helen H. Jun, "Black Orientalism: Nineteenth-Century Narratives of Race and U.S. Citizenship," *American Quarterly* 58/4 (December 2006), 1049, 1048–49.

5. As Historican Nayan Shah has argued, "The terms and possibility of exclusion or inclusion depend upon the performance of norms of gender, sexuality, and domestic space. In order to be a candidate for inclusion, the previously unreformed have to prove that their conduct makes them worthy of participation in society and governance" (*Contagious Divides: Epidemics and Race in San Francisco's Chinatown, American Crossroads* [Berkeley: University of California Press, 2001], 254).

6. As theorist of transnational feminism M. Jacqui Alexander reminds us, "loyalty to the nation as citizen is perennially colonized within reproduction and heterosexuality" (*Pedagogies of Crossing: Meditations on Feminism, Sexual Politics, Memory, and the Sacred* [Durham, N.C.: Duke University Press, 2005], 23).

7. Ibid.

8. Daniel B. Wood, "Rising Black-Latino Clash on Jobs," *Christian Science Monitor,* May 25, 2006, 1.

9. These links between family and citizenship are especially clear during war efforts. Robert B. Westbrook, for instance, has shown that the state and corporations exploited familial obligations—duties to the family in which they were raised, raising, or would raise in the future—to convince U.S. Americans to support World War II ("Fighting for the American Family: Private Interests and Political Obligations in World War II," in *The Power of Culture: Critical Essays in American History,* ed. Richard Wightman Fox and T. J. Jackson Lears [Chicago: University of Chicago Press, 1993], 195–217).

10. Angie Chung, "Young Latinos Add Their Voices to the Immigration 'Movimiento,'" *Oregonian* (Portland, Ore.), April 14, 2006, A1.

11. Mireya Navarro, "Between Gags, a D.J. Rallies Immigrants," *New York Times,* April 30, 2006, 12.

12. Ibid.

13. As theorist of race and sexuality, Roderick Ferguson explains, "the citizen is a racialized emblem of heteronormativity whose universality exists at the expense of particularities of race, gender, and sexuality" (*Aberrations in Black: Toward a Queer of Color Critique* [Minneapolis: University of Minnesota Press, 2004], 12).

14. Sharon McNary and Douglas Quan, "Day of Protest: Anger over Immigration System Comes to Head; Boycott Plans Expose Deep Island Divide," *Press Enterprise* (Riverside, Calif.), May 1, 2006, A1.

15. Holly K. Hacker, "Hispanic Students to Peers: Stay in School, Register to Vote," *Dallas Morning News,* May 1, 2006, 1.

16. Erin Aubry Kaplan, "They're Our Jobs Too: A New Union Contract in L.A. Recognizes That Hotels Have to Hire More African Americans," *Los Angeles Times,* October 25, 2006, A17.

17. Swarns, "Growing Unease for Some Blacks."

18. Daniel B. Wood, "Rising black-Latino clash on jobs," *Christian Science Monitor,* May 25, 2006, 1.

19. Yvonne Abraham, "Immigration Hits Home in Lynn: Blacks Voice Fear of a Loss of Jobs," *Boston Globe,* April 16, 2006, A1.

20. Joel Dresang and Tannette Johnson-Elie, "Immigration Rights Debate Unveils Rift: Some African Americans Fear Fewer Job Prospects," *Milwaukee Journal Sentinel,* May 28, 2006, D1.

21. Abraham, "Immigration Hits Home in Lynn."

22. James Kyung-Jin Lee, *Urban Triage: Race and the Fictions of Multiculturalism* (Minneapolis: University of Minnesota Press, 2004), xxviii.

23. The Dominican Republic–Central America Free Trade Agreement (DR-CAFTA) was implemented in July 2006, and only a couple months later, in September 2006, over 6,500 workers lost their jobs because U.S. companies relocated parts of production to Central America. Every U.S. Congressman representing the districts where these U.S. jobs were lost supported DR-CAFTA (Todd Tucker and Andrew Wolf, "CAFTA's Textile Promises Begin to Unravel," in *Monitoring Report: DR-CAFTA in Year One,* ed. Stop CAFTA Coalition, 31–31, September 12, 2006, at http://stopcafta.org [retrieved January 18, 2008]).

24. From 1993 to 2000, ConAgra's profits increased 189 percent, from $143 million to $413 million, but small Canadian farm bankruptcies and delinquent loans were five times higher in 2001 than before NAFTA. In the United States, 33,000 small farms ceased to exist (Public Citizen, *Down on the Farm: NAFTA's Seven-Years War on Farmers and Ranchers in the U.S., Canada and Mexico* [Washington D.C.: Public Citizen, June 2001]).

25. Burke Stansbury, "El Salvador: First in the Race to Implement DR-CAFTA, First to See Negative Effects of 'Free' Trade Agreement," in *Monitoring Report: DR-CAFTA in Year One,* ed. Stop CAFTA Coalition, 7, September 12, 2006, at htpp://stopcafta.org (retrieved January 18, 2008).

26. The changes to Guatemala's intellectual property laws will make medicine unavailable to the poor. According to Doctors without Borders/Médecins sans Frontières, the treatment for patients with HIV/AIDS depends on providing generic antiretrovirals. Doctors without Borders pays U.S.$216 per person a year for the same combination of drugs that Guatemala's social security system pays U.S.$4,818 to GlaxoSmithKline per person a year (Doctors without Borders/Médecins sans Frontières, *New Guatemalan Law and Intellectual Property Provisions in DR-CAFTA Threaten Access to Affordable Medicines,* March 10, 2005, at http://www.doctorswithoutborders.org/pr/2005/03-10-2005.cfm [retrieved January 18, 2008]).

27. According to a study by Jeffrey S. Passel for the Pew Hispanic Center, we

can deduce that NAFTA dramatically increased the number of people entering the United States without authorization. He notes that each year between 1990 and 1994 averaged 450,000 people entering without authorization, while from 1995 to 1999 the average increased to 750,000 a year, slowing down to only 700,000 per year from 2000 to 2004 (*Estimates of the Size and Characteristics of the Undocumented Population,* Pew Hispanic Center, March 21, 2005, 1, 8).

28. Drug offenders represented 49 percent of the growth, and public-order offenders represented 38 percent (Paige M. Harrison and Allen J. Beck, "Prisoners in 2004, NCJ 210677," *Bureau of Justice Statistics Bulletin,* October 2005, 10).

29. Ibid., 8.

30. Jesse McKinnon, *The Black Population in the United States: March 2002,* Current Population Reports Series P20-541 (Washington, D.C.: U.S. Census Bureau, 2003), 1. This number is the noninstitutionalized population of all ages and both genders.

31. Daniel Kanstroom, "United States Immigration Policy at the Millenium: Deportation, Social Control, and Punishment: Some Thoughts about Why Hard Laws Make Bad Cases," *Harvard Law Review* 113 (2000), 1889–1935.

PART III

Immigrant Acts

The title of this section is taken from Lisa Lowe's magisterial book, *Immigrant Acts: On Asian American Cultural Politics* (Durham, N.C.: Duke University Press, 1996), in which she sets forth the myriad ways that Asian immigrants to these shores have struggled for identity and power, and in doing so, have transformed the meaning of citizenship for all Americans. The three essays in this section examine the formation of various immigrant rights organizations. Immigrant activists offer a different model of political action. Immigrant workers, according to Glenn Omatsu (in this volume), transform what is possible by their vision of society and their practice of "militant humility." At this writing, we are witnessing an explosion of such immigrant acts. This moment holds out great possibilities for the transformation of democratic citizenship.

The mobilizations around immigrant rights during the spring of 2006 emerged from a specific historical context. House Resolution 4437, popularly known as the Sensenbrenner bill, proposed an increased militarization of the U.S.-Mexico border, further criminalization of undocumented migrants, and new restrictions on humanitarian aid to immigrants and refugees. This bill expressed a surge of nativism that combined post-9/11 fear of foreigners with the anxieties of many Americans about economic downturns caused by the continued exportation of many white-collar and blue-collar jobs overseas.

Leading off this section, sociologist Pierrette Hondangneu-Sotelo and Coalition for Humane Immigrant Rights of Los Angeles (CHIRLA) Director Angelica Salas (chapter 9) consider the mass mobilizations in Los Angeles in spring 2006. They trace the emergence of immigrant rights activism against the recent history of nativist politics and restrictionist immigration policy. Technological developments such as the use of the internet and cell phones and the key role of Spanish-language DJs facilitated these mass mobilizations, they argue. As a component of the current transnational moment, such "democracy technology" points to changes in the practice and significance of politics in general. Following the piece by Hondagneu-Sotelo and Salas is a reprint of the 1954 pamphlet *A Documented Story of Police-State Terror against Mexican-Americans in the USA*, by Patricia Morgan of the Los Angeles Committee for the Protection of the Foreign Born.

In chapter 10, Christine Neumann-Ortiz, Executive Director of Voces de la Frontera, a workers' center and immigrant rights organization in Milwaukee, Wisconsin, explores the genesis of immigrant rights organizing in that city. Neumann-Ortiz discusses the transformation of Voces de la Frontera from a newspaper on the Texas-Mexico border to a Wisconsin institution responsible, in large part, for the largest labor mobilizations in the state's history. In conveying what she calls "the essence of what the immigrant rights marches meant to so many people," she relates several stories of participants in the 2006 mobilizations, taking into account the stories of individual immigrants, as well as the consequences for those who left work to make history on those days.

This section concludes with a particular vision of the ways in which individual immigrants offer alternative approaches to politics. In chapter 11, longtime activist, scholar and teacher Glenn Omatsu documents the alliance formed between Latino/a and Korean workers in the grocery stores, markets, and restaurants of one neighborhood in Los Angeles. Omatsu suggests that immigrant workers like Max Mariscal and Jung Hee Lee draw on ideas of culture and politics influenced by their experiences in their nations of origin. Their "militant humility" provides an alternative model of politics for low-wage workers, offering new approaches to labor organizing and community empowerment.

CHAPTER 9

What Explains the Immigrant Rights Marches of 2006?

Xenophobia and Organizing with Democracy Technology

Pierrette Hondagneu-Sotelo and Angelica Salas

During the spring of 2006, millions of people, most of them Latino immigrants of various nationalities and ages, took to the streets to raise their voices and placards demanding justice in immigration reform. The marches were in favor of immigrant inclusion and civil rights—specifically, the right to legal status. Among the protestors were many people without legal, authorized immigration status. Cries of "Hoy marchamos, manana votamos" (Today we march, tomorrow we vote), and placards demanding "Full Rights for Immigrants!" but also "We Love U.S.A. Too!" filled the streets. Many of the marchers wore white, to symbolize peace, and carried American flags. Hundreds of marchers in Los Angeles wore a t-shirt featuring the imprint of El Cucuy, a popular Spanish-language DJ who was instrumental, along with a few of his DJ colleagues, in disseminating the call to get out in thc streets. The t-shirt succinctly summarized the rationale behind the marchers' claim to legalization: "This nation was built by immigrants! And that's it!" New immigrants were claiming the right to legal status, and ultimately American citizenship, not on the basis of existing laws but on the basis of their economic contributions as immigrant workers.

These largely Latino mobilizations peaked on April 10, 2006, with "The National Day of Action for Immigrant Social Justice," when immigrant rights marches and rallies occurred in over sixty cities. The mainstream media was taken aback by the dimensions of the marches and by the simultaneity of large demonstrations in New York City, San Francisco, Chicago, and many smaller cities. In fact, not only the English-language media but also political pundits, social movement observers, and political scientists were caught by surprise. But this movement did not drop out of the sky overnight. The marches were not spontaneous. These had been quietly brewing, nurtured by key grassroots leaders and organizations for many years.

We argue that three themes explain the development of this massive immigrant rights mobilization. First, different tributaries flowed into the immigrant rights marches of spring 2006. A long process of organizing by people in many sectors, including organized labor, legal advocates, traditional civil rights leaders, different religious organizations, and an emerging sector of immigrant rights activists allowed for these manifestations to emerge. Bringing the different strands together into a finely coordinated national effort was a long-term process. Second, the immigrant rights movement developed in reaction to growing restrictionism. It emerged in reaction not to growing immigration but, rather, in response to the urgencies posed by racialized nativism (directed largely, but not entirely, against Mexicans), xenophobia, and restrictionism. Third, national coordination and mobilization of the masses hinged on the harnessing of communications technology for democracy. These included Spanish-language radio broadcasts and the dedicated efforts of a handful of Los Angeles–based but nationally distributed DJs, themselves Mexican and Central American immigrants, and the dissemination power of communications technologies. Telephone conference calls and the long arm of Spanish-language radio emerged as the new democracy technology, as important disseminators of information. At the local level, cell phones and internet technology helped bring youth to the streets. These tools enabled networking and tightly coordinated collective action, allowing for the mass, nationwide mobilizations for immigrant rights.

The Legacy of Immigrant Exclusion and Restrictionism

The burgeoning immigrant rights movement has emerged in tandem with and in response to restrictionist immigration laws and legislation. For this reason, we begin by noting the legal legacies and dimensions of contemporary immigration to the United States. Our starting point is this: The United States is a nation of immigrants with a long legacy of anti-immigrant and blatantly racist exclusion laws. In fact, the nation's first major federal immigration law was one of explicit racial exclusion, the Chinese Exclusion Act of 1882. With a few exceptions, U.S. immigration laws have been more about promoting exclusions, barriers, and quotas rather than integration, social cohesion, and inclusion.

Still, there are distinctive periods of immigration legal history. The period from about 1965 to 1980 was one of liberal reform in immigration law in the United States. That liberal era was inaugurated by the 1965 Immigration Act, which ended racial exclusions for Asians and promoted family reunification and a new quota system as the basis for obtained legal entrance and permanent residency. This was followed by the 1980s Refugee Act, which sought to uncouple U.S. foreign policy from decisions about who to admit as refugees.

Since the 1980s, we have seen a barrage of anti-immigration legislative effort and administrative decisions, and the new immigrant rights movement emerged in response to these efforts. In this time, new immigrants to the United States have faced hostility in workplaces, talk radio, newspaper editorials, and the legislative corridors of political power. This hostility has been codified in immigration laws. Beginning in the 1980s, a steady stream of immigrant restrictionist legislation has been enacted. Highlights of key restrictionist legislation of recent decades include the Immigration Reform and Control Act (IRCA) in 1986, with its attempt to diminish the undocumented immigrant population through the implementation of employer sanctions; California's Proposition 187, which sought to control and diminish undocumented immigrants by denying public education and health services to undocumented immigrants and their children (this ultimately proved unconstitutional); and the federal 1996 Illegal Immigration Reform and Immigrant Responsibility Act (IIRIRA), which curtailed the rights of both unauthorized immigrants and legal permanent immigrants.

Immigration law remains the jurisdiction of the federal government, but in recent years we have also seen the emergence of anti-immigrant vigilante groups, such as the Minutemen and Ranch Rescue. Simultaneously, we have also witnessed efforts by state governments to restrict immigrants by denying driver's licenses to undocumented immigrants. Municipalities have joined the restrictionist bandwagon by passing laws against renting residential units to undocumented immigrants and by authorizing local law enforcement authorities to enforce federal immigration laws. Mexicans and Latino immigrants have become the favored targets.

While racialized nativism, xenophobia, and restrictionist efforts have been many faced, multipronged efforts, the mass marches in favor of immigrant rights during the spring of 2006 were in direct response to one particular proposed national bill, H.R. 4437, introduced in December 2005, and colloquially known as the Sensenbrenner bill. H.R. 4437 included provisions for fortifying 700 miles of fence at the U.S.-Mexico border; new fines and fees for legal residency applications; the imposition of a minimum sentence of ten years for those using fraudulent documents; deportation for legal immigrants convicted of DUI; and criminalization of anyone assisting undocumented immigrants, potentially even priests or social workers who teach English classes or offer food and water. While H.R. 4437 galvanized both the restrictionists and the immigrant rights advocates, it is important to acknowledge that it was only the latest in a long line of anti-immigrant legislative efforts.

By the spring of 2006, an estimated 12 million immigrants were living in the United States without authorized legal status. The majority of them were people embraced by U.S. labor markets and employers but legally excluded through immigration law. The immigrant rights movement of spring 2006 focused on this fundamental flaw in the U.S. immigration system: the subordination, disenfranchisement, and partial inclusion of millions of immigrants. The primary demand centered on gaining front-door legal status for 12 million people. Below, we detail how this unfolded.

Immigrant Rights Advocacy in the 1980s: Providing Legal Service

Advocates have been working for immigrant rights for many years. These advocates and activists, drawn from ethnic communities, legal services, labor organizing, and religious sectors, have generally found themselves reacting to legal and policy assaults on immigrants. The first big formation and national coordination of immigrant rights efforts came in response to legislation of the 1980s, which intended to deter illegal immigration by imposing employer sanctions at the workplace on employers who hired immigrants unauthorized to work legally and which included an amnesty-legalization provision.[1]

With IRCA, the undocumented immigrant population was cast into two groups: those who would qualify for legalization and those who would be criminalized at the workplace. In response to these new uncertainties and opportunities, legal service providers, advocates, and community organizers responded with services, outreach information, and advocacy. And as communities across the country grappled with similar issues, immigrant rights coalitions cropped up in all major U.S. cities.[2] In California, the Coalition for Humane Immigrant Rights in Los Angeles (CHIRLA) emerged, bringing together many different organizations. Similar coalitions devoted to promoting immigrant rights and services emerged in San Francisco, New York State, Massachusetts, Chicago, and Texas.

These citywide and statewide coalitions worked with national organizations like the National Network for Immigrant and Refugee Rights (NNIRR) and the National Immigration Forum. The National Network, based in Oakland, California, served as a grassroots think tank, providing leadership on organizing around immigrant issues, and it served as a forum through which the citywide immigrant and refugee rights coalitions could share information and develop strategies to advance their cause. The National Immigration Forum provided policy updates, organized national lobby days, and directed legislative advocacy in Washington, D.C.

The period of the 1980s was marked by responding to the urgencies and contingencies of IRCA. For the first time, "immigrant rights" entered the lexicon. These organizations and their leaders were involved in some lobbying efforts, but providing services for amnesty-legalization needs consumed most of their time. As soon as IRCA was signed into effect in November 1986, community centers and churches in undocumented-immigrant neighborhoods were filled with lawyers and service providers explaining the barrage of documents, forms, and fees that successful applicants for legalization would need. Groups such as U.S. Catholic Charities, the International Institute, One Stop Immigration, and Hermanidad Mexicana used both paid staff and volunteers to help Mexican immigrants navigate the confusing federal instructions required by amnesty-legalization provisions. There were some efforts at organizing the undocumented immigrants, who would not qualify for amnesty legalization.

Meanwhile, civil rights organizations such as the Mexican American Legal and Educational Defense, American Civil Liberties Union, and National Association of Latino Elected and Appointed Officials (NALEO) sought to document and deter the most egregious employment discriminatory outcomes of IRCAs I-9 forms. To reiterate, most immigrant rights efforts during the 1980s, however, were directed at providing legal services.

The 1990s: Toward an Organizing Model

Organizing for immigrant rights as a strategy took off in the mid-1990s. This was largely in response to the devastating effect of IIRIRA and Welfare Reform in 1996. Both pieces of legislation demoted undocumented immigrants, as well as legal permanent residents.[3] Before this moment, much of the effort around immigrant rights had been toward providing services with sporadic mobilizing, as was the case against Proposition 187 in California.

In the 1990s, more efforts were directed at organizing immigrants to become involved in the public sphere around particular issues. One arena that galvanized momentum in the 1990s was the citizenship movement. In the 1980s, IRCA allowed 3.1 million persons to obtain legal status, and when California's Proposition 187 placed undocumented immigrant relatives of those newly legalized people in jeopardy, many newly legalized people opted to naturalize as U.S. citizens. "Citizenship USA," a national campaign to streamline the naturalization process, was supported by Democrats such as President Bill Clinton, and the philanthropist George Soros supported citizenship efforts by funding new campaigns.

The 1990s also witnessed an upsurge in innovative labor organizing for immigrant workers toiling on the margins, usually in low-wage, highly exploitative jobs in informal-sector labor markets. In Los Angeles, the Garment Workers Center spurred organizing among immigrant workers toiling in sweatshops, and the Justice for Janitors campaign successfully organized janitors, mostly Latino immigrants; in addition, the Service Employees International Union (SEIU) organized nearly 100,000 mostly immigrant homecare workers into the union as Local 434B. Meanwhile, CHIRLA became a staging ground for labor organizing among immigrants working as day laborers and domestic workers. A national organization of day laborers was eventually established.

On the other side of the country, the Long Island Workplace Project brought undocumented immigrant workers together to fight for fair wages, dignity, and safe working conditions. From Los Angeles to Long Island, undocumented domestic workers and day laborers won job improvements and new social recognition.

2000: Organized Labor Moves from Exclusion to Inclusion

Organized labor's turn toward an inclusive immigration politics also contributed mightily to the growing immigrant rights movement. After decades of declining rates of unionization, a revitalized labor movement emerged in the United States at the turn of the millennial century. Spearheaded by progressive leaders working at the grassroots level and in the AFL-CIO, the movement gained momentum with the rise of service sector unions; the concerted cultivation of community allies; and a new commitment to organizing women, minorities, and immigrant workers.[4]

The decision to support immigrant workers and to strive to organize them represented a 180-degree turn in labor's approach. Overnight, immigrants went from being seen as organized labors' nemesis and lower-wage competitor to becoming part of organized labor's winning card.[5] As established labor unions sought to organize hotel and restaurant cooks, housekeepers, and janitors, they achieved major success. We have seen this new face of the labor movement and its organizing and integration of immigrant workers chronicled in newspaper headlines, weekly newsmagazines, and even a docu-drama style movie, *Bread and Roses.*

Part of organized labor's new strategy involved the concerted cultivation of community support, such as the support of clergy, laity, and students. Building these new alliances allowed organized labor to meet with immigrant rights organizers. This was quite significant. Immigrant rights organizers and community activists had been working for immigrant rights for years, but until then, and with a few notable exceptions, the union leaders had remained tone deaf. When organized labor began singing the tune of immigrant rights, new coalitions emerged among people from community groups, religious organizations, and the labor movement.

Then, to promote a new amnesty legalization and build momentum for repealing employer sanctions, the AFL-CIO sponsored a series of public, regional forums in New York City, Atlanta, Chicago, and Los Angeles, where immigrants gave testimonies. On June 10, 2000, some 20,000 people packed the Los Angeles Sports Arena to participate in this event. Unions, community organizations, and church congregations supported the forums, bringing their respective constituencies together and building momentum for an immigrant rights movement. Students, congregation members, and rank and file workers came together to voice their support for a massive legalization program. The unions also sparked a national postcard campaign, recruiting 1 million people to sign and send postcards to Washington in favor of legalization, just before 9/11. Other sectors joined in this effort, including the Roman Catholic Church and Mexican hometown associations.

Labor organizers with connections to Latino immigrant communities proved to be central players in this new movement. Organizers such as Miguel Contreras, Fabian Nunez (then with the Los Angeles County Federation of Labor), Eliseo Medina, and Maria Elena Durazo came from Mexican immigrant families and had been influenced by the Chicano movement and the United Farm Workers.

Durazo, for example, emerged as a strong leader who helped bring "immigrant rights" to the core of the AFL-CIO. The child of Mexican immigrants, and one of ten siblings who had worked in California's agricultural fields, she stems from roots that are strikingly similar to those of Cesar Chavez. Durazo, trained as a lawyer, began her labor-organizing career in garment sweatshops and then moved on to organizing hotel and restaurant workers.[6] As she later testified before Congress, when she began as an organizer with Local 11 she witnessed not only unfair treatment of the immigrant workers by the employers but also by the union:

> I got hired as an organizer at Local 11 in 1983 and for 4 years I witnessed a Union deteriorate right before my very eyes. The leadership of that Local had a policy of exclusion. 70% of the members are immigrants from Mexico and Central America. The meetings were held in English only; the publications were sent out in English only and members rarely attended meetings. The office closed down at 4pm—the time most members were getting off their shifts.[7]

Durazo led a rank and file effort to change union leadership and policies. The cooks, dishwashers, and housekeepers she organized were, like those in the garment industry, predominantly Spanish-speaking, Latino immigrant workers. Under her leadership, Local 11 emerged as a union at the forefront of the struggle for Latino immigrant worker rights, a union not shy about using aggressive tactics, such as strikes, boycotts, and fasts.

It was under Durazo's HERE (Hotel Employees and Restaurant Employees International Union) leadership and influence that the national AFL-CIO undertook the ambitious Immigrant Workers Freedom Ride campaign in the fall of 2003. Inspired by the "freedom riders" of the civil rights movement of the 1960s, this campaign involved busloads of union supporters traveling from ten cities throughout America to converge on Washington to lobby Congress and show broad support for immigrant civil rights. Designed also to teach Latino immigrant workers about African American civil rights struggles, the bus riders descended on the city to push for amnesty legalization. Initiated by HERE, the freedom ride won support and participation from religious groups and leaders, community groups, immigrant rights activists, and local and national politicians.

Religious Support for Immigrant Rights

Religion has provided a wellspring of support for immigrant rights advocacy in the contemporary United States. Consider these facts. All of the major, mainline religions have issued statements in favor of antirestrictionist reform. Among the most prominent are the pastoral letters issued by the U.S. Conference of Catholic Bishops. In 2000, they issued a statement declaring, "We advocate for just policies that respect human rights of immigrants," and stated opposition to policies that attempt to stem migration but do not "adequately address its root causes."[8]

In 2003, together with the Mexican bishops, they issued a historic joint statement, "Strangers No Longer: Together on the Journey of Hope." Citing New and Old Testament and Catholic social teachings, the statement focused primarily on the world's largest and longest-running labor migration, U.S.-bound Mexican migration. While recognizing the right of a sovereign state to control its borders, the statement's declaration is unabashedly in favor of migrant rights. If people are unable to find employment in their home societies, the bishops declared, then "they have a right to find work elsewhere in order to survive. Sovereign nations should provide ways to accommodate this right."[9] Building on this earlier momentum, in June 2004, the U.S. Conference of Catholic Bishops launched the Justice for Immigrants campaign, laying a moral foundation for comprehensive immigration reform.

Consequently, religious leaders were visible and vocal in the immigrant rights marches of 2006. Cardinal Roger M. Mahony, the leader of the nation's largest archdiocese in Los Angeles, garnered national media attention when he denounced the Sensenbrenner bill as "un-American." He publicly stated that he would urge priests to resist orders to ask immigrants for legal papers, and during Lent he asked Catholics to fast and pray for social justice in immigration reform. He and his organization cosponsored an immigrant rights march on May 1. In the marches of spring 2006, the Catholics were joined by Presbyterians, Muslims, Lutherans, and Episcopalians, among others. The National Hispanic Christian Leadership Conference, an organization of Latino Evangelical ministers led by the Reverend Samuel Rodriguez also threw their support behind immigrant rights and even pushed the National Association of Evangelicals to issue a statement in support of immigration reform.

Comprehensive Immigration Reform and the Fair Immigrant Rights Movement (FIRM)

The Coalition for Comprehensive Immigration Reform (CCIR) was formed by national and local immigrant rights, labor, and community leaders and policy makers in 2004. The board of directors included immigrant rights activists from different sectors—labor unions, such as SEIU and UNITE HERE!, as well as immigrant rights coalitions from Los Angeles, New York, and Illinois and law centers and policy groups such as the Asian American Justice Center and the National Council of La Raza. Based in Washington, D.C., CCIR's goal was to pass progressive immigration legislation.

The New American Opportunity Campaign (NAOC) was launched as a legislative campaign for comprehensive immigration reform and as an alternative to the purely punitive and restrictionist proposals. The key organizing principles for NAOC include the following commitment to immigration reform:

1. Encourage comprehensive reform
2. Provide a path to citizenship
3. Protect workers (U.S.-born and immigrant workers)
4. Reunite families
5. Restore the rule of law and enhance security
6. Promote citizenship and civic participation[10]

The Fair Immigrant Rights Movement (FIRM) was launched in May 2004 as the campaign of the Immigrant Organizing Committee (IOC). The IOC was a coming together of over thirty immigrant and nonimmigrant organizations from across the nation whose priority was organizing immigrants to change workplace conditions and reform immigration policy. The IOC prioritized building alliances with other antipoverty groups.

The participants involved in CCIR and FIRM were scattered across the country. While spatial distance could potentially hinder nationally coordinated efforts among so many disparate organizations, the geographical distribution of these organizations was also an asset, assuring greater outreach. But this would require close communication and coordination, and new communications technology facilitated this. Bimonthly telephone conference calls allowed key leaders in Washington and in the major cities where immigrant rights activism was more developed to discuss the issues. This allowed advocates in more distant, smaller immigrant communities located in places like Nebraska, Rhode Island, and Connecticut to listen in and become informed of the rapidly changing political context, and then to coordinate commensurate strategies. This resulted in a tight web of communication among community-based organizations, unions, advocates, and policy makers.

From the period of December 2004 to May 2005, the strategy was to develop a strong bipartisan bill on immigration reform. Community-based organizations, labor, religious, and business sectors were all involved, and this effort resulted in the Kennedy-McCain bill (S. 1033, the Secure America and Orderly Immigration Act), with specific provisions for legalization. Delicate negotiations were brokered among different sectors and communities. Advocates targeted legislators to gain their support and endorsements.

Advocates for comprehensive immigration reform had planned to introduce the bill in the Senate, but Katrina and two U.S. Supreme Court nominations garnered attention first. Things seemed to be moving smoothly until Senator Sensenbrenner introduced his bill, which he had been working on for about a year, before the immigrant rights advocates introduced theirs. Once again, immigrant right organizers were put on the defensive. This new urgency to the immigrant rights cause prompted the flurry of immigrant rights marches and rallies.

The Marches and Rallies of Spring 2006

Immigrant rights activists needed to show strong public support against the Sensenbrenner bill. On March 7, 2006, the National Capitol Immigrant Coalition organized a march of 40,000 in Washington, D.C. On that same day, NAOC announced a National Week of Action around immigrant rights for March 20–27. Through conference calls, organizers around the country were urged to mobilize rallies and protests in favor of progressive immigration reform. Both the NAOC and FIRM, for example, organized bimonthly and weekly conference calls that included as many as 300 simultaneous participants listening in as organizers shared reports from their cities.

Massive marches and protests in favor of immigrant rights ensued in late March and on April 10 and May 1. In Los Angeles, 500,000 took to the streets on March 25. On April 10, "The National Day of Action for Immigrant Social Justice," marches and rallies took place in more than sixty cities around the United States. And on May 1, more than 1 million people gathered in protest rallies throughout the country. While professional advocates and organizers from community-based groups, unions, and religious congregations had laid the groundwork, and had used conference calls and face-to-face meetings to coordinate their efforts, an unlikely group of advocates stepped to the fore at the last minute to bring out the masses: Spanish-language DJs on commercial radio.

How the Bogeyman, Tweetybird, and the Baboon Got People to the Streets

Commercial radio, either in English or Spanish, does not usually promote protest or social justice advocacy. But in the spring of 2006, that changed when three enormously popular Spanish-language DJs in Los Angeles adopted the immigrant rights cause. "El Cucuy" (the Bogeyman, also known as Renan Almendarez Coello), "El Piolin" (Tweetybird, Eddie Sotelo), and "El Mandril" (the Baboon, Ricardo Sanchez) are three extraordinarily popular morning DJs. They are all immigrants from Mexico and Central America. Sotelo says he entered the country illegally in the trunk of a car in 1986 before getting legal status in the 1990s. After they were approached by organizers of the March protests, they put their weight behind the cause and even tried to outdo one another, promoting the protest, featuring immigrant rights advocates on the air, and hosting audience call-ins on all sorts of immigration legal matters.

Latino immigrant workers do watch Spanish-language television and read newspapers, but radio is a form of media that is particularly important to this community. This is a population that is hyperemployed, with many adults holding two or three jobs. Radio is easily accessible to people traveling to work in cars and trucks or listening at work places. The DJs also enjoy a kind of rapport with their listeners that TV news broadcasters and newspaper writers do not. These DJs come from similar immigrant backgrounds as their listeners, and they have a particularly close rapport with their audiences. Not surprisingly, Arbitron reports have consistently shown that the shows of these DJs are the highest-rated radio programs in *any* language in Los Angeles. In recent years, as Mexican and Central American immigrant workers have fanned out to fill labor demands in poultry processing plants, furniture factories, construction, and services in new destinations in the Southeast and Midwest, these DJs' radio programs have been broadcast throughout the nation.

Ethnic media is important in immigrant communities, but most ethnic media is taken up with entertainment and advertisements. This was true of their radio shows, which typically featured, until spring of 2006, a mix of ribald, sexually picaresque humor on the Cucuy show and music, skits, and humor on the Mandrill show. These were and largely remain talk-entertainment shows with call-ins, loud gags, and recorded laugh tracks. In March, a group of immigrant rights organizers in Los Angeles (including Jesse Diaz, Gloria Saucedo, Angela Sanbrano, Angelica Salas, and Javier Rodriguez) went on El Piolin's morning show to tell the public about the proposals of the Sensenbrenner Bill. El Piolin, Eddie Sotelo, decided to call a summit with his rival DJs to urge them to get the word out. By March 16, 17, and 18, 2006, the DJs were telling their listeners to call the offices of Senator Diane Feinstein and to join in solidarity for the March 25 immigrant rights march.

Immigrant rights organizers made regular appearances on the Spanish-language DJ shows. Angelica Salas, executive director of the Coalition for Humane Immigrant Rights in Los Angeles, found herself appearing as a regular guest, through a call-in, on the 6 A.M. El Piolin show, answering immigration questions from listeners, providing legislative updates, and urging people to attend the upcoming marches. Public service announcements on Spanish-language television followed.

These radio shows expanded from purely commercial entertainment venues to constituting nothing less than a big democratic town hall meeting on immigration reform. Listeners called in with questions about how the proposed reforms would affect them and their families, were educated about the legislative proposals, and received, quite literally, their marching orders. While the DJs broadcast out of Los Angeles, their shows and information reached Latino immigrant listeners in Houston, Las Vegas, Minnesota, and Idaho.

What Explains the Mass Marches?

The efforts of organizers working from different sectors, the urgency of responding to restrictionist legislation and sentiment, and the democracy technology explains why rallies in favor of immigrant rights occurred in over sixty cities on May 1, 2006. While the goal of a nonpunitive, comprehensive immigration reform that will feature legalization has not yet been reached, the manifested groundswell of support for immigrant rights is unlikely to wither. All of the conditions that gave rise to it are still in place. The commitment to organizing for immigrant rights is still visible among professional advocates in the Washington beltway and among grassroots organizers in labor, churches, and community-based organizations around the country. These groups are now better networked and better acquainted with one another, although there have been the inevitable conflicts that come with coalition work. The harsh restrictionism exemplified by the Sensenbrenner bill has not disappeared. And finally, not only is the technology of conference calls, radio airwaves, and cell phones still with us, but the organizers have learned the power of mobilization through this communications technology. The celebrity DJs have discovered their power as leaders and have used this to further an agenda of democracy, civil engagement, and legal inclusion.

Social movement scholars always want to know why collective moments for social change emerge when they do. As we have shown in this essay, the immigrant rights movement already had several decades of traction before the massive street debut in the spring of 2006. The union leaders, clergy and laity, professional advocates, and grassroots community leaders who laid this foundation are still working in the trenches. So what explains the marches?

More than resource mobilization, political opportunity structures, or new creative framing of grievances, the massive immigrant rights mobilizations of spring 2006 are best explained by the confluence of three factors. This includes long-term organizing from many sectors, the urgency of reactively responding to proposed legislation, and the powerful communications technologies (conference calls, cell phones, and the airwaves). In an effort to search for explanations, and to understand why and how this was possible, we should not overlook the most stunning fact: this was an instance of people at various stages of stages of legality and partial inclusion demanding full inclusion for themselves and for their communities. While the meaning of citizenship is changing in the context of globalization and transnationalism, it is clear that millions of immigrants are not consigned to remaining in legal limbo and partial inclusion. For them, immigrant rights is nothing less than citizenship rights.

NOTES

1. Simpson-Mazzoli legislation, with employer sanctions at its centerpiece, was introduced in the 1980s. It subsequently morphed into the Simpson-Rodino Bill, which eventually became the Immigration Reform and Control Act (IRCA) of 1986. IRCA mandated employer sanctions but also provided provisions for amnesty legalization for those immigrants who could prove they had resided continuously in the United States for five years or who could prove they had worked a certain amount of time in agriculture.

2. These groups came out of efforts to respond to the legal and service needs of the some 3.1 million immigrants who were able to qualify for legal status under IRCA's new amnesty-legalization provisions.

3. IIRIRA created devastating losses for new immigrant communities and, for the first time, rolled back the rights of legal permanent residents. The main advocates in Washington D.C., such as the National Immigration Forum and the National Council of La Raza, responded directly by trying to safeguard the rights of legal permanent residents, asylum seekers, and immigrants with temporary legal authorization. This was something of a triage system. While the needs of legal resident immigrants received attention, the needs of undocumented immigrants were ignored.

4. On the contemporary resurgence of labor and efforts to mobilize immigrant workers, see Hector L. Delgado, *New Immigrants, Old Unions* (Philadelphia: Temple University Press, 1995); Ruth Milkman, *L.A. Story: Immigrant Workers and the Future of the U.S. Labor Movement* (New York: Russell Sage Foundation, 2006); Immanuel Ness, *Immigrants, Unions, and the New U.S. Labor Market* (Philadelphia: Temple University Press, 2005).

5. Organized labor, with the exception of the International Workers of the

World (the Wobblies), has a long legacy of immigrant and racial exclusion in the United States. In fact, the unions were key in promoting anti-immigrant exclusionary laws. Samuel Gompers built the American Federation of Labor as an organization reserved for white, male, U.S.-citizen workers, and the AFL steadfastly opposed immigrant workers, especially Chinese immigrant workers in the late nineteenth century. Similarly, Dennis Kearney's Workingman's Party advocated exclusion of Chinese immigrant workers and promoted vigilante violence against them. Later, the United Farm Workers Union, under Cesar Chavez, initially viewed Mexican immigrant workers as a threat and a wage-cutting competitor to U.S.-born Mexican migrant farm workers. Later, the UFW changed this policy and organized both U.S.-born and Mexican-born farmworkers. For most of the twentieth century, however, organized labor continued to see immigrant workers as a threat, not as a potential source of solidarity.

6. By 2006 Durazo was the executive secretary-treasurer (the leader) of the Los Angeles County Federation of Labor, representing 850,000 union members and 350 local unions.

7. Maria Elena Durazo, *Public Testimony to the Subcommittee on Employer-Employee Relations Committee on Education and the Workforce U.S. House of Representatives, Wednesday, July 21, 1999,* at http://www.house.gov/edworkforce/hearings/106th/eer/ud72199/durazo.html (accessed May 24, 2006).

8. U.S. Conference of Catholic Bishops, *Welcoming the Stranger among Us: Unity in Diversity,* Pastoral Statement, November 15, 2000, at http://www.usccb.org/mrs/welcome.shtml (accessed May 24, 2006).

9. U.S. Conference of Catholic Bishops and Conferencia del Episcopado Mexicano, *Stranger No Longer: Together on a Journey of Hope,* Pastoral Letter Concerning Migration from the Catholic Bishops of Mexico and the United States, January 22, 2003, at http://www.usccb.org/mrs/stranger.shtml#1 (accessed May 24, 2006).

10. Coalition for Comprehensive Immigration Reform, *CCIR Principles,* at http://www.cirnow.org/content/en/about_principles.htm (accessed November 4, 2006).

Shame of the Nation

A Documented Story of Police-State Terror against Mexican-Americans in the USA, 1954

Patricia Morgan

Published by the Los Angeles Committee for the Protection of the Foreign Born, this 1954 pamphlet on Operation Wetback resounds in the current period. Like the raids conducted by the Immigration Customs Enforcement (ICE) branch of the Department of Homeland Security in the current period, Operation Wetback targeted undocumented migrants and political subversives. Hundreds of thousands of Mexican Americans were deported under this program.

Note about the Author

Patricia Morgan worked for the Los Angeles Committee for the Protection of Foreign Born during the 1950s.

We are all descendants of immigrants.
—F.D.R.

In April, 1954, President Eisenhower appointed a military man, a retired U.S. Army General like himself, as Commissioner of the United States Immigration and Naturalization Service, a post traditionally held by a civilian.

Late in May, Congress confirmed this appointment.

The man is Lieutenant General Joseph M. Swing, known to reputable newsmen as "a professional, long-time Mexican hater." Swing was with General John ("Blackjack") Pershing on the United States' punitive expedition into Mexico, an "expedition" which kept U.S. troops on Mexican soil from February 1916 until March 1917. He is a field artillery and airborne troops expert and prior to his recent appointment was Commanding General of the U.S. Sixth Army in Syngman Rhee's South Korea.

On June 14—American Flag Day—U.S. Attorney General Herbert J. Brownell, Jr., head of the U.S. Department of Justice of which the Immigration and Naturalization Service is the deportation arm, announced that a militarized campaign, "the Government's biggest offensive against Mexican 'illegals' in history," was about to begin.

Legal weapon used by the attackers was the U.S. Immigration and Nationality Law (the Walter-McCarran Act of 1952). This law, purporting to codify all existing immigration and naturalization laws into one law, simple and easily understood, instead, in the words of U.S. Senator Herbert H. Lehman "pushes to extreme and inhuman length the doctrine that aliens have no guaranteed rights in this country."

Of this racist law, the Reverend Joseph J. Lamb, Director of the Diocesan Bureau of Social Service, Inc., in Providence, R. I., has also said: "I am quite shocked and surprised in seeing Hitler's principles retained in our immigration legislation, particularly after we have fought a war to eradicate his ideas."

The Walter-McCarran Law was passed in the midst of the war in Korea and at the end of a five-year "anti-alien" drive in which the U.S. Justice Department had suffered numerous court setbacks in seeking to deprive noncitizens of their constitutional rights. It jumbles together all existing immigration laws and adds many shocking provisions, exposing its sponsors' bias and hatred of all foreign-born Americans.

Indeed it is believed by many that the Justice Department itself helped to draft many sections, if not the entire law. It, together with its predecessor the McCarran Law (the Internal Security Act of 1950), has already been used against thousands of noncitizens. Now Mexican-Americans, long the object of unconstitutional attacks by immigration authorities, were to be its mass victims.

Reports told of "reinforced ranks" of border guards and patrols; of plans to "flush out" Mexican workers in the fields and industrial plants and to institute terror "raids" in Mexican-American communities. In Los Angeles, advance reports said, the Elysian Park Recreation Center, a city playground for children and adults, was being readied as a "security facility"—a concentration camp if you please—to hold the rounded up workers pending their transport "to stockades" in Nogales, Arizona, and final dumping over the border. A quota of 40,000 Mexican-Americans was set for the California district by Brownell and General Swing and accepted by local immigration authorities.

I

Under the Attorney General's personal order and under General Swing's personal command, again in the words of Brownell and immigration officials, "flying squadrons" of U.S. deputies "swept" through the fields, factories and communities "to ferret out . . . to capture . . . to herd over the border" defenseless Mexican laborers. Federal agents (the dreaded Los Federales, long-feared and despised by the Mexican people), invaded private homes in the dead of night, frightening and routing from their beds men, women and children. Business places were raided and their owners —many of them longtime U.S. citizens—were pushed about; customers and employees were dragged away by immigration authorities. Street cars and buses were stopped and their riders interrogated. U.S. planes swooped down upon fields at near-ground level to "spot" terrorized field workers who, thus fingered, were picked up by deploying U.S. deputies.

"Due process" was ignored in this giant mass man-hunt. Illegal arrests without warrant; illegal grilling of citizens and noncitizens alike without right to counsel; unlawful jailings without public hearings or the right to bail and summary, wholesale deportations was the rule.

Terror reigned in the great, fertile southlands, lands made rich and fruitful by the toil of these Mexican laborers. Such was the terror as to cause one immigration attorney of long practice to protest to President Eisenhower and Attorney General Brownell that the Constitution was being "trampled upon" by Government agents and agencies. Such was the terror as to prompt this same attorney to appeal to Governor Goodwin Knight as the head of the State to act to protect California residents from such crass violation of the California Constitution and the State's civil code.

The protesting attorney in his letters cited typical cases to disprove statements of local immigration authorities who had said that in the mass roundups of "more than 20,000" Mexican people to date, "everything is according to law."

He told how one client, who had lived in Los Angeles for two years and elsewhere in the United States for several years previously, had been arrested at three o'clock in the morning on the day the stepped-up raids officially began.

The attorney wired the Los Angeles immigration department, asking an immediate hearing for his client. No word came back from Herman R. Landon, district director of the immigration service. At 4 P.M. the next afternoon, the attorney, on inquiry, was informed that his client "no doubt had been shipped by truck across the border to Mexico."

Reporting the incident, the attorney added, "we have not yet heard from the United States Immigration Service."

Another, a Mexican-American employer—a U.S. citizen if you please; for 20 years a member of the Los Angeles Mexican Chamber of Commerce and with 36 years' residence in Los Angeles—was pushed aside and told by U.S. agents "we don't need a warrant here" when he stated his rights and tried to bar unlawful entry.

One employee, this businessman said, was grabbed up and taken away without opportunity to draw his salary; customers were forced out before they paid for their meals and private premises of U.S. citizens were searched illegally.

Federal agents also invaded private homes without warrant, the attorney said, entering bedrooms where women and children were sleeping, flashing lights in their faces and behaving in such a frightening manner that one woman became so ill a doctor had to be called.

All these cases are supported by affidavits on file with District Director

Landon and could be multiplied a thousand-fold in this reign of terror unleashed by the U.S. Immigration and Naturalization Service. "A condition prevails here which is tantamount to martial law," the immigration attorney, whose cases are cited above, wrote the President and Attorney General. He further declared: "Under these circumstances, it appears that all constitutional rights have been suspended in California and that homes are being entered without warrant of arrest and papers and documents and persons seized and arrested and driven out of the country without any legal process or opportunity to exercise any legal or constitutional rights and that no person of Mexican descent in California or surrounding area is safe and secure . . . and that no person has any guarantees that he can obtain a hearing under legal process to determine whether or not he has any rights to remain in the United States."

The attorney added: "Never has such action been taken before in peacetime. Only in war have the constitutional rights of people been so suspended. There is no guarantee that attacks, begun against Latin Americans, cannot be repeated again and again against all Americans. To stop these attacks all Americans must protest."

His was not a lone voice. Community service organizations representing Los Angeles citizens sent delegations to Landon to protest in behalf of the nearly 500,000 Mexican-Americans who live in this area.

Representatives of the Los Angeles Jewish community, whose 300,000 members recall with horror other pogroms and other concentration camps wherein thousands were tortured and killed, also called upon London and Attorney General Brownell to end the terror. Japanese residents, which number 110,000 in Los Angeles, remembered the U.S. Relocation Camps where they were imprisoned during World War II, and joined in the protests, as did trade unionists and representatives of other community, nationality, cultural and civic organizations.

The Los Angeles Committee for Protection of the Foreign Born, upon public revelation of the hitherto "top secret" plans for the mass deportations, immediately:

- Addressed an open letter to the Attorney General denouncing the object of his "campaign" trip to Los Angeles, immediately preceding the mass deportation drive. Copies were sent to organizations, civic officials and to the press.

- Organized a picket line before the Elysian Park U.S. "concentration camp" and two other picket lines on succeeding days before the Immigration and Naturalization Service headquarters in downtown Los Angeles.
- Sparked delegations from community trade union, nationality, cultural and civic organizations—both Mexican-American and Anglo-American—who visited London to protest the illegal mass roundups, the illegal failings, the illegal mass deportations and the establishment of the Elysian Park "security enclosure."
- Organized a mass protest meeting in East Los Angeles, an area which is largely populated by Mexican and other minority peoples.
- Distributed 85,000 leaflets in Spanish and English, protesting the roundups, together with a Spanish-English brochure, "Know Your Rights," which was particularly welcomed in the Mexican-American community.
- Sent letters and press releases to Spanish-language and English newspapers and periodicals, setting forth the story of terror, with facts, facts to arouse the members of the Mexican-American community and all other decent-thinking Americans; facts to galvanize them—and you—into immediate, united, protests against the Government's unconstitutional actions.
- Printed for circulation—with a minimum objective of 10,000 signatures—a petition in Spanish and English addressed to Attorney General Brownell, requesting him "to stop these militarized police-State practices" and "to act instead to give all who live and work here—citizens and noncitizens alike—full protection under the Constitution which was designed to protect all."

II

Who are these Mexican workers?

Why do they come here?

The answers lie first and finally in the history of conquest and exploitation of Mexico and its people by the United States.

At the end of the U.S.-Mexican War of 1846–48, Texas, California, Arizona, New Mexico, Utah, Colorado and parts of Montana—all of which belonged to Mexico—were seized by U.S. force-of-arms and annexed to the United States.

The Treaty of Guadalupe Hidalgo, which ended this unjust war, established for the Mexicans living in this conquered territory the rights of culture, religion, property and political rights.

It was established in the treaty that land grants given by the Mexican Government would be respected: that future international disagreements would be settled by mutual and peaceful negotiations and that the people of the two republics would live as good neighbors, perpetually at peace.

But the United States Government, once the treaty was signed, consistently ignored it. The lands and mines of the Mexicans were invaded, their customs violated, their political rights invalidated. The lands of the enormous territory seized from Mexico were concentrated in a few hands and the despoiled farmers were converted into farm hands for the new landlords.

By legislation and long practice, barriers have been set up which today, as through the years, are designed to make economic, cultural and political outcasts of the Mexican people, whether Mexican nationals, naturalized or U.S.-born citizens.

Although Mexico lost economic and political control through the U.S. conquest, annexation did not stop the traditional flow of Mexican colonists into the region now defined by a new border, the Rio Grande. With the discovery of gold and the extension of the railroads the economy began to accelerate. The basic labor force was provided by the Mexican people in the area, supplemented by others moving northward as the demand for labor increased. This movement continued at an increased tempo, particularly as agriculture developed.

Large-scale agriculture in the Greater Southwest was only possible because of this ready flow of labor from Mexico and because of the available labor provided by the Mexican people who lived in the annexed territory. The Mexicans were dispossessed of their land and their property by many kinds of unscruplous schemes such as illegal foreclosures, falsification of deeds, entrapment into sale of land without knowledge of owners, illegal confiscation of land and downright murder.

From the end of the U. S.-Mexican war until 1924, there was comparatively free movement across the border. Many Mexican-Americans now up for deportation or being hunted and hounded or already deported by the

U.S. immigration service, entered the U.S. in those early years. Many came with their parents on payment of a small head-tax and with no requirement for registration, particularly of minor children. (Average length of time in the United States of the Mexican-Americans now being defended by the Los Angeles Committee for the Foreign Born, is 34 years.) Proof of entry for many is virtually impossible as records were seldom accurate.

In 1917, the United States passed the first overall immigration law. However, it had scarcely been passed before the U.S. Secretary of Labor (May 23, 1917) suspended certain provisions of the law—including the literacy test, the contract labor clauses and the payment of a head-tax—to admit Mexican agriculture laborers on the premise of an agricultural labor emergency.

On June 12, 1918, further exceptions were made to permit employment of Mexican laborers on maintenance of railroad ways and lignite coal mining. From the year 1880, 70 percent of the section crews and 90 percent of the extra gangs on the principal western railroads have been Mexican laborers.

In July, 1918, more exceptions were made to permit Mexican workers to enter the United States to erect certain government buildings. In 1919, provisions were again modified by request of the beet sugar producers. Between 1917 and 1921, 73,000 Mexicans came in under a U.S. Labor Department "emergency waiver."

Thus began a pattern, a pattern wherein the guiding principle has been to obtain "a labor supply which on one hand is ready and willing to meet the short term work requirements, and which, on the other hand, will not impose social problems once the needed work is done and the job is over." [Among these "social problems" which employers have sought to evade are such benefits as social security, unemployment insurance, disability benefits, old age pensions, relief,schooling, health, etc.—*Ed.*]

Union organization, likewise, is apparently classed as a "social problem" by U.S. importers of Mexican labor. As far back as 1918, the U.S. Bureau of Immigration reversed the official trend of encouraging migration from Mexico, by deporting all striking Mexican copper miners. Their union, the Western Federation of Miners, was broken and union organization of copper miners in the area was held back for more than 20 years (until World War II) with consequent depressed, under-scale wages.

In 1921, while the first immigration quota legislation was being prepared, representatives of the United States were on hand to tell their need and dependence on Mexican labor. When in 1924 the quota system of immigration was tightened, the restrictions were not applied to Mexico upon pleas of U.S. employers.

From 1923 to 1926, the immigration of Mexicans into this country was greater than had been expected, raising again the demand to include them in the quota restrictions. Employers, however, from all of the Southwest, including California, joined forces to guarantee the incoming flow of Mexican labor. None of the restrictive bills, proposed in 1926, was passed.

In 1929, a policy of administrative restrictions was adopted. "Whereas in the twenties we absorbed a Mexican population of about 1,000,000, in the thirties we disgorged [*sic*] almost 500,000 people of Mexican origin," according to the President's 1951 Commission Report. "Great numbers of these, becoming disemployed in the United States, were repatriated in destitution," the presidential report adds.

A "Starve the Mexicans Out" policy was boldly announced by Los Angeles relief officials as a "cure" for the depression. The choice was "voluntary" repatriation or get off relief.

"During the forties, the northward flow started again," the presidential report continues. "Months before Pearl Harbor, farm employers in the Southwest and in California initiated demands that administration of the immigration laws be adjusted to allow entry of Mexican workers. . . . Our Government responded and again, as in World War I, we turned to Mexico."

The first International Agreement between the United States and Mexico, providing for emergency importation of the Mexican nationals demanded by U.S. growers, was signed in August, 1942. Congress appropriated public funds for recruitment, transportation, placement and supervision of Mexican workers. This wartime emergency farm labor program extended through 1947. In those years some 219,000 Mexican nationals were brought in as agriculture workers, at public expense, by the United States. At the peak of the program in 1945, California had 63 of the total Mexican workers in the U.S.; 90 at seasonal peaks. "In effect, the Government was the labor contractor," the Commission report says.

The Commissioner of Immigration and Naturalization, with the approval of the Attorney General, under the authority of the Ninth Proviso to Section 3 of the Immigration Act, which determines the basis for excluding noncitizens in general, "shall issue rules and prescribe conditions . . . to control and regulate the admission and return of otherwise inadmissable aliens applying for temporary admission."

"The Immigration and Naturalization Service, the United States Employment Service and its Farm Placement Service, and the Department of State have all rendered assistance to private employers contracting otherwise inadmissable aliens for temporary farm employment," the report says.

The report also points out the startling fact that "legalization of workers, already here illegally, has constituted the bulk of (U.S.) contracting activities since 1947. "For infraction of our immigration laws, some have been prosecuted in the courts and sent to prison, but most of those who have been apprehended were simply allowed to make a voluntary departure. Others, of no different offense, and no less guilt, in numbers sufficient to meet all, or the majority of, legal recruiting needs have been given contracts after a token departure to Mexico in lieu of conventional deportation or voluntary departure.

"The illegals were given identification slips in the United States by the Immigration and Naturalization Service which entitled them, within a few minutes, to step back across the border and become contract workers," the Presidential report explains. The United States, having engaged in a program giving preference in contracting to those who had broken the law, had encouraged violation of the immigration law. Our government thus has become a contributor to the growth of an illegal traffic which it has responsibility to prevent.

This was done by the same Immigration and Naturalization Service which now is callously rounding-up Mexican workers by the thousands. Is it any wonder that Mexican nationals, who know the immigration department's hypocrisy from their own experience or that of their fellows, continue to come here illegally?

III

Americans, opening their newspapers one morning in early February this year (1954), read the shameful news. They read that United States

Government negotiators, on the eve of signing a new International Agreement, had summarily broken off talks with Mexico and had taken unilateral action to bring in Mexican farm laborers in direct defiance of the Republic of Mexico.

They read how United States border guards, backed by the tear gas, side arms and high pressure hoses of Imperial County Sheriffs deputies and Calexico, Calif., city police and firemen, had turned back 7,000 Mexican nationals whose only crime was the desire to work.

They read how other U.S. officials, officers of the United States Immigration Service and the U.S. Department of Labor—acting again to defy the Mexican government—herded 500 workers over the border into the U.S. to fill landowners prescribed quotas.

IV

U.S. Immigration officials, however, continue to disregard the few protections still maintained under the present laws, in their deportation moves against people of Mexican citizenship.

The Los Angeles Committee for Protection of Foreign Born, drafting a bill to remove these inequities, points out that special legislation is necessary to prohibit the lawless behavior, the terror, the police-state raids of U.S. Immigration authorities against Mexican workers and their families.

Mrs. Josefina Yanez, executive secretary of the Committee's Eastside Branch, declared recently:

> The role of the immigration authorities—their dragnet operations wherein they swoop down upon fields, factories and entire communities—is so well-known and feared in any Mexican community that the word "Los Federales" (the Federals) strikes terror not alone to the non-citizen but to Mexican-American citizens of the first, second and third generations.

Among the Mexican-born Americans now being defended against the McCarran Act deportation by the Los Angeles Committee, seven have been in this country for well over 40 years; three have lived in the United States for more than 30 years; three others have lived here over 20 years.

Seventeen have U.S.-born families, including sons, daughters and grandchildren in every branch of the U.S. Armed Forces.

Twenty-two of them are trade unionists, members of the CIO Steelworkers Union, the AFL Laborers Union, CIO Packinghouse Workers Union, independent International Longshoremen's and Warehousemen's Union, CIO Shoeworkers Union, Railroad Brotherhood Unions and others.

Steelworker, machine operator, packinghouse worker, tool grinder, railroad worker, furniture worker, sheet metal worker, moulder, shoe worker, laborer, fruit picker, fruit packer, agricultural worker: the roster of Los Angeles' Mexican-born deportees is adequate proof that the Walter-McCarran Law is aimed straight at the heart of American labor.

With this law, under pretext of hunting "illegals" and "subversives," immigration service officers serve as a terroristic police force in Mexican communities, as a strike-breaking, union-busting force in the fields, shops and factories.

It is not easy, under the ever-changing U.S. immigration laws, to prove U.S. citizenship or legal permanent residence status. Not everyone has proof at hand of his place of birth or evidence of legal entry. Furthermore, against those who have such evidence there still remains the charge, under the McCarran and Walter McCarran Laws, of former membership in the Communist Party, the Workers Alliance and its Unemployed Councils of the early Depression '30's. Proof of these ugly facts is shown in four typical case histories of Los Angeles' Mexican-born deportees:

Justo Cruz, 66, is a skilled machine operator in a Santa Ana County woolen mill. He came to the United States with his family as a young man of 19 years. His father and mother died here. His two children were born here. Justo Cruz helped build the railroads of this country; he worked in the fields and orchards, tilling and harvesting the million-dollar crops of the big U.S. growers. In the 1933 Depression, when agricultural workers —if they found work at all—were paid as low as eight cents an hour, 75 cents for a sun-rise to sun-down day, Justo Cruz, with thousands of other impoverished workers, joined the Workers' Alliance. Together with members of the Alliance's Unemployed Councils, Justo Cruz fought for relief for the jobless, against arrests and evictions, for the social security and unemployment insurance that is taken for granted by every U.S. worker today. The Workers' Alliance (a product of the Depression '30's, no longer existent today) and other organizations which fought for jobs and to get living wages and working conditions; to end discrimination against minorities, including Mexican citizens and noncitizens, now have been declared "subversive" by the U.S. Attorney General. Membership, when Cruz and other workers joined the Alliance in the early '30's, was perfectly legal. Today, retroactively under the Walter-McCarran Law, it is a "crime," punishable by deportation if a noncitizen or a naturalized citizen; by fine and prison sentences if a U.S.-born citizen.

Acting under the Walter-McCarran Law and its predecessor, the McCarran Act, U.S. immigration officers first went to Cruz' employer and tried to get him fired from his job.

His employer replied: "If business gets so bad that I have only two men working in the mill, one of them will be me. The other will be Justo Cruz."

Failing in this, the immigration department authorities arrested Cruz. He was taken to Terminal Island, the immigration department's Los Angeles' detention center. There he was kept on $5000 bail. But Justo Cruz, and three others from Orange County arrested at the same time, had learned how to fight in those depression years. As a member of the Orange County Community Chest in Santa Ana, as a member of the Mexican Festival Association and the Funeral Benefit Society in the Santa Ana Mexican community, Cruz had become known throughout California as a leader. He fought against segregation of Mexican children in the Orange County schools. When his townsmen learned of his arrest, they rallied to free him. Together with the Los Angeles Committee for Protection of Foreign Born they managed to raise the staggering sum of $16,000 bail for Cruz and the other three victims.

The Committee's panel of lawyers fought through the hearings wherein the same U.S. Immigration Service whose officers had harassed, arrested and imprisoned him now served as prosecutor, judge and jury. These officials scorned the facts of Cruz' long and honorable residence (45 years) in this country; his contributions to the U.S. as a hard-working laborer and skilled workman. They ignored the hardship which Cruz' deportation would cause his two motherless U.S.-born children, both tubercular and depending for their very lives on their father's earnings and care.

Justo Cruz, on December 18, 1952, was ordered deported to Mexico.

Delegations of trade unionists, nationality groups, and community leaders voiced protests and attorneys went to the U.S. Bureau of Immigration Appeals, fighting to win a stay of deportation.

Though again ordered to surrender for deportation on January 28, 1953, Justo Cruz is still here. Application for suspension of the deportation order now rests with Attorney General Herbert Brownell who has authority under the hardship clause of the Walter-McCarran Law to grant Cruz a permanent stay.

Hear now the story of Maria Cruz, widow of Jesus Cruz who was deported last year only to die in Mexico. Mrs. Cruz, now 51, was brought with her mother and older sister to the U.S. by her father at the age of five and has lived here continuously. She is the mother of two children already made fatherless through deportation and death. Her son, Joseph, is one of our nation's heroes who won the much-prized Oak Leaf Cluster as a U.S. Air Force gunner who distinguished himself in many hazardous fights over Germany in the thick of the fighting of World War II. Her second son, Carlos, 14, is in junior high school. Both are U.S.-born citizens.

Maria Cruz has broken no laws. She entered this country legally, paid the small crossing fee and was registered with her mother and sister as required. When the Walter-McCarran Act became law, she registered as demanded and, again meticulously obeying U.S. law, always carried her registration card with her.

When her registration card was stolen by a purse snatcher, as a law-abiding, legal resident, she reported it to the police and to immigration authorities. When she asked for a substitute card, she was seized bv the U.S. immigration authorities. "Just a couple of questions, so that you can get your registration card back," they falsely told her.

Instead they questioned her, harassing her for three solid hours while exhibiting her dead husband's picture. The questioning summed up to demands that she act as a stool pigeon against her own husband and against his friends and associates.

Four months later Federal agents came to her home and arrested her. Only her war-decorated son's angry protests stopped a matron from the immigration office from inflicting further insults by searching her for "weapons and narcotics." Maria Cruz, honorable, respected, legal and law-abiding resident of the United States for the past 46 years, was held in Terminal Island on trumped up charges, including "illegal entry" and—a newly thought-up charge since her original questioning—"membership in the Communist Party."

This latter charge, it appeared from the questioning, was based on the fact that she had once belonged to the CIO Cannery Workers Union and had been active in that union in the early days of CIO organization in California.

While at Terminal Island, Mrs. Cruz—whose soft, dark eyes spark with anger at indignities against others—talked with penniless young Mexican women, who had come to seek jobs in this country and were being held for $500 bail by immigration authorities. They told her of the rude, pawing hands of immigration officers in the corral at San Ysidro, hands which had insultingly "covered our whole bodies while the officers called us ugly, dirty names." No matron was on duty, they declared, at the border detention center.

She also talked to a Canadian woman, married to a U.S. citizen and who had lived here for 26 years. Her son is now serving in the U.S. Navy. Yet this woman, too, was held for deportation under terms of the Walter-McCarran Law.

Should Maria Cruz be deported, her U.S.-born sons would be orphaned, with the sole alternative exile from their land, the United States, the country that one brave son has heroically fought for.

Agapito Gomez, now 46, has lived in this country since he was 21. He worked for the Santa Fe and Southern Pacific railroads as a section hand for the sum of 3 1/2 cents per day, living in the miserable boxcar quarters that the multi-million dollar companies think good enough for thousands of Mexican workers that labor on their right-of-ways. Later, he worked at grueling, back-breaking labor, picking celery, cabbage and cauliflower on the fertile truck farms around Downey, Norwalk, Montebello and Gardena. His pay was 10 cents an hour, $7.50 weekly.

Agapito Gomez believed he belonged here. He had a permit card showing permanent residence and the right to stay. His wife, Sophia, is U.S.-born, his two children, Georgia and Albert, were born here.

It was not easy to save on the $35 per week he made as a farm laborer in the costly war years of the early '40's. But Sophia and Agapito saved and stinted and finally bought a little house. Later, by dint of more hard pinching, they bought another with a big yard for the children.

When, during World War II, the United States needed manpower and industry opened its doors to minority labor, Gomez went into a steel foundry. He became a crane helper and joined the union, the United Steelworkers of America, CIO.

Then came the McCarran Act. The witch hunt began. Honored families of the Southwest; permanent, legal residents; parents of U.S. native-born children, were pilloried because they had once belonged to a relief organization or had joined in early efforts of the CIO to organize workers in field and factory.

Gomez was one of these. On December 17, 1951, two immigration service agents came to Agapito Gomez' Norwalk home. They wanted names: names of his fellow-unionists, names of organizations and accounts of his past activities.

When Agapito Gomez refused to become an informer, they took away his prized permit card. These men, sworn to uphold the Constitution and the country's laws, did not tell Gomez his rights, including the right against illegal search and seizure of property and the basic right of counsel.

Nine months later they returned. This time they arrested Gomez, took him to Terminal Island, held him on $500 bail. His wife appealed to the Los Angeles Committee for Protection of Foreign Born, which services deportees. Two days later bail was obtained for his release.

The panel of attorneys which works with the Committee filed motions with the Bureau of Immigration Appeals and in the Federal Courts for a stay of the deportation order, pending court review.

On November 29, 1953, Gomez was again arrested and ordered to surrender for immediate deportation. Again attorneys obtained a restraining order, this time in the Federal District Court in Washington, D.C. Agapito Gomez is now temporarily free on $1000 bail, pending judicial review.

Also living under threat of deportation and separation from his wife, his friends and the land which he has called his own for over 40 years is another Mexican trade unionist, Jose Noreiga.

Noreiga, now 67 years old, came to this country when he was 25. As a construction worker in Texas and California and, later, as a longshoreman at the Los Angeles harbor, he learned the importance of unions to the worker. In 1928, Noreiga joined the longshore union, then the International Longshoremen's Association (ILA). Arrested, with hundreds of other strikers in the maritime strike of 1923, Noreiga served a short jail sentence and, returning to the docks, found himself blacklisted. He went to San Bernardino, worked in a packing shed and during the depths of the depression was responsible for raising thousands of dollars in food contributions for needy workers and their families.

Noreiga returned to the docks in 1937 and again went on strike in the maritime struggle along the Pacific Coast which culminated in the formation of the International Longshoremen's and Warehousemen's Union (ILWU). During the war years, he continued maritime work as an active member of the Wilmington unit of Warehousemen's Local 26. His harassment by immigration officers started in 1952 with interrogations at his home. A year later his Coast Guard Port Security Pass was taken away, which meant that areas in which he could work were limited. In February of this year, he was arrested and held at Terminal Island detention center on $2000 bail.

As with Justo Cruz, Mrs. Maria Cruz, Agapito Gomez and many others, objectives of the immigration officers were made plain in the questioning of Noreiga. His union activities; his work in the San Bernardino community among "Hooverville" dwellers, impoverished victims of the great depression; the books he read, made him suspect with U.S. immigration officers. They even questioned the presence on his wall of a picture of the great Mexican liberator, Benito Juarez, who can be compared to Washington in our country.

Fellow-members of the Longshoremen's and Warehousemen's Union rallied to Noreiga's defense. A Jose Noreiga Defense Committee was formed in Local 26. Aim of this Committee was not alone to stop the deportation of fellow trade unionists, but to fight for total repeal of the Walter-McCarran Law.

Every school child learns the date and the facts of the infamous Alien and Sedition Acts of 1798. Then, as now, reaction linked the words "foreigner" and "seditious" to hound, to arrest and to jail those who dared dissent. Again, at the end of World War I, the foment of union organization brought brutal employer reprisals culminating in the sinister Palmer Raids of the early 1920's.

There again Americans of foreign birth—emigrants from Eastern Europe who had crossed the ocean to work—were chosen as targets; there again workmen's halls and homes were raided and hundreds were rounded up for mass jailings.

The Alien and Sedition Laws were swept off the statute books by an aroused citizenry and with them went the President who sought to put himself above the will of the people.

In the Palmer Raids it was an ambitious Attorney General who aspired to become a President of the United States. He found himself sent, by an angered public, not to the White House but to political oblivion.

Today the parallel is obvious, in the harassment, the warrantless arrests, the mass deportation of Mexican-Americans the same forces, the same reasons lie behind these lawless acts; acts facilitated by the nearness of the Mexican border, by modern means of transportation such as the "Operations Airlift" used by the U.S. Government to transport and summarily dump Mexican nationals into the interior of Mexico. (Although boxcars have not been neglected for this purpose.)

The deportation drive against the Mexican people, left unchallenged for years by the U.S. labor movement and others who have shut their eyes to its dangers, is now being extended—with the aid of the iniquitous Walter-McCarran Law—to other foreign-born communities.

From deportation of the non-citizen, it is only a short step to the denaturalization of naturalized citizens and to the jailing and disfranchisement of native-born U.S. citizens.

The Los Angeles Committee for Protection of Foreign Born was organized in September, 1950, following passage of the McCarran Act (the Internal Security Act of 1950), predecessor of the Walter-McCarran Act (the Immigration and Nationality Act of 1952). When the Walter-McCarran Act was passed, the Committee saw, in the Act's features, a weapon for brutal use by McCarthyites, in and out of Government, not only against foreign-born minorities in general but most particularly for use against Mexican-Americans, whether U.S.-bom, naturalized or Mexican nationals who are noncitizens.

The Committee was cognizant that the accessibility of the U.S.-Mexican border and the U.S. Government's own long established policy of mass importations of agricultural workers to suit the growers' needs, had attracted thousands of Mexican laborers here, with or without contract.

The Committee knew the long history of harassment, wherein thousands of people of Mexican birth, as well as U.S. citizens of Mexican descent, have lived in terror of deportation though many of these thousands were long-time and virtually life-time residents, with established homes and U.S.-born wives and children.

With this harassment stepped up by Federal agencies under the discriminatory provisions of the Walter-McCarran Law, problems of the Mexican people became of paramount concern to the Committee. A community branch was opened in East Los Angeles. From this office the Committee functions to rally new forces and, with them:

- To oppose the continued violation of civil rights against the Mexican people in the Southwest; the illegal mass round-ups; the unlawful grilling of citizens and non-citizens without right of counsel; the arrests without warrant; the illegal failings without public hearings and the right to bail.
- To stop the breaking up of families which makes wives widows, and children orphans; to preserve the sanctity of the home against unlawful invasion and illegal searches and seizures; to prevent loss of jobs and livelihood, the lowering of wages and the imposition of indecent living and working conditions through deportation and the threat of deportation.
- To protest the militaristic police-state actions and to work to end for all time these un-American practices by all agencies of the U.S. Government.
- To defend victims of the McCarran Act, the Walter-McCarran Law and the mass deportation drives of the U.S. Government. To provide to each Mexican deportee and to each deportation case the most meticulous defense as far as judicially possible in the courts while raising maximum support for each case in the area of public opinion.
- To work for complete repeal of the Walter-McCarran Law and other oppressive and discriminatory legislation and for enactment of new immigration laws, designed to encourage and protect non-citizens and naturalized citizens as well as U.S.-born citizens.
- To promote better relations and understanding between the foreign born and those who are born U.S. citizens, in order to perpetuate and extend the democratic concept of liberty and justice for all, foreign born as well as citizen, regardless of race, color, nationality, place of birth or religious or political belief.

NOTES

Published by the Los Angeles Committee for Protection of the Foreign Born, then at 326 W. 3rd St., Room 318, Los Angeles 13, Calif., Telephone: MA. 5-2169. All notes deleted in this reprint. Reprinted with the cooperation of the Morris Fromkin Memorial Collection at the University of Wisconsin–Milwaukee, archivist May Yela in particular.

CHAPTER 10

¡Sí, Se Puede! Spaces for Immigrant Organizing

Christine Neumann-Ortiz

A Poem: *Sí se puede*

by Miguel Rowell-Ortiz, 15 years old

Sí se puede
Sí se puede

The chants rise above us, creating the rhythm to march for immigrant rights

Sí se puede
Sí se puede

It's March 23, 2006. Milwaukee is the third city to turn out on the streets against Sensenbrenner's HR 4437 and in support of legalization for the undocumented.

Sí se puede
Sí se puede

We cross the Sixth Street Viaduct Bridge, a beautiful arching bone white bridge, from Southside Milwaukee to the Northside. When I am almost across, I turn to look back

And see the endless crowds that keep coming . . .

Sí se puede
Sí se puede

It is like a tidal wave rising up against the inhumanity of these laws

Sí se puede
Sí se puede

No one will ever be the same. This is a turning point.

Sí se puede
Sí se puede

The preceding poem captures the essence of what the immigrant rights marches meant to so many people. Though many people participated with a common sense of justice, it is also true that each individual had a unique story to tell. I first describe the organization that coordinated the marches in Milwaukee, Voces de la Frontera, and then share some of the stories of the people who organized and participated in these historic events.

Voces de la Frontera: Our Roots

Voces de la Frontera (VF) is a low-wage and immigrant workers center with two chapters in Milwaukee and Racine and a youth chapter, Students United for Immigrant Rights (SUFRIR), is based out of three Racine high schools. Voces de la Frontera started from below due to the needs and initiative of low-wage workers.

VF started in 1994, following the passage of the North American Free Trade Agreement (NAFTA), as an organization and bilingual newspaper that supported the rights of workers in Mexico's *maquiladora* industry and promoted international solidarity, through our affiliation with the Coalition for Justice in the Maquiladoras (CJM). During that time, I was a student at the Chicano Studies Department at the University of Texas–Austin. Given our proximity to the border, I had the opportunity to meet maquiladora workers who had organized workers' centers along the border.

The purpose of these workers centers is to educate workers about labor law and to promote collective organizing strategies. This was a critical influence on me in recognizing the value of this type of organization for low-wage immigrant workers in the United States. While all workers in the United States are vulnerable to dismissal or retaliation because of weak U.S. labor laws, undocumented immigrant workers face additional challenges. These challenges include language barriers, a disconnect with existing unions, and vulnerability because of their immigration status, which makes it easier to fire them, harder for workers to find employment (as well as not qualifying for unemployment benefits), and the threat and fear of deportation.

In 2000 VF started the Wisconsin Legalization Coalition following the historic shift on the part of the AFL-CIO, which voted to support legalization, as well as the broad support expressed at the time by the U.S. Chamber of Commerce and the U.S. Catholic Conference of Bishops.

In response to many immediate workplace problems that undocumented workers faced, including unfair dismissals due to Social Security No Match letters, exploitative conditions such as no health insurance, no health and safety protections, low wages, verbal harassment, discrimination, and retaliation for union organizing, VF members decided to open a workers' center in Milwaukee in November 2001. The founding members were clear that the purpose of the center was to educate immigrant and low-wage workers about their employment rights and policy proposals; to offer key services such as a free legal clinic, ESL (English as a second language) and citizenship classes; and, fundamentally, to promote collective organizing as a means of addressing the barriers that the Latino and immigrant community faces. Since its inception, VF has become a vehicle for the organization and a political voice for low-wage immigrant workers and their families.

Local workers started the VF Racine chapter in 2003 headed up by Maria Morales, whose family were migrant workers from Texas and who eventually settled in Wisconsin. She was the first Latina president of the Racine County Labor Council in the 1980s. As she recalls, "when I was a little girl, my father always had me translate for people and it became a way of life for me to help others." Voces de la Frontera started as a bilingual newspaper and grew into a handful of staff that, with the support of many volunteers, was able to organize some of the largest marches in Wisconsin's history.

Youth Organizing

In 2003 a local high school teacher, Al Levie, who had attended a local Freedom Rides rally with his family, initiated the Racine youth club. In turn, Levie, a social studies teacher who taught Latino and African American history, and another instructor, Ryan Knudson, an ESL teacher, started an initiative to empower low-income Latino and African American youth to connect their studies to real life issues affecting the students, peers, and families. The students and families eagerly responded to this initiative, and SUFRIR, a largely Chicano and immigrant student club, and Students United in the Struggle, an African American youth leadership club, formed at Horlick High School. The school administration supported these efforts because it has resulted in a better attitude in the student body and a decrease in the suspension rate. SUFRIR has grown to represent students at two other local high schools, Park and Cass.

These two student clubs have been at the front lines of the immigrant rights movement representing a powerful grassroots black-brown alliance that complements the community alliance in Racine between Voces de la Frontera and the local chapter of the NAACP on school funding, Get Out the Vote (GOTV) efforts, and immigrant rights.

In 2004 SUFRIR students led a 280-student walk-out in response to efforts by the school board to shut down a nonpartisan GOTV program that had been approved by the school administration. The reason for their change of heart was the fact that one week before the November elections, the Republican Party threatened school boards in various districts that supported a nonpartisan GOTV community service program in urban or African American and Latino neighborhoods with lawsuits alleging that these were partisan activities. As SUFRIR president, Xavier Marquez, recalls the day before the elections:

> I was in the office, when the principal asked my teacher to inform the students that the activity would have to be shut down. My teacher refused and told them that they would have to make the announcement. I told them, "Don't worry, I'll do it." So they wrote me a script and I got on the speaker system for morning announcements. At that moment I threw the script away and I told all the students that the event had been cancelled but I was still going to do it and those students that wanted to join me should meet me in front of the school tomorrow. The next day, the buses came and 280 students carried out the GOTV program. We would have had more students join us but those that went in the school ended up in detention and were not allowed to go outside.[1]

In the end, the local newspaper lauded the students as a true example of civic participation for what became an inspiration to many people in the community. This was not a partisan issue. It was a democracy issue. Since then, SUFRIR and VF Racine have carried out GOTV efforts in the city of Racine, winning two school funding referendums and leading a successful GOTV program in 2006 that resulted in a 32 percent increase in ten wards that have traditionally low voter turnout.

Students United in the Struggle has been similarly working on developing youth leadership among African American youth and joining SUFRIR in immigrant rights actions for driver's licenses, in-state tuition, and legalization for undocumented workers and their families. As president of SUFRIR, Breanna Stephens said in a press conference before attending a national convention of the Fair Immigration Reform Movement (FIRM):

> It really means a lot to me being here today, taking a step towards uniting black and brown people in order to create a unique bond woven together by strands of understanding and compassion. With this bond, I'm hoping to see social and economic advancement in these two cultures,

and I want more than anything for us to exceed the limits that have held us down for so many years, and go above and beyond in everything we do. In going to Washington, I want to learn more about the struggles immigrant and Hispanic people are faced with today, and by understanding their struggles, I hope they will be able to understand mine.

National Ties

VF has national affiliations specific to immigration reform with the Fair Immigration Reform Movement and the Campaign for Comprehensive Immigration Reform (also known as the New American Opportunity Campaign).

As part of a national coordinated response to Rep. James Sensenbrenner's bill, H.R. 4437, the passage of which appeared imminent, Voces de la Frontera organized three major mobilizations in 2006. The first mobilization occured on March 23, 2006, following the massive marches in Washington, D.C. and Chicago.

In Milwaukee, the first march held on March 23rd was dubbed "A Day without Latinos" and drew 30,000 people, the May 1st march and consumer boycott drew 70,000, and the September 4th Labor Day march, joining the traditional Milwaukee County labor unions' march, brought 30,000 people.

Despite assertions that the national mass marches were organized spontaneously by people, as opposed to being facilitated by local organizations, I only need to reflect on the fact that the call to action was developed at a national conference call where the discussion resulted in elevating and highlighting the criminalization provisions of H.R. 4437. Locally, VF obtained the city and police permits; coordinated through our members and allies the distribution of flyers at churches, schools, and workplaces; organized outreach to the media and to small businesses to obtain donations; organized phone banking; and trained fifty VF members as coordinators for the marches. The point in describing some of these activities is to caution against perpetuating a myth similar to the civil rights movement for African Americans that individuals like Rosa Parks simply decided one day to not give up her seat and spontaneously sparked the civil rights movement.

Where There Was Employer Support

In anticipation of the first march on March 23, 2006, Voces de la Frontera developed a letter that workers could provide to their employers explaining the reason to be excused from work that day, underlying the urgency of this civil rights/human rights issue. In some cases, we spoke with managers directly to support this request.

In one case, I was asked by some workers who manufacture tires to speak with their manager about the written request. As I saw the supervisor approach, a man probably in his late 50s, a bit of a paunch, wearing a baseball cap and blue garage-type uniform and a facial expression like a growl, I held my breath, assuming from his swagger and appearance that he was clearly not on our side.

When we sat down in his small office to talk, I was struck by his candor and sympathy. He was Polish American, and he said that he remembered when the Polish had been discriminated against when they came to this country. How the corporate office demanded quality and production, which they got with their workforce, but then complained when there were problems with their papers. He said:

> They can't have it both ways. We are like a family in this workplace. I have been to picnics with these workers; I have seen their kids grow up. I want to see somebody earn a decent wage and have health insurance and not be caught in this trap of having to change names to hold a job and not being able to get ahead. It's not right. If they left this company, the company would go under. I've told these workers they have my permission to go to the march, but they have to make up the hours on a different shift. And they better go to the march, or if not they'll have to hear from me.[2]

Immigrant workers are employed in all industries. In some industries, the numbers are much higher. Construction is one of the major industries dependent on immigrant workers. Juan, an asbestos worker who was working for a small contractor talked to the owner with his coworkers. The owner was sympathetic and gave them permission to participate in the march. But, a couple of workers said they were not going to march. When the owner heard that some employees intended to come to work, she decided to close the business the day of the march so that everyone could participate.

One worker at a meatpacking plant organized 500 workers to participate in the first march. On the day of the second march, the company closed, allowing all 1,500 workers to participate.

One of the most inspirational developments of the marches were the meetings we held with local small businesses in Milwaukee's Southside. From these meetings, over 200 businesses decided to close during the marches, in a show of solidarity with the immigrant community. This solidarity also included small businesses in Kenosha and Racine. As one of the business owners said during one of the meetings, "I have had a business for over 20 years, and this is the first time that I've seen us [small business owners] united like this." Several business owners recollected with pride, how they walked together with their workers, some in their workplace uniforms, to join the stream of people that resembled a mighty river fed by several small streams as people joined in from different streets. After each meeting, like the marches, people donated money to help cover the costs of the organizing.

Where There Was Employer Retaliation

Not all employers were agreeable to employee requests to participate in the marches. But the power of even one worker is illustrated in the story of Lolo. Lolo worked for a cafeteria and catering company. Resourceful and hard working, he did the job of three workers, was punctual, and was always available when needed. When he very respectfully made his request to participate in the march, the owner told him, "Absolutely not. You go and you're fired." But Lolo was smart and knew that his supervisor needed him more than he needed her.

The night before the march, they had an important catering event. At the last minute, one of the workers called in to say they couldn't come in. Lolo had to step in to do the bartending. In the middle of the event, he made a second request to go to the march and told her, "If you do not give me permission to go I will quit right now since you plan on firing me anyway. No one has ever given me anything for free; I have had to work all of my life to survive. You're not doing me a favor by giving me a job. I will always find work." She said, "Fine. You can go to the march."

In many workplaces, the sheer numbers of participants made retaliation impractical. In just one company, one employer threatened to fire employees who were a key part of his production line, who then told him: "We are leaving and we don't care if you fire us." When they returned, he scolded them, complaining that they had cost him $30,000 worth of production. They were given a warning but not fired. The real economic impact of these mass strikes and the boycott has not been measured, but even this story gives a glimpse of the economic impact. In another company, 132 workers walked off the job despite the threat of dismissal.

In the first march, there was greater retaliation, though still small considering the level of participation during work hours. In total, around 120 workers were fired that we knew of. In a near majority of cases these jobs were recovered. A Solidarity Fund between Voces de la Frontera and St. Patrick's Catholic Church was set up, and local businesses allowed us to put up donation boxes to help raise funds to support some of the workers during this period.

One young man named Elias needed this modest aid. He was one of the three workers fired from Applebee's. Though they had been granted permission by their supervisor and the general manager to attend the march, after they returned to their job, they were told they were fired. The economic hardship on all the workers was very difficult. When Elias was fired, he was desperate for work and got a job at a foundry that did not value job safety. His finger was cut off in a machine. They tried to save it but it wasn't possible. He had a small stump all bandaged up, and you could see in his young face all his suffering and sense of loss. He was unable to work for a long time as he recovered from his amputation. The three workers filed a complaint with the National Labor Relations Board (NLRB) with the help of a volunteer labor attorney, Mark Sweet, and the decision is still pending.

Veronica, a worker from Applebee's whose husband and brother were also fired for participating in the first march recollects, "I do not regret our decision to march. I participated that day because I felt that I was a single grain of rice and that, perhaps, if we were enough, we could tip the balance of justice on our side."[3]

Another worker, Vanessa Vara-Ramos, who faced retaliation for her participation in the first march reflects:

> I was one of many thousands of people from Milwaukee, Wisconsin, who participated in the "Day without a Latino" march. I had planned an early lunch hour with my employer at that time so that I could participate in the march. I was joined by my sister and we walked the streets chanting, "Sí se puede." I can honestly say that March 23, 2006, was one of the proudest days in my entire life—so proud to be a Latina.
>
> After returning to work that day, I was disciplined for attending this historical march. I could not accept that a written disciplinary memo would tarnish my employment record which was exemplary after seven years. Especially since I knew that my manager was racist. I decided to challenge my disciplinary warning which was later destroyed. After feeling stress for 7 months, I ended my employment with that employer. I was then able to volunteer more at Voces de la Frontera and eventually was offered a full-time position. I'm blessed to work with the same people I marched with that brisk morning of March 23.[4]

Teachers and administrators joined their students and their student's families at the risk of their own jobs. In one case, a Latina grammar school teacher employed at a local agency was not given permission to participate. The day of the march, she went to school in the morning, and there was only one student in her classroom. She told her director, "All the rest of the students have been taken out of school so they can attend the march with their parents. I am Latina and I am going to the march so you can fire me if you choose." Right after that she came to our office to help us get ready for the march. Another teacher at a different school, Caucasian, was given a discipline in her file for participating.

Where There Was Fear

Prior to the May 1st march, there was clearly an organized effort on the part of anti-immigrant groups to intimidate people from participating.

Throughout the state there were false rumors that immigration agents were carrying out raids at churches, schools, local stores, streets, and businesses. Our office was still getting calls at 9:00 PM at night from scared people asking about the raids. Though we were able to verify through site visits and discussions with immigration officials the inaccuracy of these claims, we also discovered that there was some basis for these rumors. There were witnesses who had seen people impersonating immigration officials at different locations, and this had contributed to these false rumors.

In one case, a witness saw and was approached by individuals impersonating immigration officials at a local church, Saint Adalberto. This incident led to rumors that the Department of Immigration was raiding the local churches. At another church, this announcement created a panic, causing people, lawfully present or not, to start running. One immigrant worker recollected how he was there with his young daughter when the panic started. He had flyers for the May 1st march with him. He says, "first of all, I told my daughter, if we're separated remember your telephone number, at least you are a U.S. citizen. I thought, dear God, they're going to take me away, if it's going to happen I want God to know that I tried to the end to let others know what's happening and to make a difference." As all the people ran out, he handed out all his flyers and when they were all gone, he ran out of the church with his daughter.

This strategy on the part of anti-immigrant groups backfired, resulting in an even larger number of participants in the second march of May 1. In fact, it was the largest march in Wisconsin's history to date: 70,000 people marched from the Southside to the Veteran's Park on Lake Michigan. This march was recognized by the Wisconsin Historical Society as one of the top ten historical events in 2006.

VF's first African American member joined the organization after hearing about the disgraceful tactics of the anti-immigrant groups on the news. She said, "When I heard that they were going after people in their church. I thought that was it. I had to get involved."

One worker who became an activist, and who, like many others, was key in distributing flyers and recruiting at their workplace, schools, churches, and neighborhoods, said, "Before I knew VF I was always afraid, but after I had the support to stand up for myself on a workplace issue, I was no longer afraid. I now feel confidence when I walk down the street because I know I am not alone."

For the marches our message was clear: there was nothing to lose. Losing your job was the least of your worries.

We Are Not Criminals

In the first march we had parents come to our office to cut in stencil and iron on the T-shirts the words, "I am not a criminal" for the children who would lead the march. This message was in response to H.R. 4437, which not only would criminalize the adults as aggravated felons but the children as well, creating a permanent, criminalized underclass of low-wage workers. In all the marches that followed, parents proudly brought their children up to the front. As one mother said, "even if people are afraid to fight for themselves, they will find the courage to fight for their children." These marches were fundamentally about low-wage working-class families standing united.

One father rushed happily into the office the morning of the Labor Day march, asking for a flyer with the information for the march that day. Beaming, he told how his small son had waked him up early from bed that morning, saying excitedly, "Get up Daddy, get up. Today we march." Countless parents now talk about their toddlers repeating the chant, *¡Sí se puede!* And asking, "When is the next march?"

Solidarity

As we know, it was not just undocumented workers and their families who marched; the Latino community and a broad section of society joined them. Professionals from all occupations, including attorneys, doctors, pastors and ministers joined them. All of them were threatened with the status of felon for not turning in an undocumented person if Sensenbrenner's H.R. 4437 passed. There was support from Irish, Jewish, Arabic, Hmong, African, African American, Anglo, and Native American organizations, among others. In all the marches, seniors and the disabled joined in, despite the long distances and the threat of storms. One Jewish woman shared how when she was working in a building in downtown Milwaukee, she and her coworkers and clients saw the march below, and she was so moved. She drew a big sign and put in on the glass window for the marchers to see. It said: YOU LOOK BEAUTIFUL.

But perhaps the third march is the best example of solidarity because it united a traditional Labor Day march organized by the Milwaukee County Labor Council (MCLC) and the immigrant rights march. This created a controversy within the MCLC, causing six unions, primarily in the construction trades, to boycott the event. However, this represented a minority of the unions in the MCLC. The vast majority of union members in the MCLC welcomed the immigrant community and the unions affiliated with the Change to Win federation under the theme of "Working in Solidarity." The African American leadership of the MCLC on the part of the president and secretary-treasurer was extremely meaningful for the Latino members of Voces de la Frontera.

An exciting moment occurred when the immigrant rights march was waiting its turn to file in at the tail end of the union march. As the union members passed by, there were mutual cheers of support. This moment was captured beautifully in a photograph of the *Milwaukee Journal Sentinel,* where they quote a white worker of Polish descent, saying, essentially, these workers are no different than earlier waves of European immigrants to this country; underneath the caption was a photograph of African American members of the United Steelworkers as they passed by, raising their fists in the air in a show of solidarity with Latino workers. The *Labor Press* editor recalled two memorable moments: seeing many of the union members waiting outside the Laborfest grounds to welcome the immigrant rights participants as they rounded the corner and later, after the march, seeing all the children together on the playground.

Some of the most powerful testimonies at the marches included the experience of immigrant workers themselves. One woman who experienced the transition from being undocumented to becoming a naturalized U.S. citizen shared a statement:

> In 1980, out of necessity I started working at age 14 for piecework at a large textile company in Milwaukee. Many of us who worked there were undocumented. The INS carried out a raid at the company, taking many

> workers to Chicago, even those who were legal residents but didn't have documentation with them. Many were deported to Mexico, leaving their husbands and children behind. One woman who was separated from her family, I will call her Maria out of respect, though it is not her real name. She did what any wife and mother would feel the need to do to, to do whatever was needed to reunite with her family. She decided to come back to Milwaukee, despite the dangers of crossing the border. She was traveling with two coworkers who were also separated from their families by the raid. The three of them crossed the Rio Grande together, holding hands, when the current pulled Maria under. She drowned that day, trying to unite with her family. She was a victim of a twisted system that on the one hand wanted the benefit of her hard labor while on the other, afforded her no rights.
>
> The tragedy was not only the loss of our coworker Maria, but the pain that would be felt forever by those who saw her die without being able to save her, not to mention the irreparable loss of a mother for those little children. I was fortunate enough to have found my path to citizenship without suffering deportation or death of a family member. But like so many others in our community, personal experiences like these create a lasting bond between documented and undocumented immigrants. I realize this happened more than 20 years ago. But I also know that more than 400 human beings lost their lives this past year in their attempt to find work and a better life for their families.
>
> On behalf of those former undocumented workers like myself who have gained our right to live and vote in the United States, I have a message that flows from this story. I live in the district represented by Congressman Sensenbrenner, who is making a name for himself by exploiting and fanning the flames of anti-immigrant prejudice. My message is this. I will not forget Maria. I will not be unfaithful to who I am and where I came from, and I will not forsake those who have come behind me. Sooner or later, our voices will be heard, and justice will be done![5]

Another worker, Miguel, described how in his journey to come to the United States, a six-hour journey ending up taking three days because of the increased militarization of the border. Along the way they faced many dangers. As he recalled:

> A man around 30 years of age started to become dehydrated and even though we gave him a little bit of water, his body started to shake and he could no longer walk. One of the coyotes stayed with him while we continued walking. Later the coyote caught up with us and told us he had died and he had to leave him along the side of the road. At that moment, I thought of his family who would never hear from him again. I thought of my own family and how they would survive if something happened to me. . . . Today it has been 15 days since I came to the United States, and I still reflect where is the American Dream? And worse, where is the American Dream for those people that died in the desert and for their families in the country they came from?[6]

Immigration laws also harm U.S. citizens. A U.S. citizen woman whose husband is undocumented shared her family's experience living under our current immigration system:

> I cannot imagine my husband not being here. Who will help me raise my children? My father passed away, and my mother and brother are alcoholics. I would have to cut back on full-time work and go on state assistance to get by. We are unable to obtain his residency without him returning to Mexico and remaining there for up to three years. We have five children. At the age of 14 months, our son was diagnosed with leukemia. I could not have endured this hardship alone. Our government wants us to believe that these undocumented immigrants can be sent back with no ramifications, but that is simply not true. Families will be greatly affected. Innocent children are involved and ultimately punished by the removal of a parent.[7]

Where Do We Go from Here?

The marches were successful in defeating the passage of H.R. 4437. The momentum of the marches was sustained into the 2006 elections as the chant "today we march, on November 7 we vote" turned into reality at the ballot box. The historic ethnic shift in the Latino vote in support of the Democratic Party (from 44 percent in 2004 to 73 percent in 2006) was largely due to the view by the Latino community that the Republican Party was running on a political platform of immigrant and Latino bashing and that, by and large, the Democratic Party supported comprehensive immigration reform. However, despite the Democratic Party winning a majority in the House and Senate, the movement for immigrant rights still faces an uphill battle to ensure that both political parties treat immigration reform as a priority in 2008 and beyond.

The response of the Bush administration has been to carry out raids such as those at the Swift meatpacking plants, which have exposed the inhumanity and injustice in these actions—including civil rights violations, racial profiling, and the separation of families from their children. This, in turn, has led to numerous anti-immigrant ordinances at the local level to deny access to renting apartments, city permits, school or driver's licenses, among others. In Whitewater, Wisconsin, a raid was carried out at Star Packaging on August 8, 2006. The raid resulted in the detention of a grandmother, who recalled:

> They took us to Dodge County jail. We were told to strip off our clothes and put on the uniforms. When my clothes were off, I could not control myself any longer and I started to cry. Then I started to throw up. They covered me in a sheet and took me away to isolation. I was without food, water, or clothing for 28 hours. I am diabetic. Finally, the Consular from Mexico came because my coworkers had spoken to him and they wanted to know what happened to me. He had to wait two hours to see me. I had to talk to him without clothing. He contacted the pastor at my church, and they raised the money to pay for the bond.

A husband and wife were arrested at the company. The woman was still breast-feeding her eight-month-old baby. When she told them that she needed to feed her baby. She was told, "maybe some American family can take your baby."

In addition, in 2006 the administration was able to sneak in enforcement provisions through an administrative rule change to Social Security No Match letters. This means that an employer who receives an SS No Match letter must re-verify work authorization and dismiss workers if the problem is not resolved or the employer will be considered to have constructive knowledge of a worker's immigration status. This policy, if implemented, would lead to large-scale dislocation and superexploitation as workers would be recirculated through temporary agencies as "new workers" with even lower wages and less access to insurance. This will greatly bring down the standard of living for all workers in the United States by creating an even larger pool of vulnerable temporary workers. Although the implementation of this new rule is being delayed due to opposition by employers, the impact will bring to the forefront once again the immigrant working class.

This struggle is an entrenched battle against powerful corporate interests that benefit from the exploitation of immigrant workers, for-profit prisons who stand to benefit from increased criminalization and detention, and defense contractors who benefit from the militarization of the border. The ability to divide and conquer America's working class by scapegoating immigrant workers for economic problems is of course a powerful weapon of social control.

¡Latinos callados serán deportados, Latinos unidos serán respetados!

Despite these acts of repression, the marches represented what is possible when working families are pushed against the wall. Resistance by immigrant workers to raids made national headlines by the sanctuary of Elvira Arellano in a Methodist church in Chicago. In solidarity, workers from Whitewater, Wisconsin, chanted outside of the Immigration Court, "Latinos callados serán deportados, Latinos unidos serán respetados," which translated means, "Silent Latinos will be deported, United Latinos will be respected," and holding up signs for the media and passer-bys that read, "It should not be a crime to work."

In January 2007 an interdenominational group called CLUE convened a national meeting to expand on this concept of a sanctuary movement for the undocumented. These important developments represent resistance to unjust deportations on the part of U.S. citizens and immigrant workers.

To win the justice we seek, we need to keep organizing, mobilizing, developing new leaders, and building alliances to win good immigration reform that is part of a broader social and economic justice movement for working people in the United States and around the world.

Juan Soto, a VF member, wrote a poem, "The Hymn of Voces de la Frontera," to inspire other workers to join the struggle. It is often recited at various meetings, and it seems appropriate to close this contribution with it.

Himno de Voces de la Frontera

Animo paisano, y adelante,
Hay mil obstáculos dondequiera,
Pero saldremos triunfantes,
Uniéndonos, a Voces de la Frontera.

Es gente humilde y sencilla,
De las que pocas hay,
Pienso que es buena semilla,
Pá alcanzar la libertad.

Unámonos a su causa,
Eso es lo que yo quisiera,
Que vieran que hay pura raza,
En Voces de la Frontera.

Es gente que ha sufrido,
Como tu, como yo, en la vida,
Pero siempre han sabido,
Encontrar buenas salidas.

Ahí te miran hermano,
Sin ver las clases sociales,
Ya que el país donde estamos,
Nos mire como animales.

Por lo pronto ahí te espero,
Con esa gente sincera,
Paisano yo verte quiero,
En Voces de la Frontera.

Here is a translation of the poem:

Hymn of Voces de la Frontera

Let's go brothers and sisters
There are a thousand obstacles everywhere
But we will come out of it triumphant
Uniting with Voces de la Frontera.

The people there are humble and simple
The kind that few are
I believe it is good seed
To achieve our liberty.

Let's unite to their cause
That is what I desire
For them to see people united
At Voces de la Frontera.

It is people who have suffered
Like you, like me, in life,
But have always found good ways to progress.

Brothers and sisters, there they look at you
Without seeing social classes
Even though in the country we are in
They look at us like animals.

Just for now, I wait for you there
With those sincere people
Brothers, sisters, I want to see you
At Voces de la Frontera.

NOTES

1. Xavier Marquez, interview, August 8, 2006.
2. Ed Kubacki, interview, May 12, 2006.

3. Veronica Garcia, interview, August 1, 2006.
4. Vanessa Vara-Ramos, interview, May 2, 2006.
5. Bertha Gonzalez, interview,July 26, 2006.
6. Miguel Ortega, interview, August 1, 2006.
7. Luis Alvarez, interview, July 12, 2006.

CHAPTER 11

Immigrant Workers Take the Lead

A Militant Humility Transforms L.A. Koreatown

Glenn Omatsu

When we look at the country, we see who are the ones doing this kind of low-wage work. They're not white Americans; they are immigrant workers. I think we play such an important role in U.S. society.

—Jung Hee Lee, L.A. Koreatown restaurant waitress and organizer[1]

We are tired of being mistreated, tired of being overworked and underpaid, and tired of being insulted. We deserve better work conditions, salaries, and benefits. But the most important thing is that we deserve to be treated respectfully because we are human beings, not slaves.

—Maximiliano Mariscal, L.A. Koreatown market worker and organizer[2]

Where do leaders for our communities come from? How do people develop the skills to lead communities?

In neighborhoods across the United States today, we often hear the following question: "Where are this generation's Malcolm X, Martin Luther King Jr., Rosa Parks, and Cesar Chavez?" Implicit in this question is the belief held by many in America today, especially young people, that there is a leadership crisis facing our communities and that little can be done to change society until new leaders emerge.

Actually, in our communities today inspiring, new leaders have already emerged—but they are largely invisible, except to those immediately around them. Like Rosa Parks, these new leaders show others how seemingly small acts of courage by a single person can be linked to collective mobilization against injustice. Like Malcolm X and Martin Luther King Jr., these new leaders teach others how to combine social change with personal transformation. Like Cesar Chavez, these new leaders show others how fighting for the rights of the most oppressed sectors in a community can empower all people.

Who are these new leaders, and why are they so invisible? Too often we are conditioned to look for our leaders in the wrong places. We look for them in the TV news broadcasts where reporters cover dramatic events in our cities and interview important individuals. We look for them among the ranks of politicians. We look for them among the spokespersons of organizations or from the sector of professionals in our communities, such as lawyers and business executives. But when we look for our leaders in these places, we forget one of the most powerful lessons that Malcolm X, Martin Luther King Jr., Rosa Parks, and Cesar Chavez taught us: leaders in our community emerge in "ordinary" settings. They are found in workplaces, schools, and other community gathering places. They are found in grassroots struggles around basic neighborhood needs like housing, jobs, and schools.

In this essay I tell the story of one remarkable set of leaders in Los Angeles Koreatown, a gritty, inner-city neighborhood where tens of thousands of immigrants from Latin America and Korea live and work together in a five-mile radius of densely packed apartment buildings and small shops. Like many other communities across America, L.A. Koreatown is marked by poverty, overcrowded schools, gangs, crimes, and ethnic conflict over scarce resources. Yet, amid this turmoil, several important leaders are helping people to organize collectively to solve these problems. These leaders are immigrant women and men from Korea, Mexico, Guatemala, and El Salvador who developed their leadership skills during the past decade through campaigns for justice in Koreatown restaurants, markets, and other workplaces. Because they are immigrant workers in one of the city's poorest neighborhoods, these women and men are unknown to most outside of Koreatown, and they are not yet fully appreciated even by their neighbors. Yet, their impact as leaders extends far beyond workplaces. They have redefined race relations in Koreatown, reshaped gender relations in their largely patriarchal immigrant cultures, and contributed to the development of a new, grassroots leadership model that can potentially help all communities today. Who are these inspiring leaders?

Rising from Fires of Koreatown

Our story begins in the dark weeks after the 1992 L.A. riots. The four days and nights of fire and destruction devastated many inner-city neighborhoods, including Koreatown. Officially, more than fifty people died, thousands were arrested, and more than 5,000 small businesses throughout Los Angeles were looted, burned, or destroyed.[3] Described by one researcher as "America's first multiethnic riot," the upheaval stood in sharp contrast to riots in the 1960s and 1970s that focused on conflicts between African Americans and Whites. The 1992 L.A. riots involved a rainbow of ethnic and racial groups as both victims and perpetrators.[4] The multiethnic conflict punctured the myth that had been carefully nurtured by the city's politicians and corporate executives of Los Angeles as a postmodern city of ethnic harmony. The riots highlighted a different reality: the growing gap between rich and poor and the decades of neglect by politicians and business executives of the city's poorest neighborhoods.

The riots severely affected Koreans and Latinos. Throughout Los Angeles, more than 2,000 Korean small businesses were looted, burned, or destroyed.[5] Of those arrested during the riots, Latinos represented the largest racial-ethnic group and also faced deportation by immigration authorities. They were arrested for looting, curfew violations, and simply being in the wrong area at the time of a police sweep of neighborhoods.[6] In Koreatown, the destruction of small businesses brought more than economic hardships for the owners. Many Latino and Korean immigrant workers in markets, restaurants, and other small shops suddenly found themselves unemployed.

For community groups in the areas affected by the riots, the racial conflicts provoked intense reflection about what could be done in the future to improve race relations. In Koreatown, groups ranging from business associations to churches to social service agencies launched new initiatives aimed at reaching out to other communities of color, establishing contact with politicians in mainstream society, and training merchants in cultural sensitivity.[7] In other L.A. neighborhoods, many groups came to a common conclusion: communities of color faced a leadership crisis. Thus, the groups needed to focus on leadership training. However, most leadership programs created in the period immediately after the riots adopted a model associated with corporations, the military, and mainstream politicians. As we will see later, this model of leadership is strongly rooted in western colonialism and, by its very nature, defines leaders as being a select few in society who command others.

In this tumultuous period, one new organization arose in Koreatown that would change the face of community leadership. The new group was founded one month before the riots and had the audacious goal of empowering Korean and Latino workers and mobilizing them as leaders to grapple with the challenges facing Koreatown. The new group was called Korean Immigrant Worker Advocates (KIWA); KIWA was renamed in 2006 as Koreatown Immigrant Workers Alliance to more accurately reflect its composition. The cofounders of KIWA—Roy Hong and Danny Park—were young immigrant activists who had previously been involved in international solidarity work and community organizing. They perceptively observed that Koreatown faced a vacuum: there was no organization advocating for the needs of workers. They also recognized that many Koreans entering the United States in the late 1980s and early 1990s were influenced by the massive, militant labor struggles occurring in Korea that led to the formation of hundreds of new unions and greater public awareness of workers' power. Moreover, while most researchers and journalists focused on the importance of immigrant entrepreneurs in Koreatown and the high rates of small business ownership by Koreans, Hong and Park keenly saw that 70 percent of Korean immigrants toiled as workers, often in back-breaking and low-paying jobs. Hong and Park also realized that in Koreatown these Koreans toiled side by side with Latinos, but little was being done to address their common concerns.

KIWA's first campaign was to demand emergency aid for immigrant workers who had lost their jobs at shops destroyed during the rioting. KIWA helped workers confront powerful Korean community leaders who had amassed a large relief fund from donations sent in from people around the world. Initially, this relief fund was to be distributed only to shop owners, but due to KIWA's efforts, the distribution was expanded to include workers.[8] Meanwhile, KIWA organizers had already begun laying the foundation for two major campaigns that would occupy the bulk of their work for the next decade: organizing Korean and Latino workers in Koreatown's restaurant and market industries. But how would they deal with the climate of ethnic tensions in the period after the riots?

Latinos and Koreans: Conflict or Solidarity?

In the wake of the 1992 L.A. riots, academics and journalists focused on racial conflicts underlying the unrest, especially tensions between Koreans and African Americans in inner-city neighborhoods. Those more attuned to the realities of L.A. neighborhoods—such as community organizers and community-based researchers—pointed to another and potentially more explosive source of tensions: the complex relationship between Latinos and Koreans.

Similar to Black-Korean tension, the Latino-Korean relationship involves two minority groups pitted against each other in inner-city neighborhoods. Black-Korean conflict involves a merchant-customer relationship between immigrant small businessmen who live outside the neighborhoods and an American-born oppressed minority group that historically has been denied opportunities for business ownership. Throughout the history of Los Angeles, African American and immigrant workers have been involved in competition, as well as cooperation with one another.[9] In contrast, Latino-Korean conflict involves two immigrant groups that are involved not only in a merchant-customer relationship but also a workplace relationship. In

Koreatown especially, many Korean businesses hire Latino immigrants. Like other American employers, these businesses regard Latinos as "cheap labor" to be exploited. Thus, the employer-employee relationship adds to a new dimension of tension between two new immigrant groups.[10]

The ethnic tensions are particularly evident in Koreatown's two largest industries—restaurants and markets. In both industries, Korean employers hire large numbers of Latino and Korean workers and systematically divide the workforce by race and ethnicity. In restaurants, Koreans are hired as cooks and waitresses, while Latinos are employed as kitchen helpers, busboys, and dishwashers. In markets, Korean women and men work the cash registers and in other jobs dealing with the public, while Latinos work as stockers, warehousemen, and the clean-up crew. It is also common for Korean employers to promote "ethnic solidarity" with their Korean workers, using favoritism in job assignments to create a special bond. At the same time, this "ethnic solidarity" can work against Korean workers who sometimes must endure abuse and harassment from bosses under the guise of adhering to shared cultural values. In addition, those Korean workers who are labeled "troublemakers" for fighting for their rights quickly discover they are blacklisted and unable to find a job with another Korean employer in the industry.[11]

KIWA founders, as seasoned political activists, recognized that the key to building unity between Latino and Korean workers was to help them see their common issues (i.e., their exploitation as a low-paid workforce) and to understand what divided them (i.e., ethnicity, language, and gender). "You cannot talk about race without class and look at class without race," explained Roy Hong, then KIWA executive director: "If you do that, you fall into the trap of racializing, or the other side of the coin, it becomes ethnocentric or nationalistic. We strongly feel that worker organizing should not be categorized as just an economic justice issue. It's not. It's the most effective for workers to build racial justice."[12]

Thus, KIWA promoted an expansive vision of immigrant worker empowerment. Gaining justice for immigrant workers did not simply mean gaining better wages and benefits. Gaining justice went beyond economic issues. It involved changing race relations in Koreatown, upholding immigrant rights, and fighting for decent housing and schools. Gaining justice meant transforming Koreatown. But to gain justice, new leaders and a new concept of leadership were needed. KIWA founders firmly believed that these new leaders and this new model of leadership would emerge from the ranks of immigrant workers.

Immigrant Workers as Community Leaders: Leading with Militant Humility

Neither Jung Hee Lee nor Maxiliano Mariscal fits the stereotypical image of community leader (Figs. 11.1, 11.2). Jung Hee Lee is a young immigrant mother who looks like the hundreds of Korean waitresses carrying heavy trays of boiling, bubbling pots in Korean restaurants. To strangers, Mrs. Lee seems like a quiet woman. Max Mariscal, a recent Mexican immigrant, resembles other young Latino men toiling as busboys, kitchen

Fig. 11.1. Jung Hee Lee, L.A. Koreatown restaurant waitress and organizer (center, facing camera). Courtesy Koreatown Immigrant Worker Advocates

Fig. 11.2. Maximiliano Mariscal, L.A. Koreatown market worker and organizer (right). Courtesy Koreatown Immigrant Worker Advocates

helpers, and warehousemen in Los Angeles. Like many other immigrants, Max works hard but always seems to have a smile for those he encounters. Until recently, Lee worked as a waitress in Koreatown restaurants, and Mariscal worked in Koreatown restaurants and markets. Both today are community organizers helping fellow immigrants fight for rights in Koreatown. Both today are described by many around them as having militant humility. They ferociously fight against those who exploit and oppress others, while humbly serving their fellow workers.

Mariscal and Lee are among a cadre of immigrant workers who have emerged from struggles for justice in Koreatown restaurants and markets. They embody KIWA's vision of new community leadership. They developed leadership skills by grappling with critical questions in KIWA's campaigns for justice. These questions include: How can workers unite around common interests when they are daily divided by employers through race, language, culture, and gender? How can immigrant workers, especially those who are undocumented, overcome fear to demand respect and dignity? How can immigrant workers change the perception held by most in society that they are simply "cheap labor"? How can workers challenge the prevailing patriarchal cultures of Koreans long influenced by Confucianism and Latinos long influenced by *machismo*? How can immigrant workers with very little power mobilize to fight effectively against powerful business owners? Leaders like Lee and Mariscal answer these questions through their life stories, showing others the ways their own lives have been transformed through participation in movements for justice.

Thousands of immigrants like Lee and Mariscal work in Koreatown's two biggest industries: restaurants and markets, the focal points for campaigns launched by KIWA during the past decade. The two industries have important differences. There are more than 200 Koreatown restaurants, ranging from small, family-run operations that are barely surviving to large enterprises with high profits. In contrast to the restaurant industry, Koreatown markets are dominated by six supermarkets. Five of these companies also operate as chains with branches outside of Koreatown. Although the restaurant and market industries are structured differently, they have one significant commonality: they both depend on low-wage labor of Korean and Latino immigrants. An estimated 2,000 immigrants work in Koreatown restaurants, and about 800 work in markets. The six supermarkets especially make immense profits from their workers. These supermarkets have sales volumes similar to Ralphs and Vons, Krogers, or Safeway, but they pay workers near minimum wage.[13]

KIWA's campaigns in these two industries began at different times but have now united under the current effort to gain a "living wage" for all in Koreatown.[14] Restaurant worker organizing began in the mid-1990s when KIWA began helping workers with problems such as unpaid wages, job-related injuries, and harassment by employers. Under the leadership of KIWA cofounder Danny Park, workers filed claims with government agencies. In 1997, with the help of researchers and college students, KIWA staff conducted an extensive survey of the Koreatown restaurant industry that documented widespread abuses and severe violations of labor laws, such as minimum wage, overtime, and health and safety regulations. In 1997, some 97 percent of Koreatown's restaurants had labor law violations. However, four years later, the rate had dropped dramatically to 41 percent.[15] During this four-year period, KIWA shifted its approach on worker organizing.

Rather than helping workers file claims with government agencies, KIWA encouraged workers to meet with owners to demand unpaid wages, to hold job actions such as picketing, and to speak out in community forums to gather support.

This new approach came from immigrant workers themselves, who were frustrated about long, bureaucratic delays in receiving wages owed to them after filing claims with government agencies. Perhaps influenced by militant labor struggles they had witnessed in Korea in the 1980s, the immigrants felt that "direct action" would more quickly resolve problems. The first test case occurred at Nam Kang Restaurant where a group of Korean waitresses, angry over their employer's refusal to pay them several months of wages, met with KIWA and asked for help in picketing the restaurant. The women and their families shut down the restaurant for several days. The action ended successfully when the owner negotiated with the women on their picket line and began paying the wages he owed them.[16] In the next three years, KIWA staff assisted Korean and Latino restaurant workers to organize more than two dozen militant actions at restaurants, including a ten-day hunger strike at a popular barbecue restaurant by a fired cook and a KIWA staff member and a year-long picket and boycott of another eatery for unpaid wages.[17]

KIWA's campaign in the market industry began in the summer of 2001 when twenty Latino immigrants walked off their jobs at Assi supermarket to protest a reduction in their work schedules. The workers walked one block to the KIWA office and met with KIWA leader Danny Park, who accompanied the workers back to the market where they met with the manager. The workers' grievances initiated a three-year-long union organizing campaign at the supermarket. Latino and Korean workers—with the support of Latino American and Asian American community organizations—sought to form an independent union, the Immigrant Workers Union. The Assi owner hired an anti-union consultant who stymied the workers' campaign, diverting it into courts by having management commit unfair labor practices (e.g., firings and worker harassment) and contest the results of the union representation election. In 2005, the workers and KIWA shifted the campaign from a demand for union recognition to demands for a living wage and for the rehiring of those fired. Like the restaurant worker campaign, the campaign at Assi supermarket has been defined by militant and massive actions by workers and their community supporters.

The campaign has also prompted at least one of the other large supermarkets in Koreatown to raise its wages for workers.[18]

Jung Hee Lee and Max Mariscal emerged as leaders during the restaurant and market campaigns, respectively. Their involvement in these campaigns would transform their lives and enable them to develop the "militant humility" that defines immigrant workers as leaders. Lee first went to KIWA to learn about her rights at a restaurant workers' legal clinic. In the documentary *Grassroots Rising,* focusing on Asian immigrant labor struggles in Los Angeles, she remembers her surprise in discovering that U.S. laws regarding minimum wage and health and safety applied to new immigrants.[19] Until then, she had simply accepted the long working hours, the low pay, and the dangerous working conditions. It was not long until Lee asserted her rights. After severely injuring herself from falling on a greasy floor at a restaurant, she was fired by the owner who refused her claim for workers compensation.

She began to speak out about her case and similar abuses affecting other workers at community meetings and public hearings. She began going to protests and picket lines, first as a participant and then as a speaker. Currently, she is a leader of the Restaurant Workers Association of Koreatown and is helping KIWA with its campaign for a living wage. "Organizing is not a job to me; it's a responsibility," she states. "I get satisfaction in the successes of the workers. When the workers cry, I cry."[20] In addition, she believes her transformation from a person who knew nothing about her rights into an activist advocating for the rights of all sets a good example for her children. Her children, now teenagers, have accompanied their mother to picket lines, community meetings, and public hearings for several years. She says, "As a mother, I want my children to be socially conscious and aware of how things are and to share my experiences with them."[21]

Like Lee, Mariscal once passively accepted the harsh working conditions in Koreatown restaurants and markets that employed him. KIWA's campaign at Assi supermarket changed his life. Due to his willingness to stand up for workers, both Latinos and Koreans, his fellow workers elected him president of their fledgling union. When management fired him, the workers steadfastly continued to support him. Those who know Max describe him as quiet, strong, humble, and caring. Students active in the workers' community support committee describe him in these terms:

> Maximiliano Mariscal does not look like a labor leader. He is slightly built, almost thin, and young. He is also a recent immigrant from a southern region of Mexico, where he left all of his family and friends. His quiet charisma and humility hide his central role in this campaign. He never emphasizes his own essential organizing work or the risks he has taken and sacrifices he has made on behalf of his co-workers. Instead he tells the stories of his friends and comrades who struggled with him. He never considers what he can gain personally from his position as a leader, but simply asks, "What can we gain together?" Max's quiet leadership style and the collective decision-making process he and his coworkers utilized symbolize the workers' approach to worker empowerment.[22]

Immigrant worker leaders like Mariscal and Lee help fellow workers courageously confront managers, but they also help workers deal with internal divisions among themselves. In Koreatown restaurants and markets, the most common division centers on race. For example, Mariscal recalls that in the initial stages of the campaign at Assi supermarket, he did not know if he should go to KIWA because of his previous bad experiences with Koreans: "At the beginning, we (Latino workers) didn't trust KIWA because it was Korean. Most of our experiences with Koreans were really, really bad."[23] Similarly, at the beginning of the restaurant workers' campaign, Korean waitresses who were at the forefront of militant actions often questioned the hesitancy of Latino busboys and kitchen helpers to join them in actions. In later years of the restaurant campaign, however, Latino workers were at the forefront of militant actions, while Korean workers were absent.

All grassroots social movements for justice go through ebbs and flows, and in movements involving different racial groups, it is not unusual for one group to take leadership at different times. It is also common for those in power to promote racial divisions by fostering mistrust, accentuating cultural differences, and practicing favoritism. In both the restaurant and market industries, employers and their hired consultants manipulated racial differences to block worker unity. Nevertheless, in both campaigns, worker leaders courageously opposed these attacks. In the campaign at Assi, the actions of one man exemplify the powerful ways that immigrant workers build unity between Latinos and Koreans. Chin Yol Yi was an older and respected Korean man who worked in Assi's fish department. At a key stage in the campaign, Yi wrote and signed a document advocating his support for the Immigrant Workers Union at Assi. "We get yelled at like we are criminals," Yi explained. "We want to work with dignity, without so much pressure."[24] Then, a few days later at a meeting at KIWA, he approached his fellow Latino workers. The dramatic moment is captured in an account written by community supporters:

> At the meeting Mr. Yi introduced himself to his fellow workers and explained to them what he had done. (He spoke in Korean, and his remarks were translated into Spanish and English.) He spoke of supporting the efforts of the union and rallying other Koreans to also do the same. Mr. Yi's impressive contribution was when he bowed and apologized for the harsh treatment of the Korean people to the Latino workers. "I will do anything to help the Latino workers," he stated. "As a Korean person, I apologize to the Latinos deeply." He conveyed a sincere concern and empathy towards his fellow co-workers. The impact of his statement was a trilingual moment, capturing the emotion and heart of three languages coming together.[25]

Forging a New Model of Leadership for Our Communities

The significance of immigrant leaders such as Chin Yol Yi, Max Mariscal, and Jung Hee Lee go far beyond the Koreatown restaurant and market industries and far beyond immigrant communities. Their militant humility is rooted in a concept of leadership very different from the prevailing leadership model in America that is associated with government, the military, and corporations. The prevailing model sees leadership as an individual attribute associated with a few charismatic persons who are able to command others. Historically, the prevailing model is based on western colonialism and related to the development of racism and patriarchy that are central to colonial domination. Thus, not surprisingly, American institutions built on this colonial legacy, such as corporations and the military, are marked by the historical exclusion of women and racial minorities from leadership posts. Similarly, leadership training programs based on the prevailing model focus on the development of assertiveness, independent decision-making, and the ability to manage large numbers of people.[26]

The alternative leadership model of immigrant workers is actually part of a countertradition that has existed in various forms for the past 500 years as different groups have struggled against colonialism. This alternative model is based on the struggles of indigenous peoples who fought against the advent of colonialism and whose struggle continues today through groups like the Zapatistas. It is linked to the anticolonial movements of the twentieth century in Africa, Asia, and Latin America under leaders such as Gandhi, and it is associated in the United States with the civil rights movement of the 1960s and the accompanying movements of women, gays and lesbians, and other oppressed peoples. Today, the alternative model is being further developed throughout the world mainly by two forces: by the grassroots antiglobalization movement against corporate domination and by immigrant workers in nations like the United States.

The alternative vision of leadership foregrounds human qualities very different from the prevailing patriarchal model of leadership. It emphasizes the capacity for nurturing others and bringing out their best talents, the ability to mediate conflict, the quality to both express empathy and compassion for others, and the talent for encouraging different viewpoints while upholding one's own core values and principles. This vision appreciates leadership as not a special characteristic in a few individuals but as a collective attribute that emerges and develops within a community, especially through struggles for justice. This vision of leadership emphasizes a commitment to dignity, equality, democracy, and transformation in human beings. Thus, this vision is closely associated with grassroots movements for social justice around the world.

In Los Angeles Koreatown, immigrant workers like Jung Hee Lee and Max Mariscal are further contributing to the development of this alternative vision of leadership with their emphasis on militant humility. In their conversations with others, they always insist that they are not leaders. And, from the perspective of the prevailing leadership model in America, they are right. Yet, Lee and Mariscal are always the first to militantly confront powerful oppressors in Koreatown while humbly serving fellow workers.

By understanding how immigrant workers have transformed L.A. Koreatown, we can begin to recognize the largely invisible leaders in our communities today. And, perhaps most significant of all, we can also begin to appreciate the leadership potential existing in each of us to serve our communities.

NOTES

1. Quoted in Tram Nguyen, "Showdown in K-Town," *ColorLines* (Spring 2001): 29.

2. Quoted in Jessica Kim, T. J. Lee, and Hyun-Ja Pak, "Market Workers Justice Campaign," Asian Pacific American Labor Studies, UCLA, Winter Quarter 2002, at www.sscnet.ucla.edu/aasc/classweb/winter02/aas197a/index.html.

3. Edward T. Chang, "America's First Multiethnic 'Riots,'" in *The State of Asian America: Resistance and Activism in the 1990s,* ed. Karin Aguilar-San Juan (Boston: South End Press, 1994), 101–18; Mike Davis, *L.A. Was Just the Beginning: Urban Revolt in the United States, a Thousand Points of Light* (Westfield, N.J.: Open Magazine Pamphlet, 1992).

4. Julie Ha Chang, ed., "4-29-92: Remembering the L.A. Uprising, One Year Later," *Pacific Ties, UCLA's Asian Pacific Islander Newsmagazine* (April 1993), 2; Institute for Alternative Journalism, *Inside the L.A. Riots: What Really Happened—and Why It Will Happen Again* (New York: Institute for Alternative Journalism, 1992).

5. E. Chang, "America's First Multiethnic 'Riot.'"

6. American Civil Liberties Union of Southern California, *Civil Liberties in Crisis: Los Angeles during the Emergency* (Los Angeles: ACLU, 1992).

7. Edward Park, "Competing Visions: Political Formations of Korean Americans in Los Angeles, 1992–1997," *Amerasia Journal* 24/1 (1998), 41–57.

8. Nguyen, "Showdown in K-Town," 27.

9. For example, the Justice for Janitors campaign in L.A. has largely focused on organizing Latino immigrants who now dominate the low-wage industry. At one time, this industry was heavily African American, but as the industry shifted toward subcontracting, low-wage immigrant labor replaced American-born workers. In the L.A. hotel industry, one of the central demands of the union has been for the large hotels to hire African American workers. The union is now heavily Latino immigrant, but as it has been able to successfully increase wages and benefits for workers, hotel work is now an occupation that African American

community leaders would like to open up beyond immigrant workers and Black workers.

10. Edward T. Chang and Jeannette Diaz-Veizades, *Ethnic Peace in an American City: Building Community in Los Angeles and Beyond* (New York: New York University Press, 1999).

11. Koreatown Immigrant Workers Alliance, at www.kiwa.org (accessed July 7, 2006).

12. Quoted in Nguyen, "Showdown in K-Town," 28; see also Daisy Ha, "An Analysis and critique of KIWA's Reform Efforts in the Los Angeles Korean American Restaurant Industry," *Asian Law Journal* 8 (May 2001), 1–33.

13. Koreatown Immigrant Workers Alliance, *Koreatown Restaurant Industry* and *Market Workers Justice Campaign Fact Sheet,* at www.kiwa.org (accessed July 7 2006).

14. Koreatown Immigrant Workers Alliance, *Living Wage Campaign,* at www.kiwa.org (accessed July 7, 2006).

15. Nguyen, "Showdown in K-Town," 29; Koreatown Immigrant Workers Alliance, *History of Campaign,* www.kiwa.org (accessed July 7, 2006).

16. Koreatown Immigrant Workers Alliance, *History of Campaign.*

17. Nguyen, "Showdown in K-Town," 28; Ha, "Analysis of KIWA's Reform Efforts"; Koreatown Immigrant Workers Alliance, *History of Campaign.*

18. Sang Mok Kim, "A Spread of the Adoption of the 'Living Wage' in Korean Markets," *Korea Times* (January 26, 2006), at www.indypressny/org/article.php3?article_id=2491 (accessed August 5, 2006).

19. Robert Winn, director, *Grassroots Rising: Asian Immigrant Workers in Los Angeles,* video recording (Los Angeles: Visual Communications, 2005), 56 minutes.

20. Lynne Nguyen, "Coming Lee-aps and Bounds: One Immigrant's Transformation from Mother/Waitress to Community Leader," *Pacific Ties, UCLA's Asian Pacific Islander Newsmagazine* (Winter 2006), 10.

21. Winn, *Grassroots Rising.*

22. Kim, Lee, and Pak, "Market Workers Justice Campaign."

23. Jessica Kim, Anthony T. J. Lee, and Hyun-Ja Pak, *Winning the Wage War: The Market Workers Justice Campaign,* video recording (Los Angeles: Asian Pacific American Labor Studies, UCLA, 2002), 24 minutes.

24. Quoted in Austin Bunn, "Market Forces: Fighting for Justice and Fair Wages at Koreatown's Largest Grocery," *LA Weekly* (May 3, 2002), at www.laweekly.com/news/news/market-forces/3944/ (accessed July 7, 2006).

25. Kim, Lee, and Pak, "Market Workers Justice Campaign"; Kim, Lee, and Pak, *Winning the Wage War.*

26. For a fuller discussion of the difference between the prevailing model of

leadership and the alternative model, see Glenn Omatsu, "Making Student Leadership Development an Integral Part of Our Classrooms," in *Teaching about Asian Pacific Americans: Effective Activities, Strategies, and Assignments for Classrooms and Communities,* ed. Edith Wen-chu Chen and Glenn Omatsu (Lanham, Md.: Rowman and Littlefield, 2006), 183–94.

PART IV

Questions of Democracy

Questions of immigrant rights are essentially questions about democracy and citizenship. By advocating for their rights as citizens and noncitizens, immigrants have transformed the nature of U.S. democracy since the early twentieth century.

What rights do migrants across national boundaries possess? If, as t-shirts at the marches during the spring of 2006 proclaimed, "no human being is illegal," what does this mean? Are immigrant claims to equal opportunity to be staked in terms of human rights, or are the rights of immigrants, documented or not, a key component of national citizenship? This section addresses these questions.

In chapter 12, the lead article for this section, legal scholar Victor Romero explores "the federal-state divide" in immigration policy. While the federal government has the power to regulate immigration, local governments implement regulations governing the lives of citizens, legal residents, and undocumented migrants. The U.S. Supreme Court has resisted efforts, like the one made by the state of Texas in *Plyler v. Doe* in 1982 or in California by the passage of Proposition 187 in 1994, to deny equal protection to noncitizens. On the other hand, particularly in recent years, many local governments have responded to the presence of immigrants in places like Hazleton, Pennsylvania; New Haven, Connecticut; and Green Bay, Wisconsin, by implementing policies designed in some cases to affirm their presence, and in others, to limit their rights. Romero explores the tension between such local initiatives and federal policy in the context of contemporary debates over immigration policy.

Following Romero's contribution, chapter 13 looks at a specific aspect of conflict between federal and local policies over the rights of immigrants. Although federal law currently defines undocumented students as foreign for the purposes of public university admission, ten states have passed statutes allowing undocumented students who graduate from high school in their states to attend their colleges and universities as in-state residents. The essay explores the ways in which students have organized to advocate for such policies. While a federal DREAM (Development, Relief and Education for Alien Minors) bill has been introduced without being passed more than once in the Senate, many states and immigrant rights advocates have acted independently to ensure the access of immigrant students to higher education and opportunity.

In chapter 14, historian Jeanne Petit moves the focus on immigration and democracy back in time, examining the ways that American Catholics in the early twentieth century advocated for the rights of Catholic immigrants. This advocacy, she argues, led members of the National Catholic Welfare Congress to expand their ideas of citizenship, leading them away from the focus on racial fitness popular with restrictionists at the time and toward an expansive idea of democracy and inclusion. Petit's argument makes clear parallels to the contemporary position of Catholic leaders like Los Angeles Cardinal Roger Mahoney, who calls on Catholics to offer humanitarian aid to all migrants, regardless of legal status.

In chapter 15, Fred Tsao, Policy Director for the Illinois Coalition for Immigrant and Refugee Rights (ICIRR), looks at the ways in which different communities define their identities and strategize for survival. He writes of the ways diverse immigrant groups in the Chicago area have found common cause in the struggles for legalization and access to citizenship and political power. Chicago's substantial Latino, Muslim, Arab, Polish, African, and Irish communities have realized that many of the specific community issues facing each group are actually connected to those faced by other communities in the area. Tsao documents the successes of the alliances formed by diverse immigrants in Illinois and discusses the ways in which such coalitions are transforming the politics of the state.

Tsao's contribution is followed by ICIRR's announcement of a drive for naturalization and voter registration, a major component of ICIRR's work to aid legal permanent residents to become citizens and vote. Along with the documents from the National Network for Immigrant and Refugee

Rights in Part I, this document provides a broad context in which to understand immigrant political organization.

In chapter 16, the final article for this section, immigration lawyer and legal scholar David Cole traces the restrictions on civil liberties for immigrants since the bombing of the World Trade Center in 2001. Focusing on the treatment of immigrants from the Middle East since 9/11, he argues that the pursuit of national security cannot justify the impairment of the human rights of immigrants without also impairing the rights of citizens and the functioning of democracy itself.

This section ends with a 1950 piece by Abner Green of the American Committee for the Protection of the Foreign Born, "The Deportation Terror: A Weapon to Gag America."

CHAPTER 12

Who Should Manage Immigration—Congress or the States?

An Introduction to Constitutional Immigration Law

Victor C. Romero

The Federal-State Divide over Immigration Power

Scanning today's headlines, airwaves, and weblogs, it's easy to conclude that the United States is in a fairly anti-immigrant mood. From new federal laws authorizing the creation of a 700-mile border fence to increased security at airports and seaports, from calls for fewer immigrant visas to crackdowns on undocumented workers, Americans are clamoring for the president and Congress to prioritize comprehensive immigration reform. Yet, in small towns and some states around the country, a growing number of local governments are no longer willing to wait for the federal government to act. Places like Gaithersburg, Maryland, and Hazleton, Pennsylvania, are formulating their own solutions to the age-old problem of how to balance the needs of their communities against the desire to welcome and assimilate productive newcomers.

Often, these local governments have drawn the line at legal immigration, arguing that residents without the proper documentation have no right to be in the United States and, accordingly, have no right to live and work in their communities; opponents argue that immigration laws are the exclusive province of the federal, not local, government, and that these anti-immigration ordinances are little more than a modern form of racial profiling against a demographic that has become increasingly Latin American in flavor. Given that noncitizens immigrate to the United States and yet settle in specific local communities, which government—federal or state—should be in charge of regulating this ebb and flow of people? Assuming that both national and local entities have a role to play, whose policies prevail should there be a disagreement between the two?

Constitutional Immigration Law and the Federal-State Divide

For constitutional lawyers, two primary sources of the authority of the government are the text of the Constitution and the decisions of the U.S. Supreme Court interpreting that text.[1] In this introduction to "constitutional immigration law," I explore both of these sources in an attempt to discern the powers of the federal and state governments over noncitizens.

The Text of the Constitution

The text of our Constitution has something to say about immigration (when noncitizens may enter the United States and when they must leave) and citizenship (who gets to be a U.S. citizen), although what it says is not entirely clear, nor does it specify how national laws regarding migrants coexist with local laws affecting the same. On the one hand, Article I, which outlines the powers of the federal lawmaking body, Congress, appears to include some power over foreigners. Article I, Section 8, Clause 4 authorizes Congress to create a "uniform Rule of Naturalization," establishing that the House and Senate are responsible for drafting laws that allow qualified noncitizens to attain full U.S. citizenship.[2] Yet, aside from references to the "migration and importation" of slaves,[3] the Constitution says nothing about congressional power to regulate the voluntary movement of noncitizens into and out of the country, which is at the heart of immigration law.[4]

On the other hand, the Constitution says even less about the power of the states over noncitizens and, indeed, appears to limit their power. The Thirteenth, Fourteenth, and Fifteenth Amendments—the so-called post–Civil War Amendments—were originally intended to ensure equal treatment of the newly freed slaves, but, by their terms, guarantee rights to all "persons." Specifically, the Fourteenth Amendment provides that "no State . . . shall deprive any *person* of life, liberty, or property, without due process of law; nor deny to any *person* within its jurisdiction the equal protection of the laws." For instance, a state may not incarcerate a foreign national without first giving her a fair trial (due process), nor may it punish her just because she's from another country (equal protection). The Framers could have limited rights against state encroachment to U.S. citizens only but instead chose to extend these to all *persons*. In addition, these same due process and equal protection rights have been read to restrict the federal government just as they do the states.[5]

In sum, even though Congress has the power to create rules governing citizenship, the text of the Constitution does not explicitly give it authority to regulate immigration. Moreover, even assuming Congress has such power over migrants, it is also required to provide them, as "persons," due process and equal protection of the law. Similarly, states and local governments are subject to due process and equal protection restrictions but are not explicitly or implicitly conferred power over immigration.

The Opinions of the U.S. Supreme Court

With such textual ambiguity, it is useful to turn to the Supreme Court's interpretation of the Constitution for further guidance. As the final interpreter of the Constitution, the Supreme Court has deferred to Congress and the president in the development of federal immigration policy, creating what has become known as the "plenary power doctrine": it is not the

Court's role to second-guess the political branches' rules as to when noncitizens may enter and must leave the United States.

The plenary power doctrine traces its roots to the U.S. Supreme Court's 1889 decision in *Chae Chan Ping v. United States.*[6] Chae, a Chinese citizen and long-time resident of the United States, wished to return to China for a visit. Before his departure, he secured a certificate from the U.S. government, permitting him to return. After Chae left with certificate in hand, Congress passed the Chinese Exclusion Act, barring all Chinese from entering the country. On his return, Chae presented his reentry certificate, but he was denied admission into the United States on the grounds that the new Exclusion Act revoked his permission to enter. Chae sued, but the Supreme Court was not sympathetic. The Court ruled that, as a sovereign nation, the United States had the right to decide whom to exclude and that decision making process rests solely in the hands of Congress and the president. If these political branches of the federal government thought it unwise to continue the immigration of Chinese nationals, then it was not for the Court to second-guess this decision because, as a noncitizen, Chae had no right to enter the United States despite having lived here for twelve years.

The Court extended its holding in *Chae* in *Fong Yue Ting v. United States,*[7] decided four years later. Like other Chinese residing in the United States, Fong had been required to prove that he had lived here for at least one year, through the testimony of a "credible white witness," otherwise he would be deported back to China. Due to cultural and language barriers, most Chinese did not have white acquaintances, and while they had many Chinese persons who could testify on their behalf, the government would not credit their testimony. The Supreme Court upheld the white witness requirement, extending *Chae*'s reasoning to the deportation context: Just as the Court had no right to substitute its judgment for that of Congress in *Chae,* neither could it outlaw the white witness requirement to foil Fong's deportation.

It is difficult to read *Chae* and *Fong* outside their historical context. Long valued for their reliability and strong work ethic, the Chinese had been the backbone of the railway system, providing the labor necessary to extend the rails out West. Once the work was done, however, European-Americans began to focus on the "otherness" of the Chinese. Both the

Exclusion Act in *Chae* and the white witness requirement in *Fong* embody the xenophobia evident in the Court's own words: "If, therefore, the government of the United States, through its legislative department, considers the presence of foreigners of a different race in this country, who will not assimilate with us, to be dangerous to its peace and security, their exclusion is not to be stayed because at the time there are no actual hostilities with the nation of which the foreigners are subjects."[8]

This broad deference to the federal government, however, was met by a contemporaneously robust defense of minorities' rights not to be discriminated against by state and local governments. In *Yick Wo v. Hopkins,*[9] the Court struck down a San Francisco ordinance that, while race-neutral on its face, had the effect of discriminating against Chinese nationals in their operation of local laundries. In issuing these permits, the city had denied all the Chinese laundromats' applications. The Court ruled that the Fourteenth Amendment's Equal Protection Clause was broad enough to extend its protection over not just the newly freed slaves but also the Chinese noncitizens who suffered racial discrimination.

Note that the Court did not defer to the *local* government's authority to indirectly regulate the Chinese in *Yick Wo,* although the xenophobia and distrust of the foreigner was similarly evident in both *Chae* and *Fong,* cases in which the *federal* government prevailed. It is these three nineteenth-century decisions that have formed the basis for constitutional immigration law ever since: The Court has consistently held that, in the United States, it is the *federal* government that holds power over immigration—the movement of noncitizens into and out of the country—and that state and local governments hold no such power. And so, when localities attempt to pass laws that discriminate against the foreigner (so-called alienage laws), the Court will more strictly scrutinize those laws as attempts to usurp Congress's exclusive power over immigration.

Exceptions to the Federal-State Divide over Immigration Power

This federal-state divide over immigration power has remained relatively constant since those early cases, although a few exceptions have emerged here and there. The first sign that the Court would overturn congressional will arguably appeared in *Shaughnessy v. United States ex rel. Mezei.*[10] Decided during the outset of the Cold War, the *Mezei* case involved rather curious facts: Ignatz Mezei, a longtime U.S. permanent resident, returned to Romania to attend to his ailing mother. On his return, immigration authorities detained him at his port of entry on Ellis Island, suspicious of how he spent his time behind the Iron Curtain.

While the Court affirmed Mezei's indefinite detention as within Congress and the president's exclusive purview, it also issued the following statement, opening the door ever so slightly to judicial intervention: "Courts have long recognized the power to expel or exclude aliens as a fundamental sovereign attribute exercised by the Government's political departments *largely immune* from judicial control."[11] Although it proceeded to cite the Chinese Exclusion Act cases and uphold the government's detention of Mezei, the Court also provided a glimmer of hope to future litigants by reserving for itself a small role in reviewing political branch action, perhaps in cases in which very little due process was afforded the noncitizen.

While the *Mezei* dicta has not developed into strict judicial review of immigration laws, over time, the Court has placed limits on congressional power in two important respects: by interpreting immigration statutes in ways favorable to the noncitizen, and by requiring that other federal laws outside the immigration rules—so-called alienage laws affecting benefits such as Medicare—make reasonable sense. A relatively recent example of the first exception is the *Clark v. Martinez*[12] case, in which the Court broadly interpreted Congress's immigration detention statute so as to include a presumptive six-month limit on the ability of the government to detain a noncitizen who it seeks to exclude from the United States.

At issue in *Clark* was the status of over 2,000 Mariel Cubans who, having never been formally admitted into the United States, had been held for many years pending attempts by the government to return them home. These 2,000 were part of an initial group of over 120,000 refugees who fled Mariel, Cuba, by boat but were now being removed because of their criminal activity or severe mental illness. Recognizing that the *Mezei* case gave Congress the power to unilaterally exclude noncitizens and therefore hold them indefinitely, the Court invoked the Due Process Clause as an outside limit on congressional will, reading the applicable statute in a broad way so as to protect the Mariel Cubans from being indefinitely detained.

Similarly, the second exception—that alienage laws make sense—has long been used to test Congress's power to draw distinctions among noncitizens for purposes of allocating federal benefits. In *Mathews v. Diaz,*[13] for instance, the Court upheld a Medicare law that allowed for certain older noncitizens to qualify for supplemental insurance benefits based on whether they were permanent residents who had resided in the United States for at least five years. Declaring the law "reasonable,"[14] the Court reminded the litigants of its limited role in reviewing legislation affecting noncitizens: "In this case, since appellees have not identified a principled basis for prescribing a different standard than the one selected by Congress, they have, in effect, merely invited us to substitute our judgment for that of Congress in deciding which [noncitizens] shall be eligible to participate in the supplementary insurance program on the same conditions as citizens. We decline the invitation."[15]

In contrast to the deference afforded the federal government, the Court has strictly reviewed state and local laws that affect noncitizens' lives, on the theory that noncitizens do not immigrate to any individual state or locality but, rather, to the United States as a whole. Thus, the Court has been unwilling to tolerate state and local laws that discriminate on the basis of alienage in the distribution of public benefits such as welfare or education, invoking the words of the Fourteenth Amendment requiring equal protection of the laws for all.

Plyler v. Doe[16] stands as perhaps the high-water mark of this principle; in *Plyler,* the Court struck down a Texas law that denied free public education to undocumented students in primary and secondary school. In contrast to the *Mathews* case in which the Court was willing to uphold the federal government's economic justification for drawing distinctions among noncitizens based on their immigration status and length of residency, in *Plyler,* the Court thwarted the state's desire to conserve its resources by not providing a free public education to undocumented children. Ruling it a violation of the Fourteenth Amendment's guarantee of equal protection under the law, the Court decried the Texas statute for targeting innocent children whose unlawful presence in the United States was solely the product of illegal choices made by their parents. Moreover, the majority was concerned that the law would create a permanent underclass of illiterates without substantially showing what negative impact on the state economy might result from these children's access to free education. In short, the difference between *Mathews* and *Plyler* appeared to be the difference between which entity—the federal or state government—was attempting to draw distinctions between and among noncitizens.

The sole exception to this stricter scrutiny of state alienage discrimination has been when local entities have wanted to reserve certain occupations that go to the heart of self-government. For instance, in *Cabell v. Chavez-Salido,*[17] decided the same year as *Plyler,* the Court ruled that California could require that its peace officers—including probation officers —be U.S. citizens, noting:

> The exclusion of [noncitizens] from basic governmental processes is not a deficiency in the democratic system but a necessary consequence of the community's process of political self-definition. Self-government, whether direct or through representatives, begins by defining the scope of the community of the governed and thus of the governors as well: [Noncitizens] are by definition those outside of this community. Judicial incursions in this area may interfere with those aspects of democratic self-government that are most essential to it.[18]

Based on their review, the Court determined that peace officers in California exercised a sufficient amount of sovereign power so as to warrant reserving such positions for U.S. citizens only.

The Future of Constitutional Immigration Law: A Shift from Federal to State Power?

This contrast in the deference historically granted the federal government over noncitizens and the strict review with which states have been subject will be closely watched over the next few years as more states and local governments seek to exercise control over noncitizens in their midst. With the federal government physically and fiscally unable to precisely control the flow of noncitizens, with state and local governments most immediately and directly affected by the influx, and with government control increasingly shifting from the national to the local, we are likely to see more state and local laws that burden noncitizens, especially those who are here without documents.

Traditionally, immigrants were disproportionately concentrated in but six states—New York, New Jersey, Illinois, Florida, California, and Texas. In recent years, however, more and more noncitizens are populating states from Oregon to Ohio, in industries as diverse as construction, factory work, and agriculture. In many ways, the current anti-immigrant rhetoric mirrors the concerns surrounding the Chinese during the late nineteenth century. While the strain on the public fisc and concerns about crime are often cited as official reasons for opposing immigration, some also wonder about the assimilability of this new immigrant wave, many of whom are from Latin America. In communities across the United States unfamiliar with this influx or concerned about its volume, state and local laws have been proposed, and sometimes passed, ostensibly to protect local residents and control the migrant flow. The crucial question for constitutional immigration law, then, is whether the Supreme Court will abide by this devolution in immigration control from the federal government to the states.

State and Local Responses to Immigration

To put this theoretical concern in pragmatic context, it is worth exploring several recent state and local responses to immigration, which may be placed into two general categories: an enforcement approach and an assimilation approach. After articulating both responses, we will examine two other contexts in which states and local governments have had to grapple with immigration.

The Enforcement Approach

Hazleton, Pennsylvania, was the first local government to successfully pass a strong immigration enforcement ordinance designed to discourage the influx of undocumented migration into that community. Located some 100 miles northwest of Philadelphia, Hazleton has experienced a large influx of Latino immigrants over the years. The killing of a local resident by two undocumented migrants prompted the town mayor to seek passage of arguably the toughest anti-immigration law ever enacted by a local government. This self-titled "illegal immigration act" punishes local entities that house or employ undocumented migrants; another ordinance establishes English as the official language of Hazleton. The city argues that these measures are necessary to protect their residents from the fiscal burden that undocumented persons have placed on the municipality because the federal government has failed to effectively enforce the nation's immigration laws. Opponents and immigrant rights advocates worry that local governments are usurping not just federal immigration law but also federal housing and employment laws and are basing their policies not on sound empirical research on the supposed ill effects of migration but, instead, on racial prejudice against Latinos.

A second enforcement approach has been the creation of cooperation agreements between federal immigration authorities and state police in Alabama, Florida, and Los Angeles County; others are likely to follow. Congress has passed laws specifically allowing states and local governments to enter into partnerships with immigration officials to help supplement the federal authorities' meager enforcement resources. Unlike unilateral ordinances like Hazleton's, such agreements bear the imprimatur of Congress; courts, therefore, may well defer to the federal legislature's historical plenary power. And while immigration advocates are justifiably concerned about the ability of state officials to effectively enforce national laws, under these agreements, local police are required to undergo specific training in federal immigration enforcement.

The Assimilation Approach

Instead of emphasizing immigration enforcement, other state and local governments have decided to embrace undocumented persons, recognizing their contributions to the community. In New York City and San Francisco, local authorities have passed policies that provide sanctuary for undocumented persons against federal immigration enforcement. This approach respects Congress's traditional prerogative as the legislative body charged with immigration policy, while refusing the federal government's invitation to provide local government resources to assist their interior enforcement efforts. For example, the New York City Police Department will not ask for one's immigration status when investigating an alleged crime.[19] New York does not trivialize immigration violations; however, it believes that the health and welfare of the community extends to all, regardless of the legality of their presence in the United States.

Another method of assimilation has come by way of providing undocumented students affordable access to post-secondary public schools. Because the Supreme Court's decision to effectively require free public education to all in *Plyler v. Texas* did not extend to colleges and universities, many outstanding graduates who excelled in our nation's public high schools have found the doors to higher education shut to them because they are here illegally. Some advocates estimate the number to be as high as 65,000 students a year,[20] some of whom were valedictorians of their high school classes who did not realize they were undocumented until they began to prepare their applications to college.

A handful of states, including Texas and California,[21] have passed laws to partially cure this problem by allowing even undocumented residents to avail themselves of in-state tuition, thereby making college affordable to some. These laws typically require that students be graduates of high schools within the state, having attended there for at least three years. In addition, undocumented students must submit affidavits attesting that they will file for lawful immigration status as soon as they are able. While a helpful first step because they make college more affordable, these laws fall short of providing full relief for undocumented students because, as we learned earlier, only Congress can pass immigration laws that would change their status.[22]

Communities in the Middle: Current Challenges to Immigration

In between these two extremes of enforcement and assimilation lie several other local communities struggling with how to best address the issue of current migratory pressures on traditionally low-immigrant receiving states. In Gaithersburg, Maryland, and Herndon, Virginia, both suburbs of Washington, D.C., the question of whether to appropriate local funds toward the construction of day-laborer centers has developed into a heated debate. In both communities, migrant laborers—some of whom are reportedly undocumented—gather on street corners and at local churches to provide cheap day labor for small businesses and individuals. This issue has deeply divided communities: some have argued for providing employment centers for these individuals where they can receive English-language instruction and access to sanitary restroom facilities, aside from a centralized location where prospective employers and employees can congregate. Opponents, however, question the wisdom of spending scarce municipal resources on supporting people who are illegal residents in the United States.

Regardless of which side one prefers in this debate, it is beyond doubt that to ignore the issue of immigrant integration in our communities is to invite trouble. The case of Tifton, in southern Georgia, provides a cautionary tale. While its website welcomes viewers to "The Friendly City,"[23] a sordid incident that occurred in the fall of 2005 belies that cheery greeting. Since 1995, Tifton has seen a large influx of Latino migration, many of whom flocked to the area to work the local farms. As has happened in many communities, the native African American population has lagged substantially behind the white majority, leading to the creation of gangs and other urban blight. In 2005, three African Americans were charged with the murder, assault, and rape of several migrant farmworkers; reports noted that the victims were particularly easy targets because of their cultural isolation and often marginal immigration status, which would lead to them keeping their earnings in their trailer homes rather than in banks.

Had Tifton community leaders had the foresight to allow these immigrants to open bank accounts with their foreign identification cards,[24] or for local nonprofits to issue debit cards like the "Sigo" as has been done elsewhere,[25] perhaps the immigrants would not have been as vulnerable; moreover, had Tifton been more proactive in assisting their poor and minority residents, perhaps the conflict between these two groups may not have escalated to this degree. It is, of course, easy to speculate after the fact; the important point, however, is for other communities to learn from the Tifton experience and explore ways by which such tragedies can be avoided. To that extent, the day laborer center debates in Maryland and Virginia are a step in the right direction toward a more proactive and direct approach toward assessing the impact of immigration on local communities.

Conclusion

Outside immigration law, the Supreme Court in recent years has appeared to cede more control toward state and local governments in a variety of contexts, from its view of the Commerce Clause[26] to the enforcement of civil rights laws under the Fourteenth Amendment.[27] Whether this devolution of power to the states extends to the regulation of noncitizens remains to be seen. Given its steady movement toward ceding to states power over what used to be considered national concerns, the Supreme Court may well decide to allow local governments to preserve economic resources for U.S. citizens and foreigners lawfully present, thereby eroding the protections of *Plyler v. Doe.* Immigrant advocates, therefore, must find new and creative ways to harness the plenary power doctrine for their clients' benefit while invoking the Constitution's individual rights protections that extend not just to citizens but to all persons.[28]

NOTES

1. For example, *Marbury v. Madison,* 5 U.S. (1 Cranch) 137 (1803) held that it was the Court's duty to "state what the law is."

2. In addition, the Fourteenth Amendment guarantees citizenship to all born within U.S. territory.

3. U.S. Const., Art. I, Sec. 9, Clause 1: "The Migration or Importation of such Persons as any of the States now existing shall think proper to admit, shall not be prohibited by the Congress prior to the Year one thousand eight hundred and eight, but a Tax or duty may be imposed on such Importation, not exceeding ten dollars for each Person."

4. Some have argued that the immigration power is implicit in Congress's power to "regulate Commerce with foreign Nations," although the text appears to focus more on market transactions than on migration. The exchange of goods between nations can be accomplished without a corresponding exchange of people (U.S. Const., Art. I, Sec. 8, Clause 3).

5. *Bolling v. Sharpe,* 347 U.S. 497 (1954), held that the equal protection provisions of the Fourteenth Amendment applied against the federal government by way of the Fifth Amendment's Due Process Clause which limits federal government action.

6. *Chae Chan Ping v. United States,* 130 U.S. 581 (1889).
7. *Fong Yue Tang v. United States,* 149 U.S. 698 (1893).
8. *Chae,* 130 U.S., at 606.
9. *Yick Wo v. Hopkins,* 118 U.S. 356 (1886).
10. *Shaughnessy v. United States ex rel. Mezei,* 345 U.S. 206 (1953).
11. *Id.,* at 210.
12. *Clark v. Martinez,* 543 U.S. 371 (2005).
13. *Mathews v. Diaz,* 426 U.S. 67 (1976).
14. *Id.,* at 83.
15. *Id.,* at 84.
16. *Plyler v. Doe,* 457 U.S. 202 (1982).
17. *Caball v. Chavez-Salido,* 454 U.S. 432 (1982).
18. *Id.,* at 439–40.
19. "Mayor's Office to Combat Domestic Violence," *Special Issues: Immigrants,* at http://home2.nyc.gov/html/ocdv/html/issues/immigrants.shtml (accessed July 2006):

> Challenges faced by immigrant victims of domestic violence are especially relevant in New York City where 36% of the population is foreign born, and over 120 different languages and dialects are spoken. Immigrant women may be less likely to report abuse than non-immigrant women due to language barriers, cultural differences, and a fear of deportation if they are not legally documented to live in the U.S. Young, foreign-born women in New York City have been found to be at greater risk of being killed by their partners than any other group of women. Very often, no one knows about the abuse until it is too late. It is the policy of the New York City Police Department not to inquire about the immigration status of crime victims, witness [*sic*], or others who call or approach the police seeking assistance.

20. For example, Jeffrey Passel, *Further Demographic Information Relating to the DREAM Act,* Urban Institute, October 21, 2003, at http://www.nilc.org/immlaw policy/DREAM/DREAM_Demographics.pdf (accessed July 2006).
21. Cal. Educ. Code § 68139.5 (West 1989); Tex. Educ. Code § 54 (Vernon 1996).
22. Immigrant advocates have therefore lobbied Congress repeatedly to pass a bill to adjust these students' immigration status, the most well known of which is the "DREAM Act," which stands for "Development, Relief, and Education for Alien Minors." As of this writing, this act has not passed.
23. You may view Tifton, Georgia's website at www.tifton.net.
24. For example, the *matrícula consular* is a national identification card issued by the Mexican government. The *matrícula* has been accepted by many private

and public establishments throughout the country (Rachel L. Swarns, "Old ID Card Gives New Status to Mexicans in U.S.," *New York Times,* August 25, 2003). While Congress passed the REAL ID Act in 2005 to ensure the integrity of public identification cards such as state driver's licenses, it is unclear what effect the act will have on the *matrícula,* especially when accepted by a private, as opposed to public, agency. Much litigation over the act's scope will certainly ensue when its ID provisions take effect in 2008.

25. The "Sigo" card "is a special debit card, provided not by a bank but by a nonprofit worker center [in New York], enabling hundreds of immigrants without checking accounts or credit cards to keep their cash somewhere safer than beneath their mattresses. The card also makes it easier to shop at stores as well as online" (Steven Greenhouse , "Immigrants Wary of Banks Put Faith in New Card," *New York Times,* December 30, 2006).

26. For example, *Lopez v. United States,* 514 U.S. 549 (1995) (ruling unconstitutional a federal act criminalizing possession of a firearm proximate to a local school district); *United States v. Morrison,* 529 U.S. 298 (2000) (striking down portions of the Violence against Women's Act as usurping state civil rights laws).

27. For example, *City of Boerne v. Flores,* 521 U.S. 507 (1997) (limiting Congress's section 5 enforcement power under the Fourteenth Amendment); *Board of Trustees of University of Alabama v. Garrett,* 531 U.S. 356 (2001) (holding that states are not required to comply with portions of Americans with Disabilities Act, and that records reflected congressional overreaching).

28. Specifically, immigration advocates will need to work harder at the state and local levels to educate and inform their communities of why the blanket targeting of noncitizens, even the undocumented, is ill advised, chiefly for four reasons: (1) devoting untrained local resources to complex federal immigration enforcement wastes taxpayer dollars; (2) effectively "deporting" undocumented adults from the community burdens their U.S. citizen relatives, especially children; (3) solely targeting undocumented persons is unwarranted and undesirable profiling that could sweep up the most marginalized persons (e.g., the disabled and the elderly) in its scope; and (4) a better solution to concerns over community crime or resource allocation would be to work directly with migrant groups and their advocates to create a more narrowly tailored solution.

CHAPTER 13

The Undergraduate Railroad

Undocumented Immigrant Students and Public Universities

Rachel Ida Buff

> It is difficult to understand precisely what the state hopes to achieve by promoting the creation and perpetuation of a subclass of illiterates within our boundaries, surely adding to the problems and cost of unemployment, welfare, and crime. It is thus clear that whatever savings might be achieved by denying these children an education, they are wholly insubstantial in light of the costs involved to these children, the State and the Nation.
>
> —Chief Justice William Brennan, *Plyler v. Doe*, 1982

In 1982, the United States Supreme Court ruled in *Plyler v. Doe* that states cannot deny undocumented children a K–12 education.[1] Writing for the majority, Justice William Brennan asserted the right of these children to equal protection under the

Constitution, rejecting the state of Texas' claim that their immigration status rendered the students outside the constitutional definition of personhood. Responding to this judicial assertion in the Illegal Immigration Reform and Immigration Responsibility Act (IIRIRA) of 1996, Congress dictated that "illegal aliens" cannot be considered residents of a state for the purposes of assessing tuition at public institutions of higher education unless residents of all other states also qualify for in-state tuition. Subsequently, ten states, including Illinois, have adopted bills to provide in-state tuition to undocumented students; eighteen more have similar legislation pending.[2] Two states, Alaska and Virginia, have introduced legislation further restricting the access of immigrants to public higher education.[3]

The contradiction between liberalism's commitment to equality and justice for all and the necessity of reinforcing national boundaries accelerates in an increasingly transnational global political economy, intensifying a long-running culture war over the position of "aliens" in the national community. The emergent clash in the contemporary politics of immigration is as evident at the walls being built at the U.S.-Mexico border as it is at our public universities and statehouses. On the one hand, free trade agreements secure the mobility of capital, while, on the other hand, the enduring clamor for immigration reform and immigrant responsibility limit the movement of people across borders and, increasingly, within the nation-state. These contradictions produce a class of semipermanently stateless low-wage workers. Immigrant rights' advocates speak of "globalization from below," in which workers would migrate freely, transforming the definitions of citizenship itself as they do so, but national policies have tended to reinforce militarized borders and increasingly limited definitions of citizenship.[4]

This contradiction also generates a conflict between the lived experiences of these workers and their legal status. For example, many of the undocumented students whose access to education has been shaped by Section 505 of IIRIRA have lived in one community in one state, attending high school, making friends, and hanging out the laundry, for most of their lives. In many cases, they are as fluent in English as in their mother tongue. They are what I call *denizens*—inhabitants of a place with established claims to rights in that place—even though they lack formal access to the full rights of citizenship. Deeply engaged in their communities, as residents, students, neighbors, and community members, these students have limited access to higher education and, therefore, to traditional pathways of immigrant mobility and community enhancement.

The historical evolution of citizenship in the United States has always entailed the existence of those who do not benefit from its protections and rights. Denizens have inhabited this nation, sometimes for generations, without the benefit of political representation or cultural recognition. Myriad examples include African Americans, excluded as slaves from the constitutionally mandated census count for representation; Asian immigrants, first allowed to become citizens after World War II; and American Indians, deemed members of "domestic dependent nations" in 1830 and hence excluded from both political representation and diplomatic relations.

While citizenship confers official rights of representation, its absence has not meant a historical lack of political subjectivity on the part of denizens. Instead, denizens have constantly challenged the boundaries of citizenship, in many cases expanding them and in other cases forcing the state to publicly articulate its justification for their ongoing exclusion. Across the history of American citizenship, denizens have pressed for inclusion. In doing so, they have transformed the notion of citizenship itself.

In 1857, Dred Scott claimed before the U.S. Supreme Court that, because of his migration from the slave south to the free state of Illinois and the territory of Minnesota, he and his family were free people. The Court responded that, as a slave and as a person of African descent, Dred Scott was ineligible for the rights of citizenship. In Minnesota territory, Scott had married a woman named Harriet. They subsequently had two daughters: Eliza, born on a steamboat on the way back to slavery just north of Missouri, and Lizzie, born inside the slave south. Part of Scott's suit against his owner, John Sandford, involved Sandford's assaults against Harriet, Lizzie, and Eliza and the rights of the family to legally protect themselves.

Writing for the majority, slave-owning Chief Justice Roger Taney asserted that Scott and his family had no right to sue John Sandford and no claim to citizenship. The federal government's role was to protect the institution of slavery and the property rights of slave owners over the individual rights of enslaved persons. The Court's decision against Dred Scott mapped him, Harriet, Lizzie, and even Eliza, who was born north of Missouri, as denizens of the United States, ineligible to citizenship and legal standing. Under slavery, they had no political subjectivity and no rights to family unification.

Just as Dred Scott and his family constituted nonpersons for the Supreme Court in 1857, undocumented migrants, and even their citizen allies, become in the current moment presumptively suspicious. In 1857 Chief Justice Roger Taney upheld a slave regime most Americans now view as unjust. But the security of the border between the United States and Mexico, the maintenance of national citizenships, and the policing of infractions like undocumented migration are key components of a contemporary regime of homeland security and neoliberal trade policy. Challenging these policies, like crossing the border, violates the boundaries of this regime. What does this mean, then, for denizens?

The issue of access to public higher education raises the question of political subjectivity for denizens. Like Dred Scott, students have challenged their current status under federal law. And, just as the Supreme Court decided in 1857 that the status of Dred Scott and his family was determined by the boundaries of slavery, current federal laws mandate that undocumented students be considered by state universities to live outside the boundaries of the states in which they are residents. Thousands of enslaved Africans and African Americans did not take their cases to court, instead fleeing the slave regime. With the aid of free people in an organized social movement, some of the enslaved sought freedom in Canada by traveling what has historically been known as the Underground Railroad.

Confronted with a denial of their right to an affordable education,[5] undocumented students face public institutions charged with scrutinizing and excluding them. Like the Underground Railroad, traveling the Undergraduate Railroad entails both an organized, public movement and quieter, often fraught, work to accommodate students at universities.

Denizenship and the Struggle for In-State Tuition

While the Court in *Plyler* affirmed some of the grounds for the state of Texas' claims, acknowledging the rights of states to protect themselves from the negative economic consequences of illegal immigration, the ultimate decision focused on the rights of all inhabitants of the state, including illegal immigrants, to due process and equal protection. The state of Texas had asserted that illegal immigrants could not be considered persons. But the Court invoked some of the landmark exclusion-era cases governing the rights of Chinese immigrants as "aliens ineligible to citizenship" in distinguishing between the act of violating immigration law and the possibility of losing personhood. While stating that public education is not a fundamental right, the Court found that the exclusion of undocumented children from the public schools violated their rights to equal protection under the Constitution.

Significantly, in terms of the rights of denizens, the court emphasized the potential fluidity of identity of denizens, from undocumented person to legal resident; from denizen to citizen; or, potentially, as an educated denizen with some stake in American civil society. This acknowledgment of the lived experience of migration contrasts with a long history of idealist border and immigration policy, in which discourses of "zero tolerance" construct a fantasy of a border and a state devoid of the undocumented migrants so central to the national economy.

If the arguments made by the Supreme Court in the majority decision in *Plyler* were extended to the issue of access to higher education to undocumented students, then these students would be able to attend state universities at in-state tuition rates. The Urban Institute estimates that about 65,000 undocumented students graduate yearly from high school in the United States.[6] In-state tuition has been painted as an economic catastrophe for the states by restrictionist opponents of undocumented student access, although the cost of allowing undocumented students access to this benefit has been found to be slight in states where it applies. Rather, the states allowing undocumented students in-state tuition have had increases in enrollment in public universities, ultimately increasing their revenue. Staggering estimates of the cost of allowing undocumented students access to in-state rates have tended to rely on the false premise that the state would thus lose their out-of-state tuition monies. Instead, most undocumented students, confronted with these costs, are not able to continue their educations.

Like most college students, undocumented students experience in-state tuition as an economic issue. Lacking social security numbers, these students are not eligible for federal student loans or financial aid. Sources for funding the education of these students are exceedingly limited. In the context of escalating tuition prices, paying out-of-state rates is often a deal breaker for them, resulting in not attending college. This barrier constitutes a slap in the faces of people who have spent ten or fifteen years attending school and creating lives and identities in a particular community.

For the state, policing the status of incoming university students offers a site of surveillance, where undocumented communities are, of necessity, visible and hence subject to regulation. The Department of Homeland Security requires universities to report the presence of foreign students on campus. When denizens are considered as foreign students, this puts them in a double bind, making them vulnerable for deportation. And for these students, this presents a dissonant note in educations informed by dominant discourses of naturalization and meritocracy.

Section 505 of the Illegal Immigrant Reform and Immigrant Responsibility Act (IIRIRA) of 1996 prohibited states from charging undocumented resident students in-state tuition rates unless they provided the same benefit to U.S. citizens in the same circumstances. Responding to this, Dick Durbin (D-Ill.) introduced the Development, Relief, and Education for Alien Minors (DREAM) Act in 2001. The DREAM Act would offer undocumented students residing in the United States since the age of fifteen or younger "conditional" immigration status. Under this status, these students could attend public colleges and universities at in-state rates. After six years, if a student completed two years in good standing at a four-year institution, graduated from a two-year program, or served two years in the military, he or she would be granted permanent legal residence: a green card.[7]

Immigration reform passed by the Senate in the spring of 2006 would have adopted the provisions of the DREAM Act as federal law. However, given the distance between the Senate bill and the House bill, the backers of which tend to see the undocumented as social parasites at best and dangerous criminals at worst, it may be some time before the DREAM Act is ratified. Meanwhile, student and immigrant rights activists have been busy. Their struggles connect the politics of denizenship to the ongoing discourse of citizenship and immigrant rights.

The Undergraduate Railroad

In Illinois, students across the state were involved in the struggle to get a statute allowing undocumented students to attend the state university at in-state tuition rates. Signed into law by Governor Rod Blagojevich in May 2003, the Illinois statute stipulates four criteria for applicants for in-state tuition: they must have attended school in Illinois for at least three years; they have to be graduates of an Illinois high school; they must have resided in the state with a parent or legal guardian; and they must fill out an affidavit stating that if they are not citizens or legal residents, they will apply for legal residency as soon as they are eligible.[8] Consistent with the IIRIRA stipulation, this law is applicable to anyone applying to the University of Illinois system—out-of-state students, as well as undocumented immigrant students. Legally, all ten states with statutes must be in similar compliance with federal law. With these statutes on the books, university administrators have been able to initiate steps to open some state sources for financial aid to these students.[9]

The campaign to win approval of this statute in the Illinois statehouse centered on the politics of denizenship. Diane Mora, a student organizer at the University of Illinois–Urbana-Champaign, described the mobilization of the surrounding community around the issue of student access to in-state tuition: "They feel that they can voice their opinions now, that they can do something that will make some kind of benefit or change in the long run . . . so there's less fear . . . it hits close to home."[10] For denizens of Urbana-Champaign, including students as well as both legal and undocumented residents of the surrounding community, the issue of in-state tuition was precisely about defining a claim to the state and its resources as their home. As the community in this university town mobilized, then-chancellor Nancy Cantor became a statewide leader in the campaign for a statute for in-state tuition for students.

Alheli Herrera, now an organizer for the Illinois Coalition for Immigrant and Refugee Rights, described how she got involved with immigrants rights at the age of twelve. Her neighborhood, Chicago Lawn/West Lawn, became mobilized around issues of local safety. Working with the Southwest Organizing Project, they petitioned city hall to close a bar that had been causing problems for residents of the neighborhood. As denizens of this multicultural neighborhood came together around quality-of-life issues, they also became concerned with immigrant rights. In light of the deportations and increased scrutiny of people of Middle Eastern origins after 9/11, Polish Americans, Irish Americans, Arab and Muslim Americans, and Latino/as on Chicago's Southwest side began to see immigrant rights issues as *neighborhood* issues.[11] Neighborhood meetings at churches and community centers came to include immigrant rights as a topic of concern.

Students from Chicago neighborhoods and small communities like Urbana-Champaign began to collect testimonials and create a fact sheet to press the issue. High school students from around the state came to Springfield to provide testimony to state legislators. When the bill finally came to a vote in the spring of 2003, it passed by a vote of 112 to 4 in the House and 55 to 1 in the Senate.[12]

Community mobilization around the issue of in-state tuition, in Illinois and in the nine other states that have passed similar statutes, has connected the everyday acts of denizenship—of belonging to a place and caring about one's neighbors and community—to the broader issues of access to education and civil rights in general. The ratification of these ten statutes has also been the ratification of the active membership of undocumented immigrants in their communities and, by extension, in the United States. These statutes represent a realist position on immigration similar to the one espoused by the Supreme Court in *Plyler v. Doe.*

The U.S. Army has been more than eager to accept noncitizen young people as recruits and even has a program of posthumous naturalization to honor them.[13] Or these high school graduates—valedictorians, musicians, C-students alike—pursue the many jobs always open to undocumented immigrants in America in the service sector, agricultural labor, and domestic work. As Brennan underscored in *Plyler,* this condemns denizens to the most difficult and least remunerative jobs in society. This is the real function of the idealist, anti-immigrant discourse: to constantly invoke a fantasy of an absolutely sealed border in service of the criminalization and marginalization of those who cross it. The undocumented, then, are vulnerable to low-wage, nonunion jobs; to an "all volunteer" military that preys on those with the fewest options; or, to the wasteful gulag of the prison-industrial complex.

Access to higher education is a time-honored component of immigrant mobility. Milwaukee community leader Jesus Salas explained his interest in the in-state tuition issue in Wisconsin by connecting his life's work in migrant labor and community empowerment. For him, access to education is a component of a broader access to collective bargaining and the

American Dream.[14] State Representative Pedro Colon spoke of denizen students as a source of talent, as "human capital" unprotected by the transnational escalation of free trade for corporate capital.[15] The local consequences of this transnational omission are significant for the University of Wisconsin system in general.

To date, despite efforts on many levels, Wisconsin does not have a state statute granting in-state tuition to undocumented denizens. Led by Regent Jesus Salas, a lifelong activist for the rights of migrant workers, the UW Board of Regents passed a resolution in 2004 allowing undocumented students to apply to receive a waiver of out-of-state tuition. As of 2004, undocumented students who apply and are accepted into the UW system can petition, along with athletes, musicians, and graduate students, for a remission of out-of-state tuition rates. The number of such remissions available each year is exceedingly limited.[16]

In many ways, the politics of in-state tuition for undocumented students parallel the controversy over immigrant rights in general in the contemporary period. In addition to national issues of citizenship and belonging, the issue of students' rights invokes specific questions about legal residency in the state: a key aspect of denizenship. The story of the struggle for in-state tuition in Wisconsin brings student advocates into conversation with university regents and politicians. It puts the discourse of denizenship and lived experience into a heated dialogue with an idealist politics of national and state identities.

During the 1970s, activists in Wisconsin struggled to define migrant workers as legal residents. These migrants often come to Wisconsin and other Midwestern states for a few months during the summer, as part of the seasonal agricultural cycle. In 1976, the state legislature passed a bill authorizing tuition remissions for the children of migrant workers. If out of the previous five years, a student's family had worked in Wisconsin during all or part of three of them, these students were to be considered residents.[17] Based on similar legislation in Minnesota, this bill reflects the lived experiences of migrant workers, who under more traditional definitions would not be considered legal residents. This realist perspective on residency and rights constitutes one position on the question of denizenship in Wisconsin. The migrant student provision in the Wisconsin state statutes is one antecedent for current struggles for in-state tuition rights.[18]

Another position invokes the idealist perspective, which takes the idea of "illegal aliens" literally to mean that undocumented denizens are violating the law by their very existence in Wisconsin. National organizations like the Federation for American Immigration Reform (FAIR), funded by the transnational Pioneer Fund,[19] have often come into Wisconsin to exert their influence in defining who should be considered a state resident.

As in other states, the push for a statute came from undocumented students. Wisconsin State Representative Pedro Colón remembered being approached at a Milwaukee legal clinic by the principal of South Division High School. That year's valedictorian had been undocumented, the principal said, and the student wanted to attend the university but could not afford it. The principal wanted to arrange a meeting for Colón with some students in this situation and their parents.[20] After meeting with the principal and students, Colón became involved in trying to get a statute through the Wisconsin state legislature. The struggle to pass such a statute points to the contemporary contradictions of denizenship and immigration politics.

As Colón lobbied at the statehouse, a provision to allow in-state tuition for undocumented students in the UW system was put into the 2001–03 biennial budget during conference committee negotiations. Then-Governor Scott McCallum had agreed to sign the budget, including the undocumented student provision, into law. But just before he was to sign it, McCallum received a letter from FAIR, advising him that he would be in violation of federal law if he allowed undocumented students to receive in-state tuition rates and, further, that this bill "will ultimately encourage more illegal immigration to your state. This will require more tax dollars from a growing number of Wisconsin citizens who are dissatisfied with their state's immigration policies."[21] In language paraphrasing the letter he had received from FAIR, McCallum vetoed the provision.

Subsequently, in 2003, with support from ten Democrats and three Republicans, Colón introduced Assembly Bill 95. Paralleling the DREAM Act, this bill would have allowed undocumented students to attend UW at in-state rates, provided that they sign an affidavit stating that they apply for permanent residency as soon as they became eligible. High school and college-age students in Wisconsin rallied in support of AB 95. Forty-five students from Horlick High School in Racine attended a hearing on the bill in Madison.

Mock Graduation, 2003

Despite overwhelming support for the bill in public hearings, the bill never received a stand-alone hearing by the legislature. Subsequently, Governor Doyle inserted an in-state tuition provision into the 2005–2007 budget. Extensive lobbying by the Coalition for America's Families, a Wisconsin school choice, pro-life, tax relief organization[22] resulted in a vote along party lines in the Joint Committee on Finance to remove the provision from the budget.[23]

The day after this vote, the Coalition for America's Families aired an advertisement in Milwaukee in which a woman speaking Spanish-accented English laments Governor Doyle and Democratic support for undocumented students. The woman speaks angrily to the camera, advising the public that she and others "played by the rules," in their pursuit of the American Dream. The ad claims incorrectly that allowing undocumented students in-state tuition would cost $368 million. It concludes as she says:

> We followed the rules. We became citizens. We worked hard to save money. So our daughter will be the first one in our family to go to college. We shouldn't have to pay more taxes to fund illegal aliens. It's hard enough to save the money to send our own children to go to college.[24]

Placing this one woman as the spokesperson for a mythically unified and legalized Latin community, this ad embraces the idealist position on immigration and the American dream. Like other Americans, it asserts, *legal* immigrants play by the rules and value tax relief over all. Such immigrants have no relation to undocumented people, whose education is so costly and who do not play by the rules. This ad is inaccurate, both in its representation of the Latino/a community and of the cost of allowing the undocumented access to in-state tuition. But the idealist position exerts a powerful sway in contemporary politics.

With this climate and with only the Salas resolution to work with, administrators and students across the UW system are put in a bind. When they attend workshops facilitated by UW personnel at high schools and middle schools across the state, students are asked to fill out information cards. These cards often ask the students their social security number and whether or not they are citizens or legal permanent residents. There are no estimates about how many students decline to fill out these cards or to express further interest, fearing that giving such information may jeopardize their security or that of their families. UW personnel working in recruitment, enrollment, and admissions are put in the awkward position of trying to reassure students who may have such concerns without being able to directly address these issues in their public presentations. Like other immigrant students in the post-9/11 context, undocumented students risk enhanced surveillance by the forces of Homeland Security.[25] An undocumented student who runs a stop sign risks more than a traffic ticket, as Wisconsin implemented the REAL ID Act in summer 2007, revoking the access of the undocumented to drivers' licenses. For these students, of course, such risks involve deportation and the loss of the places they have learned to call home.

An undergraduate railroad does exist. There are people within the system who direct undocumented students (who so identify themselves) about how to navigate the admissions process and how to apply for the crucial tuition remission, which is adjudicated by a specially appointed board at each campus. But because there is no state law, there is no record keeping to track these students and no official procedures to help them navigate a university system that is intimidating to most recent high school graduates. At UW–Madison, one advisor pointed out to me, an undocumented student might be able to be accepted to the university and receive a tuition remission. But Madison dormitories require students to give their social security numbers in order to receive a room key.[26]

If globalization from below and the eventual reinterpretation of citizenship in light of the realities of transnational political economy is one endpoint of contemporary progressive organizing, acknowledgment of the full rights of denizen students represents a halfway point. If denizen students in the United States attend public universities and return to their neighborhoods, whether within the United States or abroad, they stand to contribute education and leadership to these diverse communities. Globalization is a reality for those who cross borders, as well as for those who sit in boardrooms. Educated citizens are a universal good, costing little; the deprivation of education has always been expensive and unjust.

NOTES

I gratefully acknowledge support and inspiration from the Morris Fromkin Research Award at the University of Wisconsin, Milwaukee; editorial and creative support from Wendy Kozol; and the time and commitment of the many people I interviewed in the course of this research.

1. *Plyler v. Doe,* 457 U.S. 202 (1982), at www.tourolaw.edu (accessed January 23, 2006).

2. The other states are Texas, California, Utah, Washington, New York, Oklahoma, Kansas, and New Mexico.

3. National Immigration Law Center, "Chart of In-State Tuition Bills," at www.nilc.org (accessed February 24, 2006).

4. Robert Lovato, "Envisioning Another World: Integración Desde Abajo," *Nation* 282/9, March 6, 2006, 22–26; see also Tim Costello, Jeremy Brecher, and Brendan Smith, *Globalization from Below* (Boston: South End Press, 2000).

5. The right to an education is affirmed in Article 26 of the United Nations Universal Declaration of Human Rights, which has yet to be ratified by the United States. Available at http://www.un.org/Overview/rights.html (accessed September 22, 2006).

6. Jeffrey S. Passel, *Further Demographic Information Relating to the DREAM Act* (Washington, D.C.: Urban Institute, 2003).

7. National Immigration Law Center, *DREAM Act: Basic Information,* April 2006, at http://www.nilc.org/immlawpolicy/DREAM/dream_basic_info_0406.pdf (accessed September 21, 2006).

8. *In State College Tuition Now Available for Undocumented Immigrant Students,* Fact Sheet (Chicago: Illinois Coalition for Immigrant and Refugee Rights, 2002).

9. Diane Mora, student, University of Illinois, Urbana-Champaign, telephone interview by author, April 17, 2006.

10. Ibid.

11. Alheli Herrara, organizer, Illinois Coalition of Immigrant and Refugee Rights, telephone interview by author, July 26, 2006.

12. Center for Policy Alternatives, *Immigrants' In-State Tuition,* at http://www.stateaction.org/issues/issue.cfm/issue/Immigrants-Tuition.xml (accessed September 24, 2006).

13. Lisa Marie Cacho, "Alien Others: Asian and Latina/o Relational Racializations in Discourses of Immigration," panelist (sponsored by the American Studies Association Committee on Ethnic Studies) American Studies Association, Atlanta, Georgia, October 2004.

14. Jesus Salas, interview by author, August 10, 2006.

15. Pedro Colon, interview by author, August 27, 2006.

16. At UWM, for example, the fiscal pool available to fund tuition remissions amounts to 2 percent of the prior year's nonresident enrollment monies. Sources: Chancellor Carlos Santiago, in meeting with author, Christine Newman-Ortiz, Javier Tapía, Bill Velez, and Carmen Cepeda, July 17, 2006; also Christine Fairbank, Student Services Specialist, UWM Enrollment Services Office, interview by author, August 30, 2006..

17. Salas interview; Carlos Reyes, Assistant Director, UWM Enrollment Services Office, interview by author, August 29, 2006. Also cited in "Resident Tuition for Undocumented Students," Minutes of the Board of Regents Meeting, June 11, 2004; courtesy of Judith A. Temby, Secretary, Wisconsin Board of Regents.

18. Reyes interview.

19. For example, Jean Stefancic, "Funding the Nativist Agenda," in Juan F. Perea, ed., *Immigrants Out! The New Nativism and the Anti-Immigrant Impulse in the United States* (New York: New York University Press, 1997), 119–35. Actually, the Pioneer Fund is a good example of a transnational valuing of human capital: its board members are drawn from a transnational pool of Anglophone racialist academics (http://www.pioneerfund.org/Board.html [accessed October 1, 2006]).

20. Pedro Colón, interview by author, August 27, 2006.

21. Letter from Dan Stein, Executive Director, FAIR, to Governor Scott McCallum, August 3, 2001. In "In-State Tuition" file of Representative Pedro Colón, Statehouse, Madison, Wisconsin. Andy Janssen, Research Associate to Representative Colón, pointed me to the letter and its parallels to McCallum's veto. Janssen had to obtain this document through the Freedom of Information Act, as McCallum's office refused to share it with Colón's office.

22. See their webpage at http://www.coalition4families.com/About_Us.aspx (accessed October 1, 2006).

23. Office of Pedro Colón, "Timeline for In-State Tuition for Undocumented Students in Wisconsin," in "In-State Tuition File."

24. Coalition for America's Families, "College Tuition," aired May 22, 2005. Available at www.wispolitics.com under their adwatch section (accessed October 1, 2006). Andy Janssen pointed me to this source.

25. Chaiti Sen, "And Now They Come for the Students . . . ," *ColorLines* 5/3 (Fall 2002) 4–6.

26. Reyes interview.

CHAPTER 14

Our Immigrant Coreligionists

The National Catholic Welfare Conference as an Advocate for Immigrants in the 1920s

Jeanne Petit

At an Ash Wednesday Mass in 2006, Cardinal Roger Mahony of the Los Angeles Archdiocese pledged to initiate a campaign of civil disobedience if Congress passed a law making it illegal to give assistance to undocumented immigrants. In an editorial in the *New York Times,* he complained that through this sort of legislation, Americans "scapegoat [immigrants] for our social ills and label them as security threats and criminals." He argued that speaking up for the "dignity of millions of our fellow human beings" is "our Gospel mandate, in which Christ instructs us to clothe the naked, feed the poor and welcome the stranger."[1] His stance emboldened the protest against the law, leading to the March 25 demonstration in downtown Los Angeles attended by more than half a million protesters.[2]

Mahony was not the first leader of the American Catholic Church to wade into immigration policy debates. The bishops, priests, and laymen and women of the National Catholic Welfare Conference (NCWC) became some of the most outspoken critics of U.S. immigration policy in the 1920s.

American bishops formed the NCWC in 1917 out of a desire to promote Catholic interests during World War I, and the organization soon became the public voice for American Catholics on numerous political and social issues, including immigration restriction.[3]

In 1924, they called on American Catholics to protest the Johnson-Reed Act, which, among other things, set up stringent quotas for immigrants from southern and eastern European countries. In a 1924 speech, Bishop William Turner of Buffalo spoke in defense of immigrants in ways similar to Cardinal Mahony. Turner argued that the church needed to express "constant concern for the true welfare of her children" and speak out against anti-immigration "devices conceived in hysteria and applied in petulancy and passion." For Turner, though, the stakes of immigration policy extended beyond the humanitarian rights of immigrants. He disparaged the supporters of the law who saw immigrants from predominantly Catholic countries, like Poland and Italy, as racially inferior to Anglo-Saxon Americans, and he called on native-born Catholics to stand up for "our immigrant co-religionists."[4]

Bishop Edmund Gibbons of Baltimore echoed this sentiment, saying that the Johnson-Reed Act was "unconsciously or consciously a prejudice against the Catholic immigrant." More than that, though, he believed that the restrictive quotas "not only wrong[s] the immigrant but injure[s] our own country." The strength of America, he wrote, derived from the willingness of the nation to welcome all to its shores and become a "magnificent mosaic of the common aspirations and liberty of mankind."[5]

In this essay I argue that in challenging the 1924 Johnson-Reed Act, Turner, Gibbons, and other members of the NCWC did more than defend the rights of their "immigrant co-religionists." They also made a case for an expanded conception of U.S. citizenship, one based less on race and more on an ideological consensus in which Catholics could share. Historians of immigration have emphasized how restriction legislation like the Johnson-Reed Act represented the triumph of "racial nativism," since it privileged the "Anglo-Saxon" or "Nordic" races of northern Europe, restricted southeastern Europeans, and totally excluded Asian immigrants.[6] The NCWC's participation in debates about the law, however, demonstrates that the 1920s immigration policy had implications for American religious identity as well as race.

Catholics in particular saw it as a challenge to their citizenship status and their racial legitimacy. The bishops, priests, and laymen and women of the NCWC sought to influence the debate over the law in 1924, and during the rest of the 1920s, they worked to amend it in two specific ways. First, members of the NCWC invoked Catholic teachings to protest the harsh impact that the law had on immigrant families, cruelly separating husbands and wives, parents and children, for years. Second, they challenged the racial reasoning of anti-immigration politicians, at least where it concerned the racial construction of southeastern European immigrants. They emphasized that the Catholic Church could provide a model for the racially diverse United States, since it was "the Church of all peoples, all races, of all nationalities."[7]

The debate over the Johnson-Reed Act began in the post–World War I era of Red scares, 100 percent Americanization campaigns, and the rise of the Ku Klux Klan.[8] Republican Representative Albert Johnson of Washington State introduced the bill in 1923, and he intended it to establish comprehensive immigration restriction.[9] While earlier legislation had curtailed Asian immigration, this law called for the total exclusion of any immigrant who did not meet the requirement of the Naturalization Act of 1790 that citizens be "free white persons."

Southeastern European immigrants *were* considered legally white, but the Johnson-Reed Act specifically targeted them for exclusion. While an earlier 1921 law set quotas limiting immigration of any European nationality to 3 percent of that nationality's number in the 1910 United States census, the 1924 Act changed the quota to 2 percent of the 1890 census. The reason for this, according to the authors of the law, was to dramatically reduce immigration from southern and eastern Europe, since they were not present in great numbers before the early twentieth century. Moreover, Clause 11 of the law stipulated that after 1927, the total number of immigrants would be limited to 150,000, using quotas based on the "national origins," of the total population, thereby privileging immigrants from England.[10] The law did not exclude immigrants from the Western Hemisphere, however, at the behest of Southwestern Congressmen who wanted to maintain the flow of farm laborers from Mexico.[11]

When the Johnson-Reed Act was introduced in Congress in 1923, American Catholics were feeling defensive about their status in the nation.

The leaders of the NCWC were mostly middle-class descendents of Irish Catholics, whose nineteenth-century ancestors had fought, and mostly won, battles to be considered white. In the early twentieth century, however, the numbers of Catholics had grown through the large infusion of southern and eastern European immigrant Catholics, many of whom were considered racially suspect in the United States.[12] Supporters of the bill were upfront in stating that the purpose of the law was to exclude these undesirable races because they were a threat to the nation. Johnson, the bill's sponsor, flatly asserted that "'American' blood was incompatible with foreign blood, that any mixing between these two would destroy the quality of the country's native stock."[13]

When they first reported on the law to their members in 1923, the NCWC leaders immediately noted that the bill targeted nations with predominately Catholic populations. An editorial in the *NCWC Bulletin* stated that, based on the 1890 census, the proposed changes would "materially curtail the immigration from the East and South of Europe while only slightly reducing the number of those who may come from the North and West." As an example, the editorialist explained that the quota for Italians would decrease from 42,000 to 4,000. The end result would be that "we shall have fewer of the peoples classified as non-Nordics and, theoretically at least, greater numbers of Nordics." At this point, though, the author of the editorial retreated from any direct judgment, saying "the Nordics, it would seem, are to be preferred as being the more desirable . . . which may or may not be true. The wisdom of thus restricting immigration need not be touched upon here at this time." The editorial concluded by declaring it was just informing readers of the trends in the legislation.[14]

By early 1924, when the passage of the bill appeared imminent, the NCWC launched an official protest to congressional leaders, written by Bruce Mohler, head of the NCWC's Immigration Bureau.[15] Mohler's statement made two major objections to the bill.[16] First, he complained about the humanitarian crisis that the law would cause by excluding the wives and children of immigrants already in the United States. While the bill allowed the wives and minor children of native-born and naturalized citizens to enter outside of the quota, the wives and children of resident aliens, as well as the parents of citizens, were subject to the quota, even if the alien had declared his intention to become a citizen.[17] Even though family members would be given privileges within the quota, this was not enough for Mohler. He insisted to the Congressmen "that a family as a unit must be considered and that it is our primary duty to provide for this union of husband and wife and all of their unmarried children."[18]

Second, he asserted the NCWC's opposition to the bill's racial reasoning, describing it as a "distinctive and deplorable departure from our enduring traditions as a nation," because "the proposed bill involves an evident discrimination and substantial injustice to certain particular nations . . . nothing can cloak the arbitrary unfairness in selecting the 1890 census against that of the 1910 as a possible basis for establishing the immigration quotas." In the end, Mohler's protest had little effect. The Johnson-Reed bill passed in 1924 with overwhelming majorities in the House and Senate and was quickly signed into law by President Calvin Coolidge.[19]

The passage of the law did not end the NCWC's opposition to it. During the rest of the 1920s, they sought to keep, in the words of Bishop Gibbons, the "Catholic point of view" before Congress by proposing changes to the law that would harmonize with Catholic values and interests.[20] By 1925, different departments and bureaus within the NCWC started to advocate for amendments to the Johnson-Reed Act that would ameliorate the problem of separated families caused by the law. The members of the Immigration Bureau, especially those who worked at Ellis Island and other ports, wrote articles for the *NCWC Bulletin* describing "unbelievable tragic situations" of families torn apart by bureaucratic tangles.[21] An editorial decried the exhaustion of quotas from eleven European countries, which, they said, indicated that "these countries represent the largest number of *separated families.*"[22]

In 1927, when Congress was considering a bill to allow immediate family members of resident aliens to immigrate outside of the quotas, Bishop Joseph Schrembs, who headed the Department of Lay Activities, wrote a letter to all members of Congress in support of it and appealed to the sanctity of the family. Schrembs argued that "the natural ties of fatherhood, motherhood and childhood are bound together by a bond so strong of both natural and divine law that it would seem brutal to separate them by any positive law of human making."[23] Congress, Schrembs believed, should not exercise the power to pull apart what God had joined together.

Members of the NCWC asserted that amending the law to support a Catholic view of the family would not only relieve individual suffering but also strengthen the nation. In 1928, Bruce Mohler, Director of the

Immigration Bureau, and Agnes Regan, Executive Secretary of the National Council of Catholic Women, testified before the House Committee on Immigration and Naturalization hearings in support of the bill that would allow family members to enter outside of the quota. Mohler declared that he could not argue "for adjusting the immediate welfare of the family without at the same time arguing for the welfare of our country." He played into fears of communism and argued that separated families could create "a great cause of social unrest and perhaps a deep sore of radicalism."[24]

Agnes Regan made even stronger links between the family and the health of the nation. She argued that "a state flourishes by everything which makes its citizens better and happier." Excluding wives and children put the nation at risk, for "without a family, a man is adrift. He has not that anchor which is so essential to the life of a man—a home." Regan declared that the United States, and Congress in particular, had a national duty to alleviate the problem, saying that "when it is within our power to enable [immigrant families] to become united we are responsible for keeping them separated. . . . If they cannot bring their families here, I say we are responsible for the result."[25]

Besides serving as an advocate for immigrant families, the NCWC also challenged the racial logic of the 1924 law by taking a strong stand against Clause 11 of the act, which was due to go into effect in 1927. The law called for the president to form a committee including the Secretaries of State, Labor, and Commerce, which would portion off immigrant quotas by the percentage their "races" (i.e., nationalities) made of the entire U.S. population, based on the 1920 census. As the deadline was approaching in 1926, however, the president's committee struggled about how to implement the National Origins Clause, and Congress postponed it for two years to 1929. During these years, the NCWC campaigned against these quotas and the whole idea of "national origins."

It would seem that the NCWC would find the national origins quotas based on the 1920 census to be fairer than quotas based on percentages of immigrants in the 1890 census. Indeed, as defined by the president's committee, the number of immigrants from a few southeastern European countries, including Italy, would increase slightly. The problem for the NCWC, however, was twofold. First, based on the "national origins" from the 1920 census, over 73,000 of the 150,000 total immigrants would be from one country, Great Britain, while the quotas from more Catholic northern

European countries, particularly Ireland and Germany, would be less than one-half of their previous numbers.[26]

For some American Catholics, the realization that Irish and German Catholics would be excluded cut to the quick. Bishop T. W. Drumm of Des Moines wrote to Father Bruce Mohler, the Executive Director of the NCWC, in disbelief about the drop in the German quota, and asked,

> Why refuse admission to these splendid peoples? Who wishes to keep them out? What can I do to push for immediate modification? . . . Everybody I've talked to—all high-class American men—have said "it is a shame," "'a crime," "the worst thing we could do," etc. sic similiter, in keeping out these intelligent, industrious peoples.[27]

Irish American and German American Catholics wanted to believe that their ancestors had played a role in building the United States and that they had become unquestioned members of the nation, and the National Origins Clause threatened this belief. This issue gets to the root of the problem of national origins for the NCWC—it institutionalized the notion that "Anglo-Saxons" were truly American and that the status of other races, particularly those from Catholic countries, was lesser.

The leading figure in the NCWC's campaign against the National Origins Clause was William Montavon, the head of the NCWC's legal department. Between 1926 and 1929, the year the National Origins Clause went into effect, he wrote a series of articles that attacked what he described as a "hateful" law.[28] First, he made the practical argument that determining racial origins by subdividing the United States into "component racial parts" was "an impossible task."[29] He pointed out that to determine the quotas, the president's committee examined names in the census and tried to determine an individual's "nation origins" based on that. Montavan then asked:

> If [an immigrant] is descended from parents of different nationalities and they in turn are descended from parents of still different nationalities, so that the individual descendent today is a composite of four, six or a dozen nationalities who will say what is his national origin or what fraction of him is to be included in computing the quota to be granted to each of the nations from which he is descended?"[30]

He argued that the difficulty, indeed impossibility, of determining national origins based on census records would convince "our Nordics that, after all, the founders may have been right when they decreed that in our Republic no man should be discriminated against for reason of his race."[31]

This idea—that racial diversity and racial tolerance was at the root of American identity—became the crux of Montavon's argument against the National Origins Clause. He believed that the "amalgamation of the people derived from many racial and national sources" gave the United States "a population homogeneous and united in its political aspirations and having a capacity for industrial organization never attained by any other nation."[32] However, he argued, the National Origins Clause could "result in the division of our population along racial lines and thus destroy that very homogeneity which it is intended to preserve."[33] In 1929, when National Origins quotas were about to become a reality, he wrote:

> For a century and a half our nation has grown strong and has prospered in peace and in war under the motto *E Pluribus Unum.* Applied to immigration and to the population growth of the nation, that motto visions a condition utterly unlike that of the "hundred percenters" who advocate the national origins law.

He protested that the law created a "snobbish division of the nation into 'old stock' and 'new comers.'" Instead, he declared that the American ideal was about a people "all sharing the same responsibilities and enjoying the same rights" who were "happy in the thought that others may be admitted to share with them the blessings and duties of citizenship." This vision of the nation allowed for participation of diverse American Catholics who, while not Anglo-Saxons, could still be true Americans by their adherence to a common ideology. Yet the National Origins clause, according to Montavon, "destroys that vision [by] driving an artificial line of cleavage through the life of the nation."[34]

Montavan's inclusive vision, however, had limits. Historians like Mae N. Ngai have shown that even as the Johnson-Reed Act established quotas that stigmatized southeastern European immigrants, it also "solidified the legal boundaries of the white race."[35] Neither Montavan nor anyone else in the NCWC protested the part of the Johnson-Reed Act that totally excluded Asians and allowed no way for Chinese and Japanese immigrants to reunite with their families in the United States. They said nothing about the part of the National Origins Clause that excluded "descendents of such persons as were involuntary immigrants"—meaning African Americans—from consideration in the quotas, which was a way to exclude all African immigrants.[36]

In essence, the NCWC did not simply want to defend the rights of their "immigrant co-religionists" from southern and eastern Europe. They also wanted all Americans to consider those immigrants to be unquestionably white. In limiting their concern to European immigrants, the members of the NCWC were participating in what historian Matthew Frye Jacobson describes as the shift from "Anglo Saxon exclusivity" to a "pattern of Caucasian unity."[37] They wanted to racially legitimize Catholic immigrants, especially those from southeastern Europe, as a way to legitimize the Catholic Church in the United States.[38]

Even in their selective concern for immigrants, the members of the NCWC did offer a more encompassing vision of U.S. citizenship than that offered by proponents of restriction, and they tied this vision to their identity as Catholics. They called on American Catholics not to apologize for their religion but, instead, to promote their church as a model for national unity. One 1929 article pointed out:

> [Because the Catholic Church includes] representatives of all nationalities and all races [it] is a Church universal; it has marked with the sign of the cross people of all the world. Similarly, the United States is being formed of people of all the world and is a nation universal. The membership of the Catholic Church in the United States is a sample both of the membership of the Church universal and the citizenship of a nation universal.[39]

Using this kind of reasoning, the NCWC maintained that American Catholic Church served as a model for the diversity in the United States, and they insisted that their goal was to have all races—or at least all races from Europe—to be included on an equal basis, with the Catholic Church showing the way.

In the end, the NCWC failed in their specific battle against the 1924 Johnson-Reed Act. Immigration continued to be severely restricted, families continued to be separated, and quotas continued to be based on

National Origins. Yet they had a larger goal than changing the law. They wanted to ensure that all American Catholics would be respected as citizens and become a political force in the nation.

By 2006, when Cardinal Mahony spoke out in defense of undocumented Mexican immigrants, that goal of the NCWC had largely been achieved. By the end of the twentieth century, American Catholics had entered the political, economic, and social mainstream of the nation, and their status as citizens is no longer in question on the basis of their religion. The church of today, however, is facing different challenges, mostly coming from within. More and more, native-born Catholics had turned away from the church as they became critical of church teachings, especially on issues like sexuality and the role of women. Between the 1950s and 2000, attendance at Mass dropped from 74 percent of Catholics to 25 percent.

In recent years, though, the church has seen areas of growth, and most of it is among Latino Catholics, especially those from Mexico. In a December 2006 article for the *New York Times Magazine,* David Rieff pointed out that 39 percent of the total Catholic population in the United States is Hispanic, and most of those are immigrants. The church's fate, Rieff argued, "has become inextricably intertwined with the fate of these immigrants and their descendents."[40] Thus Mahony's advocacy, like that of the NCWC in the 1920s, is about more than defending immigrants. It is also about defending the American Catholic Church.

NOTES

1. Roger Mahony, "Called By God to Help," *New York Times,* March 22, 2006, A25.

2. John Pomfret, "Cardinal Puts Church in Fight for Immigration Rights," *Washington Post,* April 2, 2006, A8.

3. The NCWC was originally founded during World War I as the National Catholic War Council and later changed its name to the National Catholic Welfare Council. In 1922, conservative bishops complained to the pope that the NCWC was usurping the authority of the Vatican and that the term "Council" suggested they could set canon law. After facing an order of suppression by the pope, the

bishops of the NCWC changed their name again to the National Catholic Welfare Conference. For histories of the NCWC, see Douglas J. Slawson, *The Foundation and First Decade of the National Catholic Welfare Council* (Washington D.C.: Catholic University of America Press, 1992); Elizabeth McKeown, *War and Welfare: American Catholics and World War I* (New York: Garland, 1988); Ronald Schaffer, *America in the Great War: The Rise of the War Welfare State* (New York: Oxford University Press, 1991) 64–74; Jay P. Dolan, *The American Catholic Experience: A History from Colonial Times to the Present* (Garden City, N.Y.: Image Books, 1987); Joseph M. McShane, *"Sufficiently Radical": Catholicism, Progressivism and the Bishop's Program of 1919* (Washington, D.C.: Catholic University of America Press, 1986); Elizabeth McKeown, "The National Bishop's Conference: An Analysis of Its Origins," *Catholic Historical Review* 66 (October 1980), 565–83.

4. "Around the Conference Table: The Church and Americanization," *National Catholic Welfare Conference Bulletin* 6 (September 1924), 4.

5. Bishop Edmund Gibbons, "Review of the Work of the NCWC Legal Department," *National Catholic Welfare Conference Bulletin* 8 (October 1926), 5.

6. John Higham, *Strangers in the Land: Patterns of American Nativism, 1860–1925* (New Brunswick, N.J.: Rutgers University Press, 1955/1994), 316–24. For other works on the racial implications of the law, see Desmond King, *Making Americans: Immigration, Race and the Origins of the Diverse Democracy* (Cambridge: Harvard University Press, 2000); Gary Gerstle, *American Crucible: Race and Nation in the Twentieth Century* (Princeton: Princeton University Press, 2001); Mai M. Ngai, *Impossible Subjects: Illegal Aliens and the Making of Modern America* (Princeton: Princeton University Press, 2004), esp. chapter 1 "The Johnson-Reed Act of 1924 and the Reconstruction of Race in Immigration Law," 19–55.

7. This sentiment appeared in many articles in the *NCWC Bulletin.* See "Around the Conference Table: The Church and Americanization," *National Catholic Welfare Conference Bulletin* 6 (September 1924), 4; Elizabeth B. Sweeney, "Discharging the Duties of Citizenship," *National Catholic Welfare Conference Bulletin* 10 (June 1928), 29.

8. Higham, *Strangers in the Land,* 291–99; John T. McGreevy, *Catholicism and American Freedom: A History* (New York: Norton, 2004), 147. See also Lynn Dumenil, "The Tribal Twenties: 'Assimilated' Catholics' Response to Anti-Catholicism in the 1920s," *Journal of American Ethnic History* 11 (Fall 1991): 42.

9. The bill was cosponsored by Republican Senator David Reed of Pennsylvania.

10. For a full description of the act, see E. P. Hutchinson, *Legislative History of American Immigration Policy* (Philadelphia: University of Pennsylvania Press, 1981), 187–94.

11. Neil Foley, *White Scourge: Mexicans, Blacks and Poor Whites in Texas Cotton Culture* (Berkeley: University of California Press, 1997), 45–46.

12. For work on Irish-Americans and whiteness, see David R. Roediger, *The Wages of Whiteness: Race and the Making of the American Working Class* (New York: Verso, 1991), and Noel Ignatiev, *How the Irish Became White* (New York: Routledge, 1995). For work on the racialization of southeastern European immigrants in the early twentieth century, see Matthew Frye Jacobson, *Whiteness of a Different Color: European Immigrants and the Alchemy of Race* (Cambridge: Harvard University Press, 1998); Matthew Pratt Guterl, *The Color of Race in America, 1900–1940* (Cambridge: Harvard University Press, 2001); Thomas Guglielmo, *White on Arrival: Italians, Race, Color, and Power in Chicago, 1890–1945* (Oxford: Oxford University Press, 2003); Arnold R. Hirsch, "E Pluribus Duo?: Thoughts on 'Whiteness' and Chicago's 'New' Immigration as a Transient Third Tier," *Journal of American Ethnic History* 23 (summer 2004), 7–44.

13. Quoted in Kenneth M. Ludmerer, "Genetics, Eugenics and the Immigration Restriction Act of 1924," *Bulletin of the History of Medicine* 46/1 (1972), 67.

14. "Nordic or Non-Nordic Immigration," *National Catholic Welfare Conference Bulletin* 4 (April 1923), 12–13.

15. "NCWC Reports of the Administrative Committee and Departments Made at the Conference of the Hierarchy of the United States, Washington, D.C., September, 1924" (Draft Version) NCWC Executive Department Subject Files, Box 65, Catholic University of America, 44.

16. A third issue had to do with making sure men and women religious could remain in the non-quota category.

17. Roger Daniels, *Guarding the Golden Door: American Immigration Policy and Immigrants since 1882* (New York: Hill and Wang, 2004), 54.

18. "NCWC Protest against Proposed Immigration Bill," *National Catholic Welfare Conference Bulletin* 5 (February 1924), 12.

19. Hutchinson, *Legislative History of American Immigration Policy,* 194

20. Bishop Edmund Gibbons, "Review of the Work of the NCWC Legal Department," *National Catholic Welfare Conference Bulletin* 8 (October 1926), 15.

21. "In the Field of Immigration," *National Catholic Welfare Conference Bulletin* 6 (April 1925), 10.

22. "In the Field of Immigration," *National Catholic Welfare Conference Bulletin* 9 (August 1927), 9–10; emphasis in the original.

23. Joseph Schrembs to Members of Congress, February 12, 1927, NCWC Executive Department, Numerical Files, no. 145, International Affairs, Immigration, 1927, CUA.

24. "Statement of Bruce M. Mohler, Director of the Bureau of Immigration of

the NCWC, Washington D.C.," *Hearings before the Committee on Immigration and Naturalization, House of Representatives, Seventieth Congress, First Session,* Hearing no. 70.1.6 (Washington, D.C.: U.S. Government Printing Office, 1928), 15–16.

25. "Statement of Agnes Regan, Executive Secretary of the NCCW, Washington D.C.," *Hearings before the Committee on Immigration and Naturalization, House of Representatives, Seventieth Congress, First Session,* Hearing no. 70.1.6 (Washington, D.C.: U.S. Government Printing Office, 1928), 22–24.

26. For a breakdown of the quotas, see King, *Making Americans,* 208–9. Bruce Mohler described the loss of the Irish and German quota numbers in several articles in the *Bulletin*—for example, "In the Field of Immigration," *National Catholic Welfare Conference Bulletin* 8 (August 1926), 11. Other articles that emphasize the loss of the Irish and German quotas include "In the Field of Immigration," *National Catholic Welfare Conference Bulletin* 8 (December 1926); "Legislation and the People," *National Catholic Welfare Conference Bulletin* 8 (December 1926), 7; and "Legislation and the People," *National Catholic Welfare Conference Bulletin* 8 (July 1926), 9.

27. Bishop T. W. Drumm to Bruce Mohler, November 30, 1929, NCWC Executive Department Numerical Files, no. 145, International Affairs: Immigration, CUA.

28. "Legislation and the People," *National Catholic Welfare Conference Bulletin* 8 (December 1926), 7.

29. "Legislation and the People," *National Catholic Welfare Conference Bulletin* 8 (February 1927), 7.

30. William F. Montavon, "The Seventieth Congress," *National Catholic Welfare Conference Bulletin* 10 (April 1929), 4–5.

31. "Legislation and the People," (February 1927), 7.

32. William F. Montavon, "Legislative Review of the Sixty-ninth Congress," *National Catholic Welfare Conference Bulletin* 8 (August 1926), 5.

33. William F. Montavon, "Congress and Immigration," *National Catholic Welfare Conference Bulletin* 7 (March 1926), 10.

34. William F. Montavon, "Shall the National Origins Law Be Enforced?" *National Catholic Welfare Conference Bulletin* 10 (May 1929), 26.

35. Ngai, *Impossible Subjects,* 7. Court cases dealing with naturalization also show, in the words of historian Ian F. Haney Lopez, "the imprecisions and contradictions inherent in the establishment of racial lines between Whites and non-Whites" (*White by Law: The Legal Construction of Race* [New York: New York University Press, 1996], 2).

36. Hutchinson, *Legislative History of American Immigration Policy,* 189. For work on how American Catholics confronted questions about African Americans during the first half of the twentieth century, see David Southern, *John LaFarge*

and the Limits of Catholic Interracialism, 1911–1963 (Baton Rouge: Louisiana State University Press, 1996); John T. McGreevy *Parish Boundaries: The Catholic Encounter with Race in the Twentieth Century Urban North* (Chicago: University of Chicago Press, 1996); and William C. Leonard, "A Parish for the Black Catholics of Boston," *Catholic Historical Review* 83/1 (1997), 44–68.

37. Jacobson, *Whiteness of a Different Color,* 94.

38. The NCWC did not address the question of Mexican immigration in this context because Mexicans were not subject to the quotas at this time as they were from the Western Hemisphere. The organization did, however, speak out against the anti-clerical revolutionary government in Mexico and tried to shape American diplomacy on the issue (Matthew A. Redinger, *American Catholics and the Mexican Revolution, 1924–1936* [Notre Dame: University of Notre Dame Press, 2005]).

39. "Our Common Catholic Work during 1929—A Symposium: Some Common Catholic Problems and Responsibilities Calling for Catholic Action, Part 3," *National Catholic Welfare Conference Bulletin* 10 (March 1929), 14.

40. David Rieff, "Nuevo Catholics," *New York Times Magazine,* December 24, 2006, 41.

CHAPTER 15

Building Coalitions for Immigrant Power

Fred Tsao

This article discusses how my organization, the Illinois Coalition for Immigrant and Refugee Rights (ICIRR), has sought to organize immigrant communities across ethnic lines to build power and shape policy. I begin by describing the demographic context of our work, then discuss our overall strategy, as well as specific examples of coalition building across immigrant communities and beyond.

The Immigrant Population in Illinois

More than 12.4 million people lived in Illinois as of 2005. Of these, 1.7 million, or 13.6 percent, are foreign-born, and 1.5 million are the U.S.-born children of immigrants. About one-half of Illinois' immigrants entered the United States between 1995 and 2005. New immigrant arrivals account for 51 percent of the state's net population growth since 2000, and nearly 60 percent of its growth between 1990 and 2000.[1] Illinois' immigrants break down by immigration status into three major categories: approximately 425,000 are undocumented; another 500,000 are lawful permanent residents (LPRs), or green card holders; and 735,000 are naturalized citizens.[2]

Illinois immigrants now come from all corners of the globe: about 48 percent are from Latin America, 24 percent from Europe, 24 percent from Asia, and 2 percent from Africa. While Mexican immigrants make up the largest national group (695,000, or 41 percent of the total foreign-born population), Illinois is also home to 150,000 immigrants from Poland; 104,000 from India; 80,000 from the Philippines; and large populations from China, Korea, the former Soviet Union, the former Yugoslavia, Germany, Italy, and Pakistan.[3] It would be a grave mistake to think of Illinois' immigrants as just Mexican or just Latino.

Illinois' immigrant population has historically concentrated in the city of Chicago. While metropolitan Chicago is still home to 93 percent of all of Illinois' foreign-born residents, far more now live in the Chicago suburbs (984,000) than in the city (590,000).[4] Immigrant communities are emerging in places like Waukegan, Elgin, Aurora, and Joliet, satellite cities of Chicago that are growing again due to the influx of new immigrant residents. More dramatically, 30 of Illinois' 102 counties experienced an increase of more than 100 percent in their immigrant populations between 1990 and 2000; Cass County witnessed a 1141 percent surge in its foreign-born residents, as immigrants came to work in food processing plants in the county seat, Beardstown.[5] Small rural communities like Cobden, Arcola, and Mendota are now home to growing immigrant communities.

The dispersion of Illinois' immigrants translates into much greater potential political influence. Nine of 19 Congressional districts had populations that were at least 10 percent foreign born, including the district of former House Speaker Dennis Hastert west of Chicago.[6] Similarly, 55 of the 118 legislative districts for the Illinois General Assembly had at least 10,000 immigrant constituents.[7] The shifting demographics within many of these districts, particularly those in the Chicago suburbs that have long been held by Republicans, provide an opportunity for immigrant voters to tip the balance of power on both state and federal levels.

Vision and Strategy

ICIRR's vision is summarized in fig. 15.1. This vision seeks to convert what could be negatives about our state's immigrant population into positives. Diverse communities that could fragment as they pursue their own interests exclusively are instead producing strong coalitions around shared goals. Dispersed immigrants might not be numerous enough in many areas to elect their own representatives, but they could provide crucial margins of victory in swing districts. The inability of the majority of immigrants to vote, rather than disempowering them, instead has motivated them to mobilize in other ways and to pursue opportunities for citizenship.

In realizing this vision, ICIRR has used two basic principles of community organizing: understand and appeal to the self-interest of various constituencies, and build a sense of solidarity among them through relationships and collective action.

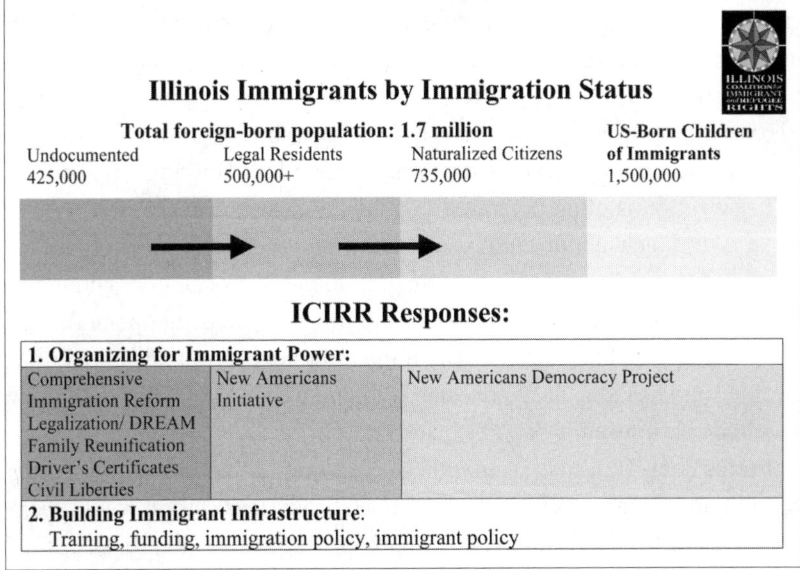

Fig. 15.1. In this chart, ICIRR documents the proportions of foreign-born denizens of the state. ICIRR's strategy for immigrant rights emphasizes naturalization and citizenship, so that immigrants become voters and can affect policy. *Source:* Illinois Coalition for Immigrant and Refugee Rights; for more information, see www.icirr.org, "Take Action!"

Undocumented Immigrants: Legalization

One of ICIRR's major focuses is moving undocumented immigrants into legal status. ICIRR began to work on legalization for the undocumented in spring 2000. This push, part of a larger national effort, came after the AFL-CIO executive committee reversed the labor federation's historical stance opposing immigration and endorsed legalization. Locally, this effort culminated in a march in downtown Chicago that drew 10,000 participants—at that time, the largest demonstration in Chicago in at least thirty years.

ICIRR's work on legalization continued despite the September 11 terrorist attacks. On the state level, we won a major victory in May 2003 with the enactment of H.B. 60, which enables undocumented students to attend state colleges and universities at in-state tuition rates.[8] ICIRR has also worked to win driving documents for undocumented immigrants. On the federal level, ICIRR has vocally advocated for the DREAM Act, sponsored by Illinois Senator (and new Senate Majority Whip) Richard Durbin, which would provide undocumented students the opportunity to gain legal status and continue with their education and careers. Introduced again in Congress in fall 2007, the DREAM Act has failed to garner adequate support. We have also continued to push for more comprehensive federal legislation like the Secure America bill introduced by Senators John McCain and Edward Kennedy and Illinois Congressman Luis Gutierrez in 2005.

Legalization is often portrayed in media and seen in the general public as an issue solely about Latino, or even more specifically Mexican, immigrants. Mexicans indeed make up roughly 56 percent of all undocumented immigrants, with other Latin American immigrants making up another 22 percent.[9] Leadership from Mexican immigrant advocates fueled the immigration marches in Chicago on March 10 and May 1, 2006, that each drew hundreds of thousands of participants.

In this context, it may seem unlikely that non-Latino immigrant groups would join in support of legalization. Specifically, legalization would seem unappealing to Asian immigrants, many of whom face long backlogs for themselves and their family members. Because of high demand and a statutory cap limiting any single nation to no more than 7 percent of the numerically limited visa categories, immigrants from China, India, and the Philippines generally must wait even longer to immigrate than those from most other nations. In the most extreme case, the wait for immigrants sponsored by U.S. citizen siblings is eleven years for most of the world, but twenty-two years for the Philippines. Such backlogs could lead to resentment that undocumented immigrants would jump ahead of the line if the federal government were to enact legalization.

ICIRR has nevertheless won the support of local Asian American organizations for legalization, including the Korean American Resource and Cultural Center, the Chinese Mutual Aid Association, the Indo-American Center, and the Asian American Institute. In part, this support is due to the inclusion in most legalization proposals of provisions that address the backlogs. The McCain-Kennedy bill, for instance, would increase the number of visas available within the backlogged visa categories so that anyone currently in the backlog would wait no longer than six years. This combination of interests, under the rubric of "comprehensive immigration reform," provides a vehicle for these Asian American organizations to back legalization.

Such support is not simply a matter of brokering interests, however. Asian American leaders recognize the need for legalization in their own communities. Approximately 1.5 million immigrants from Asia lack legal status.[10] Most of these immigrants, from Korea, India, Pakistan, and the Philippines, arrived in the United States on short-term visas as students, tourists, or temporary workers and never left. Indeed, many of these immigrants are highly educated but must work at lower-skilled jobs because they lack legal status. These newcomers would clearly benefit from legalization. In this context, the backlogs are not a source of resentment but a symptom of a more general dysfunction in the immigration system that provides inadequate opportunities for legal immigration.

At ICIRR, this support among Asian American leaders has taken the form of an active Asian Caucus, which, led by the Asian American Institute, launched a postcard campaign in May 2006 in support of comprehensive reform that would address legalization and backlogs. This support also translated on the ground in significant Asian participation in the historic spring 2006 marches in Chicago.

The Muslim community provides another perhaps unexpected source of support of legalization, again due to a blend of self-interest and solidarity. On the surface, one would expect Muslim communities to be concerned primarily with the effects of the federal initiatives undertaken since the September 11 attacks in the name of national security. Having faced this barrage of attacks, why would these communities advocate for legalization, an issue that would not appear to affect or benefit them?

The president of the Council of Islamic Organizations of Greater Chicago (CIOGC), Abdul-Malik Mujahid, provided the best answer to this question. Writing to promote the May 1 immigration marches, Mujahid recognized that federal post-9/11 initiatives fell particularly hard on immigrants, many of whom overstayed their students or visitors visas. The U.S. Justice Department detained many of these individuals on immigration violations even as their suspected of links to terrorist activity proved groundless. Most dramatically, the federal "special registration" program targeted men from twenty-four predominantly Muslim nations who entered the United States on temporary visas. Of the more than 83,000 men reported to INS offices during this program in late 2002 and early 2003, some 13,000 were arrested and placed into proceedings for removal.[11] "Undocumented status became a handy reason to punish Muslims, who were deemed guilty for 9/11 by association," Mujahid wrote.[12]

In Mujahid's view, Muslim advocacy for legalization is a matter not only of protecting their community but also of seeking justice for all immigrant groups: "This is about fairness, dignity and an end to the hypocrisy that ignores illegal immigration when it's convenient, but chooses to crack down harshly on it when it's expedient." As Muslim immigrants came under suspicion after 9/11, so did undocumented workers who were swept up in federal enforcement activities like Operation Tarmac, which targeted undocumented workers at airports.[13] Mujahid called for Muslims to stand in solidarity with Latino and other immigrants in defense of civil rights and in support of immigration reform. Responding to calls from the CIOGC, the Chicago chapter of the Council on American-Islamic Relations, and other Muslim organizations, approximately 10,000 Muslims joined in the May 1 march in Chicago.

Other ethnic organizations have likewise joined in support of legalization. During 2006, Irish immigrant organizations emerged as key backers of immigration reform. While the numbers of Irish immigrants in the United States is relatively small, the undocumented Irish population is significant and, more important, increasingly vocal. So vocal have they been in reaching out to election officials of Irish descent, including Senators Kennedy and Durbin, and others that their efforts garnered national attention.[14]

Legal Immigrants: Citizenship

The second major part of ICIRR's vision is moving legal immigrants toward citizenship. Illinois is home to 404,000 legal immigrants who, because they had been LPRs (legal permanent residents) for at least five years, were eligible for U.S. citizenship.[15] Yet an average of fewer than 30,000 immigrants in Illinois were naturalizing each year during the period from 2000 to 2005.[16] A nation that is serious about making immigrants full members and about upholding democracy should make more strenuous efforts to enable immigrants to naturalize.

ICIRR has responded with the New Americans Initiative (NAI). Launched in 2005 with the support of Illinois Governor Rod Blagojevich (himself the son of a Serbian immigrant), Illinois Congressman Luis Gutierrez, and the Latino Caucus of the Illinois General Assembly, this state-funded program provides $3 million a year toward a coordinated citizenship campaign, including community and media outreach, application assistance, legal services, and classes to prepare applicants for their citizenship interview. The focus of these activities is citizenship workshops organized monthly in Chicago and suburban communities, and regularly elsewhere across the state. Through December 2006, NAI had conducted 249 workshops and completed more than 18,500 naturalization applications. NAI contributed to the surge in naturalization applications in Illinois during 2006: applications surged in February 2006 to 3,280 compared with 1,963 in February 2005, and overall rose 23 percent from the first half of 2005 to the first half of 2006.[17]

While Mexican and other Latino immigrants make up the majority of eligible LPRs, citizenship is available to immigrants regardless of national origin and is prized by all immigrant communities. It seems only natural that a broad range of community organizations participate in NAI and have joined in advocating for its continuation. These organizations serve not just Latinos but also Poles, Russian Jews, Chinese, Koreans, Arabs, Bosnians, Muslims, and African refugees.[18] The collaborative nature of NAI, with various organizations working on different aspects of the workshops and initiative operations, also brings together disparate types of agencies, including ethnically based social service providers, community-organizing projects, immigration practitioners, schools, and media, particularly foreign-language outlets serving immigrant communities.

Cross-ethnic alliances have also proved important in advocacy on citizenship-related issues. Latino, Polish, Chinese, Korean, and other communities joined ICIRR in protesting long application backlogs in the late 1990s. Many of these communities have more recently come together to denounce initiatives by the immigration service such as higher fees and a tougher citizenship test, initiatives that ICIRR likens to a "second wall" that would unduly block the way for many immigrants seeking citizenship.[19] Since such citizenship barriers cut across ethnic lines, they offer useful opportunities for organizing across these lines.

Naturalized Citizens and U.S.-Born Children of Immigrants: Voting

The final part of ICIRR's overall strategy involves moving naturalized citizens and the U.S.-born children of immigrants toward voting and civic engagement. This work builds on Latino successes in Chicago, where Latinos have elected aldermen, state representatives and senators, and a U.S. Congressman. But as noted above, immigrants are dispersing beyond Chicago, establishing communities in the suburban collar counties and throughout the rest of the state. ICIRR has proven that when voters from immigrant families turn out to vote in united cross-ethnic blocs, they can swing elections toward immigrant-friendly candidates on the state and federal levels.

With this strategy, ICIRR undertook massive nonpartisan voter registration and turnout efforts in 2004 and 2006. In 2004, the New Americans Vote campaign ran fifteen electoral mobilization operations in immigrant communities throughout Chicago and in emerging communities such as Aurora, Elgin, and Waukegan. These efforts targeted not only voters in heavily Latino areas but also Muslim, Chinese, and Korean enclaves and multiethnic areas on Chicago's north and southwest sides and in the northern Chicago suburbs. In one area, organizers built coalitions between south Asian and Filipino immigrants. In others, the campaign brought together Latinos and Muslims.

The campaign often targeted its messages to specific groups based on their particular interests: for Muslims, attacks on civil rights; for Asians, immigration backlogs; for Latinos, legalization. Yet ICIRR trained the immigrant electoral activists together and also brought all the communities together on several occasions. A September 2004 rally that made one final push for voter registration highlighted families from each of these communities standing together to call on immigrants to register and vote. The end result was 27,054 new voter registrations and 62,486 additional immigrant voters who had not voted in the previous two election cycles. In suburban Elgin, the local state representative came within 350 votes of losing reelection due to the increased turnout among Latino voters in the district. The following spring, one of the Elgin leaders, Linda Ramirez Sliwinski, won her race for village trustee in nearby Carpentersville, the first Latino candidate to serve on the village board.

ICIRR returned to many of these communities in 2006, working again throughout Chicago and in the collar counties with Latinos, Koreans, and Muslims and in multiethnic areas. The campaign registered 16,556 voters and increased turnout among immigrant voters in some communities by as much as double over the expected levels. This increased turnout helped a Latino Democrat defeat a long-time anti-immigrant Republican state representative in the northwest Chicago suburbs.

The effect of this electoral work has been enormous. Since 2004, in addition to the three races already mentioned, pro-immigrant Republicans have been reelected in two state representative districts; one long-term anti-immigrant Republican Congressman, Philip Crane, was ousted; and two U.S. House seats that had previously been safely Republican each came within 6 percent of electing more immigrant-friendly Democrats. Statewide, pro-immigrant Governor Rod Blagojevich won reelection, while Jim Oberweis, who ran virulently anti-immigrant campaigns for U.S. Senate and Illinois governor, was soundly defeated in the Republican primaries for both offices.

Beyond Immigrant Communities

Even if bound together by shared interests and solidarity, immigrant communities still make up a minority of the body politic. Building effective coalitions for immigrants must therefore involve outreach to nonimmigrant communities and institutions. Fortunately, ICIRR has forged alliances with several key constituencies that share our understanding of and interest in advancing immigrant rights.

Faith institutions have been particularly responsive. The Catholic Archdiocese of Chicago, home to increasing numbers of Latino parishioners, many of them recent immigrants, has actively participated in national and local advocacy efforts. The Northern Illinois Conference of the United Methodist Church (whose bishop, Rev. Hee Soo Jung, is a Korean immigrant), the American Jewish Committee, and the Jewish Council on Urban Affairs have also worked with ICIRR to spotlight the need for immigration reform. For these communities, justice for immigrants is a matter of faith, based on principles of welcoming strangers and caring for the most vulnerable.

Labor unions have also worked closely with ICIRR, particularly those that seek to organize immigrant workers in low-wage occupations: SEIU (immigrant janitors), UNITE HERE (immigrant hotel employees), and UFCW (immigrant food service workers). These unions seek to improve wages and working conditions for all workers and recognize that such efforts will continually fail as long as industries are able to threaten undocumented workers because they lack immigration status and to drive wedges between these workers and other low-wage workers.

ICIRR has also established initial linkages with the business sector. These include relationships with some trade associations representing the restaurant and landscaping industries, as well as the U.S. Chamber of Commerce. These business groups have joined in advocating for legalization because they need workers to fill jobs in their growing sectors of the economy.

We have begun working as well with African American communities. Rev. Jesse Jackson vocally endorsed the immigration marches in Chicago and even invited ICIRR's board president, Juan Salgado, to speak on his weekly television broadcast. Jackson frames his support for immigrant rights in terms of bolstering wages and working conditions for all workers and addressing poverty in sending countries like Mexico so people will not need to immigrate to survive.[20] ICIRR youth leaders also participated in the August 2006 conference commemorating the fortieth anniversary of the Chicago Freedom Movement, when Dr. Martin Luther King joined local civil rights leaders in campaigning to end local housing segregation. The conference's youth organizers witnessed the struggles of immigrants firsthand from seeing their classmates, many of whom are undocumented students whose lack of status threatens to thwart their education and careers. In addition, African immigrant and refugee groups such as the United African Organizations have helped to build bridges to African American elected officials. Significant numbers of refugees for Sierra Leone and Liberia and immigrants from Nigeria and Ghana live in heavily African American communities in the Chicago area and can appeal to African American legislators as constituents.

Finally, ICIRR has established strong ties with elected officials on the state and federal levels. Several represent immigrant-heavy districts, including U.S. Representatives Luis Gutierrez (who is of Puerto Rican descent) and Jan Schakowsky and the Latino members of the Illinois General Assembly, and many are themselves immigrants themselves or children of immigrants, including Governor Blagojevich and U.S. Senators Durbin and Obama. Even without such direct ties, political leaders and political observers also pay attention to immigrant votes and organizing and the difference they can make to their candidates and parties come election time.

Public Policy Results

These strategies have put Illinois in the forefront of the immigration debate. Illinois' congressional delegation has taken strong leadership on immigration issues. Rep. Gutierrez helped draft the Secure America comprehensive reform bill. Sen. Durbin sponsored the DREAM Act. Sen. Obama has supported legalization and was involved in developing the Senate compromise bill that emerged in spring 2006. Rep. Schakowsky has been outspoken in advocating for immigration reform and improved performance from the immigration service, and with Rep. Gutierrez has vocally protested higher immigration fees and other obstacles to citizenship.

On the state level, the impact has been even more impressive. In addition to H.B. 60 and the New Americans Initiative, the Illinois General Assembly passed and Governor Blagojevich signed legislation that recognizes foreign consular identification documents; cracks down on abusive day labor agencies, many of whose victims are undocumented immigrants; creates the AllKids health insurance program that covers children regardless of immigration status; and authorizes universal preschool for all children.[21] At ICIRR's November 2005 Immigrant Justice Convention, Blagojevich also signed an executive order mandating creation of a comprehensive state strategy to bring immigrants into Illinois' economy and American society.[22]

Conclusion

Through a combination of appeals to self-interest, relationship building, and collective action, ICIRR has built a strong, effective coalition that embraces the diversity of immigrants in Illinois. While much remains to be done, we hope that our example provides a model for similar alliances in other states and localities. Only by building such coalitions across and beyond immigrant communities can we win public policies that will move immigrants toward full membership in our community.

NOTES

I gratefully acknowledge the assistance of Joshua Hoyt, ICIRR's executive director, in reviewing and editing this article.

1. Data from the U.S. Census Bureau American Community Survey: Census 2005, Tables S0502, "Selected Characteristics of the Foreign-Born Population by Period of Entry to United States (Illinois)," and S0602, "Selected Characteristics of the Native and Foreign-Born Populations (Illinois)"; Census 2000, Table QT-P14, "Nativity, Citizenship: Year of Entry and Region of Birth (Illinois)"; Census 1990, Table DP-2, "Social Characteristics (Illinois)." Tabulated by Rob Paral and Associates, 2006.

2. *Estimates of the Unauthorized Migrant Population States based on the March 2005 CPS* (Washington, D.C.: Pew Hispanic Center, 2006), at http://pewhispanic.org/files/factsheets/17.pdf (accessed June 3, 2006); U.S. Census Bureau American Community Survey.

3. U.S. Census Bureau American Community Survey: Table B05506, "Place of Birth for the Foreign-Born Population—Universe: Foreign-Born Population Excluding Population Born at Sea."

4. U.S. Census Bureau American Community Survey. Metropolitan Chicago includes Cook, DuPage, Kane, Lake, McHenry, Will, Kendall, and Grundy Counties.

5. Louise Cainkar and Moushumi Beltangady, *The Changing Face of Illinois* (Chicago: Illinois Coalition for Immigrant and Refugee Rights, 2002), at www.icirr.org/publications/changingface.pdf (accessed June 3, 2006).

6. U.S. Census Bureau American Community Survey.

7. Rob Paral and Michael Norkewicz, *Metro Chicago Immigration Fact Book* (Chicago: Roosevelt University Institute for Metropolitan Affairs, 2003).

8. An Act Concerning Higher Education, Public Act 93-0007 (2003).

9. Jeffrey S. Passel. "Estimates of the Size and Characteristics of the Undocumented Population" (Washington, D.C.: Pew Hispanic Center, 2006). Estimates are based on U.S. Census Bureau Current Population Survey, March 2005.

10. Ibid.

11. Thirty-six federal initiatives that targeted immigrants in the name of national security in the two years after the September 11 attacks are catalogued in the ICIRR report *Losing Ground: The Loss of Freedom, Equality, and Opportunity for America's Immigrants since September 11,* at http://www.icirr.org/publications/losingground03.pdf (accessed June 3, 2006).

12. Abdul-Malik Mujahid, *Why Muslims Must Join America's Growing Immigration Movement,* at http://www.ciogc.org/pages/Perspectives/3014/pageDetailPB.html (accessed June 5, 2006).

13. Among the twenty-five airport workers arrested in Chicago as part of Operation Tarmac on December 10, 2002, was Elvira Arellano, who has since received national attention for seeking sanctuary in a local church to resist her court-ordered deportation.

14. Nina Bernstein, "An Irish Face on the Cause of Citizenship," *New York Times,* March 16, 2006.

15. Joshua Hoyt, Fred Tsao, Rob Paral, *Today We March, Tomorrow We Vote!* (Washington, D.C.: Center for Community Change, 2006). Tabulations performed by Rob Paral based on American Community Survey 2001–4, at http://www.icirr.org/index_files/tomorrowwevote.pdf (accessed January 4, 2007).

16. U.S. Department of Homeland Security Office of Immigration Statistics, *2005 Yearbook of Immigration Statistics* (Washington, D.C.: U.S. Department of Homeland Security, 2006).

17. Figures compiled by U.S. Citizenship and Immigration Services for Chicago District, September 2006.

18. A complete list of NAI participating agencies is on the NAI website at http://www.icirr.org/nai/orgs.html.

19. More information about this "second wall" campaign is at http://www.icirr.org/stories/secwall.htm.

20. "Wage War on Poverty, Not Immigrants," *Chicago Sun-Times,* March 28, 2006.

21. Consular Identification Document Act, Public Act 94-389 (2005); An Act Concerning Finance, Public Act 94-511 (2005); An Act Concerning Insurance, Public Act 94-693 (2005); Covering ALL KIDS Health Insurance Act, Public Act 94-1497 (2006).

22. The executive order and the reports produced by the policy initiative it launched are available at www.immigrantintegration.org.

PRIMARY SOURCE

Illinois Coalition for Immigrant and Refugee Rights, June 26, 2006

36 S. Wabash, Suite 1425
Chicago, IL 60603
312.332.7360 voice, 312.332.7044 fax, www.icirr.org

For Immediate Release—Press Release

Immigrant Leaders Launch Massive Citizenship and Voter Registration Campaign: Collective of community organizations, union trades, corporate and business leaders to support immigrants in the quest for political power

CHICAGO, IL (June 26, 2006)—"The Opportunity Is Now: Participate, Become A Citizen, Vote"; that was the message sent to Chicago's nearly 500,000 immigrants who are eligible for citizenship by Congressmen Luis Gutierrez and Jan Schawkowsky when they joined dozens of leaders of immigrant groups, business and community organizations on Monday to announce a "massive citizenship and voter registration drive."

Although Independence Day draws near, for immigrant populations nationwide, July 1 will be a powerful symbol of patriotism, since its recent declaration as "National Citizenship Day." This declaration has ignited new political movements with the state of Illinois in the lead. Today, in preparation for July 1, the Illinois Coalition for Immigrant and Refugee Rights (ICIRR) will launch "The Opportunity Is Now" Campaign, which will include massive citizenship workshops and voter registration drives statewide. Branded with the slogan of "Participate, Become a Citizen, Vote," this campaign will be used to build on the momentum gained by recent marches through large-scale citizenship workshops, voter registration drives, and direct actions in support of comprehensive immigration reform.

The national campaign to increase civic participation of immigrants will assist eligible legal permanent residents become U.S. citizens. "This new initiative will provide a meaningful and critical step toward U.S. citizenship for thousands of men, women and children across the country, so that they too can fully share in the rights that citizens enjoy and also help shoulder the responsibilities," added Gutierrez. "It will allow these men and women to better protect their families and to better advocate for the best interests of our immigrant community and our country," said Congressman Gutierrez

On July 1, at Little Village High School, 3120 S. Kostner Avenue, over 1,000 legal permanent residents will be assisted in filling out citizenship applications. This event will have the participation of Congressmen Luis Gutierrez and Congresswoman Jan Schakowsky who will also help legal permanent residents in their quest for citizenship.

In addition to beginning the path for citizenship, July 1 will also be a celebration for new U.S. citizens who went through the naturalization process through the New Americans Initiative (NAI), a citizenship program sponsored by the State of Illinois and administered by ICIRR. "Citizenship is the key that can help thousands of immigrants in Illinois open the door to a full participation in our society. The opportunity is indeed now. Governor Blagojevich has worked hard with the Illinois Coalition for Immigrant and Refugee Rights, and with elected officials and community leaders to create new opportunities for hard-working, law-abiding immigrants. The Governor's New Americans Initiative opened the gate to help drive thousands of immigrants to seek the benefits of citizenship and exercise their new rights in our democracy," said Esther Lopez, Gov. Blagojevich's Deputy Chief of Staff.

July 1st continues to be a day for celebration as ICIRR launches the "We are America Immigrant Democracy Summer" campaign, a voter registration program targeting the immigrant population in Illinois, which combines training, organizing and electoral civic engagement. "This movement will not only be a march in the streets, it is a march for full citizenship—it is a march to the polls," said Juan Salgado, president of the Illinois Coalition for Immigrant and Refugee Rights.

The centerpiece of ICIRR's strategy is the organization's collaboration with community organizations throughout the city and suburbs, with ICIRR as the umbrella organization for collaborations between highly diverse immigrant-led organizations, such as Instituto del Progreso Latino, the Council of American-Islamic Relations, the Chinese Mutual Aid Association, and the Korean Resource and Cultural Center. These are only a few of the many community organizations that collaborated with ICIRR in one of the most successful voter registration and mobilizations campaign in the country—our New Americans Vote '04, which registered over 27,000 new immigrant voters and drove over 62,000 immigrants to the polls on Election Day. These organizations are continued collaborators for the upcoming "We Are America: Immigrant Democracy Summer" campaign, the youth component of our larger electoral strategy for increasing civic engagement and building immigrant political power.

The Immigrant Democracy Summer fellows include young, bright, energetic people who will be encouraging citizens to vote as an act in continuation of the marches and their goals. This integrated, nonpartisan citizenship and voter registration, education, and mobilization campaign will feature 19 youth—mostly immigrants or the children of immigrants—as field organizers running the day-to-day activities of a large-scale voter registration and GOTV campaign. In close collaboration with host community organizations and ICIRR, the youth organizers will write campaign plans, register voters through door-to-door canvassing and site registration, and learn the technical requirements of working with complicated voter files for voter targeting and tracking. From July to November 2006, ICIRR's goals are to:

- Create 10,000 new citizens
- Register 15,000 immigrant voters
- Mobilize 50,000 immigrants to the polls on Election Day in November

Among these fellows, Germain Castellanos, a child of Mexican immigrants, will be working in Waukegan, the city in which he grew up. "We will reach out to potential voters every weekend, every day, door to door, at churches, and in their neighborhoods, to make sure that those who can, will exercise their right to vote. We can change the political landscape of Illinois and the country," Castellanos said.

Many organizations, trade unions, and businesses are part of the July 1st event and sponsors of the "We Are America Immigrant Democracy Summer" including the State of Illinois, Illinois Hispanic Chamber of Commerce, Second Federal Savings, Western Union, Univision Radio, Illinois Restaurant Association, SEIU Local 1, La Raza Newspaper, Polish Television Chicago/Polvision, Hoy Newspaper, UNITE HERE Local 1, Su Casita, American Jewish Committee, Anti-Defamation League, and Mexican American Legal Defense and Educational Fund (MALDEF).

Additional citizenship workshops will be taking place throughout the state on the same day in Aurora, Mendota, and Bloomington, creating awareness of the importance of citizenship and voting among the immigrant communities in Illinois.

The Illinois Coalition for Immigrant and Refugee Rights is a statewide coalition of 130 organizations dedicated to promoting the rights of immigrants and refugees to full and equal participation in the civic, cultural, social, and political life of our diverse society.

For more information about citizenship, call 1-877-792-1500 or visit www.newamericans-il.org or ICIRR's website www.icirr.org or call Catherine Salgado at 312.332.7360 ext. 35 or 630.362.6202.

CHAPTER 16

Their Liberties, Our Security

David Cole

> To those who pit Americans against immigrants and citizens against non-citizens, to those who scare peace-loving people with phantoms of lost liberty, my message is this: Your tactics only aid terrorists, for they erode our national unity and diminish our resolve. They give ammunition to America's enemies, and pause to America's friends.
>
> —Attorney General John Ashcroft, December 6, 2001

On January 24, 2002, the U.S. military transported John Walker Lindh, a young American raised in Marin County, California, and captured with the Taliban on the battlefields of Afghanistan, to Alexandria, Virginia, where he was to be indicted in a civilian criminal court for conspiring to kill Americans. White House spokesman Ari Fleischer announced that "the great strength of America is he will now have his day in court." Represented by some of the best criminal defense attorneys in the country, Lindh raised substantial constitutional challenges to his prosecution, and the government ultimately dropped its most serious charges against him in exchange for a plea agreement.

At the same time, the military was holding 158 foreign-born Taliban and al Qaeda prisoners at a military base at Guantanamo Bay, Cuba, in eight-foot-by-eight-foot chain-link cages. A widely circulated press photo depicted the prisoners bound and shackled, with bags covering their heads and eyes, kneeling on the ground before U.S. soldiers. They were initially held incommunicado, without charges, without access to lawyers, and without any judicial review. President George W. Bush announced that he categorically determined that the Guantanamo detainees were not entitled to the protections accorded prisoners of war under the Geneva Conventions, and Secretary of Defense Donald Rumsfeld dismissed concerns about their treatment with the assertion that they were "being treated vastly better than they treated anybody else over the last several years." Two months earlier, the president had issued a military order providing that al Qaeda members and other noncitizens could be tried by military tribunals, in which the military would act as prosecutor, judge, jury, and executioner, without any appeal to a civilian court.

The difference between the treatment afforded John Walker Lindh and his fellow Taliban and al Qaeda prisoners held at Guantanamo rested on the fact that Lindh was, as the press nicknamed him, "the *American* Taliban." When Attorney General John Ashcroft announced the charges against Lindh, a reporter asked why Lindh was being tried in an ordinary criminal court rather than before a military tribunal. Ashcroft explained that because Lindh was a U.S. citizen, he was not subject to the military tribunals created by President Bush's order. As a purely legal matter, the president could have made U.S. citizens subject to military commissions; citizens have been tried in military tribunals before, and the U.S. Supreme Court expressly upheld such treatment as recently as World War II. But the president chose to limit his order to noncitizens.

Several months later, however, this form of "military justice" was extended to U.S. citizens, as the government asserted the right to hold two citizens—Yaser Hamdi, captured in Afghanistan, and José Padilla, arrested at Chicago's O'Hare airport on suspicions, later disavowed by the government, that he might be planning to set off a radioactive "dirty bomb"—as "enemy combatants," without charges, without counsel, without trial, and without judicial review.

Both the president's initial choice to limit military justice to foreign nationals and his subsequent extension of that authority to U.S. citizens are emblematic of how the Bush administration has responded to the terrorist attacks of September 11, 2001. While there has been much talk about the need to sacrifice liberty for a greater sense of security, in practice the administration has far more often selectively sacrificed *noncitizens'* liberties while retaining basic protections for American citizens. All too often, it has sought to avoid the difficult trade-offs between liberty and security by striking an illegitimate balance, sacrificing the liberties of noncitizens in furtherance of the citizenry's purported security. Because noncitizens have no vote, and thus no direct voice in the democratic process, they are an especially vulnerable minority. And in the heat of the nationalistic and nativist fervor engendered by war, noncitizens' interests are even less likely to weigh in the balance.

Some maintain that a "double standard" for citizens and noncitizens is perfectly justified. The attacks of September 11 were perpetrated by nineteen Arab noncitizens, and we have reason to believe that other Arab noncitizens are associated with the attackers and will seek to attack again. Citizens, it is said, are presumptively loyal; noncitizens are not. Thus, it is not irrational to focus on Arab noncitizens. Moreover, on a normative level, if citizens and noncitizens were treated identically, citizenship itself might be rendered meaningless. The very essence of war involves the drawing of lines in the sand between citizens of our nation and those against whom we are fighting. Surely in that setting it makes sense to treat noncitizens different from citizens.

I argue here that such reasoning should be resisted on three grounds. First, it is normatively and constitutionally wrong. The basic rights at stake—political freedom, due process, and equal protection of the laws—are not limited to citizens but apply to all "persons" subject to our laws. The individual rights set forth in the Bill of Rights extend to persons, the people, or the accused. Other constitutional provisions do limit their protection to citizens, such as the right not to be discriminatorily denied the vote, but the rights to due process, equal protection, free speech, and association, for example, are owed to all. Second, it undermines our security interests. Employing a double standard with respect to the basic rights accorded citizens and noncitizens is likely to be counterproductive at home and abroad because it compromises our legitimacy in both spheres and thereby fuels anti-American sentiments that are the lifeblood of the terrorists' cause against us. And third, it will pave the way for future inroads on citizens' liberties: as the government's treatment of Padilla and Hamdi has already illustrated, what we let our government do to immigrants creates precedents for how it treats citizens.

In short, when we seek to strike a balance between liberty and security, we should respect the equal dignity and basic human rights of all persons and not succumb to the temptation of purchasing security at the expense of noncitizens' basic rights. The true test of justice in a democratic society is not how it treats those with a political voice but how it treats those who have no voice in the democratic process. Human rights are predicated on human dignity, not belonging to a particular political community; they extend to the outsider and insider in equal measure.

Sacrificing Their Liberty for Our Security: The Post-9/11 Response

"Somebody who comes into the United States of America illegally, who conducts a terrorist operation killing thousands of innocent Americans —men, women, and children—is not a lawful combatant. . . . They don't deserve the same guarantees and safeguards that would be used for an American citizen going through the normal judicial process." With these words, Vice President Dick Cheney defended the president's military order of November 13, 2001, which authorized trial by military commission of any noncitizen whom the president accuses of engaging in international terrorism or belonging to al Qaeda. The vice president's view captures much of the administration's response to the attacks of September 11. Most of its most questionable counterterrorism initiatives violate equality, the first principle of the rule of law, by imposing limitations on noncitizens' basic rights that citizens do not bear.

Secret Preventive Detention

In the first two years after the attacks of September 11, 2001, by its own admission, the administration detained over 5,000 foreign nationals in antiterrorism preventive detention initiatives. Yet five years later, not a single one of the post-9/11 detainees has been convicted of any terrorist crime.

Most of the detainees were released or deported after being affirmatively cleared of any involvement in terrorism by the FBI. But despite the fact that not one turned out to be a terrorist, thousands spent days, weeks, months, and, in some instances, years in preventive detention.

These domestic detentions were carried out under an unprecedented veil of secrecy. The government refused to release any details regarding the identity of the detainees. And the vast majority of the detainees, those held on immigration charges, were tried in proceedings closed to the public, the press, legal observers, and even family members. On orders from Attorney General John Ashcroft, all hearings were closed, no matter how routine and whether or not any sensitive issues were discussed.

Many persons were initially held for weeks or months without any charges at all. More than 317 detainees were held for more than forty-eight hours before being charged, 36 detainees were held for more than four weeks without charges, and 9 were held for more than fifty days without charges. Once charges are filed, they were generally "pretextual." And even if the charges were resolved, the individuals were kept locked up until the FBI satisfied itself that they were not connected to terrorism.

Consider, for example, Ali Maqtari. A Yemeni citizen, Maqtari was picked up on September 15 when he accompanied his U.S.-citizen wife to Fort Campbell, Kentucky, where she was reporting for Army basic training. Agents interrogated him for more than twelve hours and accused him of being involved with terrorists. Maqtari took and passed a lie detector test, but he was detained on the highly technical charge that he had been in the country illegally for ten days while changing his status from tourist to permanent resident. The government never offered any evidence linking him to terrorism or crime of any kind. It merely submitted a boilerplate affidavit from an FBI agent arguing that Maqtari should be detained because the investigation of terrorism is a "mosaic," and therefore, seemingly innocent facts might at some future time turn out to indicate culpability. Two months later, Maqtari was released without charges.

An internal Department of Justice investigation found that individuals were arrested on such flimsy evidence as an anonymous tip that "too many" Middle Eastern men were working in a local convenience store. The FBI would then send out agents, and if they could not immediately rule out the possibility that the men were terrorists, they would be arrested—whether or not there was any outstanding violation with which they could be charged. Then, once they were detained, the FBI would investigate to see if they had any connections to terrorism.

The Constitution does not permit detention for investigative purposes. And immigration authorities have no freestanding authority to detain; they may do so only when necessary to effectuate a noncitizen's removal from the country. When a foreign citizen agrees to leave, there is no legitimate immigration purpose to keep him detained. Yet many noncitizens were held in custody for months even after they agreed to leave, while the FBI investigated them.

The Justice Department policy was essentially to lock up first, ask questions later, and presume that the detainee was dangerous until the FBI had a chance to assure itself that he was not. The government did everything it could to keep the detainees from obtaining a hearing on the legality of their detentions, but when such hearings were held, the government justified its actions with a combination of the "mosaic" argument noted above and the "sleeper" theory. Under the latter, the fact that a suspicious person has done nothing illegal only underscored his dangerousness; because al Qaeda is said to have "sleeper" cells around the world, groups of individuals living quiet and law-abiding lives but ready and willing to commit terrorist attacks once they get the call, even the absence of evidence of any suspicious activity could be deemed suspicious.

When some immigration judges ordered that the detainees be released on bond pending resolution of their deportation proceedings, Attorney General Ashcroft changed the rules. Under a regulation issued October 29, 2001, even if an immigration judge ruled after a custody hearing that the government had shown no basis for detention, an immigration prosecutor could keep the foreign national locked up simply by filing an appeal of the release order. Several federal judges declared this rule unconstitutional, but the Justice Department kept it in place.

These tactics were possible—both politically and legally—only because the targets of this sweep were foreign nationals. Had the government locked up 5,000 citizens, none of whom turned out to be terrorists, it would be a major scandal. Because those detained were foreigners, public reaction was muted. As a result, we allowed the government to impose on foreign citizens' widespread human rights deprivations that we would not have tolerated if imposed on ourselves.

The USA PATRIOT Act

The targeting of noncitizens was further reflected in the USA PATRIOT Act, an omnibus antiterrorism bill enacted just six weeks after September 11. The act made many changes to criminal, immigration, banking, and intelligence law, but its most extreme measures are targeted at noncitizens. It made noncitizens deportable for wholly innocent associational support of a "terrorist organization," whether or not there is any connection between the individual's conduct and any act of violence, much less terrorism. Indeed, the Department of Homeland Security interpreted this provision to apply even to those who had been forced at gunpoint or otherwise to support terrorist groups.

Under this law, a pacifist immigrant who sent a book by Gandhi to the leader of a designated terrorist group to encourage him to forego violence would be deportable as a terrorist and would have no defense that his intentions were honorable.

The Patriot Act also resurrected ideological exclusion—the practice of denying entry to aliens purely on the basis of speech. That practice, common during the Cold War under the McCarran-Walter Act, led to the exclusion of such prominent writers as Graham Greene, Carlos Fuentes, and Gabriel Garcia Marquez, among many others, for their beliefs and associations. Congress repealed the McCarran-Walter Act in 1990, proclaiming that we were strong enough to permit free trade in ideas. But after 9/11, Congress again erected bars to entry based on speech. The Patriot Act denies admission to foreigners who "endorse or espouse terrorist activity," who "persuade others to support terrorist activity or a terrorist organization," or who are representatives of groups that express such views. Because of the breadth of the definitions of "terrorist activity" (virtually any act or threat of violence) and "terrorist organizations" (any group of two or more persons that engages in or threatens violence), this authority would empower the government to deny entry to any foreigner who advocated support for the African National Congress in the 1980s, for the Contras during the war against the Sandinistas in Nicaragua, or for opposition forces in Afghanistan or even the government of Israel today.

Four years later, in the REAL ID Act, Congress went still further, making the grounds of exclusion into grounds of deportation. Accordingly, permanent resident aliens who have lived here for decades can be deported if they are found to have ever been associated with a group that has used or threatened to use violence, even if their association had no connection to any unlawful or violent activity of the group.

Finally, the Patriot Act radically expanded the government's authority to detain immigrants. It gave the attorney general unprecedented power to detain foreign nationals indefinitely *without* a hearing and *without* showing that they pose a threat to national security or a flight risk. He need only certify that he has "reasonable grounds to believe" that the foreign national is "described in" various antiterrorism provisions of the Immigration and Nationality Act, provisions so broad that they would encompass a permanent resident alien who brandished a kitchen knife in a domestic dispute with her abusive husband or an alien who donated a box of crayons to a charitable day-care center associated with a "terrorist organization."

The Patriot Act also undermined citizens' rights, most notably in a provision authorizing the FBI to demand records from businesses, nonprofit organizations, libraries, and bookstores without any showing that the records concerned someone suspected of involvement in any wrongdoing. This provision, Section 215, sparked widespread objections. When the Patriot Act was reauthorized four years after its initial enactment, Congress insisted on placing additional safeguards on Section 215—but did not even discuss the much more onerous Patriot Act provisions directed at immigrants.

Ethnic Profiling

One of the most dramatic responses to the attack of September 11 was a swift reversal in public attitudes about racial and ethnic profiling as a law enforcement tool. Before September 11, polls found that about 80 percent of the American public considered racial profiling wrong. State legislatures, local police departments, and President Clinton had condemned the practice and ordered data collection on the racial patterns of stops and searches. The U.S. Customs Service, sued for racial profiling, had instituted measures to counter racial and ethnic profiling at the borders. A federal law prohibiting racial profiling seemed likely. Even Ashcroft had criticized the practice and pledged to end it.

After September 11, however, polls reported that nearly 60 percent of the American public favored ethnic profiling directed at Arabs and Muslims. The fact that the perpetrators of the September 11 attack were all male Arab and Muslim immigrants and that the attack was orchestrated by al Qaeda has led many to believe that it is only common sense to pay closer attention to Arab-looking men boarding airplanes and elsewhere. The high stakes make the case for profiling stronger here than in routine drug interdiction stops on highways. Stuart Taylor, a columnist for *Newsweek*, the *National Journal*, and *Legal Times*, and a prior critic of racial profiling, wrote shortly after the attacks in favor of ethnic profiling of Arab men on airplanes. Press accounts made clear that, whether as a matter of official policy or not, law enforcement officials and airline employees were paying much closer attention to those who appear to be Arabs and Muslims.

While the Bush Administration has spoken out against ethnic and religious stereotyping and hate crimes, its actions have sent a different message. Virtually all of the 5,000 men detained in antiterrorism initiatives in the two years after 9/11 were Arab and Muslim, and in many instances there seemed to be little other than their Arab or Muslim identity that rendered them "of interest." The FBI called in 8,000 young men for interviews in connection with the September 11 investigation, solely on the fact that they were young recent immigrants from countries with predominantly Arab and Muslim populations. The Justice Department prioritized the deportation of foreign nationals from Arab and Muslim countries under the Absconder Apprehension Initiative, again, simply because of their origin. And in its Special Registration program, the government required foreign nationals from Arab and Muslim countries to register and be fingerprinted. Such actions only encourage others to act as if Arab or Muslim identity is a permissible basis for suspicion.

Guantanamo and Military Tribunals

The administration's mistreatment of detainees at Guantanamo, Bagram Air Force Base, and elsewhere around the world has also been predicated on a double standard. When critics charged that locking up human beings indefinitely, without charges, without hearings, and without access to lawyers or courts violated their rights, the administration's response was that, as foreign nationals held outside the United States, they are not entitled to any constitutional protections.

Some of the Guantanamo detainees will reportedly be tried in military tribunals. Under President Bush's November 2001 order creating the tribunals, and under the revised rules authorized by Congress after the Supreme Court declared the initial rules illegal, only foreign nationals can be tried in such tribunals. Citizens who engage in exactly the same conduct —even on behalf of al Qaeda—will be tried in ordinary criminal court, with all the protections that attend such trials. Defendants in military trials, by contrast, can be tried and executed without conviction by a jury of their peers and on the basis of hearsay evidence and testimony obtained through coercive interrogation methods. Here, again, the Bush administration has sought to strike a balance between liberty and security by denying basic rights to noncitizens in situations where they are identically situated to citizens.

Perhaps the most extreme example of this double standard came when the Bush administration opined, in secret, that an international human rights treaty, the Convention against Torture and Other Cruel, Inhuman, and Degrading Treatment or Punishment, barred cruel, inhuman, and degrading treatment only of persons within the United States or U.S. citizens. On this theory, the Department of Defense and the CIA were free to use cruel, inhuman, and degrading interrogation tactics against any foreign national held outside our borders—including those "disappeared" into CIA "black sites" and those held at Guantanamo. The government's argument turned human rights into citizen's rights and ignored the fact that human rights attach by definition to all *human* beings by virtue of their humanity, not the passport they happen to carry. To its credit, when it learned of this double standard, Congress reversed it, in an effort led by Senator and former Vietnam prisoner of war John McCain. But the Bush administration fought Congress every step of the way and managed to ensure that the McCain Amendment had no mechanism for enforcement.

Citizens' Rights

Security proposals that implicate the rights of citizens have generally received a far more skeptical reception from the American public. The proposal to create a national identity card was discussed almost immediately after 9/11, but Congress forbade any expenditure of funds on such a program—for citizens. When Americans learned of Operation TIPS, in which the Justice Department planned to recruit 11 million private citizens to spy on their neighbors, the program was roundly criticized by voices on all sides of the political spectrum, from Phyllis Schlafly to the ACLU. And at House Majority Leader Dick Armey's insistence, the Republicans' Homeland Security bill expressly prohibited adoption of Operation TIPS. When citizens' rights are directly at stake, in other words, the legal and political processes have proven much more rights-sensitive. When only immigrants rights appear to be at risk, the system hardly blinks.

Resisting Double Standards

As a way of striking the difficult balance between liberty and security, sacrificing foreign citizens' liberties is undoubtedly tempting. It allows those of us who are citizens to trade someone else's liberties for our security. We can avoid the difficult trade-offs, and have our security and our liberty, too. But doing so is wrong as a constitutional and normative matter, unlikely to make us more secure, and virtually certain to come back to haunt us.

Bill of Rights as Human Rights

As a constitutional matter, basic rights such as due process, equal protection, and the freedoms of speech and association are not limited to citizens but apply to all "persons" within the United States or subject to U.S. authority. The Constitution does restrict the right to vote to citizens, but that specific restriction only underscores by contrast that the Constitution's other rights apply to all "persons." These are human rights, not privileges of citizenship. At the time of the framing, they were seen as divinely decreed natural rights; in today's world, they are the core of what we understand as international human rights, owed to all persons by virtue of their personhood, irrespective of their identity or the political character of their government. The U.S. Supreme Court has stated that the First and Fifth Amendments acknowledge no distinction between citizens and foreigners residing in the United States, and as recently as 2001 the Court reaffirmed that "the Due Process Clause applies to all persons within the United States, including aliens, whether their presence here is lawful, unlawful, temporary, or permanent."[1] The very fact that noncitizens lack the vote only makes it all the more essential that they receive judicial protection, as they cannot rely on the political process to consider their interests.

The best way to ensure that a fair balance is struck between liberty and security is to ensure that all our interests are considered on both sides of the balance. When measures selectively target the rights of non-nationals, the political process is bound to fail, as the balance is skewed to consider everyone's security, but the liberties only of those with no voice.

Undermining Security

Double standards are not just wrong as a moral or normative matter. They are also unlikely to make us more secure. Even granting that it is rational to assume that al Qaeda operatives are more likely to be Arab or Muslim, if we are going to identify and capture the few al Qaeda terrorists among the many millions of law-abiding Arabs and Muslims here and abroad, we need the full cooperation of those communities. The communities themselves are much better equipped to identify any terrorists residing among them than are a group of outside law enforcement officials who are largely unfamiliar with the language, culture, and community. But when we impose on Arabs and Muslims burdens that we would not tolerate for ourselves, we make the targeted communities far less likely to cooperate and simultaneously stoke anti-American sentiment. And when we single out citizens of Arab countries for treatment not accorded to other nationals, those countries are likely to be less eager to assist in the war on terrorism as well.

The United States had the world's sympathy on 9/11. Five years later, that sympathy has been squandered, and resentment against the United States is higher than it has ever been before. In some countries Osama bin Laden has a higher approval rating than George Bush. That anti-Americanism, attributable to a widespread perception that the United States has refused to play by the rules and refused to recognize the basic human dignity of Arabs and Muslims in its counterterrorist initiatives, plays right into al Qaeda's hands. Terrorist groups want their enemies to overreact, because that overreaction then fosters sympathy and recruitment for the terrorists. By most reports, al Qaeda is stronger and more dispersed than ever five years after we declared war against it. The war on terror is not working, and one of the principal reasons it is not working is that we have refused to abide by basic principles of equality in how we've gone about protecting our country.

The Illusory Double Standard

The argument that we are only targeting foreigners' rights, and therefore citizens need not worry, is in an important sense illusory, for what we do to foreign nationals today provides a precedent for what can and will be done to citizens tomorrow. When the president asserted the power to hold enemy combatants at Guantanamo, he reassured Americans that it would not apply to them but only to noncitizens. Yet shortly thereafter the administration crossed that line and asserted the same authority with respect to the two U.S. citizens, Hamdi and Padilla, that it asserts with respect to the foreign citizens held at Guantanamo.

The line between foreign national and citizen has often been crossed before. In fact, two of the most shameful episodes in our nation's history, both of which affected thousands of American citizens, had their provenance in measures initially targeted at noncitizens. The McCarthy era of the 1940s and 1950s, in which thousands of Americans were tarred with guilt by association, was an extension to citizens of a similar campaign using similar techniques against *alien* radicals in the first Red Scare thirty years earlier. The earlier Red Scare, which culminated in the arrests of thousands of aliens for their political associations during the Palmer Raids, was coordinated by a young J. Edgar Hoover, then in the Alien Radical division of the Justice Department. Hoover applied what he had learned in the first Red Scare to U.S. citizens during the second Red Scare, which targeted thousands of them.

The same pattern underlies the internment of U.S. citizens of Japanese descent during World War II. Since 1798, the Enemy Aliens Act has authorized the president during wartime to arrest, detain, deport, or otherwise restrict the freedom of anyone over fourteen years old who is a citizen of the country with which we are at war, without regard to any actual evidence of disloyalty, sabotage, or danger. The justification for that law, which the Supreme Court has upheld as constitutional, is that during wartime one can presume that citizens of the enemy country are loyal to their own country, not ours, and that there is insufficient time to identify those who are actually disloyal.

In World War II we simply extended that argument to U.S. citizens through the prism of race. The Army argued that persons of Japanese descent, even if they were technically American citizens because they were born here, remained for all practical purposes "enemy aliens," presumptively likely to be loyal to Japan. Lt. General John L. DeWitt, the driving force behind the internment orders, wrote in his report on the Japanese evacuation that "the Japanese race is an enemy race and while many second and third generation Japanese, born on United States soil, possessed of United States citizenship, have become Americanized, the racial strains are undiluted."[2] More colloquially, General DeWitt testified in 1943 before the House Naval Affairs Committee, that "a Jap's a Jap. . . . It makes no difference whether he is an American citizen or not."[3] And so we locked up 110,000 persons solely because of their Japanese ancestry, 70,000 of them U.S. citizens.

History reveals that the distinction between citizen and alien has often been resorted to as a justification for liberty-infringing measures in times of crisis. In the short term, the fact that measures are limited to noncitizens appears to make them easier for the majority to accept—citizens are not asked to sacrifice their own liberty. But the same history suggests that citizens should be wary about relying on this distinction because it has often been breached before. What we are willing to do to noncitizens ultimately affects what we are willing to do to citizens. In the long run, all of our rights are at stake in the war against terrorism.

Conclusion

In the wake of the attacks of 9/11, there may well be justification for sacrificing some of our liberties if the sacrifice will make us more secure. But many of the measures the Bush administration has undertaken after September 11 follow a disturbing historical pattern, in which the polity sacrifices not its own freedoms but the freedoms of noncitizens, a minority group with no vote, in the interest of preserving citizens' security. The post-9/11 response constitutes a reprise of some of the worst mistakes of our past. Once again, we treated people as suspicious not for their conduct but based on their racial, ethnic, or political identity. Once again, we used the immigration power as a pretext for criminal law enforcement without the protections associated with the criminal process. Once again, we undertook a mass detention campaign directed at immigrants without probable cause that any of them were tied to the specific threats that we face. And once again, we authorized the government to bypass procedures designed to distinguish the guilty from the innocent, holding secret hearings and authorizing executive detentions that challenge the most basic notions of fairness.

As politically tempting as the trade-off of immigrants' liberties for our security may appear, we should resist it for reasons of principle, pragmatism, and self-interest. As a matter of principle, the rights that we have selectively denied to immigrants should not be reserved for citizens. The rights of political freedom, due process, and equal protection belong to every person subject to U.S. legal obligations, irrespective of citizenship. As a pragmatic matter, reliance on double standards reduces the legitimacy of our struggle, and that legitimacy may be our most valuable asset, both at home and abroad. To paraphrase John Ashcroft himself: "To those who pit Americans against immigrants and citizens against non-citizens . . . my message is this: Your tactics only aid terrorism."[4] And as a matter of self-interest, what we do to aliens today may well pave the way for what will be done to citizens tomorrow. In the end, however, it is principle that should drive us: the justice of our response should be judged by how we treat those who have no voice in the political process. Thus far, we have performed predictably, but not well.

NOTES

Some parts of this essay appeared previously in the *Boston Review.* A more detailed account of this argument can be found in David Cole, "Enemy Aliens," *Stanford Law Review* 54 (2002), 953–59, and David Cole, *Enemy Aliens: Double Standards and Constitutional Freedoms in the War on Terrorism,* rev. ed. (New York: New Press, 2005).

1. *Zadyydas v. Davis,* 533 U.S. 678, 121 S. Ct. 2441, 2500 (2001); see also *Matthews v. Diaz,* 426 U.S. 67, 77 (1976) (holding that due process applies to all aliens in the United States, even those whose presence is "unlawful, involuntary, or transitory").

2. Final report of General DeWitt, quoted in Jacobus tenBroek, Edward N. Barnhart, and Floyd W. Matson, *Prejudice, War, and the Constitution* (Berkeley: University of California Press, 1954), 110.

3. Ibid.

4. Testimony of Attorney General John Ashcroft, Senate Judiciary Committee Hearing on Anti-Terrorism Policy, 106th Cong. (December 6, 2001)

PRIMARY SOURCE

The Deportation Terror

A Weapon to Gag America, 1950

Abner Green

Like the post-9/11 restrictions on civil liberties, deportation policy during the Cold War limited immigrant rights in the service of national security. Abner Green, director of the American Committee for Protection of the Foreign Born from 1942 through his death in 1954, argues, much as David Cole does in the previous chapter, that the deportation of immigrants is a threat to democracy, no matter which period is under discussion.

Note about the Author

Abner Green is executive secretary of the American Committee for Protection of Foreign Born. He has filled this post since 1942, and, previous to that, served as educational director and Washington Legislative Representative for the Committee. A native of New York, Mr. Green is also serving as a Trustee of the Bail Fund of the Civil Rights Congress of New York and has been actively engaged in the field of civil rights for the past 15 years.

The American Committee for Protection of Foreign Born was organized in 1932 and has functioned since that date as an agency assisting non-citizens and naturalized citizens with problems arising as a result of their foreign birth. The Committee maintains a Naturalization Aid Service and is currently defending more than 135 non-citizens who face deportation from the United States because of their political opinions. This pamphlet concerns itself principally with this latter phase of the Committee's work.

Published by The American Committee for Protection of Foreign Born
23 West 26th Street, New York 10, N.Y.
January, 1950
PRINTED IN U.S.A.

The Deportation Terror

Central Office File Number a-5300756 (5596/80) . . .

To the Department of Justice, that is just another file number.

But, to four-year-old George Harisiades, that is not a file number. THAT IS HIS FATHER.

To Esther Harisiades, that is her husband, the father of her two children, the sole support of their family.

And over the Harisiades home in Brooklyn hangs the threat of deportation that would take Peter Harisiades forcibly away from his family and exile him to Greece, where he faces death because of his anti-fascist convictions.

In thousands of American homes throughout the land today there is fear and insecurity as the result of the Justice Department's deportation hysteria.

The non-citizen, however, is only the first victim of the current deportation drive. It is the Bill of Rights of the United States Constitution—the rights and liberties of every American, native as well as foreign born—which will be destroyed if this deportation drive succeeds.

Regimentation

Three million non-citizens in the United States already live in an atmosphere of regimentation.

They have all been fingerprinted.

Every detail of their personal lives is on file with the F.B.I.

They cannot move from one address to another without notifying the Justice Department.

Their activities are under the constant surveillance of the F.B.I. and the Immigration and Naturalization Service.

They can be—and are—called in by immigration officials and subjected to hours of searching questioning and examination.

They are warned by Justice Department officials to discontinue membership and activity in organizations which do not have the support or approval of the F.B.I.

They are threatened with denials of citizenship, deportation, imprisonment, loss of their jobs if they do not conform with the instructions of Justice Department officials.

The most dangerous aspect of the attack on the rights of the non-citizen remains the Justice Department's deportation drive. If the Justice Department succeeds in its campaign to deport non-citizens because of their political opinions, then 3,000,000 immigrants in this country will find themselves deprived of all of their rights, and their stay here dependent on the approval of the F.B.I.

The Justice Department wants to dictate to 3,000,000 non-citizens what they shall think, what they can read, whom they may see, erecting a legal and political concentration camp around the con minds of the non-citizen population.

Our democracy will not long survive under these restrictions. Citizens will find their rights equally restricted and endangered once thought-control is imposed on non-citizens.

What Has Happened?

In October, 1946, the Justice Department started proceedings to deport Peter Harisiades because of his political opinions.

The proceedings were based on the 1940 amendment to the Immigration Act of 1918, which provides that any non-citizen who, "at any time after entry" into this country, believed in or belonged to an organization that advocated the overthrow of the government of the United States "by force and violence" should be deported.

There is no time limitation in the law. Non-citizens have been arrested for deportation after living and working in this country for 45 and 50 years.

Nor has the Supreme Court of the United States ever ruled on the constitutionality of the 1940 amendment; or even on the validity of the 1918 law providing for the deportation of non-citizens because of their political opinions.

The Justice Department *thinks* it can deport non-citizens under this law. It doesn't *know* whether it can and it will not know until there has been a clear decision by the Supreme Court.

One would assume that, if the Justice Department were interested in clearly establishing the law, it would have waited until the Harisiades case is decided by the Supreme Court. It would have waited to find out whether the law is constitutional before arresting any more non-citizens.

But the Justice Department continued arresting more non-citizens on the basis of charges identical with those made against Peter Harisiades. In these arrests, the Justice Department was motivated clearly by political considerations. The arrests, which were completely unnecessary, have been a means of creating hysteria and terror in foreign-born communities.

Non-citizens have been fired from their jobs. Their lives have been threatened by hoodlum elements. Their families have been terrorized. And all as a result of unnecessary arrests motivated by purely political considerations on the part of government officials.

As a result, more than 135 non-citizens in 19 states have been arrested in deportation proceedings; and the Justice Department has announced that it is preparing to arrest 3,500 more non-citizens.

Who Are They?

Twenty-four are women—mothers of American citizens and mothers of war veterans, wives and grandmothers of citizens.

Forty-one are men and women who have been active members or leaders of trade unions in this country.

Two are leaders of the Negro people. Four are Mexican-American leaders. One is a leader of the Jewish people. Six are leaders of the Communist Party. And leaders in all foreign-born communities in the country have similarly been selected for persecution.

Throughout the period of World War II, these were among the people the government praised and honored for their contribution to mobilization, production, and winning the war.

Today, the same government, although a different administration, rewards them for their outstanding services to the nation—with deportation proceedings.

Yesterday they were honored and today they face exile from the United States.

Almost all of those arrested in deportation proceedings are in the United States legally. Almost all have American families dependent upon them for support.

Almost all have tried in the past—and all sincerely want at this point—to become citizens of the United States. In fact, 41 of those arrested had applications for American citizenship pending at the time they were arrested.

Not one of the non-citizens arrested is charged with the commission of any act, or acts, that would threaten the government of the United States or that might endanger the safety or well-being of the American people.

They are not criminals. They are decent, hard-working, legal residents of this country—its towns, and subways, and skyscrapers, and railroads, peopled the cities and worked the factories and mines, who contributed to our culture and helped make America the foremost industrial nation in the world.

The Deportees

Peter Warhol, of Minneapolis, is the husband of an American citizen and the father of three American-born children. Pete was brought to this country 35 years ago, when he was three years old. He grew up in Minneapolis, and, in 1936, became a leader of the Upholsterers Union, A. F. of L.

After Pearl Harbor, Peter refused an opportunity to avoid service in the armed forces on the basis of his trade-union position. He was inducted into the Army and served together with his four younger brothers, all of them American citizens by birth.

While in the Army, Pete elected to go overseas with his unit in place of remaining in this country in order to get his citizenship. He felt that he could take care of his citizenship after the war.

After serving for two years, Peter Warhol was honorably discharged and a grateful government rewarded him by arresting him for deportation to Czechoslovakia. His application for citizenship is still pending.

That is the type of person who faces deportation.

Then, there is:

Leon Callow, a steelworker of Niles, Ohio, sole support of an American-citizen wife and nine American-born children—the oldest 16 and the youngest one month old . . .

Benjamin Saltzman, 54-year-old painter of New York City, one of whose sons died in Europe as a member of the armed forces of the United States during the second World War . . . Theresa Horvath, of Fairmont, West Virginia; Esther Sazer of Los Angeles; Anna Taffler, of Brooklyn—all mothers of war veterans . . . Jack Crewe, of San Antonio, Texas, faces deportation to Newfoundland, while his wife, Ada, faces deportation to England while their two children will remain in the United States since they are American-born citizens.

To each one of those arrested, deportation means separation from family and friends, exile from the land of their adoption. These people have lived and worked most of their lives in this country. William Heikkila, of San Francisco, for instance, was brought here when he was three months old and today, at the age of 42, faces deportation to Finland.

These non-citizens are Americans in every sense of the word.

They are an integral part of the American people

They lack only the technical requirement of citizenship papers—which most of them have been prevented from getting by the Justice Department—to qualify for all of the duties and responsibilities of American citizens.

Their threatened deportation violates our traditions as a people concerned with human welfare and human rights.

But basic democratic principles are also jeopardized by this deportation drive.

What Is Involved

Peter Harisiades came to the United States from Greece in 1916 at the age of 13. In his youth he worked as a water boy on the Illinois Central Railroad and later in a foundry in Beloit, Wisconsin; in a rubber factory in Akron; in steel mills in Canton, Ohio, and New Castle, Pennsylvania; in a textile mill in New Bedford, Massachusetts.

In 1925, while working in Boston, Peter Harisiades became a member of the Communist Party. During the New Bedford textile strike in 1930, when immigration officials tried to break the strike by arresting non-citizen members of the Textile Workers Union, a warrant for the arrest of Peter Harisiades was issued. (Pete was served with the warrant 16 years later, in New York in 1946.)

During the 1930's, Pete worked as a leader of the Greek Bureau of the Communist Party in New York City. In 1939, his membership was discontinued when the Communist Party dropped all non-citizens from its rolls. In 1937, Pete married an American citizen. During the second World War, he served as one of the editors of *The Greek-American Tribune*, a weekly newspaper, and traveled throughout the country to rally Greek-Americans in support of the war against fascism.

In 1944, Pete applied—for the second time—for American citizenship. Instead of considering his application for citizenship, the Justice Department arrested him in October, 1946, and held him for deportation to Greece on the ground of his past membership in the Communist Party.

Extensive hearings were held in the Harisiades case during 1947 and 1948. In December, 1948, the Commissioner of Immigration and Naturalization ordered Peter Harisiades deported to Greece on the ground that he personally believed in, and advocated, the overthrow of the government of the United States by "force and violence" and also that he had been a member of an organization so advocating.

In May, 1949, the Board of Immigration Appeals—the highest administrative body in the Justice Department—sustained the order of deportation on only one of the two grounds. The Board held that, on the basis of the record, Peter Harisiades never believed in, or advocated, the overthrow of the government of the United States by "force and violence." The Board sustained deportation only on the ground of his past membership, from 1925 to 1939, in the Communist Party.

In finding that the Communist Party is an organization that advocates the overthrow of the government of the United States by "force and violence," the Justice Department could not point to one instance since it was organized in 1920 when the organization actually advocated force or violence or taught its members any such beliefs.

The Justice Department based its findings on the literature circulated by the Communist Party, the Marxist classics, some of which are more than 100 years old.

The record in the Harisiades case is hundreds of pages long. Peter Harisiades testified at length as to his beliefs and as to what the Communist Party taught him and advocated during the years of his membership. William Schneiderman, an American citizen, whose citizenship the United States Supreme Court preserved in 1945 in its historic decision after Wendell Willkie argued on his behalf, also testified in the Harisiades hearings.

Mr. Schneiderman, who is California State Chairman of the Communist Party, discussed the principles of his organization, denied that it believes in, or ever believed in, force or violence, and completely exposed the Justice Department's charges as political persecution.

But, nowhere in these hundreds of pages did the Justice Department present so much as one iota of proof that the Communist Party believes in, or advocates, the overthrow of the government of the United States by "force and violence.

Test Case

On May 20, 1949, the Justice Department suddenly arrested Peter Harisiades and took him to Ellis Island. They had a passport for him and passage on a boat to Greece.

The Harisiades case was immediately appealed to the Federal courts and a petition for a writ of *habeas corpus* is now pending in the Federal District Court in New York before Judge Vincent Leibell.

If Judge Leibell sustains deportation, his decision will be appealed to the Federal Circuit Court of Appeals and then, if necessary, to the United States Supreme Court.

The case of Peter Harisiades has become a test case for all those 135 arrested to date and held for deportation because of their political opinions. The decision in the Harisiades case will affect the lives of all other non-citizens threatened with deportation. It will affect also the rights of all Americans because of the important political and legal issues that are being tested, because the constitutional rights of all Americans are being tested.

The Justice Department is attempting to replace the traditional American concept of democracy—that all persons in the country have equal democratic rights—with the reactionary principle that, in deportation proceedings, non-citizens do not have freedom of speech or freedom of belief.

Obviously, if non-citizens are fully protected in their right to freedom of speech and belief, Peter Harisiades could not be deported because of his political opinions. In his political activities, Peter Harisiades exercised freedom of speech and belief—freedoms which he assumed were his because the Bill of Rights accords those liberties to all persons (not just citizens) in this country.

Tomorrow, it will be naturalized citizens.

And the day after, it will be native-born citizens.

This is the path fascism took in Europe. It is the road mapped by American reaction in its drive to destroy the rights of the American people.

Guilt by Association

Peter Harisiades has been ordered deported solely on the ground of his former membership in the Communist Party, despite a clear finding that he never personally believed in, or advocated, the overthrow of the government of the United States by "force and violence."

Here, again, we have an attempt to change basic American traditions.

One of the most important concepts in any democratic system of government is the principle that guilt must be personal. An individual is responsible for what he does.

The government admits that Peter Harisiades is not personally guilty of any violation of law. He never committed any act of force or any act of violence. He never believed in—and never advocated—force or violence. Yet is he ordered deported!

How could Peter Harisiades, who never believed in force or violence, have belonged for 14 years to an organization that the Justice Department now says advocates "force and violence"?

This doesn't make sense. It mocks every concept of democratic procedure. It is an attempt to establish in American law the principle of "guilt by association." If successfully established for non-citizens, this un-American principle will be extended immediately and used as well against American citizens in order to deprive them, too, of their freedom of speech and freedom of belief.

Another democratic principle which is under attack in this deportation drive is the constitutional prohibition against ex-post-facto laws.

Peter Harisiades terminated his membership in the Communist Party in 1939. Yet, he faces deportation on the basis of a law passed in 1940.

In 1938, the United States Supreme Court held, in the Strecker case, that the government did not have the right to deport non-citizens for *past* membership in proscribed organizations.

The Supreme Court, in deciding the Strecker case, did not rule on any basic issues since it found that under the law as written in 1918, Strecker could not be deported on the basis of his past membership in the Communist Party.

Then, in 1940, Congress amended the Immigration Act of 1918 to provide that non-citizens could be deported for membership "at any time after entry" in proscribed organizations.

In 1939, when Peter Harisiades terminated his membership in the Communist Party, the government could not arrest him for deportation under the laws then in effect because of the Supreme Court decision in the Strecker case.

In 1939, Peter Harisiades was secure in his status in this country.

Then, in 1940, Congress amended the law and Peter Harisiades, continuing to do exactly the same things he had been doing, suddenly faced deportation proceedings.

This is clearly an ex-post-facto law. It violates the Constitution and, if upheld by the courts, it will undermine the security of citizens as well as non-citizens since it is one more step in the direction of destroying the Bill of Rights and constitutional liberties in this country.

Alien Testing Ground

The Justice Department is using the non-citizen as a guinea-pig in an attempt to establish dangerous and undemocratic principles.

Arrests of non-citizens are accompanied by false and misleading statements to the press.

Most metropolitan newspapers need no encouragement to use their news columns for alien-baiting and provoking hysteria against the non-citizen.

Deportation arrests secure front-page spreads and banner headlines with the aim of inflaming the publics mind against so-called dangerous alien Reds.

It is clearly the belief of the Justice Department that the American people will not come to the defense of the rights of non-citizens if non-citizens can be made a sufficiently unpopular minority.

Concentration Camp

During the past two years, the Justice Department has attempted to create a concentration camp for non-citizens on Ellis Island. It is ironical that this attempt to create America's first concentration camp should be made at Ellis Island.

There, within arm's length of the Statue of Liberty, originally a symbol of hope and a promise of freedom, is a prison camp with barbed wire and armed guards. There men and women are deprived of their liberty and our American traditions flaunted. It is perhaps also symbolical that the Statue of Liberty stands with its *back* to Ellis Island.

In February, 1948, the Justice Department arrested five noncitizens in deportation proceedings and held them on Ellis Island without bail. These five were: Charles Doyle, Gerhart Eisler, Irving Potash, Ferdinand Smith, and John Williamson. As the result of a five-day hunger strike—and thousands of telegrams as well as protest demonstrations throughout the country—the five were released from Ellis Island on March 6, 1948. During

August, 1948, the Federal Circuit Court of Appeals held that the Federal District Court must review any abuse of discretion by the Attorney General in denying bail to non-citizens held in deportation proceedings.

Thus, the Justice Department's first attempt to undermine the American right to bail was defeated. A second attempt was made in 1949.

George Pirinsky and Beatrice Johnson

In July, 1949, the Justice Department re-arrested and held without bail on Ellis Island two non-citizens—Beatrice Siskind Johnson, mother of a six-year-old daughter, and George Pirinsky, secretary of the American Slav Congress. Both Mrs. Johnson and Mr. Pirinsky were arrested originally in deportation proceedings during 1948 and released then on $1,000 bail.

Although there had been no decision in either case, they were told that their bail had been cancelled and that they were being held without bail. A press statement by the Justice Department in Washington informed the American people that Beatrice Johnson and George Pirinsky were being denied bail because the Justice Department did not want them "at liberty."

After the two had been deprived of their liberty for five weeks, the Federal District Court in New York held that the Justice Department could not deny bail to non-citizens facing deportation because of their political beliefs and ordered them released promptly on reasonable bail."

The Justice Department then demanded $25,000 bail each for Beatrice Siskind Johnson and George Pirinsky. This was "reasonable" bail—$25,000, when bail in deportation cases usually was $500 to $1,000!

Because Mrs. Johnson's daughter was returning from summer camp and there was no one at home to take care of her, bail of $10,000 was posted finally under protest for her release from Ellis Island.

George Pirinsky remained on Ellis Island for another two months while an appeal was taken in his case.

First, Federal District Judge Alexander Holtzoff held that $25,000 was "reasonable" bail. His decision was appealed.

Finally, after George Pirinsky had been held on Ellis Island for 91 days—illegally deprived of his rights and illegally deprived of his liberty—the Federal Circuit Court of Appeals reversed Judge Holtzoff and ruled that

Pirinsky must be released on bail of "not more than $5,000." Thus a second attempt to hold non-citizens without bail was defeated.

Creating False Impressions

The Justice Department demanded $25,000 bail for George Pirinsky because it wanted also to make non-citizens appear to be criminal and dangerous elements and to create a false impression in the public's mind that these non-citizens face immediate deportation.

Neither Pirinsky nor Johnson faced immediate deportation when they were arrested.

The Justice Department knew very well that neither could be deported until a Supreme Court decision was handed down in the Harisiades case.

When the Justice Department arrests a non-citizen, that is only the first step in a long administrative proceeding and then a possible court appeal.

Non-citizens arrested in deportation proceedings are not necessarily guilty when arrested. They are arrested, presented with charges, and then administrative hearings must first be held to determine whether or not they should be deported.

The Justice Department, however, is trying to establish in the public mind the idea that the very moment a non-citizen is arrested he is guilty and he is going to be deported.

That is sheer nonsense, as the Justice Department very well knows. It violates another principle of democratic procedure—that a person is innocent until tried and found guilty.

Reporting

The Justice Department is at the same time trying to make the non-citizen who is arrested in deportation proceedings feel like a criminal and guilty before he is even tried.

In order to achieve this purpose, the Justice Department is trying to impose illegal conditions for the release of non-citizens arrested in deportation proceedings.

In many respects, the Justice Department is using typical police-state measures in an effort to further regiment non-citizens and destroy our liberties.

In all parts of the country, the Justice Department has demanded, as a new condition for the release of non-citizens arrested in deportation proceedings, that the non-citizen agree to report *in person* once a week to the local office of the Immigration and Naturalization Service or local police station. This is in addition to posting $1,000 bail and, in some cases, $5,000 bail.

Five Federal judges—in New York, San Francisco, and Philadelphia—have ruled that it is illegal for the Justice Department to require non-citizens to report regularly in person.

However, only those non-citizens who have appealed to the Federal courts have been released from reporting. More than 25 other non-citizens are forced to continue to report regularly in person—in clear violation of the law. These non-citizens are intimidated by the Justice Department by threats of being re-arrested and having their bail increased from $1,000 to $5,000 or even $10,000, if they attempt to discontinue reporting.

Attack on Trade Unions

In the course of its deportation drive, the Justice Department has repeatedly attempted to use deportation to weaken and destroy trade unions.

Of the 135 non-citizens arrested to date, 41 are active members and leaders of trade unions.

During the week that New York subway workers were considering a strike for higher wages in September, 1947, the Justice Department arrested John Santo, at that time one of the leaders of the Transport Workers Union.

Just as his union was entering negotiations with employers in March, 1948, Irving Potash, leader of the Furriers Joint Council of New York, was arrested in deportation proceedings.

This pattern of using the deportation laws to interfere with legitimate activities of American trade unionists is carried out by the Justice Deparment in every section of the county.

The recent attack on the union of the Alaska Cannery Workers, in Seattle, is one more example of the anti-labor bias of Justice Department officials.

The Alaska Cannery Workers Union, F.T.A.-C.I.O., Local 7, has raised its members' wage, from $25 a month in 1934 to $250 a month in 1949. Throughout the years the Associated Farmers of California and the Alaska Salmon Industry have tried unsuccessfully to destroy this Union.

All other efforts failing, finally in 1949 the Justice Department moved in, and during September arrested for deportation to the Philippine islands the three leaders of this Union: Ernesto Mangaoang, business agent; Chris Mensalvos, educational director; and Ponce Torres, dispatcher.

Then there is the unrelenting drive against Harry Bridges—a history of 15 years of persecution because of his progressive and militant leadership of longshoremen and warehousemen on the West Coast.

Framing Trade Unionists

The use of the immigration laws to frame Charles Doyle and Pete Nelson has been perhaps the most vicious.

Charles A. Doyle, of Niagara Falls, New York, was international vice-president of the C.I.O. Chemical Workers. He is a native of Scotland and a legal resident of the United States for more than 24 years. His wife is a legally resident non-citizen and his four children were all born in this country.

Pete Nelson, of Everett, Washington, is business agent of his local of the International Woodworkers of America. He is a native of Sweden and a resident of the United States for more than 25 years. His wife and two children are native-born Americans.

Doyle—in January, 1948—and Nelson—in October, 1949—each went to Canada on regular business of their unions. Doyle went to Canada for a regularly scheduled meeting of the international executive board of his Union and Nelson for a regularly scheduled international convention of his Union.

Before leaving for Canada, they each obtained re-entry permits and the assurances of the Immigration and Naturalization Service that they would have absolutely no difficulty in re-entering the United States.

However, both Doyle and Nelson were barred from the United States when they tried to re-enter the country. *Their re-entry permits had been cancelled after they left for Canada.*

Both Doyle and Nelson re-entered the United States without permission and were then arrested and held for deportation because they insisted on their right to rejoin their families in this country and return to their union jobs.

They both still face deportation and Charles Doyle faces in addition a one-year sentence in a Federal penitentiary for entering the country "illegally."

Naturalized Citizens

Naturalized American citizens are also being subjected to questioning, harassment and intimidation by the Immigration and Naturalization Service. Once an immigrant becomes a citizen, he is no longer under the jurisdiction of the Immigration and Naturalization Service. But, the Service is using all kinds of tricks, and depending also on the citizen's lack of familiarity with the laws of this country, to deprive naturalized citizens of their rights.

In all parts of the country, naturalized citizens are being called in to the local offices of the Service and questioned illegally by immigration inspectors. They are being visited by F.B.I. agents and are subjected in their own homes to illegal questioning and intimidation.

This is part of the Justice Department's program to destroy the rights of naturalized citizens. The Department has announced that it is preparing to initiate proceedings to revoke the American citizenship of 238 naturalized citizens on political grounds.

Part of General Attack

The deportation drive and the hysteria against the foreign-born are an essential part of the concentrated drive on the rights of all minorities in the United States and the general assault on the liberties of the American people.

Lynchings of Negro people in the South. . . . The "loyalty" program for government workers. . . . The Hollywood 10. . . . Increased police brutality against the Negro people in industrial centers and against Mexican-Americans in the Southwest. . . . The Los Angeles 21 and the Denver 6. . . . Increased anti-Semitic propaganda. . . . The Trenton 6. . . . The attempt to jail the leaders of the Communist Party because of their ideas. . . .

These—together with the deportation drive—are part of the general attack on the rights of all Americans who believe in peace and the democratic way of life.

The Foreign Born

The foreign born have been selected for special persecution because of the vital role they play in the democratic life of our country.

The immigrants helped build this country. With their sweat and blood, with their lives, they helped build the cities and factories, laid the railroads and developed the industries. Today, they still comprise a large section of the nation's working force and the majority of them are to be found in the basic industries—in coal, auto, steel, rubber.

The immigrant, having come here seeking democracy, has often fought to strengthen our democracy. As a result of his personal experiences in Europe, the immigrant is keenly aware of the meaning of oppression and is often to be found in the ranks of the labor and progressive movement in this country.

The concentrated drive against the foreign born is clearly an attempt to terrorize them and to separate them from other sections of the American people, to deprive the American people of these natural allies in the fight for peace and democracy.

The Justice Department wants to prevent the foreign born from participating in the present-day fight against reaction—in the fight for housing, trade-union rights, relief, peace, democracy, and all other progressive aims to defend and extend the welfare and well-being of the American people.

It is therefore the duty as well as the responsibility of every person in this country—and, in the first instance, of native-born Americans—to fight to defeat this attack on the rights and liberties of the foreign born.

Fight for Citizenship

The fight against the deportation hysteria is basically a fight today to win American citizenship for all three million non-citizens now in the country.

Almost every one of the 135 non-citizens arrested in deportation proceeding has tried on one or more occasion in the past to become an American citizen.

They didn't become citizens because they were prevented from doing so as the result of the red tape and discrimination that is a part of the naturalization process.

This red tape and discrimination, as well as the educational and literacy requirements, prevent hundreds and thousands each year, and discourage many thousands of others, from becoming American citizens.

The naturalization of all three million non-citizens now in this country would *strengthen our democracy* and make it more difficult for reaction to persecute or terrorize the foreign born.

An Old Story

The attack on the rights of the foreign born follows a pattern which has been pursued by reactionary government officials in every period of American history when they have been confronted with an economic or political crisis.

Reaction has always attempted to use the non-citizen as a scapegoat in very much the same way that Hitler used the Jews in Germany.

Shortly after the founding of this country, in 1798, the Federalist Party enacted the Alien and Sedition Laws in an effort to maintain itself in power. But, under the leadership of Thomas Jefferson, the American people wiped these vicious laws off the statute books and the Federalist Party out of the political life of the country in 1800.

Shortly after the first World War, the American people were shocked by the infamous Palmer Raids of 1920 and A. Mitchell Palmer, the Attorney General who carried out the raids and hoped to have himself elected President as a result, went into oblivion, a disgraced political figure.

Then, during the early years of the depression, in 1931, the then Secretary of Labor earned himself the name of "Deportation" Doak. But, again, the American people refused to be diverted from the solution of serious economic problems by a deportation drive and turned the alien-baiters out of office.

Today, again, the American people are haunted by an oncoming economic crisis and the administration in power is faced with a political crisis in its foreign policies.

Another crisis—another deportation drive. Reaction has only one answer to the problems faced by the people and that is to divide and terrorize them and to divert their attention by stimulating hysteria and discrimination.

The Fight against Deportation

The Justice Department's deportation drive will be tested in the Federal courts on the basis of the case of Peter Harisiades. But this is not a problem that can be left to the courts alone to decide. The deportation drive is not just legal; it is also a political drive on our rights and liberties as Americans.

It is the responsibility of the people of this country to defeat by their protests and demonstrations the Justice Department's drive on the rights of foreign-bom Americans. It is the responsibility of the people also to guarantee that each attempt by the Justice Department to terrorize the foreign born meets with defeat.

The American people will respond to this fight for the rights of the foreign born once they are aware of the issues that are at stake. The American people will defeat this hysteria because they will recognize that not only their rights but also their very existence and the democratic future of this country is jeopardized by this hysteria.

The 135 non-citizens arrested in deportation proceedings because of their political opinions are being defended by the American Committee for Protection of Foreign Born, an organization which has carried on the fight for the democratic rights of non-citizens and naturalized citizens for the past 18 years.

Today, the Committee urges all Americans—regardless of their political beliefs—to join in the fight to preserve the rights of the foreign born as essential to the continued existence of American democracy.

Defeat Deportation Hysteria

The deportation hysteria is contrary to the democratic traditions of our country. Unless it is defeated, it will serve to undermine and destroy the democratic aspirations of the American people.

The deportation drive can be defeated. It must be defeated if the American people are going to move on the road of peace and democracy and progress to a better America for all persons, regardless of race, color, creed, nationality, place of birth, or political opinion.

Those are the goals for which Americans gave their lives in the war against fascism. That is the America for which we must continue to fight if the generations to come are to live in a free America dedicated to liberty and progress.

NOTE

Reprinted with the cooperation of the Morris Fromkin Memorial Collection at the University of Wisconsin–Milwaukee, archivist May Yela in particular.

PART V

Afterwords

The authors in this collection have shown how the concept of "immigrant rights" draws on, contradicts, and complicates existing categories of citizenship and nation. In the early twenty-first century, with free trade agreements facilitating the mobility of corporations and migrants crossing international borders to seek refuge and opportunity, even such complex categories undergo change. This book concludes, then, with two broad visions of the ways we have come to imagine citizenship and nationhood. Implicit in both essays are ways these imaginings might be transformed to become more egalitarian.

Looking back to the Mexican-American War and the resulting annexation by the United States of a vast parcel of formerly Mexican territory, literary critic Donald Pease (chapter 17) traces the violence of Walt Whitman's national imaginary in which Anglo-American sovereignty was legitimized and Mexicans, along with newly colonized Mexican Americans, were dehumanized. For Pease, Whitman's egalitarian American construction of the nation was possible only by exalting the violence of the Mexican-American War and celebrating American troops as martyrs and liberators. Mexicans, then, become, in Whitman's famous "Song of Myself," villainous and unworthy of full citizenship: a predictor of things to come, as many Mexican Americans in the Southwest were disenfranchised from political, social, economic, and cultural rights after 1848. For Pease, this violence toward Mexicans constitutes the conditions for the emergence of the category "illegal imigrant" some eighty years later. The terrors of war and disenfranchisement are thus entwined in the emergence of American national unity.

Like Pease, ethnic and women's studies scholar Monisha Das Gupta (chapter 18) notes the ways that the Treaty of Guadalupe Hidalgo in 1848 imposed citizenship on Mexican Americans. For Das Gupta, the nation comes into existence only through such violent acts. Therefore, citizenship always entails coercion. With this awareness, Das Gupta traces three "rights discourses": citizenship, migrant, and indigenous. Drawing on the history of Hawai'i, which has often pitted native Hawaiian sovereignty against the claims of Anglo-American settlers and predominantly Asian migrants, she follows these discoures, examining the ways that they contradict and illuminate one another. For Das Gupta, citizenship depends on the same violence and division that creates nation-states. Justice, then, might evolve from the hybrid identities those who have been colonized invent to describe their histories.

CHAPTER 17

The Mexican-American War and Whitman's "Song of Myself"

A Foundational Borderline Fantasy

Donald Pease

In *A Forgetful Nation: On Immigration and Cultural Identity in the United States,* Ali Behdad has established a heretofore unrecognized connection between U.S. culture's mythical representation of itself as an "Immigrant Nation" and the negation of the history of the violence inflicted against immigrants that this self-forgetful representation necessitates.[1] "Immigrant America" has always been a myth rather than a historical fact. This foundational national fantasy projects the ways that Americans want to represent themselves to the rest of the world. This origin myth is not remembered. It is reproduced through a scene of the nation's founding that represents what Americans want to believe about themselves. What Americans want to believe requires the erasure of historical facts that contradict such beliefs.

With the publication of *A Forgetful Nation,* Behdad interrupts the recollection of this foundational fantasy. Instead, he reminds the nation of historically factual violence inflicted on immigrants. Behdad's critique of this dimension of the national myth involves a demonstration of the ways in which Walt Whitman's populist form of assimilationism eclipsed cultural differences and economic inequalities so as to celebrate the nation as a sacred geography populated by unique and free individuals.

In what follows, I build on Behdad's revisionist reading of the relationship between Whitman's poetry and and the nation's foundational fantasy. My observations turn on two interrelated claims: that colonial violence constituted the disavowed underside of the nation's foundational myth, and that this underside was the site of enunciation for Walt Whitman's celebration of the United States itself as the greatest poem. Walt Whitman associated "Song of Myself" with the effort to establish the United States' hemispheric sovereignty, and he deployed this foundational fiction to delineate a border between the United States and Mexico at the extraterritorial site that he forged out of his account of the Battle of Goliad. Further, Whitman's foundational fiction was structured in the belief that the immortality of the national state required the production of the mortalized body of Mexico as its underside, and Whitman deployed this foundational narrative to obscure the conditions from which he constructed and policed an imaginary border separating the United States and Mexico.

I begin with an effort to explain Whitman's association of his literary project with the effort to establish the United States' hemispheric sovereignty in the military campaign that President James A. Polk ordered General Zachary Taylor to undertake against the state of Mexico from 1846 to 1848. This effort obliges me to begin with a discussion of the editorials that Whitman wrote while working for the *Brooklyn Eagle* from 1846 to 1848.[2]

Whitman first gave expression to the United States' presumption of the hemisphere itself as a national entitlement in an editorial he composed for the May 2, 1846, edition of the *Brooklyn Eagle* in which he characterized the memories of the Alamo and Goliad as violations of that presumption:

> May 2, 1846 The massacre at the Alamo, the bloody business at Goliad, the red butcheries which the cowardly Mexicans effected whenever they got the people of Texas in their power during the course of the sanguinary contest, should be avenged more signally than ever outrage was avenged before.... The Whigs have laudation for them (the Mexicans),

> but not a word for the sacred martyrs whose bones yet whiten the soil of San Antonio de Bexar, whose blood reddens the river that wets its borders. At the Alamo they preferred death by sword to subjugation—so the difference between the two was that the latter accepted the conditions of the peace but the former did not and the latter ended with same fate as the former.[3]

In this editorial, Whitman relocated the origins of the Mexican War in the scene of the war crime that reputedly took place at Goliad, Texas. The Battle of Goliad was part of the Texas Revolution that culminated in the Independence of Texas in April of 1836. This battle marked the conclusion to a much larger battle that took place in Coleta, Texas, on March 19–20, 1836. On March 27, 1836, some 354 American prisoners from the battle were executed under the command of General Santa Anna. The soldiers at Goliad differed from those at the Alamo in that they had voluntarily agreed to become prisoners of war. The difference between the mass deaths at the Alamo and Goliad was that the soldiers who died at Goliad signed a treaty of surrender but the former did not. Yet the militia at Goliad met the same fate as did those at the Alamo.[4]

After thus redescribing Goliad in terms of the Mexicans' violation of the rules of war, Whitman generalized the scene of the war crime to include the entirety of the territorial state of Mexico. Therefore, Mexico became a just target for the United States' acts of retributive violence. In describing the militia who were executed at Goliad as sacred martyrs whose blood called out for vengeance, Whitman evoked the memory of Goliad to reestablish a norm of U.S. hemispheric dominance that recognized no other sovereignty.[5] The militia's voluntary surrender at Goliad rendered that site extraterritorial to both the United States and Mexico. The men who were interned at Goliad were rendered utterly vulnerable to the will of their captors. At the most intimate level of their being, they were given over to a field of power that conditioned them absolutely.[6]

Although Whitman represented General Santa Anna's violation of the treaty of surrender as grounds for the derecognition of Mexico's standing as a sovereign state, it was in fact the Texas Rangers' acts of looting that had violated the sovereignty of the Mexican state. The Texans' offer of surrender at Goliad had embroiled the general in an intractable contradiction. After the fall of San Antonio on December 30, 1835, Santa Anna issued a punitive decree, declaring that all "armed foreigners who entered Mexico with the intention of attacking the government would be executed as pirates upon capture." General Santa Anna had published the edict of San Antonio so as to avoid the political difficulties in which the Texan militia taken as captives at Goliad subsequently embroiled him. He could not treat the Texans as prisoners of war without transforming what he described as "their acts of piracy" into a war between sovereign states. And Santa Anna could not treat the Battle of Goliad as an incident in a war between sovereign nation-states (rather than a police action involving small bands of pirates) without also changing the status of the Texas militia into representatives of the U.S. government.[7]

The United States achieved its self-declared standing as the sole agent of hemispheric sovereignty at the outset of the so-called Mexican-American War when it deprived the Mexican state of the power to exercise control over its populations and spaces.[8] After the United States stripped the Mexican government of this capacity, it reduced the peoples of Mexico to the condition that Girogio Agamben has described as zoe, or raw biological life. In the editorials that he published in the May 6 edition of the *Brooklyn Eagle,* Whitman reduced all of Mexico into a terrorizing geography inhabited by nonhumans from whom the citizens of the United States society had to be defended:

> May 6, 1846 Though Mexico is called a Republic, the inhabitants have neither the real possession of true liberty nor any tangible idea of it. As a people, their character has little or nothing of the noble attributes of the Anglo-Saxon race (we say this more in regret than in contempt for it is true), never developing the sturdy independence of the an English freeman, their Spanish and mulatto ancestors have lent them craft, subtlety, passionate spite, deceit and voluptuousness enough—but no high patriotism, no doubtless devotion to great truths, no energy to overcome obstacles, no lusty independence, preferring a home in the wild to giving up even a trifling principle. The Mexicans are a hybridous race withal. Only a small proportion are of purely Spanish or any other European extraction. Nine-tenths of the population are made up of various intermixtures formed from white, Indian and black parentage, in all its mottled varieties. Nothing possessed by such a people can stand for a moment before such a power as the United States.[9]

By way of the characterizations of them that he included in his May 8th editorial, Whitman placed Mexican peoples as having the inherent capacity to be killed.[10] In passages like the following, Whitman arrogated the power to break into the domains of hemispheric life, armed with the biopolitical power to decide who would live and who would die:[11]

> May 8, 1846 We who pay shot for our soldiers want something for our money—some little glory in one way or another; a dozen or twenty dead mestizos now and then, at least. In all conscience, we cannot think General Taylor justified unless he transmits the account of a skirmish out of which our tongue-patriots can manufacture the glory, forthwith.[12]

Following this biologization of the conflict, the practice of Anglo-Saxon freedom entailed the right of conquest of the Mexican territory. Upon describing the Mexicans as a "hybridous race" who were perforce lacking in the "noble attributes of the Anglo-Saxon race," Whitman endowed Zachary Taylor's army with the biopolitical mandate to accomplish the United States' sovereign right to propagate the empire of liberty by whatever means necessary.

In Whitman's opinion, Goliad marked the loss of the U.S. presumption of the hemisphere itself as a national entitlement. Whitman invoked the memory of Goliad to reestablish a norm of geopolitical dominance in the hemisphere. The United States constituted its wholeness out of the systematic derecognition of the sovereignty of other state territories.[13] In the editorial he published eleven days later, Whitman recalled the racializing stereotypes to which he had reduced the peoples of Mexico so as to effect the ineradicable equivalence between Anglo-Saxon liberty and the conquest of Mexican territory:

> May 19, 1846 Any body with brains in his head cannot help seeing that the United States must conquer. Why what a comparison. This republic, the richest nation on earth—the fullest of means, of men, of moral power—running over with the elements of which great victories are made—the nation of nations—this to be pitted against such a state as Mexico—a land of zamboes and mestizoes—distracted, impoverished, with no reality about it—when the very freedom they are fighting for is not understood—where the officers and priests are despotic and the

> people slavish! What can be expected of such a contest, while the natural laws are not suspended? and what doubt can there be of who will win the day?[14]

In his reflections on sovereignty, Agamben focuses on what he describes as the concealed points of convergence between the juridico-political and the biopolitical models of power. In *Homo Sacer,* Agamben traces the origins of the biopolitical body that he calls bare life to a figure known in Roman law as the *homo sacer,* defined as "he who can be killed with impunity but who cannot be sacrificed." This figure, Agamben explains, "names what is included within the juridico-political realm precisely as what must be excluded from it."[15]

Now it is Agamben's contention that the inclusion of bare life in the political realm constitutes the original, if occulted, core of sovereign power. "It can even be said," Agamben explains, "that the production of a biopolitical body is the original activity of sovereign power."[16] What Agamben called the *nomos* of the camp describe spaces in which individuals are reduced to bare life insofar as they are included within the calculations of the state only in order to be abandoned by those calculations. As I hope to demonstrate, Agamben's thesis has another powerful historical example in the exclusion of Mexicans in the zone of abandonment that was quite literally productive of the United States border in the middle of the nineteenth century.

Now in proposing that Goliad be construed as the strange location from which Whitman's "Song of Myself" was enunciated, I need to explain the relationship between the space from within which Whitman sings and celebrates and what Agamben calls a sovereign exception. The exception "is an element in law that transcends positive law in the form of its suspension.[17]

Agamben elsewhere explains the paradoxical relationship between localization and ordering in general and specifically with references to the constructions that produced the representations of the New World. According to Carl Schmitt, the connection between localization and ordering that is constitutive of the nomos of the earth inevitably produces a region or zone that is excluded from law. Such spaces assume the shape of free and juridically empty space in which the sovereign power no longer knows the limits fixed by the territorial order. In the classical epoch of the

Ius Publicum Europeam, this zone corresponded to the New World, which was identified with the state of nature in which everything was possible.[18] Agamben concludes:

> The state of nature and the state of the exception are nothing but the two sides of a single topological process in which what was presupposed as external (the state of nature) now reappears as in a moeibus strip, on the inside (as the state of exception) and the sovereign power is this very impossibility of distinguishing between inside and outside, physis and nomos, nature and exception. The state of exception is this not so much a spatio-temporal suspension; it is rather a complex topological figure in which not only the exception and the rule, but also the state of nature and the law, the outside and the inside pass through one another.[19]

The border that Whitman produces between the United States and Mexico produces a concrete instance of this complex figure.

The border that Whitman imagined is not a state of chaos or an arbitrarily achieved boundary line that negates the localization-ordering activity of sovereignty. The border is the concrete figuration or projection of an imaginary membrane: it specifies something included within the juridical order as a zone of indistinction between the chaos of barbarism to which Whitman consigned the state of Mexico and the normal state of U.S. civil society, between an outside that is brought within as what must be excluded from the normal order.

In his several accounts of the Battle of Goliad, Whitman deployed his representations of it to represent quite literally the underside of the national territory—a space of generalized violence that he included within the territorial United States to delineate what its civil order must exclude so as to render discernible the differences from the Mexican territories that Whitman characterized as not civilizable:

> May 11, 1846 We have dammed up our memories of what has passed in the South years ago—of the devilish massacres of some of our bravest and noblest sons, the children not of the south alone, but of the north and west—massacres in defiance not only of ordinary humanity, but in violation of all the rules of war. Who has read the sickening story of

> those brutal wholesale murders, so useless for any purpose except gratifying the cowardly appetite of a nation of bravos, willing to shoot down men in the hundreds in cold blood—without panting for the day when the prayer of that blood should be listened to—when the vengeance of a retributive God should be meted out to those who so ruthlessly and needlessly slaughered His image.[20]

Now in becoming the virtual historical witness to the Texans' martyrdom, Whitman inhabited the zone of indistinction between the dead and the living, nature and culture, barbarity and civilization that Whitman's several accounts of it have correlated with the Goliad's "out of placedness."[21] The men who lost their lives there, died in a place that, as a prisoner of war camp, named an order lacking localization in either the United States or Mexico. But this site lacking localization nevertheless becomes Whitman's means of territorializing the border in between the United States and Mexico.

Cut off from the condition of national belonging, the men interned there experienced that condition as a vulnerability to an alien field of power that exercised absolute control over their life and death. But in Whitman's narrative of their fate, the Texans who were killed and the Mexicans who killed them underwent a drastic change in their biopolitical status. Whereas the Mexicans reduced the Texans to the condition of bare life, Whitman, in his retelling of their story, effected their transformation of these "sacred martyrs" into the representatives of the sovereign desire for freedom on which the U.S. body politic was founded. Whitman thereafter represented the state's appropriation of this Mexican territory during the U.S.-Mexican War as redress for the martyrdom sustained by the U.S. citizens who occupied it.

Overall, Goliad named the space in which the Texans who were reduced to the condition of raw biological life produced the pretext for Whitman's transfiguration of the entirety of the United States into the sovereign exception. If Whitman deployed that pretext as the grounds for the U.S. reduction of the state of Mexico into the condition of bare life in the editorials that he wrote between May 2 and May 19, in the editorial that he composed on May 11, he reconfigured the event itself as a dammed-up memory that required the Mexican-American War as the agency empowered to accomplish its release.

But as this memory underwent a translation from his editorials to the poetry, Goliad's status as a place that lacked placement within a territorial site enhanced its powers of integration. Whitman did not annex this site within his poem; he redeployed this space that was excluded from the territories (Texan and Mexican) in which it was located as the site for the singing of the song of myself. In celebrating their deaths at this site, Whitman construed the "martyr's' pent-up desire for secure placement" as the affective energy that would enable him to integrate the whole of the territorial United States within this site of internal exclusion. The transition from the prose to the poetry might as a consequence be described in terms of Whitman's effort to construct a medium that would rechannel the memory flows condensed in Goliad.

In the following lines from section 34 of "Song of Myself," Whitman depicted the Texas Rangers' desire for belonging as more internal to both the Northerners and Southerners who died at Goliad than the ideological conflicts that then divided the country. Although it was external to the territorial United States, it constituted the condition of its boundednes, as well as —in its capacity as a form of surplus inclusivity—its force of integration:

> Now I tell what I knew in Texas in my early youth,
> (I tell not the fall of Alamo,
> Not one escaped to tell the fall of Alamo,
> The hundred and fifty are dumb yet at Alamo)
> 'Tis the tale of the murder in cold blood of four hundred and twelve
> young men.
>
> Retreating they had form'd in a hollow square with their baggage for
> breastworks,
> Nine hundred lives out of the surrounding enemy's, nine times their
> number, was the price they took in advance.
> Their colonel was wounded and their ammunition gone.
> They treated for an honorable capitulation, receiv'd writing and seal,
> gave up their arms and march'd back prisoners of war.
>
> They were the glory of the race of rangers,
> Matchless with horse, rifle, supper, courtship,
> Large, turbulent, generous, handsome, proud, and affectionate,

Bearded, sunburnt, drest in the free costume of hunters,
Not a single one over thirty years of age.

The second First-day morning they were brought out in squads and
massacred, it was beautiful early summer,
The work commenced about five o'clock and was over by eight.

None obey'd the command to kneel,
Some made a mad and helpless rush, some stood stark and straight.
A few fell at once, shot in the temple or heart, the living and dead lay
together.
The maim'd and mangled dug in the dirt, the new-comers saw them
there,
Some half-kill'd attempted to crawl away.
These were despatch'd with bayonets or batter'd with the blunts of
muskets.
A youth not seventeen years old seiz'd his assassin till two more came
to release him.
The three were all torn and cover'd with the boy's blood.

At eleven o'clock began the burning of the bodies;
That is the tale of the murder of the four hundred and twelve young
men.[22]

As the narrative of an event that was included within the song but could not be included within the national narrative, the story Whitman recounted in section 34 of "Song of Myself" deterritorialized the site that the Battle of Goliad previously occupied in the national imagination. Whitman then reterritorialized this place as an extraterritorial site that designated the transition from the state of nature to the national culture. The loss of the battle became the gain of a permanent need to compensate for loss with an endless trooping forth of the figures through whom the memory took place. As a site memorializing the battle that resulted in the sacrifice of young men for the land they desired to integrate within the Republic of Texas, Goliad named a territory that transcended the nation's capacities of integration.

After Whitman recounted General Santa Anna's successful defense of Goliad against the incursions of Texas militia who were intent on annexing it as part of the Republic of Texas. Whitman deterritorialized the site that the Battle of Goliad previously occupied in the national imagination. It previously existed as the account of a group of Texas militia who in 1836 were ordered executed by General Santa Anna after their commander, Colonel James Fannin, had agreed to terms of surrender offered them by General Urrea. When Whitman recollected the battle in the 1855 version of "Song of Myself," he transformed it into the site in which he found the surplus reserve of freedom. Whitman thereafter included it as a sacred event, an event that had formerly been excluded from the national territory. The narrative materialized the extraterritorial site that designated the transition from the state of nature to the national culture. Here we find Whitman in a sacred threshold space in between the dead and living, in between U.S. territory and the territory of another, freedom. At this limit the distinction between American and the national Other was reinscribed as the difference betweeen the assassinated and their assassins.

Although the contours of the event are as Whitman describes them in this passage, he nevertheless leaves out significant dimensions of the story. For one thing, he has omitted the contentions of the men who did not wish to surrender. In Whitman's account, the denial of their intending consciousness was monopolized by their captors rather than their commanding officer. But the man who negotiated the terms of surrender at the Battle of Goliad was Colonel James Fannin, the officer whom Sam Houston had accused of betraying his country for having ordered the Alamo mission stripped of food, medicine, and munitions and for thereby having rendered it virtually defenseless in relation to the offensive of General Antonio Lopez de Santa Anna. Moreover the general with whom Colonel Fannin had negotiated the terms of surrender, Jose Urrea, initially disobeyed Santa Anna's order that no prisoners be taken alive and Santa Anna had to appoint another general to carry it out.[23]

Goliad, in fact, names a space of contested memory. Every aspect of Whitman's account of the battle is subject to dispute. The American men Whitman celebrated as "sacred martyrs" to liberty; the Mexicans he characterized as marauders and mercenaries intent on looting and ravaging their landscapes. The behavior that Whitman described as "martial valor,"

Mexican historians described as robbery. Whereas it was the Americans whose invasion of Mexican territory had, in fact, violated the sovereignty of the Mexican nation, Whitman invoked international treaties protecting prisoners of war to support the claim that it was the men's sovereign rights that were violated. Whitman's selective memory thereby resulted in the transformation of the agents of colonial aggression into the victims of a war crime. At the site of this reversal, Whitman enshrouded forms of colonial violence into the enchanted relations between oppressors and victims that facilitated the disavowal of U.S. colonial violence. But for Mexican poets and historians, the Battle of Goliad brought the history of U.S. illegal occupation of Mexican lands into stark visibility.[24]

Goliad continues to be traversed by collateral memories of the events that took place there. But these contradictory memories do not merely haunt the site with vexing questions about the verisimilitude of Whitman's account. They also introduce histories that would recharacterize Manifest Destiny as the mythological guarantor of U.S. colonial violence. In doing so, Whitman appropriated the site of Goliad as a sacred space of memory in which he commemorated the Texan martyrs who gave their lives there. In so doing, Whitman deactivated the Mexicans' memory of the event so that he might restrict his affective investments to the Texas revolutionaries who died there.[25]

In bearing historical witness to the mass execution of the "race of rangers" at Goliad, Whitman converted them into sacrificial victims. Their deaths for its sake materialized the ideal of liberty in whose name they had died. His act of recounting their story released the Texas Rangers from the memories of the U.S.-Mexican War in which they had been dammed up. Those memories were recollections of the Mexican War. More specifically, memories of a defeated Mexico continue to haunt this site of memory. The Mexicans had forcibly disconnected the Americans from the condition of historical belonging. But Whitman's deactivation of the Mexican memory has effectively ceded the Rangers who died there imaginative possession of the site.[26]

What I find most compelling about Whitman's account of the Battle of Goliad is its placement in the poem. Whitman's account of the battle takes place within a series of passages in "Song of Myself" wherein Whitman's identification with the bodies of the wounded, the impoverished, the enslaved, or imprisoned bodies ruptures the continuity between the self, body, and nation his song had accomplished. Whitman's most accomplished critics and interpreters have characterized the sequence of passages that begins with the assertion "agonies are one of my changes of garments" and that concludes with the phrase "I sit shame-faced and beg" as contradictory to the logic of celebratory idenitification underwriting the rest of the poem.[27]

Whitman's account of the Battle of Goliad describes the rationale for the conflict as ungrounded in any cause other than the act of lawlessness whereby the Mexicans violated the rules of war. Whereas the violence performed by "the race of rangers" was recognizably human, the violence the Mexicans committed was unrecognizable as human activity. In representing the Mexicans' violence as the illegitimate productions of unlawful combatants who violated the rules of war, Whitman represented their actions as grounded in nothing but this illegal use of force. This representation was designed to remove them from the precincts of the human community and thereby construct them as unworthy of human entitlements. Whitman designed this narrative to set a frame around the losses that could be accepted as human losses in a way that placed the Mexicans outside the realm of the human and the grieveable.[28]

But if a democracy is describable as a narrative community, Whitman's narrative is procedurally a nondemocratic speech act. Whitman's account has eliminated any place for reasoning that would characterize his facts as inaccurate and its norms invalid. In this passage Whitman has produced the efficacy of his narrative out of the exclusion of the Mexican as the third-party narratee.[29]

When Whitman abstracted his story of the events that took place at Goliad between March 18 and March 27, 1836, from its dialogical relationship with competing accounts of the event, he overrode alternative representations of the issues for which the subject matter of the poems becomes the sole representative. Whitman's mode of recounting has restricted the addressees of his story to everyone except the Mexicans whose violation of the treaty protecting prisoners of war has removed them from the precincts of intersubjective exchange.[30]

When he completes the narration with the phrase "that is the story of the murder of the 412 young men" he invests *that* with a force that predetermines the narrators and addressees, as well as what can and what cannot be passed on as a narratable memory. Having been described as figures who are unable to keep their words, the Mexicans have already been set in a space that had been excluded from the hegemonic narrative community. When Whitman represents them as unable to act on the treaty that has obliged them to treat the men as prisoners of war, he has represented the population of Mexico as given over to a realm of being that is beyond the pale of civil relations.

It is at this site of refused dialogue that we discern the complicity between Whitman's poetry and the state's practices of colonial violence as their shared invoking of the ideals of American freedom to justify imperial annexation. The control over the transmitted memory of what took place at Goliad was a crucial function of the state apparatus whose political and legal frameworks gained public consent through the monopoly it exercised over the field of narrative possibilities.

In Whitman's song, the Rangers who had been deprived of any part of the earth's territory became the part through which the sovereign body of the people was reintegrated. But Whitman's reintegration resulted from his reduction of the entirety of Mexican territory into a borderland, a geography that could not be included.

At the site in which he experienced the demand to remember the Goliad dead, Whitman literally regenerated the U.S. body politic out of forgetting Goliad as an instance of colonial violence and remembering it as the site of celebratory enunciation of his song. His self is sung into existence here as the poetic medium through which the Texans' absolute longing for freedom constitutes the affective substance at the core of what Whitman calls "me myself." The singer celebrated "me myself" through the celebration of the dead out of whose infinite longing for freedom the living were reborn. It is their rebirth as the tropes of Whitman's song of celebratory memory that constructs the U.S. nation as the work of memory of the dead by the living and the living by the site of sacred memory.

In restaging the events that took place at Goliad as a sacrificial ritual, the poem transformed the soldiers' unachieved longing for freedom into the revelation of the intentionality of the manifest destiny that reintegrated a whole national self. This ritual furnished the national myth of manifest destiny with an aesthetic resolution. It rendered the heterogeneous events into symbolic moments that expressed an underlying cultural unity that reterritorialized the Mexican state into an underdeveloped substrate of U.S. national culture.

In rendering the Texas settlers' colonial violence the precondition for the emergence of the immortal body of American liberty, Whitman constructed the illusion of the immortality of the U.S. nation-state out of the mortality of the Mexican state. The transition from this substrate (of the Mexican state of nature) to the empire of liberty took place through the practices of Anglo-Saxon freedom exercised by the Rangers that rendered U.S. liberty indistinguishable from the right to hemispheric sovereignty.

Before the Civil War, the United States feared the loss of control of its borders. The crisis of the border created a simulated prefiguration of the Civil War in which the imagined community of the nation willingly participated in the state's politics of exclusion. Whitman's account of the Battle of Goliad carries a representation of "us and them" in a symbolically violent discourse that reproduces the stereotype of the Mexican as the wretched refuse of the earth. The perpetual threat of Mexican invasion inscribed a notion of differences in the national community that installed a permanent state of emergency where concepts of national citizenship and state sovereignty were ritualistically reaffirmed and that regulated an exclusive and exclusionary national identity. If Goliad names the permanent site of nascence from the state of nature to the empire of liberty, this site of permanent emergency might also be described as continuing to haunt our own time.

NOTES

1. Ali Behdad, *A Forgetful Nation: On Immigration and Cultural Identity in the United States* (Durham, N.C.: Duke University Press, 2005).

2. *The Collected Writings of Walt Whitman: The Journalism*, Vol. 1: *1834–1846*, ed. Herbert Bergman, Douglas A. Noverr, and Edward J. Recchia (New York: Peter Lang, 1998).

3. Ibid., 342.

4. "Surrender and Massacre at Goliad," in Thom Hatch, *Encylopedia of the Alamo and the Texas Revolution* (Jefferson, N.C.: McFarland, 1999), 99–106.

5. Judith Butler discusses U.S. norms of dominance with an account of the ways in which those norms are experienced most profoundly at the instant of their loss: "What kind of loss is this? It is the loss of the prerogative, only and always to be the one who transgresses the sovereign boundaries of other states, but

never in the position of having one's own boundaries transgressed" (*Precarious Life* [New York: Verso, 2004], 39). Throughout these notes, I have associated Butler's reflections on the relationship between matters of U.S. sovereignty at the time of the U.S. war in Iraq with Whitman's editorials at the time of the U.S.-Mexican War so as to follow Walter Benjamin's dictum that the task of the critic is "to blast a specific era out of the homogeneous course of history" and to "grasp . . . the constellation which his own era has formed with a earlier one" ("Theses on the Philosophy of History," in *Illuminations: Essays and Reflections,* ed. Hannah Arendt [New York: Schocken, 1968], 263).

6. Butler discusses this condition of primary vulnerability within the context of prisoner of war camps in the chapter "Violence, Mourning, Politics" of *Precarious Life,* 19–49.

7. Discussion and quotations in this paragraph from "Atrocities Committed during the Texas Revolution," in Hatch, *Encylopedia of the Alamo and the Texas Revolution,* 41–42.

8. For a splendid account of Tejanos's perspectives on the United States' violation of Mexico's sovereignty, see Arnoldo DeLeon, "Tejanos and the Texas War for Independence: Historiography's Judgment," *New Mexico Historical Review* 61 (April 1986), 137–46.

9. *Collected Writings of Walt Whitman: The Journalism,* 1:349.

10. "Whose lives count as grievable lives? What makes for a grievable life?" Judith Butler correlates these questions with reflections on Foucault's association of the state's biopolitical power with the decision over who will it let live and let die (*Precarious Life,* 20—21).

11. "If a life is not grievable, it is not quite a life; it does not qualify as a life and is not worth notice. It is already the unburied, if not the unburiable" (Butler, *Precarious Life,* 34).

12. *Collected Writings of Walt Whitman: The Journalism,* 1:354.

13. "When the United States acts, it establishes a conception of what it means to act as an American, establishes a norm by which that subject might be known. In recent months a subject has been instated at the national level, a sovereign and extra-legal subject, a violent and self-centered subject; its violence constitutes the building of a subject that seeks to restore and maintain its mastery through the systematic destruction of its multilateral relations, its ties to the international community" (Butler, *Precarious Life,* 34).

14. *Collected Writings of Walt Whitman: The Journalism,* 1:366–67.

15. Giorgio Agamben, *Homo Sacer: Sovereign Power and Bare Life,* trans. Daniel Heller-Roazen (Stanford: Stanford University Press, 1998), 8, 11.

16. Ibid., 6.

17. Schmitt, cited in ibid.,15, 17.

18. Ibid., 35–36.

19. Ibid., 37.

20. *Collected Writings of Walt Whitman: The Journalism,* 1:359.

21. On a discussion of the ways in which Whitman's various accounts of these events served his performing the role of cultural diplomat, see Kirsten Gruesz, *Ambassadors of Culture: The Trans-American Origins of Latino Culture* (Princeton: Princeton University Press, 2002), 121–35.

22. *Walt Whitman: Complete Poetry and Collected Prose,* ed. Justin Kaplan (New York: Library of America, 1982), 226–27.

23. "Surrender and Massacre at Goliad," in Hatch, *Encylopedia of the Alamo and the Texas Revolution,* 99–106.

24. For discussions of these distinctions, see Fernando Alegria, *Walt Whitman en HispanoAmerica* (Mexico City: Ediciones Studium, 1954), and Mauricio Gonzalez Garza's notorious 1970s exposé of Whitman (*Walt Whitman: Racista, Imperialista, Antimexicano* [Mexico City: Malaga Collection, 1971]).

25. For a discussion of the significance of this deactivated memory to the historical transmission of the events that took place there, see DeLeon, "Tejanos and the Texas War for Independence."

26. Gonzalez Garza describes Whitman's predatory imperial memory in *Walt Whitman: Racista, Imperialista, Antimexicano.*

27. Philip Fisher discusses the significance of these passages in the chapter "Democratic Social Space" in *Still the New World: American Literature in a Culture of Creative Destruction* (Cambridge: Harvard University Press, 1999), 82–86.

28. Butler evokes a sense of the inequities in what she calls the normative conditions of vulnerability with the following unanswered question: "Could the experience of a dislocation of first World safety not condition the insight into the radically inequitable ways that vulnerability is distributed globally?" (*Precarious Life,* 30).

29. Enrique Dussel writes movingly about the inherently nondemocratic dimension of communicative acts that are otherwise construed as rational and noncoercive: "There is no liberation without rationality, but there is no critical rationality without accepting the interpellation of the excluded, or this would inadvertently be only the rationality of domination" (*The Underside of Modernity: Apel, Ricoeur, Taylor, and the Philosophy of Liberation,* trans. Eduardo Mendieta [Amherst, N.Y.: Humanity Books, 1996], 36).

30. For a discussion of the ways in which this exclusion guarantees the rationality of the narrative community, see Dussel, *Underside of Modernity,* 28–29.

CHAPTER 18

Rights in a Transnational Era

Monisha Das Gupta

The post-9/11 treatment of immigrants in the United States, particularly those of South Asian and Middle Eastern descent, has reanimated an interest in the civil rights entitlements of those who, regardless of their immigration or citizenship status, are perceived as threats to U.S. national security. The imagery of the civil rights movement was powerfully and repeatedly invoked by activists and the liberal mainstream media alike in 2006, when hundreds and thousands of immigrants marched in the spectacular rallies across the country between March and May. They were protesting proposals in Congress to make felons out of an estimated 11 to 12 million people who lived and worked in the United States but were undocumented. Many hailed this mobilization and these acts of civil disobedience on the part of immigrant students and workers to be the new civil rights movement.

While the demands for legalization are racialized as a Hispanic issue, those for due process and First Amendment rights are raised most dramatically in the case of South Asians and Arabs, who at this moment are profiled as terrorist. Both sets of demands, when cast as civil rights, display the unquestioning belief in citizenship as the privileged route to rights. In these contestations over who can belong to the nation and what rights immigrants can have, indigenous perspectives remain obscured. Native American scholar and activist Andrea Smith observes, "By instituting repressive immigration policies, the U.S. government is once again asserting that it—and not indigenous nations—should determine who can be on these lands"[1] Furthermore, she shows that the media only cover those indigenous views that shore up support for increased border controls.

In this chapter, I juxtapose three types of rights talk—migrant, indigenous, and civil. The first two question the adequacy of the third. Full citizenship, which is the goal of civil rights–oriented visions of justice, naturalizes and reinscribes the policing functions of borders that territorialize racialized, ethnicized, and gendered notions of belonging. The civil rights framework formulates the lack of or the routine violation of rights of subjects inhabiting a national space as second-class citizenship, a condition that needs to be corrected through struggles for full national belonging.[2] For indigenous peoples colonized by the United States, the struggle for sovereignty cannot, by definition, be contained within a civil rights framework that hinges on U.S. citizenship. Decolonization would mean substantive independence from the United States. The sovereign political entity that would emerge from this break need not take the form of the modern nation-state, as scholars like Andrea Smith have established.[3] For immigrants, accessing rights only through citizenship ignores the realities of border crossing in a world where neocolonialism and imperialism have led to massive displacement. When people on the move find their rights abridged at the moment of border crossing and find their mobile bodies used to bolster xenophobic nationalism, the need for rights has to be imagined within transnational flows rather than within nationally bounded spaces.

Transnationalism offers a useful analytical tool for the purpose of tracing the intersections between immigrant and indigenous struggles because it can effectively disclose the relationship of national borders to rights. I foreground this understanding of transnationalism over its more available uses that trace the interpenetration of nationally bounded spaces and the transversal social and political fields within which immigrants craft their identities and politics.[4] The conceptualization of immigrant rights without an accompanying reliance on citizenship comes out of my decade-long work with and about South Asian immigrant women's, queer, and labor organizations in the United States. The marginal social location of the members of these organizations alert them to the disciplining functions of borders, which define not only the identity of citizens but also the identity of the nation-state itself as a sovereign, self-governing entity. The immigrants' innovative methods of claiming rights outside of nation-based regimes recognize borders as power effects that determine who can have what rights. Borders produce the biopolitics that create the racialized, gendered, sexualized, and classed distinctions between nationals and aliens. This kind of rights talk is nonintuitive because it means that the immigrants fundamentally question the violence of national border setting and its creation of the citizen as the spatially rooted and privileged bearer of rights.

Transnationalism can also serve as a framework for the ways in which indigenous nations have to constantly negotiate the effects of U.S. sovereignty in the process of asserting their right to self-determination. Though indigenous people have formal U.S. citizenship, they often experience this status as an instrument of colonization. U.S. citizenship works at cross purposes with the indigenous efforts to control their governance structures, cultural practices, land, and resources. Thinking about the collision of Native and U.S. sovereignty as a transnational process reminds us that indigenous nations radically interrupt the fiction of U.S. political and territorial integrity. A transnational approach lays bare the violence of colonization inherent in the United States' ceaseless efforts at nation-making.

I focus first on two developments—the spring 2006 immigrant marches and the post-9/11 assaults on free speech and due process—to examine the way in which immigrant rights when framed as civil rights get interpellated by discourses of citizenship. Having discussed the civil rights model's inability to accommodate noncitizen immigrant aspirations, I outline Native American and Native Hawaiian critiques of civil rights in light of their struggles for self-determination. Though both immigrant and indigenous rights talk reveals the links of civil rights and citizenship to border policing and colonialism, they rarely enter into dialog. This disjuncture leads to the disturbing conclusion that immigrant struggles are necessarily for civil rights and they harm indigenous sovereignty claims.

To avoid the trap of such a dichotomy, rights have to be thought within the framework of global inequality that is structured through relations of war, conquest, and economic subjugation. The ideological construction of the United States as a coherent and sovereign national space and its citizens as the rightful inhabitants manifests the structures of colonialism, which affect immigrants and Natives, though often in distinct ways. The conjuncture of border fortifications, foreign occupation, the surveillance of immigrants, and the intensified militarization of Native land that has been commented on by several authors in this volume lends urgency to a social justice agenda that can address the relationship among these oppressions.

Immigrant Rights Interpellated: Limits of Citizenship

The media coverage of the 2006 immigrant rights marches reveals the ways in which the massive protests against the criminalization of those who crossed borders without papers got quickly managed as a demand for a path to citizenship for "illegal" immigrants. The message that protestors conveyed about a thoroughly transnationalized United States with their t-shirts declaring, "We Are America," together with the profusion of flags of Central and South American and Asian nations, and the rendition of the "Star-Spangled Banner" in Spanish frightened not only mainstream Americans, who were stunned by the occupation of public space by a coalition of citizens, legal residents, and undocumented migrants, but also immigrant advocates.[5] Such assertions profoundly questioned the reproduction of national intactness through demands of assimilation. In response, the liberal media, as well as many advocates of immigrants, started to recirculate the old and comforting story of Americanization with its accompanying promise of full citizenship that offers endless possibilities for those willing to work hard.[6] As Eunice Cho documents in this volume (chapter 4), the immigrant rights movement represented divergent positions with policy-oriented advocacy groups playing by the rules of conventional and nationalist approaches to immigration. By April, organizers were reportedly scrambling around for American flags for the demonstrators to carry.[7] In the months that followed, media pundits and activists pontificated on the strategic mistake that the demonstrators made by challenging the nationalization of space through border controls that rendered the presence of immigrants "foreign." Even as the rhetoric of eventual citizenship for undocumented migrants and their assimilation started to dominate public discourse, the residues lingered of images of hundreds of thousands of people chanting "We are not criminals!" and members of the clergy marching bound to each other in plastic handcuffs.

The demonstrations, the walkouts staged by students, and the observation of May Day as a "Day without an Immigrant" vocalized the immigrant rights movement's demands to decriminalize border crossings, to protect immigrant workers' rights in their workplaces, and to allow migrants to reunite with their families.[8] While these demands were articulated specifically to reject the proposed legislation initiated in the House of Representatives that would make unauthorized entry into the United States a felony, many grassroots immigrant rights organizations operated with a clear understanding of how borders define "legal" and "illegal" immigrants, rendering the latter vulnerable to rights abuses because they are seen as lawbreakers. The problem, from the perspective of such organizations, then, centers on border setting and border policing, both of which involve state action that constructs a national space where a group of people are forced to live and work as "foreigners." This identity exists only in relation to the rightful occupants signified as "nationals," historically racialized as White.

The recognition of the punitive function of the U.S. border has long been felt for those who want to cross it but do not qualify under the requirements the state sets for entry. That migrants were primarily interested in addressing border controls is evident from the analysis of the executive director of the Central American Resource Center of Los Angeles who stated that "the protestors would prefer that the Congress passed no immigration legislation rather than criminalizing those who are here [in the United States] without documents *or creating a guest-worker program that would require millions to go home*" (emphasis mine).[9] Remarkably, though not surprisingly, demands for legalizing all cross border movements got contained and recoded as a demand for U.S. citizenship.

The enormous appeal of the "path to citizenship" embedded in President George W. Bush's guest-worker plan even among his usual detractors is symptomatic of the unquestioned legitimacy of citizenship that ties national belonging to rights. Those not directly involved in grassroots immigrant organizing, balking at the figure of 11–12 million immigrants living in their midst without immigration status, remained convinced that some kind of plan needed to be created to "legalize" illegal immigrants. Even the language of "earned legalization" that held those immigrants who qualified captive by imposing a work requirement of six additional years, and made competency in English and U.S. civics as well as registration for military Selective Service mandatory, seemed better and more humanitarian than life as an illegal.[10]

For immigrant rights activists working with undocumented immigrants and immigrants at risk, the requirement that the applicant for legalization pass national security and criminal background checks demystified the talk of the path to citizenship. Since the very category of "illegal immigrant" represents a breach of national security—a concept literally concretized in the fortification and militarization of the U.S.-Mexican border—few would be able to jump that hoop. The alignment of many progressives with the Bush plan reveals their acceptance of the naturalized category, "illegal," an existence they assume can be corrected through amnesty. The state's right to classify people as illegal remains unquestioned, as does immigrants' real need to adjust their status in order to access U.S. citizenship. Eventually, with the foundering in June 2007 of the immigration bill (S. 1639) that would have provided legalization, a guest-worker program, and increased border enforcement, the sentiment that undocumented immigrants had broken the law and thus citizenship would reward illegality prevailed in Congress.[11]

In comparison with the attempts to discursively link citizenship to rights in the case legalization, those addressing the post-9/11 assaults on the civil rights of noncitizen (though often legal permanent resident) Arabs and South Asians question whether civil rights are solely due to citizens.[12] The surveillance and profiling of these immigrants and their families, their incarceration for prolonged periods without being charged in the name of "special interest," and the lack of access to legal counsel or family members while in detention deprive them of the right to due process and their freedom of expression and association. Civil rights organizations are in the forefront of challenging the exercise of state power that blatantly target noncitizen South Asians and Arabs. These legal challenges that try to break the link between citizenship and the entitlement to civil liberties are historically continuous with Section 16 of the 1870 Civil Rights Act. This section established that all those who resided within the U.S. border, regardless of whether they were citizens, could enjoy certain rights guaranteed by the constitution. It is worth noting that Section 16 resulted from the pressures that Chinese immigrants brought to bear on Congress. Subsequent court rulings as early as 1886 (*Yick Wo v. Hopkins*) and 1896 (*Wong Wing v. U.S.*) and as recently as 2001 (*Zadvydas v. Davis*) affirm noncitizens' right to equal protection under the law and to due process.[13] However, the weakness of these guarantees in the face of national security is well demonstrated by the internment of the Issei and the Nisei during World War II and the deportation of "Communists" during the McCarthy Era.[14]

While the current litigation aims at dislodging the legal reproduction of the (racialized) birthright citizen as the sole beneficiary of civil rights, the connection is not easily broken. Political theorist and Asian Americanist John Park, in his analysis of the workings of constitutional law in the case of Asian Americans and of the debates over Proposition 187 that aimed at stripping undocumented immigrants of access to public education, health care, social services, and employment, frames the central and intractable paradox of liberal law.[15] The question of whether noncitizens, particularly those coded undocumented, have any rights and, if so, under what conditions is always debated to clarify the rights of citizens. Pointing to the ways in which the discourse of citizenship succeeded in pitting one group of people of color against another, he argues:

> When citizens spoke, they did so in a way that implicitly linked rights to citizenship—in other words, they assumed that without citizenship, persons were not entitled to rights or right-based claims. Ironically, the debate about Proposition 187 pointed to the continuation of a "civil rights vision," as the debate reduced undocumented aliens to "nonpersons," without a legitimate place in society.[16]

Furthermore, if certain restrictive measures that were meant for noncitizens infringed on citizens' enjoyment of their rights, only then was the constitutionality of such actions legitimately questioned. Park's insight, which is a devastating critique of the investment of the civil rights model in citizenship, is as true today, post-9/11, as it was in 1923 when Whites challenged the Alien Land Law imposed on Japanese immigrants for compromising their right to private property.[17] It is worth noting that the surveillance provisions of the USA PATRIOT Act authorizing wiretapping and tracking of financial transactions, educational records, and internet use have attracted the most direct public ire because U.S. citizens fear that these aspects of the "war on terror" would curb their rights to privacy and mobility.[18] Thus, the assaults on rights matter most when they curtail or threaten to curtail the entitlements due to citizens.

Indigenous Sovereignty, U.S. Citizenship, and Civil Rights

The standard narrative about the rights struggles of minoritized groups in the United States is one that traces their efforts at achieving full citizenship. Native Americans and Native Hawaiians, however, did not seek full citizenship within the United States, unlike the other groups that sought to correct their "second-class citizenship" or exclusion from citizenship. In fact, their U.S. citizenship has meant the loss of their sovereignty. U.S. citizenship was part and parcel of Native Hawaiian colonization when Hawai'i became a territory of the United States in 1900 in the wake of the illegal overthrow of the Hawaiian monarchy in 1893 and its annexation in 1898.[19]

In the case of Native Americans, U.S. citizenship was imposed on them in 1924. Native American exercise of their U.S. citizenship proved to be highly contingent on U.S. economic and strategic interest. The 1924 act further compromised Native American sovereignty, deepening their colonization and heightening the contradictions of their group status as "domestic dependent nations." As American studies scholar Rachel Buff has shown in her research, Native American World War II veterans still had to naturalize as U.S. citizens to become eligible for Veterans' Administration mortgages, which were otherwise out of their reach because of the trust relationship between Native Americans and the United States.[20] In the 1950s, the termination policy used the language of desegregation and the promise of full-fledged U.S. citizenship to end the trust relationship by encouraging Native Americans to leave the reservations for mainstream American life, by promoting private ownership of land over tribal ownership, and by seeking to scrap U.S. treaty obligations to provide health and social services to Native Americans. All of these measure attacked indigenous sovereignty.

From an indigenous perspective, U.S. civil rights, conferred to Native Americans through the Indian Civil Rights Act of 1968 and framed as liberatory, conflict fundamentally with tribal sovereignty.[21] Native American scholars Marie Anna Jaimes Guerrero and Andrea Smith analyze the ways in which the conflict over federal and tribal jurisdiction deprives Native Americans of their tribal rights and their rights as U.S. citizens. The worst casualties of the legal contradictions are Native women. Guerrero underscores the dangerous antagonism that arises out of the proprietary definitions of sovereignty and individual rights under a Eurocentric system of governance that depends on a separation of powers. Such capitalist and patriarchal conceptions of sovereignty and rights continuously undercut indigenous sovereignty.

At the core of indigenous conceptions of sovereignty lie collective accountability and reciprocity and the interrelated rights to land and culture, not in terms of private ownership but in terms of literal, not metaphorical, genealogy. More recently, Smith has pulled together and built on Native women activists' articulations of alternative visions of the nation and sovereignty.[22] These notions foreground Native epistemologies of collective accountability, mutuality, and interconnection not only among humans but also among humans and nonhumans, as well as the integrity of land, culture, and politics. These reconceptualizations part ways with the exclusive, coercive, and anthropocentric notions of sovereignty and the sovereign citizen-subject that underwrites the modern nation-state. Such understandings allow the indigenous women with whom Smith worked to call into question the United States in particular and the modern nation-state in general as the legitimate and normative form around which people are expected to organize political power. The demystification of the modern nation-state and the goal of full membership to it strips them of their veneer of equality and exposes their colonial roots. Such an exercise opens up the grounds to connect the thinking around immigrant rights and indigenous rights.

In Hawai'i, several Native Hawaiian scholars—most notably, Hauanani Kay Trask, Mililani Trask, and Davianna McGregor—have traced the severe erosion of Native Hawaiian rights to self-determination in the face of race-based promotion of civil rights.[23] Unlike Native Americans, Native Hawaiians do not have a formalized trust relationship with the United States and the accompanying arrangement of tribal governance. Thus, attempts by Native Hawaiians to control their land and resources through Native-only governance structures are easily challenged. Native Hawaiian scholar and activist in the self-determination movement Haunani-Kay

Trask eloquently explains the antagonism between the two frameworks when she argues:

> Modern Hawai'i, like its colonial parent the United States, is a settler society. . . . In settler societies, the issue of civil rights is primarily an issue of how to protect settlers against each other and against the state. Injustices done against Native people, such as genocide, land dispossession, language banning, family disintegration, and cultural exploitation, are not part of this intrasettler discussion and are therefore not within the parameters of civil rights.[24]

Such scholarship thus points to the critical distinction between race-based rights worked out within a civil rights framework and indigenous rights that are tied to land rights and sovereignty.

Several recent lawsuits challenging Native Hawaiian rights to self-determination exercised through the Hawaiian-only elections to the Office of Hawaiian Affairs (OHA) demonstrate the ways in which courts have used civil rights arguments to undermine Native Hawaiians sovereignty.[25] The OHA manages the monies generated by the lands the United States appropriated from Native Hawaiians and provides one avenue through which Native Hawaiians can attempt to exercise control over resources and policy making. Cases brought to the State of Hawai'i by a White resident and Americans of Japanese Ancestry (AJAs) charged that the Hawaiian-only election violated the Fourteenth and Fifteenth Amendments of the U.S. Constitution by making non-Hawaiian U.S. citizens ineligible for voting in and running for OHA elections. Courts ruled in favor of upholding the U.S. Constitution and its guarantees of civil rights, reducing Native Hawaiians to racial minorities and extinguishing their distinct rights as indigenous people, whose illegal colonization and unrelinquished sovereignty was recognized by President Bill Clinton in 1993.[26] The courts' and plaintiffs' invocation of civil rights, couched in the post-1965 color-blind ideology that enables claims of "reverse discrimination," clearly harms the rights of colonized indigenous people seeking self-determination.

In light of these legal developments that have favored the Asian majority immigrant population in Hawai'i, the idea that immigrant rights harm Native self-determination has taken root. Since 1954, the domiciled Asian population has dominated the state's party politics. Despite this

Democratic "revolution" that ended the oligarchic rule of the Republican Party, Native Hawaiians continue to suffer from dispossession and neglect. Haunani-Kay Trask has named this state of affairs as an indicator of "Asian settler colonialism."[27] Elaborating on her theorization of civil rights as intrasettler negotiations for power, she offers a searing critique of the ideology of the "nation of immigrants" internalized by Asian immigrants who narrativize their plantation past in terms of hard work and struggle for democracy that eventually got rewarded by socioeconomic mobility and political clout. In a state where the Asian-dominated legislature makes law that extends the power of the military and private corporations over Native lands and the civil rights of immigrant Asians trump Native Hawaiian efforts at self-governance, the relationship between Natives and minoritized non-Natives cannot be glossed over by turning to a domestic model of race relations.

Trask's call for Asian accountability for the colonized state of Native Hawaiians, passionately taken up by Asian American scholar Candace Fujikane,[28] has become focused on the racialized identity category "Asian settler colonists." Despite Fujikane's intentions of confronting colonialism, non-Natives find it difficult to move toward political action that can consistently analyze the United States as a colonial nation-state as opposed to a nation of immigrants in which racial and gender equality is achieved through civil rights. In the face of this predicament, conjoining the immigrant and indigenous analyses of civil rights can help identify the distinct mechanisms through which the United States reproduces itself as a sovereign nation-state and an imperial power at home and abroad. It becomes critical to attend to the transnational processes through which immigrants and indigenous people come to inhabit the space nationalized as the United States.

Interrogating Citizenship: Bridging the Immigrant/Indigenous Divide

The two types of rights talk—immigrant and indigenous—locate the problem with the civil rights model in its reliance on rights-bearing citizens, whose enjoyment of these rights rests on disavowing the complicated and connected histories of colonization and migration. The model is founded on the sovereign subject who lives within the sovereign state. These conceptions are exactly what erase the internal colonization of indigenous people by valorizing U.S. citizenship and its requisite assimilation; they construct certain crossings as clandestine and others as legitimate, certain people as citizens and others as aliens without de facto rights.[29]

The civil rights movement undoubtedly inspired a new chapter in Native struggles for self-determination on the continent and in Hawai'i. It connected the domestic struggles against a racist and capitalist state with the war in Vietnam, and it created institutionalized spaces in the academy that have scrutinized citizenship as a mode through which racial and gender hierarchies are ordered. But, like anticolonial movements in the Third World, the U.S. civil rights movement imagined the modern nation-state as the ideal political organization and the citizen as the ideal national subject. For those contemporary struggles that do not find their answers in U.S. citizenship, the legacy of the civil rights movement is formidable because, as we saw with the 2006 immigrant marches, it has become the benchmark for all subsequent mass mobilizations in the United States.

The nationalist tenor of a recent lecture at the University of Hawai'i delivered by the famous civil rights leader Robert Moses is symptomatic of the limits of a civil rights framework.[30] Talking about the importance of his current project to promote math literacy, particularly for Black children attending underfunded schools, Moses powerfully connected the right to public education to a defining moment during the Student Nonviolent Coordinating Committee's (SNCC) Mississippi Project when he was asked by a federal judge to explain why he was advocating the right of illiterate sharecroppers to vote. For him, this moment fused the right to education and the right to full citizenship, rights for which he has struggled all his life. Moses saw the Algebra Project as an extension of the struggles for full membership in American society because it aimed at equipping inner-city children with skills that would allow them to enter the country's economic mainstream. However, his advocacy of math literacy slipped into his promotion of a high-skilled national workforce that would keep U.S. jobs for Americans. The implicitly anti-immigrant framing, which defined math literacy as the key to cultivating and harvesting national talent, received many an approving nod. This rhetorical move and audience response displaced the legitimate anxieties about Black unemployment on to immigrants and situated "American" citizens as the rightful and deserving pool of workers.[31]

The irony of a position that continues to center citizens in a political project about popular control over public education lies in the fact that the most furious debate over universal access to K–12 schooling has been over the entitlements of undocumented children. In 1982, the U.S. Supreme Court ruling on *Plyler v. Doe* permitted undocumented immigrants the same access to public schools as citizens. Currently, immigrant rights advocates are resisting state legislative efforts to deny higher education to the undocumented.[32] Thus, Moses's otherwise inspiring call to wrest the right to education from the interpretive power of the judiciary and legislature rings hollow for denizens, a term that Buff uses to capture the peculiar existence of migrants who live, work, form dense social and political relations, and even die within the borders of the United States but have no standing or even personhood in the eyes of law.[33]

To reinforce the power of the people, Moses ended his lecture by asking his audience to stand and recite with him the preamble to the U.S. Constitution, which in the words of Haunani-Kay Trask, is "the settler document that declares ownership over indigenous lands and peoples."[34] The normative power of civil rights as the ultimate rights struggle served to erase the memory of the illegal annexation of Hawai'i by the United States in 1898. The enthusiastic declaration of civil liberties reinforced the subjugated status of Native Hawaiians, normalizing the colonization of Hawai'i. In this instance, Moses was blinded by another analytical inadequacy of the civil rights framework: its failure to recognize that indigenous people have a sovereignty-based rights agenda which is different from that of racial minorities who are encouraged to work out their rights within the nationalized space of the United States. Yet, if we step outside the domesticating terms of the framework for a moment, we recognize that African Americans, as involuntary migrants who were also forcibly incorporated into the United States, have grounds to challenge nation-based models of citizenship.

Espousing civil rights demands an investment in U.S. citizenship. The two go hand in hand. Consequently, rights claims forwarded by indigenous people *and* immigrants have to be constructively rethought outside of the civil rights framework. Scholars and activists working within this frame cast little doubt on the ultimate ability of citizenship to deliver social justice. From their perspective, citizenship simply needs to realize its capacity to provide those who reside within particular national borders equal access to rights. The justness of citizenship remains unquestioned; what is questioned is the distortion of citizenship by legal and social systems that confer power to Whites and elite men. Yet, like identities that have emerged from racial, gender, sexual, colonial, and class oppression, citizenship is an imposed and coercive category.[35]

Despite the rhetoric of government by consent of the governed, nation-states in fact bring themselves into being by coercively organizing people within bounded territories, making borders and citizenship central to the nation-states' identity and making nationalisms—in their so-called civic and ethnic incarnations—the central mechanism through which citizens are enticed to forget their imprisonment within national borders. The emotional power of national flags, national anthems, and the discourses of national belonging gives citizenship the appearance of an identity that is voluntarily embraced and fundamental to one's place in the world. Sociologist Nandita Sharma sheds light on the socially and historically constructed voluntarism of citizenship by turning to political theory that renders visible the links between colonialism and the emergence of western democracies that were inspired by the modern ideology of nationalism to construct nation-states.[36] Yet those who embrace the civil rights model consider citizenship to be liberatory rather than coerced. They continue to use a political vocabulary that decries the indignity of second-class citizenship and sings the virtues of full citizenship, even in the inappropriate cases of people who do not have formal U.S. citizenship.

Those of us engaged in struggles for immigrant rights—not to mention civil rights—need to interrogate citizenship, particularly U.S. citizenship, as the principal means of internal colonization and the organization of global inequalities that have triggered the unprecedented migration of people across the globe. The fact that racial minorities and transmigrants prize U.S. citizenship and its entitlements, and that indigenous people look for a workable nation-within-the-nation solution, is not a reflection of the United States' promise of western democracy. It is the effect of what Anthony Richmond calls "global apartheid": the systematic erosion of lifechances of those internally colonized and those in the Global South.

The deterioration of the conditions in which one is forced to live induces cross-border migrations in the desperate hope of material and physical security.[37]

Within a larger of project of decolonization, we need to trace the continuities in the apparatuses that subordinate indigenous people, nonindigenous racialized minorities, and noncitizen migrants who are often people of color. Thus, for example, in the case of Hawai'i, accountability on the part of Asians to Native Hawaiians would mean calling into question their celebration of civil rights as a method of political empowerment and their participation in structures that promote the colonization of Native peoples. At the same time, it would be necessary to remember that the American state does not stop being colonial vis-à-vis immigrants—old and new, forced and involuntary. The racialization of settler colonialism as "Asian" obfuscates the multiple operations of the colonial state. A standard colonial tactic involves developing a rank of colonized people, both indigenous and from groups brought in fill labor needs in colonial economies, to advance colonial interests. The march toward full citizenship through civil rights constitutes one such defense of colonial structures of governance. Recognizing this dimension of colonial rule does not condone Asian complicity in Native Hawaiian dispossession. On the contrary, it allows us to plot the specific relationships that people inhabiting a colonial space have with each other and with the state.

What would a thoroughgoing analysis of the United States as an advanced capitalist and an "advanced colonial state" entail? [38] How can such an analysis contend with the antagonistic framing of indigenous and immigrant rights? Any serious grappling with these questions would mean a careful accounting of how colonization works for indigenous people and how it works for all historical migrants. Migration, when undertaken by Europeans to settle native land, has been a part of colonization. It has also been part of labor recruitment. African and Asian laborers, often themselves colonial subjects, were recruited in the service of U.S. capitalism to work the land appropriated through settler colonialism. These historical practices have reinvented themselves in contemporary times. Sharma thus warns us not to conflate all mobilities with colonizing:

> Within this complexity of migration, displacement, and the simultaneous experiences of homelessness [through the creation of foreigners]

> and claims of homeyness [through citizenship], it is important that we not confuse the problem of colonization with migration per se. Colonization is first and foremost a relationship of exploitation and oppression. Colonization can be experienced both as conquest *and* as scattered crossings.[39]

If we adopt a transnational perspective to understand the politics of borders, then migration from other parts of the world to the United States cannot necessarily be equated with settling. Historically and today, policy directions in the U.S. have favored the creation of pools of temporary laborers, whose exploitability rests on the fact that the state does not grant them the right to settle. This existential reality is the stamp of the colonial/neocolonial and capitalist state on migrant lives.

Native people are also often migrants. The two social locations are not mutually exclusive. Native Hawaiians have been forced to migrate since the 1840s, either to the U.S. continent or to other countries in search of work. The history of Native American dispossession and dislocation on the U.S. continent is marked by mass migrations. To see indigenous people as simply rooted in a place disregards this very violent history. Buff's use of the term "im/migration" to compare the construction of alternative versions and public memorializations of sovereignty, citizenship, and denizenship through the Caribbean Carnival and Native American powpows in the urban United States foregrounds the violent history of relocation and termination that created Native diasporas within the United States. Her usage also renders visible the history of continuing migration from the Caribbean of people of African descent, who disappear within the domesticated category "Black." This straddling of various forms of mobility within colonized spaces that contain "domestic dependent nations" and across nations under new regimes of imperialism opens up the conceptual space to compare migrant and indigenous experiences, and, I would add, rights claims.

In the Pacific, where many nations have decolonized but continue to suffer extreme depredations imposed by regimes of development and good governance, scholars have started to map indigenous diasporas.[40] These perspectives tease out the implications of migration (historical and current) for conceptions of "Native" and "indigenous" that tend to obscure the mobility and hybridity of indigenous peoples in Oceania in favor of "tradition, stability, boundedness, authenticity, rootedness, organicism, topophilia, particularity, integrity and communalism."[41] In addition, scholarship is also being produced to trace the kinship—with its multivalent symbology of connectivity, affinity, and hierarchy—among indigenous people in the Pacific and those who were brought indentured to labor in the islands on land stolen from indigenous people.[42]

Out of the Shadows of U.S. Citizenship: Concluding Thoughts

In this chapter, I make the effort to connect critiques that sit disconnected: awareness of imperialism as a tool of global domination, the subjugation and dislocation of indigenous people in transnational contexts, and the awareness that people moving transnationally exist in dynamic relations to each other and to national space but also that their crossings and rights are always mediated by border-control techniques. I lay out two strands of thought—one developed in the context of immigration and the other in the context of indigenous sovereignty—that reject civil rights, with its locus of power in the colonial nation-state, as the path to justice. While these critiques emerge from analyzing the distinct predicament of immigrants, particularly those who inhabit national spaces without papers, and indigenous people, who are forcibly incorporated into the national body in order to erase their presence, in an era of resurgent imperialism, we need to trace the parallels between and intersections of these new formulations of rights that do not take the modern citizen-subject for granted.

The trust in citizenship ignores that citizenship itself, whether racialized or otherwise communalized and gendered, organizes space through a fine calibration of rights. Even if every citizen inhabiting a national space were to enjoy her or his full rights, it would still not dismantle the institutionalized and everyday regimes of border control that determine the rights of those who enter the United States from other nationalized spaces, as well as those who are colonized within the geopolitical boundaries of the United States. Since both indigenous and immigrant scholars and activists are in the forefront of rethinking the civil rights framework, comparing their insights can reveal common grounds for struggles against imperialism. Drawing on their work, I argue that abandoning the discourse of civil rights and citizenship in the immigrant rights movement and engaging in a thoroughgoing and historicized analysis of current forms of colonialism that gird the subjugation and displacement of indigenous people and migrants will put us on the constructive path of breaking down the perceived antagonism in the rights discourses of immigrants, whether voluntary or otherwise, and those of indigenous people. Such comparisons will allow rights discourses to emerge from the shadows of U.S. citizenship.

NOTES

I am particularly grateful to Rachel Buff, Cynthia Franklin, Laura Lyons, Richard Rath, and Naoko Shibusawa for their careful comments on this article and the helpful discussions about indigenous sovereignty, migration, and rights. A version of the chapter was presented at the 2007 Association of Asian American Studies meeting. The essay benefited from question and comments at the presentation.

1. Andrea Smith, *Conquest: Sexual Violence and American Indian Genocide* (Cambridge, Mass.: South End Press, 2005), 179.

2. I want to clarify my understanding of the civil rights framework and the U.S. civil rights movement. Technically, civil rights and the modern nation-state emerging from the western democratic principles are entangled (Jürgen Habermas, *The Structural Transformation of the Public Sphere: An Inquiry into a Category of Bourgeois Society*, trans. Thomas Burger [Cambridge, Mass.: MIT Press, 1989]). While civil rights are indeed basic to human dignity, they are inevitably caught up in the logic of western democracy, which grew hand in hand with capitalism and colonialism. Civil rights, for example, fall short of protecting collective rights to economic and social security (Richard Cullen Rath, *How Early America Sounded* [Ithaca, N.Y.: Cornell University Press, 2003], 120–72). Explicating how the Habermasian idea of a civil society implicitly provides a foil for those considered uncivilized—in the case of early American indigenous people—Rath argues that "Habermas' defense of the modern liberal nation state as a sort of last best hope for rational and equitable government sneaks in the older idea of civilization in the guise of 'civil society'" (210 n.1). I understand the civil rights movement in the United States to be a historically specific development that came out of the monumental failure of Reconstruction to guarantee African Americans their newly won citizenship rights. The movement, which started to gather force in the

mid-1950s and claimed the public sphere, did away with legally enforced segregation, disenfranchisement, and Jim Crow. It powerfully resisted White supremacist terror.

3. Smith, *Conquest,* 184–91; Andrea Smith, "Native American Feminisms, Sovereignty, and Social Change," *Feminist Studies* 31:1 (2005), 116–32.

4. For example, Yen Le Espiritu, *Home Bound: Filipino American Lives across Cultures, Communities, and Countries* (Berkeley: University of California Press, 2003); Nina Glick Schiller, Linda Basch, and Cristina Szanton Blanc, *Toward a Transnational Perspective on Migration: Race, Class, Ethnicity, and Nationalism Reconsidered* (New York: New York Academy of Sciences, 1992).

5. Robert McFadden, Laura Griffin, Judy Sheppard, Corey Taule, Elisa Williams, and Andrea Zarate, "Across the U.S., Protests for Immigrants Draw Thousands," *New York Times,* April 10, 2006, 14; Sheryl G. Stolberg, Julia Preston, and Rachel L. Swarns, "After Immigration Protests, Goal Remains Elusive," *New York Times,* May 3, 2006, 1.

6. For example, Nicholas Confesore, Janon Fisher, and John Holl, "Thousands Rally in New York in Support of Immigrants Rights," *New York Times,* April 2, 2006, 29. The article quotes a housekeeper who migrated from Argentina over a decade ago as saying, "'We came here because we love America and we want to stay here. . . . My children are American. I love my country, too, but there is no future there. Here, they can be a doctor, anything.'" Buried in the article is a statement of the Democratic Representative from New York to the Congress, Nydia Velázquez, who is quoted as saying, "We should not be in the business of criminalizing undocumented immigrants." See also the introductory paragraph of McFadden et al., "Across the U.S., Protests for Immigrants Draws Thousands," 14. The news item that reports on protests in Dallas, Birmingham, Alabama, Boise, Idaho, Salem, Oregon, and Maimi frames them as demands for "citizenship and a share of the American dream for millions of illegal immigrants who have run a gantlet of closed borders, broken families, snake-eyed smugglers and economic exploitation."

7. McFadden et al., "Across the U.S., Protests for Immigrants Draws Thousands," 14.

8. These demands that underline the inalienable rights of migrants regardless of their immigration status to their bodily integrity, familial ties, and freedom from economic exploitation and political intimidation are consistent with the 1990 International Convention on the Protection of the Rights of All Migrant Workers and Their Families that came into force in 2002. But, as Ratna Kapur observes, the convention fails to tackle the central problem of national immigration policies because "the transnationalisation of labour and migration cannot be addressed within the framework of immigration, which is based on notions of loyalty to an

identification with the nation" (*Erotic Justice: Law and the New Politics of Postcolonialism* [London: Glasshouse Press, 2005], 152).

9. Nina Bernstein, John M. Broder, and Rachel L. Swarns, "In the Streets, Suddenly, an Immigrant Groundswell," *New York Times,* March 27, 2006, 14.

10. National Immigration Forum, *Snapshot of the "Hagel-Martinez Compromise" Immigration Reform Legislation,* 2006 [cited April 30, 2006]), at http://immigration forum.org/documents/PolicyWire/Legislation/Hagel-MartinezSnapshot.pdf. According to the report, the Senate Judiciary Committee's bill proposed that those who had resided in the United States undocumented for five years prior to April 5, 2006, and had worked a minimum of three years during those five years could qualify for legalization but only if they continued to work for another six years after the enactment of the law.

11. For the main provisions of the bill, see U.S. Senate, *S. 1639: Congressional Research Service Summary,* 2007 [cited August 7, 2007]), at http://thomas.loc.gov/cgi-bin/bdquery/z?d110:SN01639:@@@D&summ2=m& (accessed August 7, 2007).

12. Susan M. Akram and Kevin R. Johnson, "Race and Civil Rights Pre-September 11, 2001: The Targeting of Arabs and Muslims," in *Civil Rights in Peril: The Targeting of Arabs and Muslims,* ed. Elaine C. Hagopian (Chicago: Haymarket, 2004), 239–255; Cherif M. Bassiouni, "Don't Tread on Me: Is the War on Terror Really a War on Rights," in *Civil Rights in Peril: The Targeting of Arabs and Muslims,* ed. Elaine C. Hagopian (Chicago: Haymarket Books, 2004), 1–5; Nancy Murray, "Profiled: Arabs, Muslims and the Post-9/11 Hunt for the 'Enemy Within,'" in *Civil Rights in Peril: The Targeting of Arabs and Muslims,* ed. Elaine C. Hagopian (Chicago: Haymarket Books, 2004), 27–68.

13. Robert S. Chang, *Disoriented: Asian Americans, Law, and the Nation-State* (New York: New York University Press, 1999), 81–82; Murray, "Profiled," 27, 250 n.2.

14. Eric K. Yamamoto and Susan Kiyomi Serrano, "The Loaded Weapon," in *Asian Americans on War and Peace,* ed. Russell C. Leong and Don T. Nakanishi (Los Angeles: UCLA Asian American Studies Center Press, 2002), 63–74.

15. John S. W. Park, *Elusive Citizenship: Immigration, Asian Americans, and the Paradox of Civil Rights* (New York: New York University Press, 2004).

16. Ibid., 142.

17. Ibid., 127–32.

18. Consistent with the nationalist tone of his other documentaries, Michael Moore, in *Fahrenheit 9/11* (2004), highlights the ways in which the civil rights of U.S. citizens are endangered in the "War on Terror."

19. See text of the Organic Act passed on April, 30, 1900, to "provide a Government for the Territory of Hawaii," at http://hawaii-nation.org/organic.html (accessed August 9, 2007).

20. Rachel Buff, *Immigration and the Political Economy of Home: West Indian Brooklyn and American Indian Minneapolis, 1945–1992* (Berkeley: University of California Press, 2001), 56–58.

21. Marie Anna Jaimes Guerrero, "Civil Rights versus Sovereignty: Native American Women in Life and Land Struggles," in *Feminist Genealogies, Colonial Legacies, Democratic Futures,* ed. M. Jacqui Alexander and Chandra T. Mohanty (New York: Routledge, 1997), 101–21. For numerous instances where Native women have not received justice in cases of sexual assault and police brutality because of jurisdictional conflicts, which reflect the clash, engineered by the United States, between civil rights and tribal sovereignty in the lives of Native peoples, see Smith, *Conquest,* 30–33.

22. Smith, *Conquest,* 177–91; Smith, "Native American Feminisms, Sovereignty, and Social Change," 120.

23. Mililani B. Trask, "*Rice v. Cayetano*: Reaffirming the Racism of Hawaii's Colonial Past," *Asian-Pacific Law and Policy Journal* 3/2 (2002), at www.hawaii.edu/aplpj (accessed February 7, 2008); Haunani-Kay Trask, *From a Native Daughter: Colonialism and Sovereignty in Hawai'i,* rev. ed. (Honolulu: University of Hawai'i Press, 1999); Haunani-Kay Trask, "Settlers of Color and 'Immigrant' Hegemony of 'Locals' in Hawai'i," *Amerasia Journal* 26/2 (2000), 1–24; Davianna P. McGregor, "Recognizing Native Hawaiians: A Quest for Sovereignty," in *Pacific Diaspora: Island Peoples in the United States and across the Pacific,* ed. Paul Spickard, Joanne L. Rondilla, and Debbie Hippolite Wright (Honolulu: University of Hawai'i Press, 2002), 331–54.

24. Trask, *From a Native Daughter,* 25.

25. The cases are *Rice v. Cayetano* in 1996, in which the Supreme Court ruled against the exclusive rights of Hawaiians to vote for OHA members; *Arakaki et al. v. the State of Hawaii* in 2000, in which the district judge granted non-Hawaiians the right to run for OHA; and *Arakaki et al. v. Lingle* in 2002, in which OHA and the Department of Hawaiian Homelands were charged with discrimination for administering programs that serve Native Hawaiians. For discussions of the implications of these cases on Native Hawaiian political and cultural self-determination, see Cynthia G. Franklin and Laura Lyons, "Remixing Hybridity: Globalization, Native Resistance, and Cultural Production in Hawai'i," *American Studies* 45:3 (2004), 49–80; Candace Fujikane, "Foregrounding Native Nationalisms: A Critique of Antinationalist Sentiment in Asian American Studies," in *Asian American Studies after Critical Mass,* ed. Kent A. Ono (Malden, Mass.: Blackwell, 2005), xvii–xxii; McGregor, "Recognizing Native Hawaiians."

26. The full text of the apology is available at http://www.hawaii-nation.org/publawall.html (accessed February 28, 2007).

27. Trask, "Settlers of Color."

28. Candace Fujikane, "Asian Settler Colonialism in Hawai'i," *Amerasia Journal* 26:2 (2000), xv–xvii; Fujikane, "Foregrounding Native Nationalisms."

29. Kapur, *Erotic Justice*, 137–76.

30. Robert Moses, "The Algebra Project: Radical Equation > Math Education > Civil Rights = Social Justice," paper presented at the Ah Quon McElrath Lecture for Social Change, University of Hawai'i, 2007.

31. See Lisa Marie Cacho's article, chapter 8 in this volume.

32. See Rachel Buff's essay, chapter 13 in this volume.

33. Buff, *Immigration and the Political Economy of Home*.

34. Trask, *From a Native Daughter*, 26.

35. Nandita Sharma, *Home Economics: Nationalism and the Making of "Migrant Workers" in Canada* (Toronto: University of Toronto Press, 2006).

36. Ibid.

37. Anthony H. Richmond, *Global Apartheid: Refugees, Racism, and the New World Order* (Toronto: Oxford University Press, 1994).

38. Guerrero, "Civil Rights versus Sovereignty: Native American Women in Life and Land Struggles," 101.

39. Sharma, *Home Economics*, 15.

40. For example, Graham Harvey and Charles D. Thompson Jr., eds., *Indigenous Diasporas and Dislocations* (Aldershot, Hampshire, England: Ashgate, 2005), in particular, Teresia Teaiwa, "Native Thoughts: A Pacific Studies Take on Cultural Studies and Diaspora," 15–35.

41. Graham Harvey and Charles D. Thompson Jr., "Introduction," in *Indigenous Diasporas and Dislocations*, ed. Graham Harvey and Charles D. Thompson Jr. (Aldershot, Hampshire, England: Ashgate, 2005), 2.

42. Katerina Teaiwa, "South Asia Down Under: Popular Kinship in Oceania," *Cultural Dynamics* 19:2 (2007): 193–232.

ABOUT THE CONTRIBUTORS

The Africana Cultures and Policy Studies Institute (ACPSI), formed in 2003 and created by a unique community of scholar-activists, holds as its central mission the task of defining the field of Africana Cultures and Policy Studies and thereby strengthening the discipline of Africana studies. This think tank intends to fill a much-needed gap in the global public sphere of knowledge creation and implementation by bridging the study of Africana cultures' phenomena with relevant application toward matters of public policy advocacy, development, and evaluation. Collectively, ACPSI scholars advance the notion that the next phase of the evolution of Africana history, culture, and studies is the clear definition, articulation, and advancement of the connection between historical culture and policy. As an institute, ACPSI is poised to lead the way in addressing vital issues of global political economy which heretofore have been neglected with regard to the policy study of Africana cultures and people. Drawing on the complementary utility of interdisciplinarity and community, ACPSI seeks to bring college and university academics, government and policy experts, journalists, theologians and black religious leaders, artists, grassroots leaders, and public and organic intellectuals into a critical engagement around important issues of our collective past, present, and future as Africana peoples.

Rachel Ida Buff teaches history and comparative ethnic studies at the University of Wisconsin, Milwaukee. She is a member of Voces de la Frontera, a workers' center and immigrant rights organization.

Lisa Marie Cacho is an Assistant Professor of Latina/Latino studies and Asian American studies at the University of Illinois, Urbana-Champaign. She is an interdisciplinary scholar, who specializes in comparative race and ethnic studies.

Eunice Hyunhye Cho is the former Education Director at the National Network for Immigrant and Refugee Rights. She is the editor and coauthor of *BRIDGE: Building a Race and Immigration Dialogue in the Global Economy.*

She also helped to coordinate NNIRR's campaign to bring grassroots migrant rights leaders to the 2001 UN World Conference against Racism and Xenophobia, and she edited and coauthored *From the Borderline to the Colorline: A Report on Anti-Immigrant Racism in the U.S.* She serves on the national steering collective of Incite! Women of Color against Violence, and on the board of the Western States Center. She is currently a student at Stanford Law School.

David Cole is a Professor at Georgetown University Law Center, a volunteer staff attorney for the Center for Constitutional Rights, the legal affairs correspondent for *The Nation,* and a commentator on National Public Radio's *All Things Considered.* A graduate of Yale University and Yale Law School, he clerked for Judge Arlin Adams on the Third Circuit. He has litigated many First Amendment cases, including *Texas v. Johnson* and *United States v. Eichman,* which extended First Amendment protection to flag-burning. In 2004, his book *Enemy Aliens: Double Standards and Constitutional Freedoms in the War on Terrorism* (2003) was awarded an American Book Award and the Hefner First Amendment Prize.

Monisha Das Gupta teaches in ethnic studies and women's studies at the University of Hawai'i. Her areas of specialization are migration, globalization, U.S. race relations, and social movements. Her recent book *Unruly Immigrants: Rights, Activism, and Transnational South Asian Politics in the United States* (2006) examines conceptions of rights put forward by feminist, queer, and labor organizations. Her other publications focus on the post-9/11 political terrain, immigrant rights, and transnational feminism.

Adam Francoeur is the Policy Coordinator at Immigration Equality, a national organization fighting for equal immigration rights for the lesbian, gay, bisexual, transgender, and HIV-positive community. He leads the national effort to pass the Uniting American Families Act, a family fairness bill that would end immigration discrimination against same-sex couples. In addition, he works with immigration coalition partners to analyze and publicize how pending immigration proposals would affect LGBT and HIV-positive immigrants. He received his bachelor's degree in international affairs from George Washington University. Before joining Immigration Equality, he worked for immigration attorneys Richard S. Bromberg and

Elizabeth H. McGrail, assisting them in preparing asylum claims based on sexual orientation, Violence against Women Act petitions, naturalization and green card applications, and nonimmigrant visa petitions.

Pierrette Hondagneu-Sotelo is Professor of Sociology at the University of Southern California in Los Angeles, where she is directing a Provost's Initiative on Immigration and Integration. Her research has focused on gender, Latino immigration and work, and religion and immigrant rights, and she is author or editor of seven books. These include a forthcoming book on religion and immigrant rights, the edited volumes *Gender and U.S. Immigration: Contemporary Trends* (2003) and *Religion and Social Justice for Immigrants* (2007), and *Domestica: Immigrant Workers Cleaning and Caring in the Shadows of Affluence* (2001), which won seven book awards.

For over a dozen years and on several continents, *Scott Long* has documented and advocated against human rights violations based on sexual orientation, gender identity, and HIV status. For five years, he lobbied the United Nations on sexual rights issues; his work led to U.N. human rights mechanisms agreeing publicly for the first time to take up gay and lesbian concerns. As program director of the International Gay and Lesbian Human Rights Commission (IGLHRC) for almost six years, he edited or coauthored reports on gay, lesbian, bisexual, and transgender parenting and on the use of sexuality to target women's and feminist organizing. He joined Human Rights Watch as a consultant in 2002 to develop a project on lesbian, gay, bisexual, and transgender rights, and in March 2004 he was hired as its director. He has written and published extensively on issues of sexuality, culture, and human rights.

Babacar M'Baye, of the Africana Cultures and Policy Studies Institute, teaches African American literature and Pan-African studies at Kent State University. His work explores the relationship between African American writers and Africa, African immigrants in the United States, race and African influences in African American literature, and hybrid identities in nineteenth-century and twentieth-century African American literature. He is currently writing a manuscript entitled "Retracing Pan-Africanism: The African Influence in Eighteenth- and Nineteenth-Century African American, African British, and African Caribbean Writings."

Isabel Guzman Molina is an Assistant Professor of communications at the Institute of Communications Research and an affiliate of the Latina/o Studies Program and Gender and Women's Studies Program at the University of Illinois–Urbana-Champaign. She received her Ph.D. from the University of Pennsylvania. Her research dealing with the representational politics surrounding gender, sexuality, race. and ethnicity in the news and popular media has appeared in journals such as *Critical Studies in Media Communication* and *Latino Studies.*

Christine Neumann-Ortiz is the Founding Director of Voces de la Frontera, a low-wage and immigrant workers center with chapters in Milwaukee and Racine, including a student chapter called Students United for Immigrant Rights with members from three high schools. Voces de la Frontera is increasingly recognized as Wisconsin's leading voice for immigration reform. She is recognized as a national leader in immigration reform, serving on the board of a national coalition of the Fair Immigration Reform Movement (FAIR) and featured in national interviews on National Public Radio and CNN. She has received community award recognitions from Labor Council for Latin American Advancement chapters in Milwaukee and Janesville; the 2006 "Do What Is Just" Award from MICAH (Milwaukee Inner City Congregations Alied for Hope); the 2006 Public Service Award from the National Association of Social Workers—Wisconsin Chapter; and the 2006 "Education: A Family Affair Award of Excellence," presented by the University of Wisconsin-Milwaukee, the State Department of Public Instruction, and the Marcus Center for the Performing Arts. She also writes a regular column in the local *Spanish Journal.*

Glenn Omatsu (glenn.omatsu@csun.edu) is a lecturer in Asian American studies and the Educational Opportunity Program at California State University, Northridge (CSUN), and also teaches classes at Pasadena City College and UCLA. He is coeditor (with Steve Louie) of *Asian Americans: The Movement and Moment* and coeditor (with Edith Chen) of *Teaching about Asian Pacific Americans.* He is active in community-based immigrant labor campaigns and other social movements for justice.

Connie G. Oxford is an Assistant Professor of women's studies at the State University of New York, Plattsburgh. She received her Ph.D. in sociology from the University of Pittsburgh. She has published a journal article in the *National Women's Studies Association Journal* and a book chapter in the edited collection *Research Methods: Choices in Interdisciplinary Contexts* that are based on her dissertation research on gender-based asylum claims in the United States.

John S. W. Park is an Associate Professor of Asian American studies at University of California, Santa Barbara. He completed his Ph.D. in jurisprudence and social policy at Boalt Hall, the School of Law at the University of California at Berkeley. He worked for a year at an immigration law firm in San Francisco before completing his Ph.D. He writes and teaches on topics in race theory, immigration law and policy, and Anglo-American legal and political theory.

Donald Pease is Professor of English, Avalon Foundation Chair of the Humanities, Chair of the Dartmouth Liberal Studies Program, and winner of the 1981 Distinguished Teaching Award at Dartmouth. He is an authority on nineteenth- and twentieth-century American litrature and literary theory. A recipient of a Ph.D. from the University of Chicago, he is the author of *Visionary Compacts: American Renaissance Writings in Cultural Context* (which won the Mark Ingraham Prize for the best new book in the humanities in 1987) and of over seventy articles on figures in American and British literature and on the culture of U.S. imperialism. He is the coeditor of *American Renaissance Rediscovered* and the editor of seven other volumes, including the forthcoming *The Futures of American Studies*. Pease is general editor of a series of books by Duke University Press called "The New Americanists." He has been awarded Guggenheim, Mellon, and Hewlett fellowships and has twice received an NEH Directorship to teach college teachers about nineteenth-century American literature.

Jeanne Petit is an Associate Professor of history at Hope College. Her research specialties are in immigration and women's history, and she is currently completing a book on gender and immigration restriction debates in the early twentieth century titled *The Men and Women We Want: Gender, Immigration and the Progressive Era Literacy Test Debates.* Her next research project examines how middle-class Catholic laywomen developed their political identities after women gained suffrage in 1920.

Victor C. Romero, Associate Dean for Academic Affairs (University Park) and Maureen B. Cavanaugh Research Professor, Penn State University, The Dickinson School of Law, teaches and writes in the area of immigrant and minority rights. He is coeditor of the anthology *Immigration and the Constitution* and author of *Alienated: Immigrant Rights, the Constitution, and Equality in America.* He has served his community as president of both the South Central Pennsylvania Chapter of the ACLU and the NAACP of the Greater Carlisle Area.

Angelica Salas is Director of the Coalition for Humane Immigrant Rights of Los Angeles (CHIRLA) and is widely regarded as one of the most gifted activists/organizers in the country today. Since becoming CHIRLA's director in 1999, Salas has spearheaded several ambitious campaigns. She helped win in-state tuition for undocumented immigrant students and established day laborer job centers that have served as a model for the rest of the nation. She led efforts to allow all California drivers to obtain a drivers license and is a leading spokesperson on federal immigration policy. One of her greatest accomplishments at CHIRLA has been the transformation of a coalition of social service providers into an organization that empowers immigrants to engage in advocacy on their own behalf. She comes by her understanding of the immigrant experience firsthand. As a four-year-old, she came to the United States from Mexico to rejoin her parents who had come to the states to find work and better provide for their family.

Robert Samuel Smith of the Africana Cultures and Policy Studies Institute is an Assistant Professor of Africana Studies at the University of North Carolina at Charlotte. He is working on a book titled *Race, Labor and Civil Rights:* Griggs v. Duke Power *and the Expansion of Equal Employment Opportunity,* which explores the continued vigilance of the civil rights legal community in garnering employment opportunities on the heels of the legislative victories of the mid-1960s. He teaches courses on African American history and on African Americans and the legal process.

Jessica Stern has been a policy analyst, community organizer, and author advocating for the rights of women and the rights of queers, and against poverty at grassroots, national, and international levels for much of the last decade. As a Ralph Bunche Fellow at Amnesty International, she collaborated on its landmark report on police brutality in lesbian, gay, bisexual, and transgender (LGBT) communities in the United States. She was a founding director of Bluestockings, New York City's only women and transgender bookstore and community space in the late 1990s. She is currently an executive board member of Queers for Economic Justice. Since joining Human Rights Watch's LGBT Rights Program in 2005, she has researched and written about violence and discrimination against LGBT immigrants, prisoners, and communities at large in the United States, Iran, Kyrgyzstan, and around the world.

Originally from Oklahoma, *Dustin Tahmahkera,* Nʉmʉnʉʉ (Comanche) and Anglo, is Assistant Professor of Ethnic Studies at Mankato State University. His current project is called "Representations of Redface: Decolonizing the American Situation Comedy's 'Indian.'" His previous degrees are in English from Midwestern State University, and his academic heroes include Vine Deloria Jr., Devon Mihesuah, and Taiaiake Alfred.

Fred Tsao is Policy Director for the Illinois Coalition for Immigrant and Refugee Rights.

Seneca Vaught is Assistant Professor of Africana studies at Niagara University. He is the current Director of Information and Technology for the Africana Cultures and Policy Studies Institute. His research interests include social policy, prisons, activism, and community development. Among several projects, he is currently completing a book addressing the influence of prisons and prison culture on the evolution of the modern civil rights movement.

Zachery Williams is Executive Director of the Africana Cultures and Policy Studies Institute. Currently, he is an Assistant Professor of African American History and Pan African Studies at the University of Akron. His research interests include twentieth-century Black intellectual thought; Black religion, race, intellectuals, and policy; Black Liberation theology/Black theology; and Black men's studies. Currently, he is working on a manuscript titled, "In Search of the Talented Tenth: Howard University Intellectuals and the Dilemmas of Race, 1926–1970." He is soon to publish a book titled, *Soul Brother: Historical Essays in Black Men's Studies*. He is also a distinguished lecturer for the *Journal of African American History*.

INDEX